BLACK AFRICA AND DE GAULLE

From the French Empire
to Independence

Dorothy Shipley White

The Pennsylvania State University Press
University Park and London

Illustrations courtesy of Photo Documentation Française,
Service Info-Sénégal, Service Information de la Cote-d'Ivoir,
Information A.O.F. Photothèque du Ministere de la France
d'Outre-Mer, Rene Vital (*Paris Match*)

Map by Vincent Kotschar

Library of Congress Cataloging in Publication Data

White, Dorothy Shipley.
   Black Africa and DeGaulle.
   Includes bibliography and index.
   1. Africa, Sub-Saharan—Relations (general) with
France. 2. France—Relations (general) with Sub-Saharan
Africa. 3. Africa, Sub-Saharan—Politics and government. 4. France—
Politics and government—1958–   5. Gaulle, Charles de, Pres. France,
1890–1970. I. Title.
DT353.5.F8W48   325'.344'0967   79-1733
ISBN 0-271-00214-X

Black Africa
and De Gaulle

Dorothy Shipley White is both a scholar and a
personal friend of the de Gaulle family. After
taking her Ph.D. at the University of
Pennsylvania, she wrote *Seeds of Discord: Free
France and the Allies,* published in both the
United States and France (in French). Since
then she has been writing articles and
reviews for French and American
newspapers and journals — and writing this
book.

French Desires:

The Discovery of Far Lands and Their Products

Slaves to Grow Sugar and Bring Profits

The Glory of a Great Empire

Success in European Rivalries and the Security It Brings

The Desire to Carry Out the "Mission Civilisatrice" and to Free
Black Africa

African Desires:

Success in Rivalries with Other Black Kingdoms and Empires

Gold and Guns from the Europeans in Exchange for Slaves

Later—Freedom from the Colonizing Powers and a Resultant Sense
of Security

The Renewal of a Purely Black Civilization and the Development
of a Strong Black Race

Preface

This book is dedicated with gratitude and affection to

Geneviève Anthonioz-de Gaulle,

niece of General Charles de Gaulle, who first suggested the subject of the book, and who has done more than anyone by her friendship and wisdom to make the author understand the life, character, and influence of a family like the de Gaulles.

Some years ɑ
the Allies, I
about a subj
and then sai
Africa, and
there? No oɪ
trip to Africɑ
expected wh
endless read
America anɗ
Empire. Hoʋ
French reach
the Africans ɪ
not widespre
background ɑ
today, could
African posse
had begun as
situation maɗ
French Africɑ
only man wh
freedom, but
concerned it.
far as possible
change. This s
the trials, suf
discovery anɗ
colonization.
independence
ment at dawn
mortal snares,

Catherine G
this belief in tʰ
periods of the
understood on
precolonial anɗ

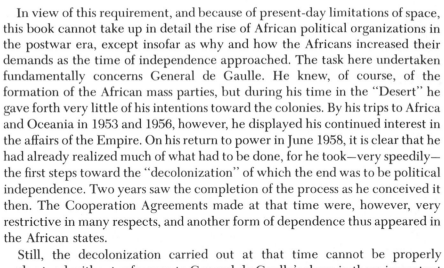

In view of this requirement, and because of present-day limitations of space, this book cannot take up in detail the rise of African political organizations in the postwar era, except insofar as why and how the Africans increased their demands as the time of independence approached. The task here undertaken fundamentally concerns General de Gaulle. He knew, of course, of the formation of the African mass parties, but during his time in the "Desert" he gave forth very little of his intentions toward the colonies. By his trips to Africa and Oceania in 1953 and 1956, however, he displayed his continued interest in the affairs of the Empire. On his return to power in June 1958, it is clear that he had already realized much of what had to be done, for he took—very speedily—the first steps toward the "decolonization" of which the end was to be political independence. Two years saw the completion of the process as he conceived it then. The Cooperation Agreements made at that time were, however, very restrictive in many respects, and another form of dependence thus appeared in the African states.

Still, the decolonization carried out at that time cannot be properly understood without reference to General de Gaulle's share in these important steps. The General's connections with and attitudes toward Black Africa are important in understanding the independence that took form at that time—1958–61. The roots of what happened then lie in history, in de Gaulle's own education, in his career, and in the newer circumstances of his return to power. By that time Indochina, Tunisia, and Morocco had obtained their independence from France, and in 1957 Britain granted independence to the Gold Coast, now called Ghana, a country right in the midst of the former French Black African states and therefore influential. In addition, Britain, Holland, and the United States had allowed their Asian colonies to become independent. When would the other dominoes begin to fall? There is no answer to that as yet, even though such a large proportion of the colonial possessions throughout the world have become independent.[3]

How the Africans felt about General de Gaulle and the French colonization of Africa, both before the era of political independence and at its opening, is important even though we realize now that the process of achieving complete independence was not terminated by political freedom. The full meaning of the change from the colonial situation of the past had not yet become apparent. One complex situation led to another, and the end is not yet.

In the writing of this book, as in work on much of contemporary history, there have been enormous difficulties, largely due to the fact that so many official and private documents are not yet available to the public. Especially in the case of General de Gaulle, whose authority and influence were so widely spread throughout the world and whose actions were subject to so much approval and also to so much hostile criticism, it has been hard to obtain information that could be called complete and objective. His papers are all immured in the French National Archives as far as is known, and it is questionable whether even a few favored individuals have succeeded in obtaining bits and pieces of them. The Institut de Gaulle in Paris believes that no one has penetrated the barrage laid down around them. According to an

Cont

official at the building dealing with the overseas dominions and territories, on the rue Oudinot (where the French Overseas Ministry used to be), the talk of opening the papers after thirty years instead of fifty is not correct. Everything from 1940 on, they say, is closed unless the director of the National Archives can be persuaded to let a researcher see a few papers.

Other records sound interesting, especially those of Free France in London, or of the Provisional Assembly at Algiers, but except for the *Journal Officiel,* both of those series of papers dated before the time when General de Gaulle's ideas had begun to change about Black Africa, for those documents terminated in 1943. The General was still a "man of the Empire" then, except insofar as his beginning acquaintance with Governor Eboué may have influenced him.

Thus the author has had to rely for information and opinion chiefly on more than two hundred interviews with the General's close associates, with a number of Africans closely associated with the governments of their countries, and also with many persons in France who were opposed to the General's policies and actions. Certain papers not often available, however, were given the author; for example, an early report of the African Party, RDA (*Rassemblement Démocratique Africain*), the "Confessions de Foi" of Lamine Guèye, the text of the Loi-Cadre, and the articles by Edwin Munger, loaned by a member of the American Embassy at Tananarive, Madagascar. Good use was made of the *Journal Officiel* of Free France, of France Combattante, of the Provisional Assembly at Algiers, and of the Fourth and Fifth Republics.

The best information, however, came from the interviews and from the many books that have now been written about the General and about the period as a whole. Certainly, better answers to some of the questions not yet clarified will be available later.

Before ending this pre-preliminary report of the giving of political independence to Black Africa, we must add a brief section explaining General de Gaulle's policies in the sixties, and try to see whether they had a lasting effect on French relations with Black Africa during the General's final years of power, and in the later period when he was no longer living. The policy of President Giscard d'Estaing should point the way to understanding what the situation is today and what it may be in the immediate future.

If time and materials are available, the author would like to undertake a more complete study of what happened in the sixties and thereafter, in order to chart the changes that have come about in the relationship between France and her former colonies. It may be possible then to consider the development of African political institutions and attitudes, and what share the General had in producing the current situation. And it may be appropriate, too, at that time to consider some of the scientific aspects, anthropological, economic, and social, that today are widening the field of history of the world and of Africa.

Dorothy S. White

Chestnut Hill, Pennsylvania
July–August 1978

In a general way, the colonized peoples have perceived that they hold only a second-class status and are condemned to inferiority, but they know, too, that they want to be on the upper level. The idea of the possession of their countries by outsiders was always painful, both to kings and commoners. However, the colonizers, in the early days at least, looked at those they had conquered as savages without souls, sometimes almost as if they were animals. Thus they justified themselves in whatever they did, and their attitudes were daggers in the souls of the blacks and other nonwhite races—daggers that remained in the wounds. The different approach of those who were really interested in the dominated peoples was not enough to prevent the break-up of a system that could not continue on a large scale because of its inner tensions. An old African proverb says, "Only a free man can work with patience because he is working for himself."[22] Colonization today has become unworkable, at least in most places.

There were many difficulties for colonizers in Africa. The geography, the climate, the living things, both animal and human, did not make life easy for Europeans. To begin with, the area the French controlled in the nineteenth century was huge—eight and a half times the size of France. Size made government extremely difficult. Four and a half million square kilometers is an almost impossible territory for relatively few administrators to govern. Before the time of railroads and airplanes, it could take a Frenchman landing in Dakar two months to reach his assignment in Chad.

Many colonies were caught between the desert and the ocean, with a shoreline indented by usable ports in only a few places. To penetrate this coast, after a long and fearsome sea voyage, the French going into Africa had to cross bars where the water dashed wildly against hidden rocks. The larger ships could not pass; passengers had to be hoisted overside in baskets lowered from the ship so they could jump the rest of the way to the sea into dugout canoes on its surface. Sometimes even skilled Africans were drowned in attempting to ride the waves over the reefs. On the return voyage, the winds were so capricious that the ships had to sail far out into the ocean before they could turn north to Europe. The prize had to be great to compensate for even those delays and risks.

Coastal West Africa is mostly low-lying, with long, muddy river estuaries that generally end in vast, almost impassable mangrove swamps. Even the great rivers are capable of swelling over their banks in the rains or drying up in the droughts. Inland, there are waterfalls and rapids. Though the plateaus that cover much of the interior at some distance from the sea are easy to enter, they fold into valleys with steep sides. Occasionally there are mountains, though only a few in Guinea or the Cameroons rise more than five thousand feet, not high enough to prevent their being crossed by man. The mountains influence Africa's climate, for they intercept the rainy monsoons from the ocean and dry desert winds, the harmattans, from the land. Perhaps they have had a psychological effect, too; when one sees the smooth sides of Mount Cameroon rising up toward heaven, close by the sea, and knows that the people of the country call it "the chariot of God," it is easy to feel that its mental effect must have been considerable.

The African climate is formidable and capricious. Sometimes it is too hot, humid, and wet, especially near the coast and in the forests; elsewhere it may be too dry. At its worst, the heat can go to more than one hundred degrees Fahrenheit, afflicting men with prostrating debility or immense fatigue. In the Congo and sometimes elsewhere, thirty feet of rain may pour down in a year. As Mary Kingsley, that intrepid British explorer and scientist of the 1890s, wrote, "There ought to be some other word than rain for that sort of thing . . . the interspaces between the pipes of water—for it did not go into detail with drops—were filled with grey mist, and as this rain struck the sea it kicked up such a water dust that you saw not the surface of the sea around you, but only a mist gliding by." Jacques Richard-Molard, the great Africanist, wrote:

> It came that night, or rather it precipitated itself desperately on the village with the speed of a White Man's machine. In an instant all the stars have disappeared under a thick blanket of black, rolling toward the west in fury, in a prodigious uproar of thunder, lightning and hurricane. The Whites say it is the "harmattan of the heights, descending like a wedge under the heavy monsoon, forcing it to rise and then to transform itself into a deluge."

"The rain," he said, "can never be forgotten." Marcel Chailley, a military man who was also a historian, wrote that it explained the country. Villages on the savannas, or huts under the great trees in the steaming undergrowth of the forests, never gave much protection to the people who lived in them. On the other hand, if there is no rain, there may be drought, causing fear and anguish at the prospect of famine. Neither are the wide savannas safe for man, with their expanse of tall grasses, their "candle-like euphorbias," spreading umbrella trees, or spiky thornbushes. They may be the haunt of great herds of antelope, wildebeest, zebra, lion, leopard, hyena, rhinoceros, hippo, or elephant. "And in worming your way in the underbrush among the creepers, there are myriads of poisonous snakes," and, as Mary Kingsley said, "you may even find yourself in a gigantic python's sleeping-place."[23]

Mary herself had to travel in a long, bulky woolen skirt, tight blouse, high-boned collar and all the rest of the Victorian equipment, yet she managed to get to the interior of West Africa three times, though she had little money and spoke no French. With her paddle she beat off crocodiles who were trying to join her in her canoe. She lived among the most hostile tribes—even those said to be cannibalistic. She jumped into the water, long skirt and all, to help her African aides push her canoe over rapids or around a corner. She became a specialist on West African fish and West African religions. She survived in spite of perils until she went to South Africa to nurse soldiers in the Boer War, and there she died. Such a waste! Many people can nurse; few are scientific explorers, and fewer still have Mary's sense of humor.

To return to the characteristics of Africa, even the insects are hostile, for they include malaria-carrying mosquitoes and the tsetse fly with its load of sleeping sickness. Both man and his animals succumbed to those small hosts of death for many centuries.

Geographers ticketed the different parts of Africa very quickly in the early days of discovery. The westernmost projection of land between two navigable rivers, the Senegal and the Gambia, was called Senegambia. Then, going east and south around the "Bulge," they named the first part of the coast Malaguette (pepper), or the Coast of Seeds. Beyond that lay the Coast of Teeth, now the Ivory Coast; after it came the Coast of Gold, and finally the Coast of Slaves. Then, passing the curve in the land, there were the Kingdoms of the Black Kings, Assinie, Benin, and, farther on, Gabon and the Congo. The whole two thousand miles of the "dog's leg" of Africa was called Upper Guinea, or the Windward Coast, because of the onshore winds there, and all to the south of the great Port of Cape Castle was called the Leeward Coast. From Calabar, near the Cameroons, to the Southern Desert stretched the fifteen hundred miles of Lower Guinea.

But the early geographers knew little of the interior of Africa. They thought the Niger River was the Nile of the west and that it rose near the Mountains of the Moon in Uganda, whereas, in reality, it takes its rise in the mountains of Guinea, the Fouta Djalon. The Senegal and the Gambia rivers were thought to be its mouths. The Congo River was also a mystery. No one had followed these rivers to their sources, and when the great streams turned or made a bend, as the Niger did, it fooled all the students and discoverers. It was centuries before these kinks in geographic thought could be straightened out.[24]

Thus the "Bled-es Soudan," the Country of the Blacks, was hard to conquer or to colonize. Death's cross was everywhere. It is not surprising that West Africa was known as "the White Man's Grave," since it really was so for a goodly number of Europeans. The story of European exploration began with the few who sailed south in the fourteenth century and increased to a very considerable number later on. Some may have died there from unknown natural causes, but many were struck down by diseases, of which there were an endless number—yellow fever, dengue, typhus, cholera, leprosy, among others. Of course, there was always malaria, for untroubled anopheles mosquitoes made happy homes in the ponds and marshes left by rivers that rose in the wet season and later returned to their banks; and, until the nineteenth century, prevention by quinine was not known. When there was no menace of disease, there might always be famine and malnutrition if the rain failed and no crops grew. Harvests were often small in any case, for the soil was poor and had few minerals. One professor wrote that "from earth and waters there rose a poisoned breath."[25]

If the foreigner survived the climate, the ferocious animals and insects, the tropical diseases, and the famines, there was still the matter of human violence, collective and individual. Many of the black peoples did not welcome strangers, and there were often wars, small or great, with the hostile tribes who raided European territories to reconquer them or to steal goods from the invaders. Sometimes rival European powers appeared. England, Holland, Portugal, Spain—all the colonizing countries—would have liked to own the coast of West Africa, and at times they fought one another for it. It is no wonder, as Hubert-Jules Deschamps has said, that with all these obstacles of nature and of human and animal life, Africa "discouraged even curiosity."[26] Indeed, everywhere the white man went, the Four Horsemen of the Apocalypse—War, Famine, Disease, and Death—rode with him.

Obviously, all those who went to Africa expected great returns for subjecting themselves to such dangers. They had all heard talk of what was to be found in Africa: ivory, skins, pepper, palm oil, and, last but not least, slaves. If they got as far as the Island of Madagascar, Ceylon, or the Indies, the list would include pearls, rubies, diamonds, and turquoise as well as silks, perfumes, ambergris, incense, or bezoar to counteract poison.[27] The catalog was enough to make men's mouths water and the hands in their pockets itch.

Above all, there would be gold—gold that came from the valleys, hills, rivers, and shores of Africa—and black men who knew where it was to be found and how to collect it, after it had been driven down the rivers by violent showers of rain in the night. In the morning, it was said, "these places are sure to be visited by hundreds of Negroe-Women naked, except a Cloth wrapped around them to hide what Modesty obligeth," and "each of them furnished with large or small Troughs or Tray, which they first fill full of Earth and Sand, which they wash with repeated fresh Water, till they have cleansed it from all its Earth; and if there be any Gold, its Ponderosity forces it to the bottom of the Trough." This information came from William Bosman, a Dutch factor, who lived several years in Africa at the end of the seventeenth century.[28]

Of course, Bosman told the other side of the story, too: how traders could be cheated by the blacks who knew how to counterfeit "Gold Dust" and the "Mountain Gold" in nuggets, too, by filling the pieces in which it was sold with copper or iron full of color, "which very much facilitates the Cheat" and "it looking so well, causeth it to pass unsuspected." However, Bosman added, one could beat or cut the gold pieces and detect the false from the true. Gold, then, was nearly as alluring as slaves, and was one of the hidden magnets that drew voyagers from Europe to West Africa.

Missionaries, too, were drawn to the Dark Continent. As one of them wrote much later, Africa offered the lure of "making a gift of that little thing which did not belong to me and which I had called my life."[29]

In short, riches and knowledge and human purposes and glory all beckoned, and men went out to find them, forgetting the menace of the White Man's Grave. Their voyages to West Africa continued through all the years from the time of the early discoverers to the Second World War. Then nationalism and the desire for independence, though little expressed up to that point, at least by the Africans, began to be spoken of openly throughout Africa, and Europeans began to realize the changed attitudes of the peoples there. A number of countries were released from the colonial relationship by the Western colonizers.[30] At last, Charles de Gaulle, who had been so long a "man of the Empire," reached Africa, gradually came to understand the situation, and began to think his way out of the old beliefs about the rightness and necessity of the domination of one people by another. His actions and those of a few others would lead to the political independence of fifteen states.

1

The Life and Death of the
First Colonial Empire of France

Who reached the White Man's Grave first? Robert Cornevin, a well-known French historian of Africa, thinks it was the French, but Herr Hennig, a German scholar, and Catherine Coquery-Vidrovitch, a French specialist on Black Africa, are both doubtful. Others think it may have been the Portuguese. Even if the French did reach Guinea with various expeditions in the fourteenth century—and that is not proven—we know that the Portuguese were there by 1434. In that year Prince Henry the Navigator succeeded in persuading his squire, Gil Eanes, with whom he had talked of the project for fourteen years, to sail around the great bulge of Africa and find out what was there. Gil did not want to go, and with good reason, for people thought that he would find there monsters without ears or noses, or those with no tongues, only a hole to suck through, and half-human things even more fearful. When he reached Guinea, he found nothing at all. It must have been a comedown. Still, not daring to return empty-handed, he plucked a few desert flowers, the Roses of Our Lady, and took them to his master.[1]

Certainly Gil had courage, and, as one of Jean Ango's men, Pierre Crignon, said, the Portuguese "must have drunk of the dust of Alexander's heart to have such inordinate ambition."[2] But perhaps they had no more than the seamen of Dieppe who worked for Jean Ango, the man who armed and supplied them so that they could set forth on voyages half around the globe, reaching even the far island of Madagascar. Some managed to return home after such voyages, but some did not. Certainly they were a gifted group, for among them were those who had studied at the Dieppe school of nautical science, or had even been in the group of poets, musicians, and dramatists who gathered around the great Ango in his town house in Dieppe or at his manor nearby at Varengeville. Dieppe was a well-known city then, with a reputation for seafaring.[3]

In 1493, Pope Alexander VI divided the world beyond the known ocean between the Spanish and the Portuguese. The French were given little or no part in it, to the annoyance of Francis I, their king. That dauntless ruler told the Spanish ambassador that the pope had no right to distribute sections of the world among kings, especially since the pontiff had not consulted France. He added that he would like to see our forefather Adam's will, and know how he had allotted the parts of the world. Clearly, Francis had swallowed some of Alexander's dust, too, or he could not have confronted the pope in that fashion.

Later, Voltaire said he didn't know which was the more remarkable—that so many lands should have been discovered or that the bishop of Rome should have given them all away.[4] For his part, Francis set up the doctrine of "permanent occupation," which has been the method of establishing modern colonization ever since, so his work lasted longer than the pope's.

But many Europeans continued to go to Africa, in spite of what they found there: even fetishes, bloody "customs" including tortures or executions for ceremonial purposes.[5] Knowledge of Africa was limited in Europe, and there were also terrible perils to be dared on the sea. Letters of marque issued by certain kings could force vessels to halt and give up the pillage they had taken, at least in an amount equal to the theft committed; or entire ships could be captured as legitimate prizes of enemy countries at war; or they might be seized by pirates.[6] One British commander was hauled before a pirate chief and asked how he had dared to resist, but he replied with such a string of oaths that the pirate chief thought it would be a sin to kill a man with such an extensive vocabulary![7] Others were not so fortunate.

Life at sea was ruthless, and the sailors knew they might never again see home. Still, for the independent French, who did not like to be governed, it was a good life.[8] There were—and still are—two kinds of Frenchmen: the home-loving and static, and the "universalists" who are always ready for adventure and, like Herzog and Cousteau, will go to mountain tops or sea depths to find it. The seamen learned geography and a little of the world, and some of this knowledge filtered back to France.

The division of the French into two kinds of personalities, the stay-at-homes and those who wandered the world, shows why it is always difficult to unite the people of France on any characteristic, except, perhaps, one: the love of power and glory. And it may explain, at least partially, why the French took and held colonies. The conditions of the time had a share in those actions, too. General de Gaulle has noted as one of his main principles that all decisions must be taken in view of the circumstances of the individual case, never merely in accordance with a previously held theory.[9]

During the first quarter of the seventeenth century, the French struggled along, relying on forts and castles they had built on the Guinea coast to maintain their presence in West Africa. After that, outfitters with powerful state-chartered companies behind them made possible the beginning of vast public or semipublic organizations that turned men's minds toward more permanent colonization. Companies of Senegal and Gambia, of Saint Malo, of Paris, and elsewhere were established, each with trading privileges in certain parts of the African coast, and together with their rivals in Africa and the Caribbean, they sponsored the beginnings of the slave trade as a system. But their success was uncertain. Wars were still frequent, and destruction by the natural causes of sun, wind, and wave was continual. Bad management and lack of interest in official circles in Paris also contributed to the failure of the French enterprises. Between 1664 and 1758 there were no less than six such companies in succession.[10]

It was Cardinal Richelieu, says Hubert Deschamps, who laid the foundations

The early French fort at Wydah (Ouidah) on the coast of present-day Dahomey.

of the First French Empire, using all his managerial ability and his desire to increase the grandeur of France by securing foreign lands and sending families out to people them. His successor, Jean-Baptiste Colbert, promoted trade interests, especially that of slavery, but even with his "magnificent ideas" the colonies often came to a bad end. His "mercantile" policy required that both import and export trade be kept exclusively to the overseas lands of France, and a sort of colonial pact grew up to insure an exclusive system of trade with the home country. The method lasted until the outbreak of the French Revolution. Colbert's other legacy was the *Code Noir*, articles drawn up legally to instruct slave masters as to how they must deal with their black charges.[11] But were his rules obeyed? We do not know.

Just before Richelieu died, he had formed a Company of the East Indies to establish a colony on the Great Island, Madagascar. Men—some good, some bad—went out to try to make it permanent. At least one French governor did not try to exterminate the inhabitants, as the Spaniards had done in some places, though he left behind him an inscription on a stone that read:

> Oh thou who comest here, heed our counsel,
> it will be useful to thee, for thy people and for thy life:
> Beware of the inhabitants! Greetings.[12]

Some were optimistic, others less so, but it seems clear that the French did better with the Africans in the Great Island than several other nations had done.[43] Still, there is a long story of misery, of wars with natives or with colonial rivals, of forgetfulness of the needs of the colonies on the part of officials in Paris, and of raids led by the French among the native villages to obtain sufficient food to remain alive. A final admission of failure came when the colonists, just as the home government annexed the island, decided they could stand their troubles no longer and went to another island, the Ile de Bourbon, part of the Mascareigne group near Madagascar, so that they might start afresh.[14] The whole system of the great companies began to fade as the century ended, and mercantilism gave way to the economic liberalism and expansion of the eighteenth century.[15]

Most important in the seventeenth century, however, was the great growth of the slave trade, though it would increase even more in the next hundred years. Equally vital, or even more so, was the change in ideas: Descartes' "atomic bomb," the belief that good judgment and good sense were "naturally equal in all men." Reason, the Light of the World, could be found in every man, and that, in the last analysis, would lead to the Declaration of the Rights of Man. Such ideas ruined scholasticism and bequeathed to men the new method of direct reasoning. In addition, the seeds of colonization, the discoveries, the colonial installations with the slave trade in the center, acted as a background for the spread of the colonial attitude in later centuries, arousing both belief in the old system and violent dissent from it.[16] From the time of discoveries on, the French believed that men were essentially similar all over the world, and that concept led to the policy of "assimilation" that was applied in the colonies. If men were all alike, why could the French not teach other more deprived races about their own civilization and persuade them to adopt it?[17]

Why did the colonized world not revolt sooner? Clearly, the Africans needed time and better armaments to revolt effectively, and, certainly, the Europeans, weakened by two world wars, and forced by later conditions to see the situation in Africa more clearly, were ready by the mid-twentieth century to accept the inevitable and join the Africans in answering the age-old questions about dependency.

Empires, like human beings, always have a birth and a death, and African empires are no exception to the rule, though most Americans, until recently, have been unaware that Africa, too, had set up empires. Ghana died in the eleventh century, and later Mali, born in the thirteenth, flourished, together with Songhai and Bornu, until well into the fifteenth. By the seventeenth, all these African empires were fading fast. However, in the 1900s such groups arose again, and they had to be conquered before the French could dominate the regions where trade, prestige, or rivalry led them. Gold, slaves, and ivory had caused these empires to become prosperous, but the tribes that composed them varied a great deal in race, cultures, and social systems. Nevertheless, they had certain characteristics that were similar.[18]

At the base of these similarities was a philosophy that was one of the chief foundations of African culture. This philosophy has generally been called Animism, and one of its chief beliefs is, and was, that the past always impregnates the present; "it is never dead." In a sense, it is a religion, for it implies obedience to a single god, who is, however, attended by a whole pantheon of secondary gods. Their duty is to supervise a harmonious world that is often broken but is restored again. It is peopled with beings who must die, but who, during their lifetimes, have special gifts of speech, together with the primal techniques of agriculture, weaving, forging, etc. In their lives there is a moral order which it is men's task to keep in harmony with itself. A multiple soul and an immaterial force exists in all of it, keeping a continuity between the living and the dead. The aged of the race serve as guides for the living and as interpreters for the dead. There are cults, rites, and sacrifices to be carried out, and custom is always a sure pathway from the past to the present and to the future.[19]

Such a society is, and was, static, but Africans have kept the advantage of a sense of the sacred, at least until exterior ideas entered their continent; even then, they retained their own essential attitudes. The spirit world is still around them, for, as Birago Diop has written: "Hear more often things than beings . . . hear in the wind the bushes sobbing, it is the sigh of our forefathers."[20]

Some centuries ago, Islam came through the desert with its prayers and holy wars and massacres; it carried with it a principle of unification, for it attested the unity of God. It superseded Animism in some places, but had little influence in the interior forests of Africa. Authority came with the Muslims through their past and their religion, and they brought with them discipline and a hierarchical structure that tended toward the unification of states.[21] In both Animist and Muslim religions, the family is a strong link in the chain, legitimating the power of relatives, both living and dead.[22]

The way the African lived was also important, for it has imposed a style of life on his descendants, at least in their homelands. The village was the largest political form of the district. Life was hard, and the gods must be propitiated into helping humankind. Work was often done in common, and possessions were likewise held in common. Tasks done, the people returned to their round or square mud huts, with a wood fire in the center and a clay bed supported by wooden walls or forks—the chief article of furniture. Gourds held food and drink, and there were a few utensils, bows and arrows, swords, and nets for hunting. G-strings and lengths of cloth protected the people from the sun. Food was uncertain, owing to flooding rivers, droughts, and the depredations of wild animals, so that moving was often necessary.[23] Africa thus became a mosaic of nationalities in many places.

The African, wrote Georges Hardy, is joyous, talkative, with a force that is almost animal. He loves music and the dance and often joins in associations. He is careless rather than provident and needs a strong authority, but he also has courage and real generosity. Moral life is intense, and religion governs all. On the negative side, he can be a cannibal, perhaps due to mystical reasons, though possibly the eating of human flesh is more often allied to famine conditions. In the *coutumes*, or ceremonies, when a king died, human beings were sacrificed, sometimes in large numbers, for on those occasions it would have been impious to make no offering.[24]

It is almost impossible for Europeans to understand both the simplicity of African life and the complexity of its religious attitudes and practices, not to mention the selling of the Africans' own peoples into slavery. But neither could the inhabitants of Africa understand European domination of other people's countries, nor the burning of their villages and the massacres sometimes carried on by the European armies in Africa.

The eighteenth century was an age of great contrasts for those Frenchmen who went to Africa, for the difference was extreme between life in France and in her African colonies. The upper echelons of the French, accustomed as they were to a life that was as "civilized" as the age permitted, found in the Dark Continent a world that seemed to them still primitive and subject to the whims of nature and to those of the human beings, both French and African, that lived there.

The meaningless, overluxurious life at Versailles foreshadowed the close of the first period of French colonization.[25] In France, the people were impoverished in some parts of the country due to higher prices, little industrial activity, and excessive taxation. New crops were introduced, requiring new tools that the peasants could not afford to buy, and the landowners wanted more money from their holdings. So France was disturbed internally, and public attention was taken off an empire that had been collected with much pain and suffering.[26] Yet wars with France's rivals in colonial waters went on and on. There were vicious quarrels between the French and the Portuguese, Dutch, English, Danes and Brandenburgers. Their agents, soldiers, and sailors fought on both land and sea, taking and retaking castles, forts, and "factories." Ships were destroyed and supplies affected. "But," says Robert Cornevin, "the beau monde at Versailles that saw lightheartedly both India and Canada leave the Empire, scarcely paid any more attention to the African trading-stations where the English were taking precedence over the momentary allies of France."[27]

Yet, because of the slave trade and the money that it brought in from the sugar plantations of America, the colonies were, to a great degree, responsible for the fine living and the lights of Paris and of all the surrounding cities and towns. And Africa had become, as Karl Marx would write later, "a sort of commercial preserve for the hunting of Blacks" in order to make such a contribution.[28]

The west coast seaborne trade was expanding with the need for Africa's most important commodity, her strong black men. New city-states appeared in the Niger Delta and Dahomey, all of them based on the slave trade. The chiefs punished European incursions when necessary, but when the supply of lawbreakers and captives ran out, and the native rulers needed firearms to make war on their neighbors and obtain men and women for the foreign traders, then they were dependent on the Europeans' equipment. Intertribal war began far inland, and the coastal chiefs became middlemen between slaver ships and the tribes of the interior. This commerce built up the prosperity of the African towns and cities, just as their European partners in the "triangular trade" brought wealth to Western Europe. Yet the Africans, too, suffered from

A convoy of slaves on their way to the coast to be sold in the days of the First French Empire.

the dangers and risks of the slave trade, for there was internal dissension between the tribes that provided the slaves. So Europe affected Africa in spite of her lack of penetration into the interior. This helped later to open the way for European conquest.[29]

An *asiento*, a defined permission to buy slaves in Africa and sell them in America under certain conditions, was granted to the Guinea Company in 1701, and the trade flourished.[30] At one time, the company carried a license to transport 38,250 slaves. In 1702, the Dutch attacked a French fort at Issinie on the Guinea coast. At the same moment, a swarm of bees attacked the French. They left all and fled, and the Dutch, thinking the fort was theirs, sent fifty men ashore to occupy it. Meantime, the French had managed to conquer the assault of the bees, and they entered the fort again by a side door and killed or took prisoner the attacking force of Dutchmen.[31] The Dutch retired; no one knows the fate of the bees. So the French kept Issinie, at least for the time.

The conflicts went on and on. The French built a strong fort at Ouidah in Dahomey, a place contested by the Dutch, the English, the Portuguese, and the Danes. But for once an international agreement was signed, settling the differences among the nations, and the French kept Ouidah. The peace there lasted twenty years. However, the French lost their chance to make their stay permanent when the captain of their force had a nosebleed and thought he had better go home. (One wonders what happened to him when he reached France!) So the Dutch and the Brandenburgers obtained the country around Ouidah until 1763, when the original owners, the Dahomeans, drove the foreigners out. They did not, however, trouble to suppress the slave trade.[32]

Senegal, as well as Guinea, was important in the eighteenth century. The new Company of Senegal, in 1696, had privileges from Cape Blanc (now in Mauritania) to Sierra Leone. It was fortunate in sending to Senegal one of the great colonial officers of France, André Brue, who went there three times between 1697 and 1723, trying to undo the damage done by the English and the Dutch and working to unite the colony. He set up forts, one in the first French post in the Western Soudan, reinstalled others, and pushed the boundaries of the colony as far south as he could. Once he was captured by Lat Soucabé, the ruler of a town northeast of Dakar, who threatened his life and then decided it would be more lucrative to hold him hostage. Somehow the government came up with the money required, the captives were released and Brue got his revenge with a blockade and military action.[33]

During the War of the Spanish Succession, Brue made a mutual aid pact with the British governor of Gambia (whose very British name was Corker), and there was peace between Senegal and Gambia during two decades—again a long time for those lands. Then, after returning to Paris for a time, Brue went back to Senegal to restore damaged forts and to try to control certain mines there. But now the French government intervened for the first time in the colonial administration, controlling the commercial companies there by royal commission, and Brue was not able to acquire the funds he needed. However, he did erect forts, and he started a trade in the kind of gum that was used in Europe as a remedy for colds, dysentery, and other ailments as well as in the textile industry. He used this gum as a means of competing with the Dutch and obtained a right to acquire it at a post at Portendick, to the north on the Senegal River. He succeeded in establishing good relations there with the local chiefs and in winning great prestige—not great enough, however, to keep him out of trouble, for his second in command accused him of thievery, saying he had carried off the company linen, spoons, and forks from the post on leaving. Though he was exonerated, such an accusation should not, it seems, have been made of a man so devoted to his task. Again he recaptured a post from the Dutch, but several other posts were lost, and he went home to France sick at heart. He ranks as a great man who could not make his greatness count as it should have. There were too many vultures standing around to tear off pieces of the land he had rebuilt.[34]

In 1763, the Treaty of Paris gave the English all of Senegal except the island of Gorée off the harbor of Dakar and a bit of the "little coast" south of the city. Other governors went to Senegal but had little or no success. Yellow fever was brought in from Guiana; the French retreated to the mainland; and, in 1791, the last company was dissolved and the administration was turned over to the state. One last ray of light came with another distinguished governor, the chevallier de Boufflers, in 1786. His fame was rather as a fine letter writer than as an administrator, for he had left his heart in Paris with his mistress, the Countess de Sabran, and his letters to her carried news and accounts of what went on in the colonies, communications that have been useful both then and now. The lovely red brick house he left on Gorée remains, too, as a reminder of a distinguished man of whatever calling. But the colony was falling into disrepair and it would not be rescued for a long time.[35]

From the far-off islands, in this eighteenth century, there came much talk of pirates around Madagascar. Among them was the celebrated Captain Kidd—

hanged at last in London, on three counts of piracy and one of murder. There were others, too, who founded the "International Republic of Libertalia" on the island, but they managed to pay no penalty. However, something had to be done about them. Count Modave, in trying to right the situation, managed to get the Paris colonial officials to let him start a small colony on Madagascar. He thought he could rule it so that the people would not know they were being ruled, but somehow the islanders found out what he was doing, and there was a scandal because he had freed some slaves. A massacre occurred, and Count Modave went back to the Indian army whence he came.

Another even stranger adventurer began by calling himself Baron Benyowski and ended by bestowing on himself the title of "Emperor of Madagascar." When the French government got around to investigating what he had done, his achievements were seen to be nothing less than catastrophic. The city he claimed to have built was a rotten palisade on a marsh with a few worm-eaten huts on it; much money had been lost; many men had died of fever. The "emperor" was sent home, but for some odd reason, he was not punished, and the government still seemed to want to colonize Madagascar.[36]

In 1765, the duc de Choiseul, then minister of foreign affairs, wrote out instructions for the colonies. They existed merely for trade, he said, and they must produce products different from those of the metropole. They were to be controlled under stiff laws that favored the mother country. There was no indication of how beneficial this arrangement was, or of what it accomplished.[37]

Part of the trouble, no doubt, was due to the kind of French people who went out to the colonies during this century. Bernardin de Saint-Pierre wrote home about this assortment of all-powerful company employees, tradespeople, sailors, missionaries, fortune hunters, bankrupts, ruined libertines, knaves and rascals, all of whom had been chased out of Europe. No wonder they could not get on with one other! Among the natives, also, there were thieves and plunderers. Life was not a bed of roses in France's overseas territories, and those who went there were not roses either.[38]

Apart from all this, the careless world of Paris continued to exist, with its excessive luxury and its neglect of its own colonial officials. Indeed, the colonies made a large contribution to all the worlds of Paris (with its merchants, black and white), in spite of the cloud of the slave trade that hung over all. Yet in France the eighteenth was called the "Century of Enlightenment."

Slavery reached its greatest height in the eighteenth century, and it lasted well into the nineteenth. The holding of slaves seems to have been in the tradition of the white race from the distant past.[39] At times, there was some limited realization that it was not right, but that understanding was only spasmodic. Slavery had been normal in Africa—and was sometimes gentler there, for slaves were taken into families and well treated—but when slaves became financially profitable, the trade became odious. The center of it was on the west coast of Africa, where slaves were brought from all over the continent—most of them probably from coastal tribes, but there were many exceptions. France did not allow slavery within her own borders, yet she did not forbid it in the islands, especially after she obtained Guadeloupe and Martinique, in 1626 and 1635, for slave labor was needed there.[40] But France and the other colonizing countries sometimes fought, each to obtain its own advantage in slavery as in other matters.[41]

Among the slaves there were men, women, and children of many varieties. Some of them had been criminals enslaved for punishment. Others were children sold in times of famine. Still others were prisoners of war, among them those captured in raids carried out by African chiefs or kidnapped by Europeans. "Buckra panyaring," it was called, and it was carried out by enticing the Africans near ships and binding them, or by quick forays at night to seize people in the coastal towns and carry them on board the slave ships. So, as Robert Cornevin says, the "infernal cycle" was begun, and military means carried it out, taking the best, young, dynamic elements of the peoples.[42] A careful study has recently been made of the numbers of slaves taken and sent to America, most of them assigned to the sugar plantations. Philip D. Curtin, author of the study, admits that none of his numbers are certain but feels, nevertheless, that they are useful. He believes that from 1761 to 1770 the French took 115,400 slaves out of Africa. The total they transported from the coastal region from 1751 to 1800 was apparently 617,800. The mortality on the ships en route to America averaged 14.3 percent, not counting the losses from shipwreck or capture at sea, but varied all the way from 7.9 to 22.4 percent. In all, the drain on African manpower from 1781 to 1790 alone probably amounted to close to 271,500. It was the all-time peak of the French trade in "Black Ivory." But Curtin gives no total figure for the numbers of slaves carried across the ocean over the years by the French.[43]

It was the manner of the trade, however, that was the most shocking fact: the long coffles of human beings chained together, led or driven from the interior to the coast; the inadequate feeding and housing of the slaves in the barracoons, where they waited for ships to take them overseas. This was bad enough; worse still was the inhuman crowding on the ships that took the slaves to the New World. Often they were chained into position one above the other, and there were unspeakable heavy punishments for any form of rebellion (of which, naturally enough, there were many incidents). And finally, the death toll by disease and suicide was extremely heavy.[44]

We cannot know who was most guilty with regard to the slave trade: the colonizers who bought and shipped the slaves; the blacks who sold them; the captains of the vessels who maltreated them; or the masters of the plantations in the Antilles and elsewhere who worked them, often cruelly. The curse of inferiority cast upon these people because of their treatment by the white race came relatively late.[45] It was used to justify the trade and also to make the Europeans feel that the way to the conquest of all Africa was open. The depopulation that the trade caused in Africa was a most serious blow to her development, and in the long run, slavery by its excesses laid one of the foundations for decolonization.

During the time of this trade in black men and women, the French felt they were doing their inferiors a favor by colonizing them. They believed they could teach the Africans something about civilization by assimilating them to the French way of life. The undoubted existence of some savage habits among the Africans helped the Europeans to justify themselves. There was certainly cannibalism in Africa, as well as human sacrifice. Europeans were used to cruelties in war, but not to those practices, and reacted with a sort of racism.[46]

The traffic in slaves was profitable, no doubt, though it is hard to be sure to what extent. However, as time went on, the costs of the companies dealing with it became absurdly inflated, and debts mounted. Gradually, important posts in Africa were lost, and the trade decreased.[47]

Through the ages, even in Roman times, there were a few individuals who disapproved of both slavery and the colonialism that was so involved with it. Some antislavery men in France were among the best minds of their periods. Pierre Ronsard, the poet, wanted native races to remain in their happy state of ignorance, virtue or vice,[48] and Rabelais, the humorous prose writer, described a free colony of "Utopians" in "Dipsodia" where all would be treated as carefully as newly planted trees.[49] Later, Montaigne feared the Europeans might have eyes bigger than their stomachs, and in embracing all "might only clasp the wind."[50] And in the sixteenth century, a courageous bishop, Bartholomé de Las Casas, said that conquest should be for conversion, not for domination.[51] Montesquieu, however, seemed sometimes for and sometimes against colonization.[52] There were others; but the man who really influenced the century was Abbé Guillaume Thomas Raynal, whose popular book informed Europe of what was happening in the colonies. He pleaded for better treatment of the Africans, though he did not ask freedom for them, and later he seems to have revised his opinions.[53] Voltaire was both anticruelty and anticolonial. He thought the blacks were inferior, but believed that decolonization was in the nature of things.[54]

Eventually, it became evident that some alterations and reforms were needed. The *Encyclopédie* of the famous *philosophes* showed the wavering character of the period, as well as the interest in intellectual matters, for example, in the science of geography. It also showed uncertainty, ignorance, and prejudice in its judgments, but, on the other hand, the *Encyclopédie* gave some idea of justice.[55] Other anticolonialist arguments were also put forward. Raynal and Anne-Robert-Jacques Turgot, the French economist, both had mentioned independence for the colonies as an idea for the future, even before the French Revolution, and their work and that of Bernardin de Saint-Pierre (author of the famous novel *Paul et Virginie*)[56] liberalized the popular attitude to slavery. Many of these influential men helped to introduce Black Africa into French literature. The foundation of the *Societé des Amis des Noirs* (Society of the Friends of the Blacks) was another important influence. The society did not ask immediate freedom for the blacks, for that was thought to presage the ruin of colonies,[57] but it is clear that the movement against slavery was well on its way by the time of the Revolution.

At the start of the Revolution, a few colonial representatives had been admitted unwillingly to the Estates General, but they were, of course, white colons whom the French were trying to tie more closely to the metropole.

However, the new constitution of 1791 excluded even those from the administration of the overseas lands, for it was planned to govern the colonies by colonial assemblies, whose actions would later be ratified by the national Assembly in Paris. There was trouble at the time in the West Indies, but some people in France, including Robespierre, tried to champion the colons. A series of liberal decrees began to be issued in 1791, when more freedom of trade was instituted. Finally, the privileges of the great companies were abolished, and rights of citizenship were granted, though few persons took advantage of that permission. But, in Africa, the colonies were nearly cut off, for England had become aggressive again, and France lost most of Senegal. There was discord and no authority in Africa or in America, and a new constitution was drawn up for colonial possessions, though it was full of restrictions. Administrators were to be named by France, the *exclusif* of trade only with the mother country would be maintained, and customs duties would be suppressed. At last, in 1794, the Convention abolished slavery, and the right of the blacks to be citizens was proclaimed.[58] Victory seemed won.

With the advent of Napoleon, however, slavery was reestablished. Napoleon had some interest in the colonies, though its basis, no doubt, was their economic possibilities. France must not let her colonies fall away as England had; they must be located in warm countries, and well managed. In addition, new lands to settle must be found. Many people felt something must take the place of the colonies that had been lost. It was important to handle colonial possessions well.[59]

Bonaparte's Egyptian expedition, with its "living encyclopedia" of learned men, was intended to ameliorate the lot of the Egyptians, to respect their customs and to separate them from their Turkish oppressors, practicing what was later called a "native policy." But Napoleon's army disintegrated, and his efforts went for nothing. Still, he was a precursor, as Deschamps says, of modern policy toward colonized peoples, promoting contemporary forms of political association as well as those of the Arab renaissance. He used methods of colonization that the nineteenth century had to rediscover slowly.[60]

Napoleon's principle in reserving many decisions for the person in command was very similar to General de Gaulle's. Like de Gaulle, he wanted to adapt decisions and consequent actions to current circumstances. He was, however, antiblack, thinking it impossible to give blacks liberty, for in his eyes they had no civilization and did not understand what a colony was. Nevertheless, Napoleon was probably "a great technician of colonization," for what he did was carried on in a way that was basically revolutionary for the colonial doctrines of the time.[61]

The emperor did not succeed in keeping the colonies, and the constitution he planned for them was never written. Just before he left power, he abolished slavery again, but under the Bourbons it was restored. Use of the off-shore islands of Africa as colonies had been suggested, but it was not carried out. So, until 1830, when Algeria became important, French interest in the colonies died, for in reality there were no more colonies worthy of the name.[62]

2

The Gathering of the Second
Colonial Empire of France: A Summary

France lost most of her First Colonial Empire to England by the Treaty of 1763 at the end of the Seven Years' War. In addition, the island of Saint Domingue (Haiti and the Dominican Republic today) was lost because of the native revolt there in 1804. Then, at the end of the Napoleonic Wars, in the Treaty of Paris of 1815, more colonies were taken over by England. After that, France held only Guiana, almost a desert; Réunion, an island without a port; the rocks of Saint Pierre-Miquelon, off Newfoundland; Martinique and Guadeloupe, whose sugar trade had diminished with the planting of sugar cane elsewhere and the rise of the sugar beet industry; and, finally, the wreckage of her efforts at colonization in Senegal, which the abolition of the slave trade had ruined.[1] It could scarcely be called an empire.

The French economy was especially poor after Waterloo, and some attempts were made to send out governors to Senegal who would try to make that colony bring in an income. But there was a fatal lack of means to that end, and hostile Africans were near at hand to make trouble. In addition, the country was not suited to the experimental plants that were tried there—except, of course, for the vines of ground-nuts, but those had to wait for a later period to become profitable. More experimentation and exploration were needed to bring in revenue.

One project alone had a good effect in the years after the wars, and that was the Catholic community and schools that Mère Anne-Marie Javouhey, founder of the Order of Saint Joseph de Cluny, and six of her nuns began in Senegal in the early twenties. Later, Mère Javouhey went to Guiana to found a center for culture for the Indians there, but her African project stands as the first missionary work in Senegal capable of enduring effect. King Louis Philippe is said to have remarked, "Madame Javouhey, but she is a great man!"[2]

Oddly enough, the additional exploration of Senegal and the nearby territories was started without any real aid from the French government. Help came through two young men who left France in 1816 on the ill-fated *Medusa*, a ship that went down on the shoals of Arguin, north of Senegal. Géricault made the scene famous by his painting of some of the ship's survivors on the rafts where many of them died. It is said that there was cannibalism among the remainder. The expedition had been sent from France to receive Senegal back from the British in accordance with the Treaty of Paris. The envoys planned, also, to develop the Cape Verde Islands off Senegal, another of those income-producing hopes that was fated to be unprofitable.[3]

Gaspard Théodore Mollien, the older of the two young men, was twenty-two when he embarked on the doomed ship. At the time of the wreck, he was taken off on a boat that managed to reach land. The sun burned the small group of refugees; they had little water and almost no food; yet somehow they reached Saint-Louis, the capital of Senegal. The English governor there had received no word that the city was now French, so he sent the little band on to the island of Gorée, in the seas near Dakar. There several of them died of fever. Mollien survived this peril, too, and soon after, having become interested in the country and the people, he took short trips into the interior. Returning to France, he persuaded some officials to give him a small grant with which he went back to Senegal. The colony's new French governor gave him a mule, a horse, and a Muslim marabout to accompany him on his expedition to trace the sources of the Senegal, Gambia, and Niger rivers.

The trip was a series of nightmares. Mollien often felt the "horrors of hunger," and he said he might easily have gone mad. He traveled among people in Guinea who knew little or nothing of the white race. They were so curious about him that they felt him all over to be sure of his humanity. Did he have a mother? Could he reproduce his kind? Was he born in the depths of the sea? He had to open fire and pretend to charge the crowd before he could get away. A local princess demanded his blanket, but when he gave her one his marabout had used, she threw it in his face, thinking it did not befit her rank.

Mollien was never really comfortable on his travels. He rode by night to avoid the heat. Thorns tore his face, he could scarcely see, but ke kept on. His horse had no food, and Mollien shared his water with him. They had to carry the mule over the streams, and the horse, shaken by a fall in the rocks, had to be lifted back on to his feet. Several times the mule was tied to their canoe during river crossings, and at last the animal drowned. But, enduring all, Mollien achieved his purposes. When he saw a European town at last, he shouted, "Land! Land!" The people rushed out to see him, wondering whether he was really a white man. Back in France he became the idol of the learned societies, for the journal he had kept was a prime historical document, a record of travels in a hitherto unknown country. He was a precursor of other explorers, but the ruin of his health seems a large price for him to pay for his fame.[4]

René Caillié, who also escaped the wreck, was a boy of sixteen with a sad history: his father had been imprisoned for a minor offense and had died before serving out his term. The mother died soon after, and René was brought up by an uncle, who wanted to make him a shoemaker. René had been jeered at by his school companions because he was the son of a convict; so he wanted to get away. He had seen the sea, and he was captivated by the stories he had read of distant lands—especially by tales of the mysterious city of Timbuktu, whence no European had returned alive. With only twenty crowns (about sixty francs) in his pocket, he managed to reach the port of Rochefort, a few miles from his home, and there he embarked as a cabin boy to sail with the fleet of the *Medusa*.

René Caillié, the first Frenchman to reach Timbuktu and return alive.

The ship he was on landed unharmed near Senegal. There he saw many passing caravans from the north and the east with their curious merchandise, and he became even more enthralled by the tales he had heard of the interior of Africa. He found out, too, that a group of men was about to leave Gambia to learn the fate of the Scotch explorer Mungo Park, who had vanished in the interior some years before. Caillié tried to join them but arrived too late in Gambia, and, worn out by the difficult climate, he took passage on a sailing vessel for Guadeloupe. After a few months, he returned to Saint-Louis of Senegal via France. He made another attempt at exploration, but his health gave way a second time. He then spent nine months with a Moslem tribe, the Brakna, learning their language and their customs. After that he wore Arab dress and called himself "Abd Allahi," the Slave of God. In 1824 he returned once more to Saint-Louis. He held a position for a time in a French garden, where he learned about plants and the weather, studied maps, found out how to calculate and draw and, above all, earned a little money. Then he applied to the governor of Senegal for additional funds for his trip, but the governor refused him aid.

Meantime, René had heard of the prize offered by the French Society of Geography for the first man to reach Timbuktu via Senegambia. Somehow, he must be that man. By this time, he had saved two thousand francs from wages earned in Senegal, and he spent most of it on cloth, tobacco, scissors, and cloves. He also bought an umbrella to give him prestige with the Africans, along with two compasses, paper, and a pencil. He did not have a watch; no doubt he did not have enough money for that, so he would have to tell time by the shadows. Thus equipped, he was ready to leave. As he prepared himself, he invented a story to tell about his "Arab" origin, for he would be in great danger if those he met knew he was a Christian; he said always that his family came from Egypt and went via France to Africa. That would explain his Arab past and also his knowledge of the French language. Then, putting his few remaining gold coins—about three hundred francs—in his belt, he persuaded a caravan leader going from Kakondy, Guinea, into the interior, to let him join the caravan. His adventure had begun.

During the first part of the trip, the mountain scenery was gorgeous and René enjoyed himself thoroughly; but then his companions took another road, and, alone, he entered a country where he feared for his life, for the people there were suspicious of his origin. Scurvy made his face almost unrecognizable; his teeth loosened from the bones in his mouth; his head seemed full of pain; gradually he became nothing but a skeleton. He had to stop traveling, but in a small village he found an old woman who was a "bone-setter," and she tended him through five months of agony, feeding him rice-water, giving him everything she could find to cure him of his illness, until, at last, he was able to pursue his journey.

Finally he reached Djenné, on the Niger River, and boarded an Arab boat for the city of his dreams. The Arabs treated him cruelly, but he dared not defend himself against blows or jibes, for he always feared discovery. But alas! when he reached Timbuktu, there was nothing there but hovels and great plains of yellow sand. The great age of Arab learning, of the university, of magnificent houses, was no more.

After a few days he resigned himself to leaving, and he took the harder way home—over the desert. He rented a camel and started out for Rabat, in Morocco. When he arrived there, he found a French consul; but the man was a Jew, and as such he feared the Arab leaders. He would not take in an unknown man in rags, his face disfigured by illness, and with no proof of his identity. So René had to set forth again, this time renting a burro and making for Tangier. There he finally found another French consul, this time a member of the Geographical Society and therefore better qualified to evaluate René's explorations. At first even this man was doubtful of him, and René had to spend a few days sleeping in stables and begging his food, for his funds had run out. But at last the consul made up his mind that this miserable wretch, with nothing but his notes—which he had taken under his cloak to hide them from the Arabs— was a real explorer. He took him in, fed and clothed him, and after a few weeks found a place for him on a vessel going across the Straits of Gibraltar to Spain. From there he could easily reach France.

In Paris, he received the coveted geographical prize, but there was doubt among some people as to whether he had earned it. The journal of his travels had to be revised, for his scientific knowledge was not sufficient to please the learned society. His health, like Mollien's, never recovered, but the government gave him posts of a sort, though he was never able to return to Africa. Neither he nor Mollien had been forced to suffer so long. Nevertheless, as Deschamps said, "they had the sort of internal illumination that makes an exceptional being."[5]

After these precursors had done their work of discovery, the real second colonial period of France began with the conquest of Algeria.[6] In time, it would produce another empire, the greatest in the world after that of England.

During the Napoleonic Wars, France had bought wheat from two merchants, one in Algiers, one in France, and the dey of Algiers had an interest in the deal. Twenty years later, the dey, receiving no payment, began to write letters to the then king of France, Charles X. The dey, a proud man, was annoyed at having no answer, and be became infuriated. One day in 1827, the French consul was at the dey's residence for an official reception. He and the consul had a quarrel about the matter; stories differ as to what they said. Suddenly the dey slapped the consul in the face three times with his flywhisk— a very obvious insult.[7] The French demanded reparation, but the dey did not trouble to appease them. He said they had asked him to give them so much that he was surprised they had not also asked for his wife. Charles X did not seem to care about the dey's fury, or his wife either, but later, when he needed better public relations in his own country, he decided to do something about it. He would invade Algeria and force reparation for the insult to France, thus gaining the prestige he needed.[8]

There was talk "about it and about"—who would lead the invasion and how would it be done? Preparations were made, some of them verging on the ridiculous; the latter included the provision of a steamboat for visitors, so that the gay crowd at the port of Toulon, where the expedition had gathered, could see the start of the navy's great armada, the long lines of ships filled with soldiers. Four hundred dogs were taken along so the soldiers could drop the poor ill-fated animals down Algerian wells to see whether the water had been poisoned. Vast quantities of matériel were collected—though those in charge of supplies forgot all about mattresses for the wounded. At last the expedition was ready.[9]

The invading army, cooped up in all the navy's boats, set forth in early June of 1830. After some delays (most inconvenient—so many officers were seasick that no one liked to descend to quarters to sleep), the armada reached the Bay of Algiers. From then on, the expedition became a serious matter. There was a battle on landing, and a great many men were killed on both sides. Two battles more, and the dey asked for negotiations. He had not known how much the French could do when they were aroused. He had to surrender, and was immediately sent into exile, together with all his harem. The war ended for the time being.[10]

As the months passed, it was decided to keep Algeria, and the army was called on again to fight for it. It took ten years to subdue the entire country; by then General Thomas Bugeaud, who had led many of the campaigns, had become a hero, and France held Algeria in a tight grip. The country was now made into three French governmental departments, containing 67 million hectares (about 2 acres each), of which only 200,000 were dealt out to the former inhabitants of the country. These lands were bound to make history, and indeed they did. They set a mold for other colonies that would be conquered later on, and the famous policy of assimilation, of trying to make the people into Frenchmen, was used there. It was applied to other parts of the Empire later on. As time went on, Algeria came to be thought of as an integral part of France.[11]

Some years later, in 1854, Louis-Léon-César Faidherbe went to Senegal as governor. He was the first promoter of a new type of colonization, and the first great workman of French expansion in Africa. When he arrived in Senegal, it had been thoroughly ruined by wars and anarchy. It needed a strong man, and Faidherbe was just the one for the positon. Four years of fighting with one of the aggressive tribes of the region, the Trarza, were required before the new governor could drive them back into the desert. Still, when the task was finished, he had forced the recognition of French sovereignty over a district far up the Senegal River. He had built a fort in an advanced position, and he had also acquired a protectorate over another region, the Walo section of the coast. Then he turned his attention to other needs of government.

Faidherbe began Franco-Muslim teaching in the schools and inspection of both Catholic and Koranic educational institutions. He tried to raise the level of the most advanced Africans by founding a school for the sons of chiefs. He began to create a city at Dakar by constructing a port and roads; introducing a steam mill, gardens, and libraries; increasing the trade in ground-nuts; and eliminating the slave system that still existed in Senegal. He adapted to his district of Black Africa the *bureaux arabes* of North Africa, in which the French officers knew Arabic, studied local customs, and "were supposed to maintain close relations with the populations whose affairs they administered."[12] Faidherbe also created the administrative *cercle* that became the chief unit of the French government in Africa. In addition, he conquered the most hostile of the Muslims who, under their celebrated leader, El Hajj Umar, were fighting a holy war—a *jihad*—against the foreign invaders of Africa. Finally, Faidherbe developed the first element of a black army, the *Tirailleurs Sénégalais*. Organized in 1838 by the French governor, it began as a small company of blacks and later fought gallantly for France in many wars. Faidherbe deserves some of the credit, for he believed in the Africans and allowed them to follow their own way of life in the army. It was one of the elements of his success.

Yet, in spite of all his efforts—for he had certainly done enough for his country—the government of France did not support Faidherbe with the troops or the funds he needed. For a long time, he received little in the line of rewards, but later, after the war of 1870, Léon Gambetta made him a "General of the Army." He had intellectual probity and tremendous energy, and he was politically active, but in spite of his great belief in Africa and these other qualities, he was harshly criticized. It was thought that he used the rather brutal military methods that he had learned in the fighting in Algeria. There is certainly no doubt that the Borom N'Dar, the great lord, as they called him, was a stern "proconsul" of a dominant empire. Some say that he remained humane in spite of the rigid discipline he exercised, though others deny this softer quality. But it cannot be doubted that he made a great advance in modernizing the government; so he has gone down in history as one of France's great colonial governors, one who commanded and developed a vast continent.[13]

After the loss of the war of 1870 and the ensuing Paris Commune, there was a period of recession in French colonial activity. France, worn out as she was after the wars with England and the Allies, could give her colonies little material aid and even less thought. It was a "sort of parenthesis in the history of colonial expansion." In 1871, there was a serious revolt in Kabylia (Algeria), the last that threatened French domination in Africa in the century. The number of French there had increased greatly, for by the century's end, there were 150,000 French in Algeria, and it seemed as if there were surely enough there to take part in the "labors and glories" of the mother country. Still, England, France's old rival, now had 22.8 million square kilometers with 280 million inhabitants in her empire, and France had only a million square kilometers with 5.4 million inhabitants. She had to catch up. The metropole's indifference to the colonies, however, went on through the decade, though interventions were required in various places because of minor uprisings. A weak new wave of colonial interest began after 1875, but it did not gain strength until after 1880. Yet it was in the decade of the seventies that colonial ideology developed, for a few men, at least, were thinking of the Empire and were working on plans for it.[14]

Perhaps the most important of these thinkers was Paul Leroy-Beaulieu, who wrote a panegyric celebrating colonialism in 1874. He explained the types of colonies that existed and the profits they might bring in. Sending capital abroad would be a prime element of progress. The peoples of the colonies should be protected, and, he added, the nation that colonizes is first among peoples, or will be tomorrow. Others, among them Ernest Renan, Gabriel Charmes, and Paul Gaffarel, seconded these ideas, saying there was nothing shocking about colonization. France would be second rate if she did not colonize. If these beliefs did not reach the people at large, still they had some effect on public opinion.[15] Other forces joined in, among them the geographical societies, whose members rose from 780 in 1873 to 2,000 in 1880 and to 3,500 in 1881.[16] There were many missionaries, too, who favored colonization because they wanted to lead less favored peoples out of their "ignorance" and help them do away with the scourges of disease and poverty. Sometimes the missionaries worked among the cannibals; sometimes they were driven out of the districts where they had been stationed; but they claimed an enormous number of conversions, and their churches, both Catholic and Protestant, approved and supported them. While some critics did not like their influence, saying that the

Africans were not really converted, others approved of their efforts.

Rivalry with the British was, however, the strongest force in reawakening belief in securing colonies, in addition to the economic reasons that always existed. New raw materials and markets were much needed. Africa was now replacing the slave trade with commerce in peanuts, palm oil, cotton, and even with the recently discovered diamonds. So the French must find more colonies before there were no more to be found. New trading posts were established even before Henry M. Stanley and Pierre Savorgnan de Brazza met at the great Pool of the Congo River in 1880. That meeting, with its subsequent division of the territory of the Congo, as well as actions of the Portuguese at the Congo's mouth, began the first stage of contention over Africa among the European powers. Others date the beginning of that rivalry with the contest of the French and English governments over the "Rivers of the South" in Guinea, a struggle that continued throughout the seventies. Still others date the rivalry from the penetration of Gabon, or from the International African Association's foundation in 1875. Some said that the contest began with a Commission for the Study of the Upper Congo, or with the British occupation of Egypt in 1880, for the French gained little by that event. Still, the meeting at the Pool of the American sent there by King Leopold of Belgium and the Italian who had been naturalized as a Frenchman was like the planting of the French flag as a guidepost to the future. It was an indication of definite intent, pointing to the division of Africa among the European powers in the last two decades of the century; so it seems a better moment from which to date the "Scramble."[17]

Sometimes the events of the eighties and nineties in Africa are called the "steeplechase," after Alfred de Musset's description of a form of English race in which the contestants ran toward a steeple in the distance. Those who took the beaten path might win; but others in the ravines would do better, providing they didn't break their necks. In France, the same period is called the "Scramble for Africa." Jules Ferry, a prime minister much interested in the colonies, spoke of it as an "irresistible movement . . . towards the conquest of new lands." Between 1880 and 1895, the share of France in Africa went from 1 million to 9.5 million square kilometers and the inhabitants of those colonies from 5 to 50 million souls.[18]

This expansion was due to explorations, national rivalries, local irritations, and, finally, to the planning of King Leopold II of Belgium. For a long time, the French navy had had to avoid conflict with Britain, for their fleet was not nearly as large as Britain's, and both countries wanted colonial lands. The French economy required more colonies and greater profits from overseas, with the use of steamers and railways instead of sailboats and camels. At home, there was the desire for scientific knowledge and the need for prestige for the "glory of the Third Republic." Much more interest in the Empire developed in these years. A colonial group (*Groupe Colonial de la Chambre*) was gathered together in the Chamber of Deputies in 1892; and in the Senate in 1898 a Committee for French Africa (*Comité de l'Afrique Française*) became a model for committees to support French interests in Asia, Oceania, and Morocco.

Studies, explorations, information, and propaganda about colonial life followed. By 1893, a commercial Colonial Union was formed, as well as a Youth League and study groups. All were aided by the schools. Many articles—scientific and cultural—poured out from the French press and from the enlarged geographical societies. A Colonial School was founded to train men for posts in the colonies, and the influence of the Empire was felt increasingly in Paris. A Ministry of Colonies was constituted in 1894.[19]

The seventies had seen the growth of the ambitions of King Leopold. A traveler, he had seen the world, and he wanted some of it for his country. At a conference in 1875 he had heard of the African explorers, and soon after, in 1876, he called a conference of geographers at Laeken, near Brussels. Plans were made to bring civilization to Africa and to combat the slave trade. The conference created an International Association for the Exploration and Civilization of Central Africa, and Leopold asked the seven nations present to set up subcommittees to further the purposes of the association. A young officer, Savorgnan de Brazza, suggested that the information about Africa be pooled, but his idea was not followed. Belgium wanted a share in the "magnificent African cake," but that was not made clear at first.[20]

Leopold then asked de Brazza and Henry M. Stanley, both already known as explorers, to go to Africa under his auspices. Stanley went, but de Brazza refused. De Brazza had trained in the French Naval School. After experience in Africa, he had organized an expedition there. Stanley, financed by the *New York Herald* and the *Daily Telegraph,* had gone into Africa to find David Livingstone, and having achieved that purpose, he had returned there twice thereafter. The third time, Leopold told him to reach the Congo before de Brazza arrived there.[21]

De Brazza, finally agreeing, started late, recruited men in Dakar, and then went on into the Congo. On September 10, 1880, he signed a treaty with Makoko, the ruler of the region. In this document the sovereignty of France over part of Makoko's territory was recognized, and a protectorate (also for France) was created over the remainder. He started for home, leaving behind an African sergeant, Malamine, with two guards. On the way he met Stanley, but did not tell him of the treaty. Stanley was angry, of course, for, arriving at the post in the Congo, he found the French flag already flying there; and Malamine made it clear that French flags could not be disturbed. Stanley could not and did not claim success, but to calm Leopold, he named a lake after him.[22] Did that have the desired effect? One wonders.

De Brazza turned over to France an immense domain in the Congo. He helped the Africans, too, by freeing slaves, and above all, he made friends among the tribes through whose domains he passed on his explorations, though the truth of the legend that no blood was shed on his expeditions has not been proven. Jean Suret-Canale believes that de Brazza, like other explorers, did not hesitate to shoot or to destroy villages. He cites a passage from Monseigneur Augouard, the bishop of Brazzaville, who wrote in his *Twenty-eight Years in the Congo* that de Brazza's secretary had committed "horrors unworthy of

Pierre Savorgnan de Brazza, the discoverer who secured part of the Congo for France.

France" and that de Brazza was responsible for his employee's actions. Monseigneur Augouard said he had documents in his hands which would bear him out.[23] We are not told, however, what this evidence was. Obviously, through his successes, de Brazza deepened old rivalries with the colonizing powers. Still, he had great personal prestige at home and abroad. He was the kind of man who could walk barefoot in the prickliest forests of the world. When briars dug into his feet, he could cut deep into his own flesh to drain the wounds of infection, though at that time no anesthetics were available. Once, when he was fired on by Africans, the bullet missed him. After that, he became a fetish to the people of the region.[24]

Jules Ferry, though he had become prime minister, did not have de Brazza's charisma. After some experience in Tunisia, having come to believe in colonization, he understood the need for new markets, for placements of capital, and for the education and general advancement of the colonized peoples. He outlined his policy in speeches in the Chamber of Deputies, in 1883, 1884, and 1885. He said that a colonial policy was an asset for the future. France must not abdicate from management of the colonial lands. If she did, she would descend from the first rank of nations to the fourth. Ferry had encouraged de Brazza, inspired reforms for Algeria, and made a French role possible during the Congress of Berlin. He interested parliament more in

Malamine, the African sergeant left in the Congo to secure the French share.

colonial expansion, though the deputies did not continue to follow him, and he lost his post after a few years.[25]

France and Germany consulted together to make the Congress of Berlin possible in 1884–85, for it was to deal with subjects vital to both: there must be freedom of navigation on African rivers, protection for traders, and plans for new occupation of African lands. To make this last motive less conspicuous, the object of bringing civilization to the Africans was clearly expressed from the beginning of the meetings. At the opening of the conference, the powers involved believed King Leopold was merely trying to obtain free trade; yet out of the conference the king managed to obtain a great domain in the Congo for Belgium. The congress also made it possible for Germany to obtain certain African lands, though France acquired but little. For England, the congress meant the loss of all hope of controlling the navigation on the Congo River. Still, the powers were, in general, favorable to increasing the influence of the International Association Leopold had founded, though the king altered that institution soon after and made the Congo into an independent state.

At Berlin, the delegates also considered the question of "effective occupation." It was to include authority to force respect of national rights. Freedom of navigation was decreed on the Congo and the Niger rivers, and opposition to the slave trade was declared. The doctrine of "hinterland" was discussed, the word meaning that the powers had rights over the populations they encountered as they pushed back the frontiers of their colonies from the coast to the boundaries of neighboring states. The use of the words "spheres of influence" spread to all European colonizing nations, constituting a sort of doctrine of a moral hinterland. To the French, that seemed to mean that they could secure a protectorate in a new region by fixing a line from the other side of which other states could be excluded. Thus, while the conference did not actually divide Africa, it made partition seem possible.[26]

Indeed, partition had already been begun by the French and the British along the Gulf of Guinea, in the Oil Rivers of the Guinea Coast, and in Gabon. Some of this was due to two Frenchmen in particular. Joseph-Simon Gallieni had pushed into the Upper Niger Valley, securing some land in the process, though the treaty he had made with Chief Ahmadu there was considered doubtful and deceptive. During his stay in the Niger country, he had been ambushed by the sultan and was set free only after six months. Later, Gallieni was sent to Senegal to repair forts on the Upper River, and, so doing, he succeeded in opening the way through Senegal to Guinea. Meantime, another Frenchman, Colonel Gustave Borgnis-Desbordes, had led a small army into Upper Senegal to the edge of the Western Soudan in 1881–82, for he feared British competition for the commerce on the Niger River. So progress was beginning toward the Soudan in West Africa. Gallieni's greatest reputation, however, came from the nine years he spent in Madagascar, suppressing a rebellion there and reorganizing the government. It is said that he remade Madagascar, for he built institutions, fixed rules of government, used men well, and adapted his principles to reality. He developed the famous system of the "patch of oil," occupying one village so that its influence would spread, seeping its way into the next. If he destroyed a village, he felt he must rebuild it at once, and he thought the "Great Island" might be a federation of units governing themselves, at least to a certain extent. He organized rather than conquered, and his attitude to the people was an advance over that of previous French administrators. His belief in France did not permit any doubt as to whether colonization was legitimate.[27]

General Louis Archinard, the commander-in-chief who followed Gallieni, completed the conquest of the Soudan in the early 1890s. He was a different type of man, for though he won his campaigns, he did not get on well with his superiors in the Colonial Department. Gallieni told him to pretend that the department did not exist, and Archinard was a good pupil. He took his own road. Having decided that he must destroy the Tokolor empire in the Soudan, he started out without instructions. Naturally, the expenses of his frequent campaigns rose. Nevertheless, his friends managed to keep him in his post for a considerable time. Some said he needed success or he would not be advanced, so he kept on "gnawing off pieces of the Soudan." The results showed. In 1888, the French Soudan contained 20 million hectares, but in 1893, it had 50 million.

Later, Archinard had to deal with Samori-Touré, the celebrated African

The signing of the Treaty of Kita. Joseph-Simon Gallieni, who opened West Africa and Madagascar to France, represented the French.

chief. The French spent eight years subduing him, and Paris got irritated and denounced the campaign against this formidable foe, but Archinard, indifferent to the opinions of the metropole, continued to do as he wished. He had some government support, but at last he was dismissed, learning of his fall only from the newspapers. There was a storm in the metropole when his dismissal was known. In the end, however, Archinard was made a brigadier-general; his insubordination was rewarded, even though he had ruined trade in the colony and doubled the costs of occupation. He was an eager "scrambler," recognizing only one method, the military column. Still, he had another side, for he loved the Africans, tried to get rid of slavery, and attempted to establish Christianity in his districts in place of both Islam and Animism. His name stands high in the annals of colonial France. [28]

The Colonial Department and the *Comité d'Afrique* wanted to tie the colony of Chad closer to the other French possessions, some of them in the east of Africa. Chad was next door to the Soudan and offered a passage near to Fashoda, the center of the district that controlled the Nile. If the French could occupy Fashoda, their lands would be more unified. The British had already put in a claim for it, but the Muslim Mahdists were installed there, and they had not been forced to leave; so the French thought they had an opportunity to obtain it. Three men tried to prepare expeditions to gain a foothold there: Captain Jean-Baptiste Marchand and two colonial officer-explorers, Parfait-Louis Monteil and Victor Liotard. But in 1895, before any of the expeditions was ready to set forth, Sir Edward Grey, the British foreign secretary, declared

Samori-Touré, the great African warrior of the 1890s. It took the
French eight years to subdue him.

that England would consider any advance in the Nile region as an unfriendly
act.[29]

The French thought Grey's declaration invalid. "Effective occupation" was
essential, and England did not have that. So France went on with her
preparations, though Gabriel Hanotaux, then French foreign minister, was not
eager to approve any of the plans proposed to take the region. Captain
Marchand's plan seems to have been preferred, possibly because he believed
that all the African colonies might be lost if the expedition to occupy Fashoda
was not carried out. The French cabinet fell, and delay followed delay, but
finally a new foreign minister, Marcellin Berthelot, ordered Captain
Marchand's expedition to proceed. More changes in government followed, but
at last Captain Marchand was on his way—supervised, it is curious to relate, by

Liotard, one of those who had expected to lead an expedition of his own. Again, more changes in France, more delays, but, in May 1896, Gabriel Hanotaux, back at the Foreign Office, said to Marchand, "Go to Fashoda, France is going to fire her pistol!"[30]

The pistol shot didn't seem to be very effective. Nevertheless, Marchand, with two hundred men and hopes of more in the future, reached Fashoda. He hung out the Tricolor on the fort, made treaties with the local African tribes and christened the stronghold "St. Louis of the Nile." In so doing, he carried out all the policies that the rather timid Berthelot, when at the Foreign Office, would have prohibited.

All appeared to be well until the British in Khartoum, farther down the Nile, found out what was happening. Then they sent two African envoys to Fashoda to announce the arrival almost immediately of the sirdar, or commander-in-chief, Lord Herbert Kitchener. Kitchener was courteous but firm. He said that his men must occupy the fort, which, after all, still belonged to the Turks, whom he represented. Marchand was equally firm, saying he had acted on instructions from his government, and that he had made a treaty with the local tribe around Fashoda. His men would rather die than give in, he said. Then Kitchener made a rather open threat of war. After all, he had two thousand troops, whereas Marchand had only two hundred, for promised reinforcements had not shown up. Everyone was polite, however, in spite of the difference of power, and Kitchener finally said they might let the two governments settle the matter. So it was left uncertain, at least for the time being. Kitchener remarked on leaving that the incident would make a noise in the world. It certainly did![31]

France was upset at this time because of general strikes and by divided opinion over the Dreyfus case. Little attention or energy was left for Fashoda. Théophile Delcassé, the new foreign minister, was furious with the British, remarking that the mission to Fashoda had begun before Grey's declaration had been issued. This was not true. Nevertheless, everyone at Fashoda remained polite. Unfortunately for France, a new cabinet came in and ordered Marchand's expedition to retreat from Fashoda. If the French had acted more quickly, this major defeat might have been avoided. The convention of March 21, 1899, that ended the incident did not help France. She lost all hope of obtaining possession of Egypt and the Egyptian Sudan, though she received a few lands east of Chad that made a tighter bond around her African Empire. Lord Salisbury, then England's prime minister and foreign minister as well, remarked: "The territories left to France are very light soil, very light. The Gallic cock, who likes to scratch the earth, can wear out his spurs there. The fertile region remains ours." It was the end of the Scramble.[32]

One good result, however, came out of the debacle of French hopes for Fashoda. Soon after, in 1904, the Entente Cordiale with England was arranged by Delcassé, and it ended the long colonial rivalry between England and France. Perhaps, as time went on, that mattered more than the defeat at Fashoda.[33]

Thus 1898 was the end of the expansion by conquest of France in Africa, and can therefore be considered as the end of the Scramble. Nevertheless, the taking of Dahomey and Madagascar happened later in the nineties, and the "pacification" of the Ivory Coast was not completed until 1917. In 1912, the French gained a free hand in Morocco, in return for allowing a free hand to England in Egypt. Finally, after the First World War, the League of Nations put Togo and the Cameroons under mandate to the French and the British, giving the Empire the greatest extent it would ever attain. The Scramble was part of the early stages of French imperialism in West Africa. It added territory to the Empire, but J. S. Hobson had not yet written his book showing how mediocre was the value of colonial trade for the metropoles. It must have been hard for the French to evaluate their gains. They still believed in imperial establishment, and they felt that political control was the right basis on which to obtain economic advantage. Thus their long-time rivalry with England seemed justified. At this time, the colonial powers thought they were dealing with "infantile peoples," and a sort of covert racism entered into their thinking about the colonies. The technological European advance deepened this attitude. They knew the Africans could not resist them; they, the Europeans, felt they belonged to a higher order.[34]

There seems no reason to blame the French for the Scramble any more than the other nations of Europe, although, without a doubt, it was they who began the race for land. England's provocations to France in the southern rivers and the Niger Valley had been endless, and the rules established by the Act of Berlin had been ignored. Naturally, the French answered by trying to be first under the wire everywhere. Henri Brunschwig, an authority on the colonial period, thinks the Scramble was a nationalist impulse to recover dignity. The French always thought they had special gifts for colonization and could succeed at it, and that the Africans could not resist successfully. It would help prestige to have an empire. Gann and Duignan think that the Scramble happened because the trade with Africa was not large at that time, and the French did not have the big navy that England possessed. Probably all these reasons were important.[35]

The colonial wars the French carried on in Africa have received very little attention in most histories. The French met stiff resistance in Africa, for the armies there were sometimes led by men of great ability, such as Samori-Touré. The initial conquest of Samori, or of anyone else, was never enough, for renewed revolts would arise after resistance seemed ended. The French did not feel that they needed any justification for fighting those wars. To them, the pursuit of empire was a righteous purpose. The men who had created the Empire were heroes. There was glory in dying for one's country.[36] Did they ever realize that the Africans were defending their own lands?

Hitherto, there had been only one way of dealing with conquered peoples— assimilation. Léopold de Saussure, writing in 1899, said that the policy of France was to make conquered peoples accept the language, the institutions— political and religious—and the moral attitudes of French civilization. Hanotaux, in 1902, added that it meant extending to regions yesterday barbarian the principles of a civilization of which one of the oldest nations in the world had a right to be proud. It was a part of the *Mission Civilisatrice* of France. Cardinal Richelieu had made this policy important, and the Revolution had adopted a belief in Reason and Universal Man. Character differences were superficial. Assimilation was the only method that worked. However, some new ideas came to the fore after a time, for the doctrine of Reason alone failed as soon as it confronted reality. Europeans thought it was an illusion to deny that there were inferior races, though they realized that assimilation was possible only if carried on slowly through centuries. After all, habits and customs matter most to a race next to their independence, and people are slow in adapting themselves to different ways of life. Saussure had seen already, at the end of the last century, that change was possible in some current beliefs.[37]

Paul Louis wrote in 1905 that colonization was for markets, capital, and exploitation, as well as for prestige for the metropole. Belief in it, he thought, had caused the invention of the theory of inferior races. Revolutionary thrusts were developing now, and the oppressed were joining forces. Colonialism had diminished the prestige of the ruling class, and Louis demanded reform of the methods employed.[38]

In 1902, J. A. Hobson, in England, had written a diatribe against imperialism, which he thought existed for the ruling class alone. It was, in effect, nationalism. It resulted in an unscrupulous struggle between competing empires, and was the chief danger of the modern state, for it meant a renunciation of higher values. Yet neither Hobson nor Paul Louis asked that colonization be abolished.[39]

In 1908, Maurice Zimmermann noted in the *Revue de Géographie* that colonization had imposed itself on the world and that it would increase. Africans would not propose independence for a long while, he believed, and many questions about the situation were still unanswered. How could men's efforts be combined, he asked, so as to be effective?[40]

Two years later, Jules Harmand pointed out that only colonies peopled by former citizens of the mother country could be self-governing, for a hierarchy of races had to be accepted. France had misunderstood the needs of the colonies and their role, and the only justification for colonialism was the good done those who had been dominated.[41]

About that time, however, others were more violent in their criticisms. One man even wrote that the colonies were a regular bear garden.[42]

The French Socialists, in advance of the English ones, condemned colonization as productive of injustice and cruelty. It was a consequence of capitalism, they thought, and their various congresses denounced the enslavement of peoples. Yet even Jean Jaurès, one of their most respected men, felt that France's civilization was superior to others and that the worst thing about colonization was the way it was carried out. Up to World War I, complaints were limited to the methods used in colonization. Socialist attitudes, however, became stronger during the war. A conference at Zimmerwald, in 1915, showed some advance in the disapproval of colonization, and with the fall of the Russian empire in 1917, the demand for self-determination for all countries began.[43]

After the First World War there was a change in some attitudes, though all that had happened was not understood immediately. Some men still wrote about the "perfect loyalty" of the people of the French colonies. No one explained why there were so many revolts in the African colonies: in the Soudan, the Volta region, Dahomey, the Ivory Coast, and Niger. It was hard, too, to recruit enough Africans for the army, and Blaise Diagne, the first black in the Chamber of Deputies, had been put in charge of recruiting. He succeeded better than the whites, though France was still supreme in Africa, and she might have been expected to do better in recruiting the Africans. In all, there were about 200,000 blacks in the French army. By the war's end, however, the French had realized that something must be done for Africa, and they started to improve facilities of various sorts in the African colonies: roads, railroads, etc. Still, it was too little and too late. The Africans had seen now that there were weaknesses in Europeans, whom they had thought all-powerful. The upsurge of their nationalism began in the interwar years.[44]

The first step in decolonization appears to have been taken after the interwar period, though some writers suggest that the earlier placement of certain countries under mandates, supervised by an international association, was a part of the decolonizing process. At the time the mandates were imposed, however, there was no general worldwide acceptance of the doctrine of self-determination. Wilson's ideas were not yet part of most people's intellectual baggage. Therefore, the chain of events during and after World War II seems to be a better date to select as the beginning of decolonization. Colonialism was at its apogee in the interwar period. Freedom for the colonies seemed far off to the colonizing powers, and the road ahead for the Empire looked clear and straight.[45]

In that era, by 1920, the French system of government of colonies had been put in place. At the summit of the Colonial Administrative Corps there was a governor, responsible to Paris, and under him the district chiefs (French) and then the territorial administrators (also French). The federations of French West Africa and French Equatorial Africa had eight and four colonies respectively. After the mandates were added, the Empire contained 7,586 million square kilometers of land and 21 million inhabitants. Each province had districts, of which there were 182 in all of Black Africa; these were divided into 300 subdivisions, and all the military commands of the region were tied to them. The Africans were represented only by the chiefs of villages, cantons, and provinces. The local administrator made the contact between the people and the upper echelons of government. He planned the budget, collected taxes, arranged for public works, and kept order. These civil servants of the bush, or *broussards*, had to cope with many African languages, diseases, poor lodgings for themselves and their people, often with a dreadful climate, as well as with the Africans themselves. The local "commandants" held all the power, and often made long trips to keep in contact with the people of their districts. They were generally isolated in the bush, and their lives would have been unbearable if they had not had a sense of creativeness in their jobs. Of course, there were among them some who could not stand the life and were unworthy of their important offices. They were plagued with drunkenness and were sadistic or otherwise oblivious to any moral code. Some even became pathological cases. After World War I, their training at the Colonial School improved, although it is said that it was never up to the quality of the "Great Schools" of France. Most of the *broussards* came from bourgeois groups, but in Africa they were aristocrats and all-powerful. Governor-General Robert Delavignette has said that they had too much power not to be corrupted by it. They were men transplanted, lonely and often quarrelsome. Some, however, kept their belief that their profession was a magnificent one, and it was they who made it so.[46]

Some infamous incidents took place in Africa under the French: burnings, murders, mutilations, etc. The Congo was famous for such horrors. There were colonizers who were corrupt, too, and they profited from the blacks, paying them paltry prices for good merchandise. Those who survived such temptations, however, and served their country and Africa well could feel satisfaction when they retired. They had had the unique experience of knowing an untouched country intimately, even though, in knowing it, they had often passed close to defeat in their purposes or even to death. One of the worst problems for all of them lay in selecting the African chiefs of their districts, for if they chose badly, they were lost in trying to govern large areas.[47] They had to deal with many sources of discontent. Among these were the requirements of forced labor, and the *indigénat*, the special code of justice applied to the Africans in Africa but not to the Europeans there. Later, these *broussards* were in the foreground of the matters that led to more vocal protest by the Africans than the government had permitted before 1945.

In France, there was little knowledge of what went on in the colonies, with the result that the French close at hand were responsible for everything that occurred. Whatever was heard in the metropole of the Africans and their difficulties was wound in France into the skein of the general belief about the inferiority of the Africans.[48]

All in all, the moment the guns grew silent, in 1945, was a turning-point in the history of colonization. The time for a revision of colonial methods had come, and the belief in colonialism itself was being questioned. The Africans had seen the difference between institutions as they were in France and as the regulations applied them in Africa. A new world was being born for colonies hitherto dominated and suppressed.

In 1940, as this situation was beginning to emerge, General de Gaulle made his first appearance on the international stage. After reviewing certain factors in his past, as child and adult, and the influences from the colonies and the outside world, we can try to determine when, how, and why his early beliefs changed, leading him to give independence to the states of Black Africa almost immediately after his return to power in 1958. General de Gaulle's unusual knowledge of history made him very much aware of the colonial past, and that is one reason for this brief survey of the First and Second Empires. De Gaulle spoke, or wrote, a number of times about Cardinal Richelieu and Jean-Baptiste Colbert; even more often about Napoleon and his deeds and ideas; and several times about the great chiefs who had fought in the colonial wars of the 1880s and 1890s; not to mention what he said about the great deeds of Savorgnan de Brazza in dedicating a monument to him at the time of the Conference of Brazzaville in 1944. There is no doubt that he knew a great deal about the colonial history of the early times, even though he undoubtedly viewed it all from the standpoint of a "man of the Empire." The past of the two empires became vital to him almost immediately after he started the Free French Movement,[49] and his early history makes it possible to understand something of his attitudes to the postwar Empire.

3

A Preparation for History

As one prepares oneself for the most difficult
examination in the world, he had prepared himself to
enter history when the moment came.

—Galante

Charles de Gaulle wrote in 1927 that our century, in less than three decades,
had seen the passage of two radically dissimilar ages with only war as a
transition.[1] Indeed, these two periods have been so different that it is an effort
even for those who have lived through both of them, and entered on a third, to
remember what that earlier horse-and-carriage era was like.

The beginning of the second age of the century came when the cannons of
"the war to end war" ceased firing and a hush fell on the torn and desolate
battlefields of France and Belgium: the need for peace seemed the only hope of
mankind. Perhaps the shock of the war would make it possible for the League
of Nations to bring about that peace. The League would have to work hard, but
many people had confidence in it at that time, and believed that it might be
able to succeed in a task in which many generations of statesmen had failed.

In postwar Europe, colonialism was at its height, teaching how to subject
and control the peoples of what we now call the Third World. Yet, little by
little, the status of the colonizing powers was being eroded. Crises in Morocco
in 1905 and 1911 had nearly erupted into a major European war. There had
been an abortive revolution in Russia in 1905, and a successful one in 1917. No
one knew what the ideology spawned by the new communism would lead to.
Other uprisings were beginning in various parts of the world, among them
Morocco, where the Rif War was not a war of European rivalries, as the
previous crises had threatened to become, but a revolt of the people.[2] And the
full effects of the recent conflict among the states of Europe had not yet been
felt or diagnosed.

During the interim period, a small fear rose now and then in some European
hearts, and had to be snuffed out. As time went on, the small fear grew into a
real dread, for it was soon evident that a permanent peace had not been
secured. However, the belief in the practice of colonization was not yet shaken.
Europe expected to carry on as she had before the war, with perhaps a few
minor reforms applied where feelings seemed to be most injured.

Of course, Europe had had a good many warnings. Nationalist aspirations
were now growing in Europe, whereas they had formerly existed for a long
period of time in the Balkan States only. There were signs of them, too, in

North Africa. In 1919, Governor Albert Sarraut had had to use a firm but persuasive tone in speaking to the Vietnamese in Hanoi.[3] The first real blows to the power of Europe had been struck during and after 1914–18, before the uneasy peace when the world began to suspect that European power was not invincible. White men were destroying each other in a manner that had not been taught them by their religion. The full effect of this knowledge was not visible until after World War II had added its human and material destruction to that of the previous holocaust. Europe's weakness was really not clear before the forties. Turning to France, to see the causes and events leading to the final decolonization of an empire that looked so strong, a glance back at the previous century is helpful.

During the last thirty years of the century, under the Third Republic, France had begun to thrive again. Industry and transportation developed; there was a solid franc to back them. Then urban progress lagged, and there was some anxiety over the increasing power of the masses, for many groups in the country were turning toward socialism and showing interest in the Second International, with its ideas of popular progress and peace. In the nineties the Dreyfus case had divided the French, demonstrating what a long and difficult task it was to obtain justice for a member of an unpopular religious minority— even in a country that prided itself on having as its motto "Liberty, Equality, Fraternity." In the first decade of the new century, the French were again divided between church and state by the quarrel over education. Nevertheless, in 1914, as the war began, national feeling rose with the spirit of *revanche,* and the people became unified. All the French gathered behind the government and were ready to fight to regain their land and their status. Once more the "Blue Line of the Vosges" had a meaning in French eyes.[4]

Charles de Gaulle, born on November 22, 1890, had doubtless felt some of the tension aroused by the dispute over Dreyfus's guilt, especially when his father lost his teaching post in a Jesuit college. That certainly laid the de Gaulles open to considerable vindictiveness and harassment. Even up to 1914, the famous case, though supposedly settled in 1906, was still causing bitter divisions in some families in France, though not in that of the de Gaulles.[5] It was an initial training in dissidence from a popular cause.

The separation of church and state in 1905 forced the Jesuits who controlled the school in which Henri de Gaulle, General de Gaulle's father, was then teaching to retreat to Belgium, and Henri became supervisor of studies in a school in Paris on the rue Vaugirard. The boy Charles went with the Jesuits to Belgium for a year,[6] but there is little other reference to this "year away from home" in de Gaulle's own writings or in those that concern him. Still, such events as his absence and the cause of it are bound to be traumatic in a Catholic family like that of the de Gaulles. Again they were on the unpopular side of a popular cause. Before he went to military school, Charles's home life was a most telling influence on the young man. The family's history and character show clearly why early environment was so important to the four sons and one daughter of Henri de Gaulle.

Charles's great-great-grandfather, Jean-Baptiste de Gaulle, born in 1720, was the first of the family to come to Paris to study law. He served as an attorney and registrar in the chancery of the king, dying in 1798. His son, Jean-Baptiste-Philippe de Gaulle, went through the Revolution as an enlightened liberal, believing in the Rights of Man and Citizen. He was imprisoned for a reason not given, but was released at the end of the Terror, and lived to see the blue, white, and red flag of the Revolution return with King Louis Philippe in 1830. His son, Julien-Philippe de Gaulle, the grandfather of Charles, went to the Ecole des Chartes, the advanced school of paleography and librarianship, in Paris, thus continuing the intellectual tradition of the family. Though he was a follower of Voltaire rather than of any religious sect, Julien-Philippe wrote a life of Saint Louis. He did this apparently because he was so moved by the deep and secure faith of his second son, Charles, the uncle of General de Gaulle, who had been paralyzed from early childhood by an attack of polio. This Charles spent his life reading, making himself a specialist in the Celtic language and even writing some poetry in that tongue. Those around him called him the "Bard of Honor." He died young, not long before the birth of the nephew who was named after him.[7] The older Charles would have been astonished to know that when his nephew, now famous, went to Brittany in 1969, he was able to recite in Celtic to the Bretons some of the verses his uncle had written. Of course, the Bretons loved it; the anti-Gaullists did not, but could not deny that Charles de Gaulle came by this accomplishment honestly.

A third son of Julien-Philippe, Jules, became an entomologist, famous in Paris long before anyone had heard of his nephew. Pierre Galante reports that when Geneviève de Gaulle, daughter of Charles de Gaulle's older brother, Xavier, was a student in Paris in the thirties, she was not asked about Charles, but rather whether she was related to Jules.[8]

The oldest son of Julien-Philippe's family—Henri, the General's father—was born in 1848. Left an orphan early, he had to take charge of his mother and two brothers. He had begun to prepare for the engineers' and scientists' school, the Ecole Polytechnique; but he had to give up a planned military career to teach and earn the family living. However, he managed to take degrees (*licences*) in both law and letters. He had to forsake all study for a time when Léon Gambetta called for volunteers in the Franco-Prussian War. Henri de Gaulle enlisted and served in the battles around Paris, being wounded in the sorties at Stains and Bourget.

Mustered out of the Mobiles de la Seine, his regiment, Henri became, soon after, a professor in the Jesuit College in the rue des Postes, preparing students for the "Great Schools," the advanced colleges of France. In 1886 he married Jeanne Maillot of Lille, whose family shared many of the traditions of his own. Five children were born of this union—Xavier, Charles, Jacques, Pierre, and Marie-Agnès. By 1970, only the one sister of the five remained to follow the coffin of her famous brother to his grave.

Today, Henri de Gaulle would be considered an extremely strict parent. The children had to be precisely on time. The slightest deviation in language that their father considered improper was reproved. They could pay little attention to themselves. They were not allowed to complain about small troubles. They must keep their attention on higher and greater matters of mind and spirit. Life was austere in more ways than one, for they lived on the fourth floor of a Paris apartment, unfashionably high up for that time. The father went out each day to teach in a long, black Prince Albert coat with a high white collar, his hands encased in yellow gloves. In spite of his strictness and his conservatism, Henri had a warm side, playing with the children and understanding their difficulties. Religiously, he was a devout Catholic, though liberal in spirit, possibly because he had such a tremendous fund of knowledge: history, literature, law, philosophy, and mathematics were all his subjects. Though severe, he is said to have been a gifted teacher. His favorite study seems to have been history, for later Charles wrote of him: "My father, a man of thought, culture and tradition, was imbued with the feeling of the dignity of France. He showed me what History really was."[9]

Conversation at the de Gaulle family table often centered on history, and so also did the walks on which the father took the children on Sunday afternoons. Sometimes he led them to the monument on the old battlefield near Stains where he had been wounded. It was dedicated to those who had died in the war, and on it was carved the broken sword of France with the epitaph: "The sword of France broken in their valiant hands will be reforged by their descendants." That monument may well have been the inspiration of the words used by Charles de Gaulle when he spoke on the BBC from London on July 13, 1940, saying: "The sword of France lies broken at the hands of those who should have been its defenders. I have picked up the shattered stump."[10] The children who saw such sights as the monument at Stains could never forget the past of their country nor the part their family had played in it.

If Henri de Gaulle wanted to share his passion for history with his children, so did his wife. She was a strong, affectionate woman, dedicating herself to husband and children. Her daughter, Madame Cailliau-de Gaulle, has written that her mother and father taught all the children the love of God together with the love of their country, and gave them a sense of their responsibilities and a will to serve. Charles's testimony was similar:

> My mother had an uncompromising passion for the fatherland. It was equal to her religious piety . . . . Nothing moved me so much as the stories of our past misfortunes: the evocation by my mother of her despair as a little girl at seeing her parents in tears: Bazaine has capitulated!

And lest they forget her grief over the general who allowed himself to be defeated in 1870, Madame de Gaulle required the children every night to pray for France and for the return of Alsace-Lorraine. The humiliation the French had suffered in losing the provinces burned deep into their hearts. The spirit of *revanche* was the result.[11]

Pierre Galante, who knows the family well, has summed up the effects of this heredity by saying that in fervor, in passion and sensibility under an icy mask, in physical temperament balanced between equilibrium and nervousness Charles de Gaulle was a portrait of his mother, though in intelligence and methods of thought he resembled his father. The surprising thing to those accustomed to studying family histories is that all the children accepted without rebellion the rather rigid and demanding situation in the family, with all that it entailed. During their lives, in spite of the strictness with which they were surrounded, they showed a closeness and affection for all the family, due, no doubt, to the warmth of their relationships. They certainly saw alike, even at the time of the Second World War, for they all stood by France and the Free French. They made the decision separately to refuse to accept the Armistice, even before they knew of General de Gaulle's appeal from London. As an evidence of their steadfastness in sticking to their beliefs, it is significant that four of the family were deported by the Germans.[12]

The importance of this portrait of family life in trying to understand General de Gaulle's thought and his actions cannot be overestimated. The heredity, the upbringing in the simple, austere environment, the strict discipline, together with that something personal which remarkable people show, and of which we do not know the origin, made the man. De Gaulle emerged from his early surroundings with an intellectual bent; a prodigious memory; a wide learning, especially in history and philosophy; religious feeling; an extraordinary amount of will power, self-control, and purpose; and certainly some egotistic appreciation of himself and what he might do in the world. His love of history· later resolved itself into a dream of glory for France and a resolve to be her servitor. He felt he must perform some signal service for his country.[13] So strong was this tendency in the General to identify himself with France that it has been hard for a great many people to credit its sincerity. Yet does not the family story make it both believable and natural?

Of course, the effects of these influences did not come all at once. One evening, when Charles was about fourteen, he announced at the table that he would be a military man. He would go to Saint-Cyr, the great military academy, to become an officer. Neither he nor anyone else seems to have doubted his decision. His resolve had an immediate effect, for he had been a "disinterested" student and a rather "turbulent" boy.[14] Now all that was left behind. Perhaps it might be close to the truth to say that a covert rebelliousness, which he had been forced to dominate to attain his purpose of admission to Saint-Cyr, remained within him. It must have been at the bottom of some of his later difficulties with people, for his human relationships were seldom smooth. There was a hostility shown by him and to him, sometimes open, sometimes hidden, that appeared at many periods in his life.

Accepted at Saint-Cyr in 1909, de Gaulle performed the usual year of training with an infantry troop under a certain Captain de Tugny. The only story known of the captain is that when he was asked why he had not made de Gaulle a sergeant, he answered, "How do you think I could name a young man Sergeant who would only feel at ease as Grand Constable!"[15]

At Saint-Cyr, the "Long Asparagus," as his companions called him, was rather isolated, and his professors were inclined to think that he was too forward in expressing his ideas. He is said to have told a friend in London later that his mother had taught him that if one had an idea, one must hold on to it.[16] He put that maxim into practice literally and continually throughout a long life. Georges Cattaui says that while at Saint-Cyr, from 1910 to 1912, de Gaulle was noted for the qualities that Hugo said were the gifts of a chief: "concision in style, precision in thought, decision in life."[17]

After Saint-Cyr, at his own request, be was attached to the regiment of Colonel Philippe Pétain. Then came the opening of the Great War. De Gaulle was wounded three times in battle and given citations for bravery. The third time, at Douaumont, near Verdun, in March 1916, he was left for dead, picked up by the Germans, and imprisoned for two years and more in Germany. At that time he was adult in his attitudes and well-trained as an officer, for when it was thought that he had fallen in hand-to-hand combat, his superior officer, in a citation, gave him the chief credit for the work his company had done.[18] He was said to be an officer without peer. So he was already making his mark in action, though his development as a thinker had not yet begun.

4

Ideas and the Man

All the dignity of Man lies in thought.
　　　　　　　　　　　　　　　—Pascal

At war's end, in 1919, when the French spoke of their lands beyond the seas in Asia or Africa, they would have said they were extremely proud of what France had done in her colonies; indeed, they still are. They felt that their work would continue, for their moral right to hold those lands was clear—at least in their own opinion. At that time, few men of importance anywhere in the world (except, of course, Woodrow Wilson) were thinking about the implications of colonizing other countries, or of the possibility of setting the colonies free. The American president had issued his Fourteen Points on January 8, 1918. In one of them, number five, he demanded

> A free, open-minded, and absolutely impartial adjustment of all colonial claims, based upon a strict observance of the principle, that in determining all such questions of sovereignty, the interests of the populations concerned *must* have equal weight with the equitable claims of the government whose title is to be determined.

Two other points were important: number three dealt with the removal of economic barriers and the establishment of equality of trade; and number five attempted to set up an association of nations to guarantee political independence around the world.[1]

The words "self-determination of nations" were not used then, but later Wilson made the points more explicit, and the plans for the peace conference contained the fateful words which Secretary of State Robert Lansing called "self-determination dynamite." Indeed, says one historian, they raised up "unrealizable hopes all over the world," for sixty million pamphlets and leaflets of Wilsonisms were scattered over all the continents.[2]

Neither French President Clemenceau nor British Prime Minister Lloyd George took the matter up with Wilson at first, for they hoped, no doubt, to make such an idealist see the light of reason in the course of time. During most of 1918, Wilson was popular in France, but when the peace conference had made what the French felt was a highly unsatisfactory treaty, they turned against him; for some years they thought no more of Wilson's "dynamite of self-determination" for conquered countries, until another war and its results gave the subject renewed significance. A few groups of Syrians and Tunisians wrote President Wilson in 1918 and 1919 asking his help toward autonomy or independence for their countries. Their yellowed, rather pathetic letters are still in the Archives of the United States, but little attention seems to have been given them. Except for a few scarcely heard anticolonialist voices in France, England, America, or the world at large, no one was talking about setting the colonies free. Albert Sarraut, a former governor and colonial minister, wrote about making colonies more valuable for the metropole and about possible limited reforms to keep the nonwhites quiet.[3] Later, Sarraut understood more of what was happening in the world.

It is odd to think that even the very word *decolonization* did not exist until recently. The *Oxford Dictionary* of 1955 thinks that one can be a *colonizer* or even a *colonialist*—one who works for colonization—but it does not offer any word for reversing the process. Neither does the *Petit Larousse* of 1954, nor the *Columbia Encyclopedia* of 1964.[4] Why look further? Clearly the breakdown of the colonial system, even while it was occurring, did not exist as an immediate possibility in most people's minds, though a statesman of the French Revolution, Anne-Robert-Jacques Turgot, had suggested that both freedom of trade and the separation of colonies from the metropole were "infinitely probable," and that friendship with former colonies was possible. "Colonies," he said, "are like fruits that cling to the tree until they have received enough nourishment: then they detach themselves." So, in Turgot's belief, "the point of view of the statesman confirms that of the economist and leads directly to decolonization."[5] But few Europeans in Turgot's day, or even much later, admitted that possibility. It was an inconvenient idea.

If others did not think about decolonization after World War I, and later, it is not surprising that a purely military man, as Charles de Gaulle then was, should not have recorded in his early writings anything about the question of freeing the colonies. After all, his training led to conquest or to protection of colonies, not to their loss. So the gradual evolution of the young officer's thought began without reference to the matter, and it began in prison.

Prison, indeed, is a very good place to think, and de Gaulle, in his various prisons, began a sort of Jacob's ladder of thought, reaching toward the beckoning light of a rather complete philosophy of action. It was a series of mental rungs or steps upward to this ideal, and all of it lay behind what de Gaulle later thought and did about colonization.

Perhaps jail life is not generally conducive to excitement or even to philosophic thought, unless the prisoner is threatened with torture or sudden death; but then, said a wartime resister, it becomes very simple to think about, for there are so few alternatives. When the door opposite to you in your cell opens, you will know whether you will go on living, or whether you will have to meet death.[6]

Also, if escape is attempted, that, too, may supercharge the atmosphere, and life will no longer seem stalled at dead center. De Gaulle tried five times to escape, but he was never successful. Each time he made an effort to get away he was caught, sometimes because of his great height of six feet four. As he himself put it, his height had let him down; and after each capture he was always put in a prison that was worse than the last one.[7] But there are certain things you can do even in prison: de Gaulle recited prose and poetry to himself, even whole plays, and he put himself through strenuous physical exercises to keep in trim. He taught some of his companions what amounted to complete courses in military history. He did a great deal of uninterrupted thinking and wrote about it. His first real product came from within the various prison walls where he was confined. That is the great importance of this period of his life— the period that ended with the Armistice of November 11, 1918, after which he was released, thin and ill, but free.[8]

So Captain de Gaulle, the "Constable of France," as his friends called him then, used his time well, whether at Szuczyn, Rosenberg, Friedberg, Magdebourg, Ingolstadt, or Ludwigshafen, which the French called *La Fille de l'Air* and the British translated as the "Escape Club." By the time of his release, some part of his first book, *La Discorde chez l'Ennemi (Discord in the Enemy Ranks)*, had been written.[9] It is not his best-known work, but is a search for the rules that have guided de Gaulle's life, the germs of two of his most important beliefs, his *idées forces*. They were the first rung of his ladder.

To begin with, he said that there is no universal system that controls military action in war; there are only circumstances and personalities. Second, he found that if the military men of a nation are allowed to make its policy, disaster must follow, for an army is only the means to put into effect the policies of statesmen.[10] These basic principles appear again and again in his writing, even in recent years. His changes in relation to the Empire and the way he carried them out are outstanding evidences of these ideas, especially in regard to the liberation of Algeria. He acted then according to circumstances, and the military was not allowed to control the executive power.

John Dryden once wrote that "mighty things from small beginnings grow," and another small step up the ladder lay in de Gaulle's first published magazine article, written soon after he went to Poland, in 1919, with General Weygand's expeditionary force, sent there to fight the Russian Communist army. In Poland, de Gaulle ranked as a major, for what was called a "zinc," or temporary stripe, was added to those of his captaincy. He spent some time in Warsaw after the fighting ended, and later wrote a few lines about watching the long queues of haggard men, women, and children waiting before the bakery shops for their weekly quota of black bread. He spoke of their famished appearance, and the "heavy looks" they cast at the carriages of the French officers, men who seemed, no doubt, so well off to a people in the depths of misery. He added that it made him realize that our civilization with all its beauties, comforts and riches, the possessions of which we have been so proud, could easily disappear under the blind fury of "desperate masses." When, in bad moments during his stay there, the thought of France came to him, he felt that she was there with them, and that the Polish people in cheering the French contingents were acclaiming France in the persons of her officers and men.[11]

Of course, Poland was not a colony, and the situation was quite different; but de Gaulle was thinking about the possible swift fading of the world he knew. This deep impression seems related to his later view of the masses of the

Empire, their great need, their semiconscious power that might so easily be unleashed against his own country. He was an observer of civilizations, and, moreover, he was aware of the possibility of their disappearance in the crucible of time. His view was not limited to the present; for he was interested in the past and the future as well.

On the less serious side, these months seem to have been one of the gayer periods of de Gaulle's life, for he frequented the salons of the lovely ladies of Warsaw and the buffets of the French officers of his mission. Though one of the fair sex described him as "that tall character who is fanning himself with his ears"—which does not sound entirely complimentary—others found him charming.[12] Perhaps he was more worldly at that time. After all, when the war began, he was just "out of school" and he had had little time to enjoy himself before he was drawn into the mud and horror of trench warfare. Also, he had not yet acquired a reputation that would cause people to criticize and rail at him; so he could take life more lightly, even though, in the war, he had seen the bitter facts of suffering and death.

All the twenties were formative years for Charles de Gaulle. He attended the War College (the *Ecole Supérieure de la Guerre*), he served on the General Staff of the Army of the Rhine, and he commanded a battalion of foot soldiers in the Rhineland.[13] There are stories that he was unusually close to his men—in one case even wearing a mourning band for a month for a soldier who had been a foundling, and who had died with no one to grieve for him.[14] But like most military men, he had to meet conditions as they were, and a subordinate was not supposed to question his superior officers. However, some personalities are possessed of unusually great intelligence and willpower, and since Charles de Gaulle was one of those, he sometimes got out of line. One famous story tells of his winning a sham battle at the Ecole de Guerre, in the twenties, by methods different from those prescribed by his commander. Winning was no virtue if you did it the wrong way, so he was rebuked—some say demoted.[15] He did not profit by the lesson of that experience. He continued to go his own road in spite of the criticisms of his superior officers. Still, as far as we know, he did not question the solid bases of the military and political life of the time—at least as regards the colonies. In the twenties, and even in the thirties, the French Colonial Empire seemed as immovable as the British hold on Gibraltar. The winds of revolt were mere whispers, easily turned aside and forced to retreat.

In an essay of 1925,[16] Charles de Gaulle spoke of the "classical epoch" when the "sense for the real" and the "taste for the true" gave durable power because the whole was adapted to national conditions of the time. If factual circumstances were not exploited, then perils might return.[17] This idea of truth to reality and adaptation to it runs through all his thought. His next step was also made in the year 1925, and though it followed the same lines, it was possibly the most important of all. The article in which it appeared was called "Doctrine *a priori* ou Doctrine des Circonstances" ("The *a priori* Doctrine or Doctrine of the Circumstances"). He explained it carefully:

The principles that regulate the use of means—economy of forces, necessity of proceeding by concentration, and, as a result, by phases or leaps, surprise for the enemy, safety for oneself—have no value (how many have said so) except in the way in which they are adapted to circumstances. . . . Moreover this statement has about it nothing specifically military—it controls every sort of action, warlike, political or industrial.[18]

This understanding of a changing world and the way it can be used—*les contingences*—can be seen whenever de Gaulle has taken a new and decisive step: in his relinquishment of power in 1946, when the circumstances were such that he knew he could not attain his ends while the government of that time continued to exist; in his changing policy toward the Empire as a whole; and especially in his relations with Algeria. In 1925, when he was thirty-five years of age, his thought was clear and definite on these vital points, and it remained so.

Of course, many other people have supported such principles, notably H. A. L. Fisher, who said in the preface to his *History of Europe*: "The play of the contingent and unforeseen is the only safe rule for the historian to observe." One might think, also, of U.S. Supreme Court Justice Oliver Wendell Holmes, who announced that "general propositions do not decide concrete cases."[19] No advance ruling can be adequate, for situations are always new.

De Gaulle went on in the same article to apply his ideas to the tasks of a "chief"—a leader. Such a man must understand, measure, and exploit surrounding circumstances. If he does, he will conquer; but if he ignores, neglects, or misjudges the contingencies, then he will be beaten, for they are the bases of his action. If a general has an excellent army, carefully deployed in battle formation, he will nevertheless be defeated if he has not been well informed about the enemy. A politician with willpower, great resources, and adequate time for planning may fail if he does not understand the character of his age. A powerful captain of industry may ruin himself if he does not comprehend the current state of the market.

For many years, said de Gaulle, French military men have tried to construct a doctrine that would enable them to make decisions *a priori*—in advance of action—but such planning cannot control events or avoid the dangers of surprise. It leads to mental indolence, an illusion that one can neglect "the mystery of the unknown." The French, who like system, the abstract, the absolute, and the categorical, have an advantage in thought, but are open to error in action. In the great period of French arms, de Gaulle said, their military men knew how to respect the concrete and ward off danger. The same century that produced the *Discourse on Method* and the development of Universal History also contained the great realistic policies of Cardinal Richelieu, the strategic objectives of Marshal Vicomte de Turenne, and the practical administration of Jean-Baptiste Colbert. Drawing a general rule from a single fact, he concludes, is a "deadly exaggeration." It shows passivity and lack of information about the enemy in our generals. In 1870, abstract rules blinded the chiefs. They had forgotten Napoleon's careful study of his opponents and all that could be learned about them. After Napoleon, said de Gaulle, "military thought slept for forty years." And later, though some men understood the contingencies and feared *a priori* solutions, they still wanted a general rule that would be adequate for all problems. They thought that such rules could be torn out of the fabric of history. Some time after 1870, when confidence had returned to France with a rebuilding of the army and with the creation of the Russian alliance, the new theory of the offensive was accepted. If the Prussians had won by boldness then, men thought, the offensive must be a good in itself; and it became a rule of action. Thus military thought moved among abstractions, leaving the terrain of reality and becoming a doctrine, an absolute metaphysic for action. The defensive might be necessary, but counterattack was the all-important procedure.

This led to the situation of 1914, when, with the army in disorder, the whole line fell back until, at the Marne, a chief who was not bound by mere theory seized a favorable opportunity and exploited it, ending the action covered with glory. The real, the positive, the use of the opportunity, thus became the great lesson of the war. In 1917–18, French leaders saw a favorable occasion. They adopted it, and thus they conquered.

After such a lesson, would they keep their distrust of *a priori* theory? It might be hoped that they would not succumb again to the absolute and the dogmatic, but using classical examples, would keep their taste for the concrete and the real. Combined with boldness and inspiration, their action might then be fruitful.[20] After all, "what has taken place once will never occur again—it might have been otherwise . . . the troubled moving torrent of circumstances escapes system as water flows through a net." Thus the knowledge of the chief has a positive value.

De Gaulle followed Henri Bergson in showing that the human spirit needs both instinct and intelligence—the latter giving the theory, the former the concrete feeling, the deep perception, the creative impulse that makes a direct contact with nature, from which sparks can burst forth. Great chiefs have always had this instinct, he says: Alexander called it his "hope," Caesar his "fortune," Napoleon his "star." Great chiefs give an impression of natural force that commands events. They synthesize thought and turn it into decision, and then, with discipline and self-control, they can coordinate the wills of others. The young Hannibal, he said, "had already assumed the indefinable splendor of those destined to great enterprises." Their prestige is the "divine element of authority." And so "intelligence supported by knowledge, instinct developed by experience, the character and prestige of the Chief, make up the action of war." The article ends by declaring that the "chain of French military force must not be broken."[21]

The central description of de Gaulle's principles ends here—at least for the articles of the twenties—though he adds a further touch or two concerning empires that carried him perhaps a step further up the ladder. In "Le Flambeau" of 1927 he suggests that immense countries exist where France might set up an empire as Rome had done. Today, he noted, the soldier is somewhat in disrepute, but he must always be the cloak of France. Again, he mentions the great number of black colonial troops that fought for France in the Great War, pointing out that they were really hoping to help their own countries, and from that they drew their courage. They would always do better when used in that way.[22]

In all of this early writing there is no word of change or independence for the colonies. De Gaulle was thinking of the safety of France and her possessions, as a military man must do. The interests of the metropole must come first. There was, as yet, no break in his firm belief that the Empire existed for France. But as the decade ended, he was posted to the Near East at his own request. There is no indication in his writing of why he asked for this assignment, though Stanley Clark says that he did it to study the problems of France in Asia Minor.[23] The time there would be an important one, for it would give Captain, now Major, de Gaulle his first experience of Overseas France.

France could not look confidently to the future, for her population was decreasing, her land destroyed, and her finances bad. Germany was beginning to menace the rest of Europe, and the new League of Nations seemed like a last hope gone.[24] The world was anything but tranquil, though it was the early thirties before the nationalist movements seemed really threatening. Few saw the clouds hanging over the colonies. For de Gaulle, experienced then in the military world only, the situation naturally turned him more and more toward belief in the French army as tbe essential shield and buckler of France.

5

The Descent to the Abyss

> International law would be worth nothing without
> troops. Whatever direction the world takes, it will not
> do without arms.
>
> —de Gaulle

At the end of 1929, for the better part of two years, de Gaulle had his first experience of the Empire when he was sent to Beirut to be on the general staff of the French Army of the Levant. How much he knew of the countries there it is hard to say; nor can we be sure that Pierre Galante is right in considering this a decisive year in the formation of de Gaulle, the writer and philosopher. At any rate, the experience increased his grasp of worlds other than his own, and must have influenced his ideas on colonization to a certain extent. He saw the French army operations in the Levant, as well as the peoples of the countries there: Syria, the Lebanon, Iraq, and Egypt. In proof of this, we have his letter of June 1930 to his friend Colonel Lucien Nachin:

> The Levant is a crossroads where everything passes by: religions, armies, merchandise, without anything's being changed. It is ten years since we came here. My impression is that we have scarcely penetrated the country at all, and that its people are just as much strangers to us—and vice versa—as they ever were. It is true that in our work in this country, we used the worst method, stimulating the people to raise themselves, and, having encouraged them, we absolved ourselves of further responsibility, though nothing had been achieved here—not the Nile Canal, nor the Palmyra aqueduct, nor a Roman road, nor an olive orchard—without the use of force. In my opinion it will be our destiny to come to that [force] or else to leave this region.

And a little later, says Gaston Bonheur, on visiting the ruins of the Crusades and before returning to France, de Gaulle wrote:

> There are people here who have never been satisfied with anything or with anybody, but who submit to the will of someone stronger than they if it is expressed, and there is a mandatory power [here] that has not yet seen what view it should take of its mandate.[1]

While in the Levant, de Gaulle, together with a comrade-in-arms, Major Yvon, wrote a brief book called *Histoire des Troupes Françaises du Levant (History of the French Troops of the Levant)*. In this brief and purely military work, the only interesting point made is that the authors found hostility to the French in the Near East among both the Turks and the Arabs. Ideas of Muslim unity had been increased by the Great War; it was an early form of nationalism. The mandate over the Levant given France by the League of Nations in 1924 had met with serious resistance in France because of the difficulties of reorganizing the army and of recruiting personnel to go to Beirut. Also, there were financial problems connected with the operations there. Still, the writers of the little book thought it must all be worthwhile, for the French presence had aided in bringing *La Paix Française* (the peace of France) to the Levant, and that, in its turn, would result in prosperity. A French general of much experience in the Levant has confirmed the fact that at that time de Gaulle was purely an army man, his mind fixed on military problems only.[2]

On his return to Paris, de Gaulle, now a colonel, assumed a position on the General Secretariat of the High Council of National Defense.[3] While he was in Paris, in the next six years, he published his most important books on the army and its significance. In a few articles he used the principles he had worked out to suggest methods to meet the needs of France in a future that was looking darker and darker.

From time to time, de Gaulle wrote a good deal about "the military spirit; there is the flame that must not die." He said that it was "part of human capital," that troops were imbued with the belief in "the abnegation of individuals for the good of the whole . . . the glorified suffering" it entailed. Its ideal was sacrifice. He believed that the military élite "should resume the consciousness of its pre-eminent rôle." Turning again to Overseas France, he wrote, "The Empire, about which we flatter ourselves, exists because of soldiers, and in the present state of things, so many riches would not weigh in our scales without the vigilance of the battalions." Perhaps this worship of military glory, this belief in force and in the necessity of war, was due in part at least to Charles Péguy, of whose work, says Crawley, "de Gaulle had drunk so deeply that he had made it his own." Péguy had written:

> Blessed are those who die in great battles
> Stretched out on the ground in the face of God.[4]

Occasionally de Gaulle would mention the Empire specifically. In 1932, in "Combats du Temps de Paix," he spoke of the outer territories that adventurous soldiers, urged on by clearsighted politicians, had conquered. France had often accepted such lands without conviction, but she had later bound them to herself. France, de Gaulle remarked, is making herself the soul of an empire. An empire exists through its soldiers, who are moved by military "virtue." He concluded that, far from being the vestiges of a past epoch, an empire is an element of modern power, for which men and materials must be drawn from the individual colonies. The courage of the chiefs, the discipline and ardor of the troops are today, as formerly, the *sine qua non* of France.[5] Force is always necessary.

A couple of years later, in 1934, de Gaulle took up the question of empires more seriously. He had realized that danger was at hand. *Vers l'Armée de Métier (Towards a Professional Army),* his most important book from a military standpoint, contains his suggestions for a mechanized force. He wrote:

> Our national existence has become that of an empire. As time goes by, this character is accentuated. The thousand bonds woven between the Metropole and its possessions overseas never stop increasing. Not only because developing the possibilities of the colonies requires more French action, but also for this reason, that the restriction of exchange between the States, a dominant feature of the time, increases the importance of new markets in our economic life every day. But while riches, instruction and liberty are growing under our aegis, we are [also] seeing the growth of movements of ideas, of passions, of interests, *whose manifest purpose is the end of our domination.* [Italics added.] Certainly, if it is given us to pursue our work to the point of progress at which wisdom comes to the élites and loyalty to the crowds, we will see populations now scarcely resigned [to us] accept union freely. But up to that point, let us remain masters, under penalty of losing everything.

And on a further page, he points out the aid that may be given by the powerful military strength existing in North Africa, provided it has been made secure by communications, good will, and incontestable authority.[6]

Thus at that time de Gaulle saw the possibility of an end to the Empire, but he still hoped to retain it, if it could be mastered by a strong authority. Albert Sarraut, then senator and minister of colonies, had written similar passages in 1931. As governor of Indochina, and in other important posts, Sarraut had been a conservative colonialist official. But by 1931 he was seeing things somewhat differently, and, to him, future dangers were apparent. He wrote that for a long time "the sparks have begun to be lighted like signal fires in the mountains," and "the crisis of colonization has begun everywhere." He also said that the men of the black race had little by little begun to dream of the day of liberation, when "they would take over the secrets of the foreign masters and use them as leverage for the independence and the riches they would no longer have to share with others." Still, Sarraut could try, even in 1931, to justify colonization as a need of human society, as a Francisizing, civilizing mission; and to do this he emphasized the duties of the colonizer as well as his rights.[7] So he agreed with de Gaulle about the movements of independence and their danger to the Empire.

In his last book of the period, *La France et son Armée (France and Her Army),* de Gaulle spoke of the lure that far-off countries had always held for the French: "Willingly or unwillingly, because of her soldiers, France takes the first rank in the rush to new lands." If he did not let his imagination wander among the peoples of occupied countries to perceive their feelings about domination, at least he realized the hardships of the French soldiers' lives in those distant places:

> Crests taken by assault, palisades attacked, [men] surprised in the depths of a ravine, calvaries [met in] climbing the rocks, solitary anguish in the desert, death and

passion of men in the bush, the forest, the marsh, cruel mornings, exhausting noontimes, dismal evenings: those are what made the empire.[8]

De Gaulle knew that public opinion was often against the Empire, though at times belief in a larger France could inspire courage and hope. Of course, the Empire cost heavily in men and money; so many thought that France should look only to the protection of the metropole. What no one saw in the thirties was the overwhelming importance the Empire would acquire after June 1940, for the French were not expecting a quick defeat.

In these prewar years, de Gaulle used every means at his command to move the writers, the generals, and the parliamentarians to perfect the defense of France. He saw dangerous gaps in the government's planning, and he asked for a more modern mechanized army than the generals had approved. The High Command still clung to the belief that the incomplete Maginot Line would defend France. A few writers and deputies helped his cause, but the necessary credits were not voted. De Gaulle was desperate at his inability to move those in command.

When the "phony war" began in September 1939, Colonel de Gaulle took command of the 507th Regiment of Tanks of the 5th French Army at Wangenbourg, in Alsace. By that time, there were a few plans for armored divisions, but no one knew whether they would be ready in time. The Colonel made one more effort, in January 1940, sending a memorandum explaining the danger to about eighty high officials in Parliament and in the government. He asked for quantities of tanks and planes, supported by infantry and artillery. However, they ignored him, thinking him a dangerous innovator. The military expert on the *Figaro* even told Wladimir d'Ormesson: "De Gaulle?—a maniac about tanks. . . . He doesn't see anything but that in the war. . . . Be reassured. What he says has no importance!" Yet, a few months later, d'Ormesson put all his confidence in General de Gaulle.[9]

During the early months of 1940, Prime Minister Edouard Daladier was opposed to de Gaulle and would not work with him. When Paul Reynaud became premier, at the end of March, though he thought of de Gaulle, he could not put him in the cabinet, as Daladier was still a minister. After the real fighting began in May, de Gaulle was made a general with temporary rank and sent to the front, with a very incomplete armored force. He was able to check the Germans in his narrow sector, and thus gave at least a small proof of the correctness of his theories. If some of his contemporaries deny the value of what he did in this action, still, he received a citation for it from Generalissimo Maxime Weygand. Previously, Weygand had never been in favor of de Gaulle, so the value of the citation can scarcely be questioned. De Gaulle was then retired to Picardy to regroup his forces, but was almost immediately called to Paris as undersecretary of war in Reynaud's revised cabinet—a cabinet from which Daladier had been omitted. The General's tenure in government was brief, for the cabinet lasted only two weeks before the fall of France put it out of of office. Still, those two weeks gave de Gaulle the right to feel and act as the last "still standing" minister of France when he went to London and set up the organization of Free France. This post was the beginning of his public life.

De Gaulle was now ready for his role in history. He had climbed to the top of the ladder of his thought, and he had a small, uncertain foothold in power. He had applied his principles, however briefly, "in accordance with the circumstances" as he found them. The outcome of the Battle of France could have been at least somewhat different if the men in the government and the army had listened to Charles de Gaulle, instead of ignoring his ideas and allowing the Germans to make use of them successfully in their armored columns. Eliot Goodman has recently written that de Gaulle's views "can be traced back to long before he came to power in France." But we have an even closer testimony on this point from de Gaulle's niece, Geneviève Anthonioz-de Gaulle, who has followed her uncle's career with the greatest attention. She has said that as a historian he was aware of the evolution of things. "It is only the adaptations of his philosophy that have altered with time."[10]

When we consider how de Gaulle felt about the Empire before the defeat of France in June 1940, his view of it must seem rather one-sided. He was looking only for the advantage the Empire might bring to France. It still seemed possible that a firm hold might keep the discontent of the Empire under control, even though that process might entail more trials, passion, and death for more French soldiers. Colonialism was still a one-way street: it was only for the colonizers. It is not very hard to understand how de Gaulle could see it then in that light. His whole energy was given to his military life, and to his effort to see that France was properly defended. Sarraut, somewhat in advance of his time, had seen even in 1919 that if France had brought education and civilization to her overseas possessions, she might in this way have brought the colonies closer to the mother country.[11] Yet, over the centuries, many Frenchmen had gone to far countries, bent on bringing the *mission civilisatrice* (civilizing mission) to the less educated hordes of Africa or Asia. There can be no doubt of the sincerity of these early missionaries, or of the fact that the French considered their civilization the highest of those man had been able to attain, and therefore worthy of being passed on to less favored races. But few saw as early as Sarraut and de Gaulle the trend toward independent status among the colonized peoples. They had not realized that a giant was waking. Edmund Burke said of the French Revolution that it had left a void, and Mirabeau called Burke very stupid, for, he said, "this void is a volcano, the subterranean agitations and approaching eruptions of which no one could neglect for a moment without imprudence."[12] Such a volcano existed everywhere in the colonies by 1940.

Most of the French did not see this trend. Arriving late at the Depression, France, in the thirties, seemed a little island of prosperity in a sea of misery. When financial difficulties came at last, there was vast unemployment and poverty. Export and production went down, the government was helpless, and there was discontent in the whole nation. A great wave of distrust of parliamentarianism began, and force seemed necessary to right the situation. Fascist leagues such as the *Croix de Feu* started up, and there were riots in the streets of Paris. But all through the decade, while France was disintegrating, Hitler was gaining in power. The Left managed to gain control for two years in the Popular Front, and there was a possibility of reform. Sit-down strikes helped the workers for a short time, but the Front lasted only two years. It had not been able to achieve any lasting implementation of its reforms. The war in Spain began, confronting Communist ideas with authoritarian ones. The result of these complicating factors was that France was divided in its thinking more than ever before. She could not act as a unit, and while she waited helplessly, Hitler broke the Versailles pact and his troops entered the Rhineland early in 1935. Britain and France were still timorous and unwilling to act in the face of aggression, and the "false peace" of Munich was the result. Soon Germany took over Austria and entered Czechoslovakia, and when she sent her armies crashing through Poland in 1939, France—in spite of her ties to Poland—did nothing to help. The war spread, and both England and France were engulfed in it.

Thus, during the whole decade, there was discontent at home and unrest in the colonies. The talk of reform was never put into action, in spite of the warnings of nationalism in the colonies, and there was also a great growth of anticolonialism elsewhere, especially in the United States and Russia. Changes might well have been expected.[13]

Edmond Michelet wrote recently that France began a long decline when she rejected Clemenceau. He had won the war of 1914–18 for his country, but she denied him the presidency in 1920. After that faithlessness, said Michelet, the road was always down-hill. At the end of the descent, "victory went away—for good this time—and she took all the furniture with her!"[14]

6

The Broken Sword of France

> For France is not alone!
> She is not alone!
> She is not alone!
> She has a vast Empire behind her! . . . She knows, she
> feels in her Empire powerful forces are afoot to save
> her honor.
>
> —de Gaulle

When defeat seemed close at hand, the Reynaud cabinet fell, on June 16, 1940, and General Pétain became premier of France. De Gaulle was unwilling to remain among the "defeatists," and may have feared arrest because of his already known desire to continue the struggle with the use of everything France had left. Together with one aide, Geoffroy de Courcel, and General Edward Spears, the British liaison officer to the French High Command, he went, in the early morning of June 17, to the Mérignac Airport at Bordeaux, where he had landed the previous day after a mission to Churchill in England. The prime minister had told him he could keep the aircraft in case he wanted to return to England; so the three men boarded the little plane, the *Rapid Dragon,* and set off for London, merely pausing briefly at Jersey for fuel.

They landed at Heston Airport near London, and as soon as de Gaulle found a room in a small hotel, the Rubens, he went to see Churchill in Downing Street. The prime minister immediately gave him permission to use the British radio, the BBC; the next day de Gaulle sent out his celebrated appeal to all Frenchmen, wherever they might be, to join him in keeping alive the flame of French resistance. De Gaulle has said that his escape was less dramatic than General Spears's story of it indicated. General Spears had made it appear that de Gaulle barely made it into the airplane as it rolled down the airstrip, pulling his aide in after him.[1] Nevertheless, when we consider the quick decision to leave, the rumor that he was to be arrested, the speedy departure, and the perilous circumstances involved, there would have been reason, in any case, to think of it as part of a "cloak and dagger" mystery.

Even in the first days after de Gaulle's flight to England, the Pétain cabinet was arranging for an armistice and setting up a new government in a new capital, Vichy. From there, it would try to control the part of France that was called "unoccupied," and it would also try to crush de Gaulle's movement and those of all other resisters.

General de Gaulle reached England before any of the others who wanted to escape the France of the Armistice and of the Occupation they knew would take place. A day later would have been too late, for the new French cabinet of Pétain disapproved his stand and would certainly have prevented him from leaving, even if they had not taken him into custody. His sudden departure took him out of their power, but in going, he cut himself off from his previous life in the army and became a deserter who would be prosecuted. Only those familiar with the great emphasis put upon obedience in the French army can realize what this meant. Yet, had he not succeeded in reaching England, there would have been no Free France, no central group, to which those who did not believe in accepting the defeat could have turned. The world now knows that on June 30 General de Gaulle was stripped of his rank and ordered to place himself under arrest at the prison of Saint Michel in Toulouse to be judged by the Council of War. The charges were refusal to obey orders in the presence of the enemy, and persuading others under arms to disobey. On August 2, 1940, he was declared guilty of treason for attempt against the surety of the state and for desertion to a foreign country in time of war; and for these crimes he was condemned to death and his property confiscated. After the first communication, he replied to the military authorities that what they said "had no interest for him whatsoever." To the sentence of death, he did not reply at all. In his *Memoirs*, he wrote later, "A Chief is always alone in the face of a bad destiny."[2]

In his first radio appeal fron London, on June 18, 1940, de Gaulle stressed the fact that France was not alone; she still had many resources and a vast Empire behind her. With this broadcast, de Gaulle became the first resister of France, and the Empire became part of his daily thought and speech. He knew now that it was the most important asset France possessed. The Empire could help to reforge the "Broken Sword of France."

For several weeks after his arrival in England, de Gaulle spoke over the BBC almost daily, and there were many such references to the Empire.[3] He tried to reach all the French in France, throughout the Empire, and elsewhere who might join "Free France," as he now called his small following in England. He wired the governors of the French colonies offering to put himself under their command, since they outranked him, but they would not come. Then, hopeless of persuading them, he spoke directly to the Empire and its peoples. It was intact in June, he said, but now Pétain and the other "Armistice-makers" had let it fall into the power of the enemy. The colonies were to be disarmed and their strategic points given up to the German and Italian control missions. The enemy would be able to take them over entirely should they wish to do so. He went on to say that the native populations, confident in France and respecting her, had become indignant, and this might mean the disaffection and revolt of all the colonies. In such a case, how would their people be fed, and how could they carry on their trade? And what would this mean to the authority of those who administered them? Later, it was learned that there was not such a great risk to the colonies, but many people believed at the time that it existed.

Then de Gaulle spoke of the peril to the French *colons* overseas, the settlers living in some of the territories. The Empire, he felt, must remain in the possession of France in spite of the fact that Vichy would be everywhere. He appealed to the governors-general, the governors, the high commissioners, and the other administrators to refuse to execute the armistices, and he called upon those who had not joined him among the French people or in the various countries of the Empire to give their help. France, the free, the courageous, must be worthy of the new France that would come after victory. He pointed out that the men in France who "were on their knees having given up the sword," and who would claim they had the right to give up the Empire, would not have fought to retain it.[4]

However, the numbers of Free France remained small. And the blow to its supporters was great when Great Britain sank a large part of the French navy at Mers-el-Kébir in early July to keep Vichy from releasing it to the Germans. Perhaps the Vichyists would not have done this, but the British feared it. Yet, "against and in spite of all," as the Free French said so often in those early days, their work continued, and it began to count.

A first small encouragement to their cause came on August 24, when the king of England was present at the first review of Free French troops at Aldershot. The king's appearance there meant British approval of the part taken by the little Gaullist army. It now numbered 7,000 men—men who were saving the honor of France by continuing resistance to Germany. The Free French could now feel that Great Britain was their ally. Yet their most important support came two days later, and it came from the Empire.[5]

Since the governors of North and West Africa had shown not only indifference but hostility toward de Gaulle, Equatorial Africa was the only hope. Early in August, de Gaulle had accordingly sent three of his most trusted lieutenants there: René Pleven, a highly placed civilian who had joined de Gaulle in the early days of Free France in London; Hettier de Boislambert, who had a great knowledge of Africa; and Major François-Marie-Philippe de Hauteclocque, later General Leclerc, an experienced army officer. Perhaps "Douglas," "Charles," and "Sullivan" (the code names of the three) could give a push in the right direction. The British would provide transportation and the use of their African territories as bases for any project attempted. On August 7 the three flew in a Sunderland seaplane, the *Clyde*, to Bathurst in British Gambia to see sympathizers in nearby Dakar, and then on to Lagos, to try to keep discouraged resisters from leaving just as help was coming. Churchill had already agreed with de Gaulle that Britain would favor Gaullist colonial commerce and would help the Free French in Africa wherever possible.[6]

While they were making their plans, Colonel René-Marie-Edgard de Larminat was arrested by a non-Gaullist commander in Syria for planning a volunteer corps to fight with the British. He managed to escape from prison with the aid of an officer and a few men of the French Foreign Legion. The sentinel outside his door was given an "urgent" letter to take to the commander, which he left his post to deliver. Seizing the chance, de Larminat slipped over a wall to a waiting car and reached Palestine. He wired de Gaulle that he would join him, and after a brief stay in Djibouti, he went on to Cairo and then to the Belgian Congo, close to the country where the Gaullists needed him. De Larminat got in touch with Commandant (Major) Colonna d'Ornano, who was with the Vichyist army at Brazzaville, in the Middle Congo, and persuaded him to desert his post and take a ferry across the Congo River to join some of the Free French at Leopoldville, on the Belgian side. There de Gaulle's adherents decided to try to take over, at one and the same time, three colonies of Equatorial Africa—Chad, Oubangui-Chari, and the Middle Congo—as well as "the Cameroons," as the two territories were called while they were divided under mandate to France and Britain.[7]

In view of their small numbers of supporters, this was a risky, almost impossible task, but the Gaullists agreed to attempt it. These plans were of prime importance to de Gaulle. First of all, he needed a capital on "French" soil to secure the effective sovereignty of France for his movement.[8] In addition, Equatorial Africa held other prizes. Perhaps de Gaulle thought most about the territory of Chad, lying in the very heart of Africa. It was landlocked, but Africa could not be crossed by air without using its facilities. It was "the turntable of the world." General Charles-Marie-Emmanuel Mangin, famous in World War I, had once said that whoever held Chad held Africa. It had great strategic value. Allied and French troops going to Egypt or the Orient could pass through it; and possession of it could force the Italians to make war on two fronts, for Chad commanded the place where their Libyan and Ethiopian armies could be joined. The Germans could not reach Nigeria and the Belgian Congo without it. Although Chad had little food or raw materials, the Free French were able to arrange with the British to supply its necessities from Nigeria.[9]

There was certainly a possibility that Chad might join Free France, for Félix Eboué was there. Governor Eboué was a son of French Guiana, the first black who had ever been named governor by the French government in Paris. There was good reason for their choice. Brought up in his home state, he had recited, like all other children, black or white, in French schools:

Formerly France was called Gaul and its inhabitants were the Gauls. Our ancestors had blue eyes and wore long heavy moustaches.

And in school, too, they chanted:

Sing, friends, of the gentle country of France
The sweet country that gave us birth
Where our joyous childhood was passed
in the arms of parents full of love.

Or perhaps they sang one of the songs Déroulède had written after 1870:

One day the lightning of battle will strike.
Then, little one, forward with heart held high!

So young Eboué and his companions had really "lived" the misfortunes of the motherland. After school in Guiana came long years of study in France, ending with several degrees; and then began a long career as an administrator in Oubangui-Chari. Eboué won his great reputation through his ability in promoting new agricultural projects and through his interest in the formulation of new policies for dealing with the peoples of the countries where he worked.[10]

Also, as an administrator in Africa, Eboué studied local customs and cultures. Even in the rainy season, he traveled into the bush several times a month to study the tribes of the various regions. Among other things, he learned about the hatred of the Germans that had followed their occupation of parts of Africa before 1914. And he knew of de Gaulle's strength among both Africans and French. Eboué had often felt the shock of racial prejudice, injury, jealousy, and ingratitude. Nevertheless, he stuck it out. He worked tirelessly to raise the level of the peoples of the countries where he was stationed. After some time he came to the notice of Paul Reynaud, then secretary-general of the colonies. Reynaud made him secretary-general of the island of Martinique, and while he was there, he was able to restore the lost prosperity of the island. Later, he went to the Soudan, and after that experience, he was made governor first of Guadeloupe, then of Oubangui-Chari, and still later of Chad. For a descendant of slaves and freed slaves, he had risen high. He had a sense of duty, a shining, smiling spirit, and an understanding of human beings that surpassed the more ordinary emotions of pride, cruelty, and envy by which so many individuals are governed.[11]

Eboué knew that the overseas lands would never have agreed to roll up their flags and wait while Berlin decided on a future for them—a lot that could be easily guessed in advance. The idea of resistance to the Armistice grew in him; so he was in complete agreement with General de Gaulle. As Danton once said, the situation needed "boldness, again boldness, always boldness!"[12]

Was it chance, or did some higher power intend that Eboué should hear de Gaulle's first appeal of June 18—an appeal that had curiously few listeners? In any case, when he heard the broadcast "a deep spiritual force led him to act," said one of his biographers.[13] Eboué knew that if Vichy removed him from command, the next incumbent of his position would be Vichyist; so, having written de Gaulle of his intention to support Free France, the governor waited for the right moment to take a stand.

While Eboué waited, René Pleven and Colonna d'Ornano (that "riotous officer and deserter," the Vichyists called him) flew on August 24 from Lagos to Fort Lamy, the capital of Chad. Success in this "capital of the bush" was anything but certain, for the Vichy government was still powerful. When the delegates landed, the long lines of troops at the airport were not reassuring. But as they left the plane, the troops presented arms and the band struck up, rendering military honors to de Gaulle's envoys; so they knew all was well. Real enthusiasm greeted them as they walked through the town. It was a provincial African city, with both white houses and straw huts and dirty, odorous streets; leather artisans at work; a dusty market and a square teeming with vehicles and animals; many Frenchmen were seen, along with Muslims saying their prayers.

When they reached the center of the town, Pleven spoke to the crowd from the steps of the government buildings. He was a good speaker, calm and persuasive, both qualities important in this far-off, superhot country where, as Maurice Martin du Gard wrote later, "the sun, the desert, and alcohol aided secession."[14]

Pleven spoke of the food that would come from Nigeria, of de Gaulle, ready to take power, and of the need for an example—a signal—for the other colonies to rise. Colonna d'Ornano followed him, telling of the expected military aid. Then there was a pause in the proceedings, for Colonel Marchand (nephew of the better known Colonel Jean Baptiste Marchand, who went to Fashoda in 1896–98), the military commander of the district, was on a journey in the bush. He was summoned back by wire next day, and Governor Eboué, together with Marchand, issued a proclamation. Because of the Armistice, the hostility of the Pétain government to Great Britain, and the isolation imposed on Chad by Vichy, Eboué and Marchand had decided to proclaim the adherence of Chad to the Free French forces of General de Gaulle. They would urge the other colonies of Equatorial Africa to follow suit. The listening crowd agreed with them.[15]

Thus the rallying of Chad was won without a shot being fired. Next day a telegram from General de Gaulle cited Chad for the Order of the Empire because of its courageous decision and its admirable resolution. Then the crowd gave way to joy, singing "The Marseillaise," marching to the presidency, drinking, crying, laughing far into the night. The first territory of the Empire had risen to fight. A part of the old France was free once more. Farther down the River Chari, at Fort Archambault, those who chose to remain under the rule of Vichy were allowed to board boats for their trip to the homeland. As they moved out on the water, and space widened between them and those remaining on the banks, who were now their "enemy brothers," the same words rose into the air from the men on bank and boat: "Vive la France!"[16]

Looking back over the years, it seems as if the rallying of Chad on August 26, 1940, must have been one of the most stirring days of de Gaulle's life. It was the beginning of the return of the Empire to the side of those who resisted Germany. The chief of Free France could not have been sure that day, in spite of all his faith in France and in her future survival, that within three years all of the colonies except Indochina would be back in the fold. But the rallying of Chad was a stirring sign that General de Gaulle's cause might succeed eventually. Two months later, he issued the declaration from Brazzaville, in the Middle Congo, setting up the legal status of Free France, in which he promised the French people the return to them—at war's end—of the power he had seized in their Empire. But the first success is the most thrilling, and it was secure, for the rains would soon begin, and the roads leading to Chad would be impassable.[17]

The reactions elsewhere were important, too. The last governor of Guiana, Jean Peset, lying seriously wounded in a hospital in England, wrote later:

> It is impossible to tell you about the enthusiasm that the news of the rallying of Governor Eboué aroused among the wounded [here]. But I keep written vividly in my memory the unbroken recollection of those moving hours when people became drunk with admiration, joy and gratitude.
>
> Eboué . . . every time thereafter that my ears have heard that glorious name, Eboué . . . I find myself transported suddenly to Great Britain, to that atmosphere delirious with hope and love.[18]

If, as Governor-General Henri Laurentie has said, "at that time Chad had two or three poor planes, a telegraph station, and a few radios, nothing else to tie its people to the world," it certainly made good use of its limited facilities![19]

The Cameroons, though under mandate to France and thus under a somewhat different regime than the rest of Equatorial Africa, still could be considered a possibility for Gaullist takeover. This was a harder nut to crack than Chad, since in July, Admiral Platon, a Vichyist, had gone to Douala, the chief port of the Cameroons, and had succeeded in persuading Richard Brunot, the governor-general, to remain faithful to Pétain. Brunot had said that he would not give the country over to Germany, the enemy of France, but that he would not rally to de Gaulle either. In short, he was a mugwump, a fence-sitter, and the people in the Cameroons interpreted this as rallying to Vichy. But the population was not content with this, and they wired de Gaulle on July 28, asking his advice.[20] Nothing had been settled, and when the emissaries of de Gaulle reached Lagos on August 7, there was no time to be lost if they wished to influence the sympathizers who had collected in the Cameroons. Some of them certainly wanted to fight, and some even wanted to attempt a *coup d'état* in the Cameroons to preserve their freedom. Brunot was not popular in Vichy. He had not fallen in with their plans, and if he were replaced, the situation might be worse. Hope of Gaullist aid among the people was waning, so time was important, especially since it was known that a new governor was on the way—and who and what would he be? There were about 630 French people in Douala, with a garrison commanded by Captain Dio, a man of real courage and decision. People were saying of the Gaullists "They're coming!" but no help had arrived.

There was a final obstacle to overcome. While Major Philippe de Haute-clocque, known later as General Leclerc, and Lieutenant Hettier de Boislambert, who were to carry out the *coup*, were preparing in Victoria, the British commander of the district, General Giffard, decided that their operation ought not to take place. The Senegalese soldiers were deserting there, he said. It was never explained why those deserters were found later on in Giffard's own regiment. But Leclerc and de Boislambert decided that the Cameroons must be taken at once, even without the approval of the British general; and de Gaulle supported them by wire.[21]

On the night of August 26–27, twenty-three Frenchmen under Leclerc and de Boislambert left Tiko harbor, in the British side of the Cameroons, for Douala. On the way, they changed into dugouts, or *pirogues,* and for fourteen hours they paddled the frail little crafts in darkness over a troubled, stormy sea. They had a frightful battle with wind and wave, but they won out. Just before dawn broke, they saw the vague outlines of Douala almost hidden in a warm, wet mist. Approaching the landing stage on the Wouri River, they heard cars starting up, as the Free Frenchmen of Douala set out to meet them. In the darkness, Leclerc and de Boislambert took some floating logs for solid ground and stepped into the water instead of onto the land, nearly drowning. However, they managed to crawl out, "wet as soup but with their resolution dry." Then they went through the town, knocking on the doors of sympathizers, whispering orders, and forming bands to meet in the post office and the wireless and railway stations. When a Gaullist tried to get them to delay their project, Leclerc retorted angrily, "I am here and I stay. I will only leave feet first. Do you understand?" So the *coup* went on, and without any opposition, the Gaullists took over the administration buildings, the militia camp, and the houses of the members of the government, who woke to find their dwellings guarded by black riflemen. Not a shot was fired.[22]

Leclerc, needing more rank than he had then acquired, tore the silver braid off one sleeve and fastened it on the other, hiding the torn material with a raincoat he carried on his arm. On the left side he was still a major, but on the right a colonel. Then he issued a proclamation on behalf of General de Gaulle, signing it as commissioner-general of the territory, and planes showered his statement over the population. The leaflet proclaimed a state of siege and said that all attempts at revolt would be suppressed. He cut all the wire services to the town and allowed no private cars on the streets. The eyes of France, her Empire, and the Allies were upon them, he said. As soon as possible, he wired de Gaulle apologizing for taking for himself a rank he did not possess. He said it would be only temporary, but that he would need reinforcements. He would continue to act energetically. Order now reigned in Douala.

Needless to say, General de Gaulle speedily made the temporary rank permanent, and he did not have to wait long for the energetic action, for it came the very next day. De Boislambert, with two companies of riflemen, took over the capital city of the French section of the Cameroons, Yaoundé, where the administrator, Michel-Raphael-Antoine Saller, a man from the Antilles, had prepared the ground for them. The colonel who had been in charge there was arrested and taken back to Douala, and on August 29 Leclerc went through the city, now lined with Free French flags, just as orders to arrest the Gaullists arrived at government headquarters from Vichy. Leclerc spoke that evening to the officers and veterans of the town, telling of the appeals that had been made to de Gaulle by the people of the Cameroons, who could not credit the defeat of France and who had felt that nothing was being done. De Gaulle had said to him "Go!" and so the new colonel had come to liberate the Cameroons.

Next day, de Gaulle wired "Warm congratulations. . . . Hang the Tricolor everywhere!" and Leclerc's name entered into history. He was introduced, as Engelbert Mveng wrote later, "to the immortality of glory."[23]

And so it happened that the 429,000 square kilometers of the Cameroons, with their 2.5 million people and their rich deposits of tungsten, coal, mica, titanium, gold, and oil, now belonged to Free France. In addition to their riches, they were an excellent strategic place from which to defend Chad.[24]

Colonel René-Marie-Edgard de Larminat was responsible for bringing over a third section of Equatorial Africa—the Middle Congo and Oubangui-Chari—to de Gaulle's movement. De Larminat was known as a man of "courage, lucidity, and determination"—"a brilliant and keen officer."[25] He certainly had those qualities and a good many more, too. He knew the importance of possessing Brazzaville, the capital and the seat of the governor-general of French Equatorial Africa. Without it and its surrounding territory, the group of colonies could not be a coherent and viable part of France. Chad and the Cameroons alone would be merely borderlands to the British part of Africa. It was the key to the whole affair, though it would be hard to take.

The only real approach to the city of Brazzaville was across the Congo via the Stanley Pool, and, of course, the opposite side of the Congo belonged to the Belgians; so no important expeditionary force could leave from there. And, thought de Larminat, a powerful military expedition would be a wrong method, in any case. Furthermore, the Brazzaville administration would know of anything that came into the country from its post at Pointe Noire, the ocean port where the rail line from Brazzaville ended. So nothing could start from the outside.

Another difficulty was that the Vichy French authorities in the capital were hostile. The declining Third Republic had put politicians instead of men of character in African posts. General Louis Husson, whom someone described as "a mediocre, pretentious, gross man of no real distinction," had been made governor of the Middle Congo in Brazzaville after the previous governor had left at the end of June. De Larminat knew Husson already and could guess what to expect from him. Whatever happened would have to come from the inside, and de Larminat himself would have to set it in motion.[26]

The five Free French "desperados," Leclerc, Pleven, de Boislambert, de Larminat, and Moitessier (a Gaullist Middle East liaison officer), planned action as they sat under a big tree on government property at Lagos. De Larminat sketched in his own part as he flew to Léopoldville on August 19 on the seaplane *Clyde*. The *Clyde* performed an additional service for him, as previously no great seaplane had landed on the Stanley Pool. The inhabitants of Léopoldville were so intrigued by the great bird that a number of them got into boats to investigate it. Thus de Larminat made many useful and unexpected contacts. Then he bent his mind to the "necessary but unpleasant rôle of being an investigator and agitator." To aid him, the Belgians loaned him a small houseboat, the S.S. *Léopold II*, for his headquarters. While he stayed in his floating office, Gaullist sympathizers crossed the Congo to see him at the risk of their lives, for Husson had placed sentinels on the banks of the river.[27]

De Larminat did not have a vast number of supporters to count on. In Léopoldville, there were a few Free French partisans and some Belgians, and, for military aid, a battalion from Chad under Major Delange, an ardent resister. On the other hand, most of the French civilians in Brazzaville would be with him, except for the men in high posts. However, his chief help in the city would come from Médicin Général Adolphe Sicé, famous for his fight against sleeping sickness. Sicé had gone far out into the bush to rally men in distant outposts.[28]

De Larminat's first action was to send Governor Husson a letter on behalf of General de Gaulle. The letter said he might choose the form under which he would rally to Free France, stating what post he would like for himself when he had done so. There was little hope of a reply to that, and, indeed, none came. Husson's only answer was to reinforce the blockade on the French bank of the Pool and to increase police surveillance. Clearly, he was not going to help. He would have to be forced by some military action from the Delange battalion. It was fortunate that Husson had reached depths of unpopularity and lack of esteem from those surrounding him; otherwise, it would not have been possible to get military men to lay their hands on a chief. Even for this, his nerve must be broken. De Larminat had learned the use of a war of nerves while he was in the Levant. Tracts could help, and de Larminat tried to send out at least one a day. A helper, Robert Wery, came every night to the *Leopold II*, took the tracts, and rolled them in bunches around his waist under a bathing suit. Then he crossed the river on his outboard motorboat and gave the documents to two men, a mechanic and a noncommissioned officer, who distributed them. They did this so secretly and so well that Governor Husson even found tracts on his desk in the morning, and on his chair when he was presiding over a football match.[29]

No time could be lost, for Husson was trying to disintegrate the Delange battalion by sending some of the men elsewhere. But its presence was the chief hope of the Gaullists. So de Larminat sent another letter which he called "a monument of impudence" to Husson. Coming from an officer to his superior, it was certainly unique! De Larminat assumed, first, that by now the general had finally read his first letter. He went on to say that Husson's indecision would disintegrate his own colony and his troops. It was essential to make him understand the situation, for tomorrow his command would be overrun individually and collectively, and he could count on de Larminat to arrange it. Clearly, Vichy and Dakar would not like that. Husson's days had been counted—but now the count was over. He could rally to de Gaulle or take refuge in Léopoldville, and if his adhesion to Free France was not received on the twenty-seventh, an offensive against him would be begun.

De Larminat remarked that by the twenty-seventh the Vichyist leader was beside himself; the war of nerves had worked, and General Husson then committed the supreme folly of threatening before he acted, though "a man of action fires and then explains himself."[30] Feverishly, Husson set up guards and patrols, arrested suspected officers, and made ready to transfer them else-where. So everyone knew that by the twenty-eighth they would be reduced to powerlessness, and "since they were not mere washrags," they drew their own conclusions. Meanwhile, the Husson patrols tramped the streets of Brazzaville that night, prepared prisons, and set up machine guns.

Then came the news of the rallying of the Cameroons, and the Gaullists would not wait any longer. One group headed for the military camp, where they lured soldiers to the mess for dinner. Then they themselves took over all the guns and ammunition the camp possessed. Armed now, they reached headquarters and found machine guns set up there, so they surrounded the area. The commander of the troops was brandishing a revolver, but a Free French officer walked up to him, hit him on the wrist, and told him to go home and stay there—which he did. The Gaullists did not lack boldness; apparently the Vichy commander did.

Then Husson retreated with a few faithful followers to Government House. The Gaullists seized trucks, filled them with armed men, and drove up to the long double-winged building, where rows of Vichy soldiers were lined up. "Surrender!" shouted the Free Frenchmen. There was a long, tense moment of silence, and then the Vichy troops let their guns clatter to the ground and gave in. Naturally, Husson was outraged. He did not wish to use force, and so he tried to take another road out. "How dare you, the son of a General, lift your hand against a general of France?" he cried. The officer to whom he spoke burst into tears, but another officer took his place and ordered his men to arrest the governor. Husson went down fighting, his glasses knocked off, his tunic torn and muddy; but the Gaullists were not abashed, and they quietly rolled him in a blanket and piled him into a truck. He left his command as nothing more than a gesticulating bundle, like a sausage in a package—a package that was soon put in a canoe and ferried across to Léopoldville. It was ignominious for a French general. Of course, he had meant to fire, but he had discovered that some of his men had filled his ammunition boxes with stones instead of munitions. So he knew he was at a disadvantage, and hesitated—the supreme fault of the weak and incoherent—and so lost his command. De Larminat, arriving in a launch flying the Tricolor with the Cross of Lorraine on it, saw Husson briefly, and then the former governor-general disappeared toward Léopoldville.[31]

At Léopoldville, Husson tried to see a medical officer about his "injuries." "See how they treat a French General!" he said. But, unfortunately for Husson, the medical officer was a Gaullist, and he replied severely, "What you need is not a doctor—it is a tailor!" And the spectators shouted, "Vive de Gaulle!"[32]

De Larminat had won. His method was good. He once said, "I followed the ball in the hope that it would pass between the goal posts without troubling myself too much about what went on at the sides."[33]

So ended what Jacques Soustelle, who has told a great deal of the story of the rallying of French Africa to the Gaullist cause, called the "Three Glorious Days of French Africa," a phrase famous ever since the three days when the partisans of Louis Philippe overthrew the regime of Charles X.[34]

These first three days of revolt contained what was probably the most important period of the war for the relations between France and Africa. In addition to what de Gaulle had foreseen he would gain by the possession of Chad, he now had a greater bargaining power with his Allies. Soon new airports and harbors with deepwater quays and new roads enhanced what Equatorial Africa had brought to Free France.[35] And the German menace to Central Africa was lifted. How great was the menace? No one knew until at the end of the war General Leclerc found among Hitler's documents in Berchtesgaden a series of maps showing the zones of Central Africa the Nazi dictator had intended to occupy in 1943.[36]

Of course, the Vichyists, realizing what they had lost, were furious; and events later did not make them feel any better, at least not until the September victory at Dakar. Things went from bad to worse for Vichy France, for on August 29, there was another bloodless revolution, when Oubangui-Chari followed the three other states of Equatorial Africa in joining Free France. And in early September, Oceania and New Caledonia were added to the new Free French Empire.

A little later, there was a revolution that was not so bloodless. Gabon, the last colony in Equatorial Africa that had not rallied to de Gaulle, was small, but it could not be left under the Pétain government. It had two good anchorages and two good airports, and it was on the edge of the Congo and the Cameroons. If it was allowed to remain as it was, the recent conquests might be lost.

According to a later account by Colonel de Larminat, now high commissioner for Africa, Governor Georges-Pierre Masson of Gabon had at first agreed to rally to de Gaulle, but some days later he withdrew his adherence, probably on the order of Governor-General Pierre Boisson of West Africa, who had clung to Vichy. A number of people in Gabon did not favor Free France at that time. They felt that Masson's agreement had been made without consultation with them; so they set up a group to maintain contact with Vichy, and the Gabonaise army sided with them. Masson notified de Larminat of his decision to change camps. There was immediate effervescence from Gaullists who were prevented from acting—some of them even had to lay down their arms. Meantime, a Vichy submarine, the *Poncelet,* a dispatch-vessel, the *Bougainville,* and a supply ship were sent over from Dakar, and forces were organized to defeat the "criminal operation" of de Gaulle. A state of siege was proclaimed. The ships were about to arrive in Mayumba—there was need for the Gaullists to hurry.

Captain Parant was sent in to conquer Gabon for Free France, and, miraculously, he took Mayumba with fifteen men. It was easy, for the guard surrendered; their commanders had gone out to dine with the chief administrator of the district! But Libreville, the chief city, was hard to win. Parant had to find enough troops to make up three detachments in order to surround it, for there were three ways into the country: two excessively bad car tracks through the forest, and a river full of rapids. None of them looked inviting.

Near Libreville, the forests are almost impenetrable. There are tsetse flies, mosquitoes and other insect pests; and when the rains come, little food can be found. Nothing can be quick there except the radio. On the way to the city, one of the expeditions took Lambaréné in the night, its defending officers having fled, leaving their riflemen behind. Their nerves had given way. Perhaps it was the terrible oppression of the great forest—where wet suns shine on land that is barely distinguishable from water. It was a harder land to live in than the Sahara Desert, more weakening and trying for the nervous system. Only exceptionally hardy individuals could survive there, where one was likely to encounter all sorts of dangers at any moment: gorgeous iridescent snakes full of venom, gorillas, hostile pygmies, panther men and their victims. Anything was easier to come by than a cooling drink![37] European men, exhausted and half crazed by a month of continuous rain, might grasp their guns and track each other around all day. They had been known to kill themselves for slight reasons.

Vichy tried hard to defend Gabon against the Free French. The ships sent by Dakar were faster than the British covering force for West Africa, and Parant had to hurry so no force could precede him to Libreville. The attack began, and in the course of it, the Vichy ships, the *Poncelet* and the *Bougainville*, were sunk. Two of their fine American planes were destroyed, the third serving as a good store of replacement pieces, or "cannibalization," as they called it then. The Free French had to wait through several weeks of skirmishes for reinforcements, but they managed to take the place in November. The Vichy commander said he would defend the "sacred soil of Gabon" to the death—to which Parant replied that he would rather die standing up than live on his knees. The poor commander could do neither for long, for he died in a plane accident three months later.[38]

The last contingent of Free Frenchmen arrived just after Libreville had surrendered, but they had not really been needed after the sinking of the Vichy ships. Five Free French planes were also shot down, and eleven men of a detachment of de Gaulle's foreign legion had been killed and others wounded.

But there were tragic notes on the Vichy side, too. Their submarine, the *Poncelet*, dived to try to attack a British cruiser, but she had to surface when detected. Her commander, Captain Saussine, was, says de Larminat, a "perfect gentleman," sending his crew to land, opening the hatches, going down into the bowels of the ship and sinking with her. De Larminat wrote later that "a Military Suicide is worth a salute, though, in the long run, one doesn't know just what the Good God thinks about it!"[39] Sadly enough, some twenty years later, de Larminat himself committed a military suicide, shooting himself when de Gaulle required him to take part in the judgment of some of his fellow officers after the Algerian War. It is only fair to say that de Larminat, then a general, had been going through a depression before this occurred.

There were other tragic notes to the Gabon affair. The former governor of Gabon, Masson, he who reneged on his decision to support de Gaulle, was found hanged by his own bedsheet from the curtain rod of his cabin in the boat carrying him back to France. He had said he would not survive if blood was shed for Gabon. De Larminat remarked that Masson could have found a more useful death if he had joined the fighting contingent of de Gaulle's forces.

And there was a final postscript to it all. René Labat, who had been in charge of the Vichyist groups set up in Gabon before the campaign, wrote bitterly that Gabon had to fall in order to regild the tarnished escutcheon of de Gaulle, and to rebuild Britain's pride after the disaster at Dakar in September. Labat was sent as a prisoner to Lambaréné. He has said he was insulted and struck by the Gaullists. No doubt he suffered terribly, as did the other prisoners, from the heat in their prison. Some of them escaped and reached a Spanish island. Did these men survive? No one knows.[40]

All in all, de Larminat wrote later, the expeditions with their expert timing, their success, had been a "happy game of chess."[41] And they were very heartening for the Gaullists. Pleven summed it up: "The first time after the Armistice that I saw hope on the faces of the French was when the papers announced that a part of the Empire had taken up arms again."[42] The Gaullist success kept the Tricolor waving. And the advantages that accrued were legion, for in addition to bringing to Free France an empire of 1.7 million square miles with a population of 6.327 million, possession of French Africa secured its important resources: cacao, coffee, palm oil, bananas, kernels, timber, tin, plumbago, wolfram, mica, iron, gold, cattle, butter, hides, cotton, nickel, lead, and chrome. The list was almost endless. It was an episode of the greatest importance, for it enabled de Gaulle to confirm his position, to remain, and to conquer.[43] It helped Free France to change from a mere movement to a government.

Who made this feat possible? De Larminat wrote that it was neither General de Gaulle nor the five men who had gathered at Lagos and planned the taking of those colonies. It was the French, Europeans, and Africans who woke to a sense of honor, courage, and fidelity that their belief in France had aroused in them. "The Africans," wrote de Larminat, "joined in with enthusiasm, they belong to a noble race which by nature reveres and practices the virtues of our virtuous chivalry,—courage, loyalty, charity. Through all the episodes of the colonization, they have always known the distinction between the greedy trader and the officer, the doctor, the functionary, the missionary who brought order, justice and progress in a disinterested manner." An African chief had said to him that he would give all to the French rather than to the Germans, and de Larminat noted, "There was the crux of the problem, it was humanity versus brutality that explained the revolt of Equatorial Africa against the Hitlerian menace."[44]

There were other witnesses to the keenness of the feelings of French Africans. Henri Laurentie was then in Chad as aide to Governor Eboué. He was sure, he wrote, that at first the Africans did not understand the depth of conscientious feeling in the French, but did realize it later. They knew that a heroic path had been chosen by those who refused to accept the Armistice, and they felt in tune with it. Africa, Laurentie thought, leaned naturally toward Gaullism.[45] They had proved that in their welcome to General de Gaulle when he visited Chad in October 1940.

Indeed, it was Equatorial Africa that affirmed the refusal of the defeat, and, of course, it was General de Gaulle who began the organization of that refusal. From this time on, de Gaulle would speak of "our Equatorial Africa," and he would say that the crime of the Armistice-makers was to have capitulated as if France had no Empire. After this, the Empire would assure the continuance of the war, and that war would be won. "Now," he said, "France, new France, great France, go forward!"[46] The reforging of the Sword of France had begun.

7

Storm Clouds Gather and Retreat

> The question was to know whether an intact Empire of
> sixty million people would contribute in any way to the
> struggle for the life or death of France.
>
> —de Gaulle

After the "Three Glorious Days" de Gaulle tried to lead France forward, but
the next step was on the dark side of the ledger. In early August, de Gaulle had
persuaded Churchill to help him set up an expedition to take Dakar, whose
port, nearest to America of any place in Africa, would be of great value to the
Allies. If they did not take it, Vichyists might. It would be important to them in
recapturing Gaullist Africa. There was also a cache of French government gold
near there, in the city of Kayes, that would be useful in the battle of the
Atlantic that was just getting under way. Dakar was, in fact, a capital de Gaulle
would have chosen before Brazzaville.

There were delays in the start of the plan, and reports of leakage about the
project by some of the Free French in England. When the combined British
and Gaullist forces neared Senegal, six Vichy warships had come in from the
Mediterranean and were "made fast with awnings spread" in the harbor of
Dakar.[1] They held men and munitions and were too powerful to be dealt with
by the smaller British-Free French contingents. And there were not as many
Gaullist sympathizers in Dakar as had been reported. Soustelle, in his narrative
of the battle, blames this on the British, but others have blamed it on de
Gaulle.[2]

De Gaulle had sent leaflets to be dropped on the city by planes, asking for
support for the Allied forces in their attack on the town "to keep it for France
and to save it from famine."[3] But alas for the Free French! These messages were
not heeded. It is to be remembered that up to this time Dakar was tightly
controlled by the Vichy authorities—much more tightly than Churchill or de
Gaulle recognized. They had not believed that emissaries under a white flag
would be attacked and arrested when they tried either to land in the city or to
take the airport. Some, at least, of their troops were fired on when an attempt
was made to put them ashore on the nearby beach of Rufisque. If one officer
was loyal to Free France and put dummy bullets in the place of live
ammunition, other groups had real fire power. And a Vichy cruiser lay off shore
in the fog close at hand. De Gaulle knew that if he stayed where he was, his
little army would be destroyed. So, aided by the fog, he made his escape.

Churchill, told by President Roosevelt to try the expedition but to be sure to win, insisted the British cruisers must stay and make another try. However, when one of them was badly damaged he dared not risk more losses, and the order for the withdrawal of the entire expedition came at the end of three days.

The results of this failure were dreadful for de Gaulle, especially since they worsened his relations with his Allies. The British thought that talk by Free French sailors or military men in an English restaurant had given the alarm, causing what was called the "resounding defeat." It was a "gigantic error," said the press, a "heartbreaking business," wrote an English writer. De Gaulle had gone there "expecting bouquets of flowers but he was met with shrapnel . . . he was showered with a stream of sarcasm." It was a setback to the entire movement, though among Africans it appears to have caused sympathy rather than criticism. Even Churchill's acceptance of the blame—for the Vichy cruisers reached Dakar through bad errors on the part of the British Admiralty—did not nullify the damage to the Free French movement.[4]

De Gaulle, leaving Dakar in his flagship, the *Commandant Duboc*, defeated instead of victorious as he had hoped, turned south to the Cameroons. He would go to the port of Douala and plan for the future after his first great defeat. He did not know how he would be received there, but as his boat approached the city of Douala on the Wouri River, he saw a great crowd standing on the wharf, the intense heat of the tropical sun beating down on them and lighting up their many-colored garments and kerchiefs. They were talking and gesticulating, and before the civilians stood a line of black riflemen in khaki shorts with red belts. A single figure was visible in front of this guard of honor, their commanding officer, Colonel Leclerc. There was a brief unforgettable ceremony, which one of the *compagnons* of Free France who was there that day has described:

> The first vessel that arrived opposite Colonel Leclerc stopped suddenly. On its bridges and its poop decks, up to the very top of its superstructures, soldiers in khaki with colonial helmets, armed with rifles and submachine guns, were standing motionless and rigid at attention, drawn up according to their rank. They stood elbow to elbow, like a human pyramid, its base on the decks, its summit rising high into the sky, impressively steady. For several seconds this extraordinary spectacle made its effect on the crowd. . . .
>
> Just at this moment, Leclerc presented his bared sword, shining with a thousand fires in the light of the midday sun. Then, on the ship, among these statue-like warriors, a man appeared, an immense man, all in white. He made his way among the ranks, crossed the gangplank and approached Leclerc. The latter, tracing a glittering parabola in the air with his sword, saluted the tall figure towering over him. The Chief drew the colonel to him with both arms, giving him a long embrace.
>
> A hurricane of cries rose from the crowd like a great storm, swelling measurelessly, drowning out the shrill sounds of the bugles and "The Marseillaise." . . .
>
> General de Gaulle straightened up and looked for a moment at these men and women, at these whites and blacks wildly shouting his name and the name of France, waving their arms frantically, throwing handkerchiefs, pieces of cloth, flowers, little flags into the air, their eyes nearly out of their sockets, their mouths twisted, their bodies shaking with convulsive trembling.

Then General de Gaulle bent toward them, holding his hands high above his head—and there was delirium. He collected himself, and calmly moved to the flag where he stood at attention. In his shining eyes there seemed to be a "fugitive sweetness . . . his emotion in discovering the new France . . . where he had never hoped to find . . . such a spontaneous outpouring of hope and love. Quietly he turned and slowly began to review the troops." For the Free French it was indeed a miraculous reward for all their misery, all their thwarted hopes. Now they felt that victory lay ahead.

Suddenly there was a cry, "You are at home and there is plenty of red wine for you here," and a great celebration began. If there was a rumor of rebellion later against the Free French, it was caused by a few malcontents. The people at Douala were heart and soul for de Gaulle.

De Gaulle had gone there quoting Adolph Hitler, "A people may be beaten, but when a people and its leaders accept defeat, they are forever lost. On the other hand, if a handful of men do not accept defeat, everything may be hoped for." Now, at least, Free France had a foothold on which de Gaulle could plant an administration and a military base. With the Free French still behind him, he could look forward to a future. After Dakar, he had suffered scorn; now he found loyalty and devotion. He must keep to the path he had laid out.[5]

So Charles de Gaulle went on again. He wrote General de Larminat at Lagos, then toured the country, profoundly touched by the sympathy he met. Africans are noble, he said, and his gesture woke a response in them. It was a cleansing for his spirit.[6]

However, de Gaulle was undoubtedly much embittered by the failure of the Dakar expedition. He is said never to have doubted that it was the reason why the Allies did not allow him to share the secrets of their landings in Africa—and there is every reason to suppose that he was correct in this supposition.[7] Yet somehow his resolution to continue on the path he had set for himself did not die, though he must often have doubted the possibility of success. When he first met de Larminat, then commissioner for Equatorial Africa, soon after the Dakar fiasco, he said to him, "Well, we go on?" and de Larminat answered, "No question about it, Equatorial Africa and the Cameroons are behind you to fight to the end."[8]

The Free French girded up their loins for the combat. From Brazzaville, over the "modest" ill-equipped radio, the instrument a writer once said was made of "a piece of string and a sardine tin,"[9] the General spoke again. He broadcast to the world a "declaration" and a "manifesto" which established a Council of the Empire and a constitutional basis and representation for Free France. The council would maintain fidelity to Free France, and the General promised to return at war's end the power he had taken upon himself. The Free French, he said, knew what hard duties the safety of the Empire would impose on the faithful native populations. In this way, the enemy, or Vichy, or even the Allies would not dare to set their hands on any part of what should by rights belong to France.[10]

During the last months of 1940, things were a little better for the Free

French. By then they had 35,000 troops, 1,000 aviators, 60 ships in their merchant marine, and 20 warships in their navy.[11] Did it matter if de Gaulle had been condemned to death and stricken from the rolls of the Legion of Honor? No, not for him—he was beyond the reach of his enemies—but there were, alas, some of his followers in France on whom such sentences were carried out. However, the movement itself had now become a useful military entity for the Allied cause. If de Gaulle had "begun at zero,"[12] he had come a long way. He would never forget African sympathy and all that it had done for him in his darkest days after Dakar. It was his first experience of real African feeling, and it touched him deeply. There is no doubt that it influenced him for the future.

Before he returned to London in late November, de Gaulle spoke again over the radio from Brazzaville, "speaking," he said, "to the shade of Marshal Foch." If the Free French tore the Empire piece by piece from the enemy to keep it for France, it would be in accordance with the orders of Foch, and it would give the *patrie* its share in the victory as the marshal would have wished; for the Empire now contained 60 million people guarded by 500,000 soldiers— all of which would be returned to the motherland at war's end.[13] Again, from London, at the end of November, he insisted on the need of bringing all the Empire and all of France back into the war, "to give France back her arms, her liberty and her grandeur." He remarked on the sound of the Empire starting up and the fact that if it all worked together, there would be a great French victory. The parts of the Empire that had not yet joined would find Free France beside them. In his *Memoirs* he said later:

> What was more, the national liberation, if accomplished one day thanks to the forces of the Empire, would establish links of solidarity between Metropolitan France and the Overseas Territories. If, on the contrary, the war were to end without the Empire having made any effort to save the Mother Country, that would be the end, without a doubt, of the work of France in Africa.

But if some part of Africa joined his effort, the enemy would know there was no easy conquest there—nor could the Allies step in.[14] Curiously enough, the Empire did make the effort, but in spite of that, and partly because of it, much of the work of France in Africa would end, for in their contacts with the Europeans the Africans would learn a great deal about the vulnerability of the nations of Western Europe.

During all this time there was no doubt in his mind, as far as we can learn, that the Empire was part and parcel of France—she owned everything in it. This gave de Gaulle confidence for the future. It gave him real trumps for the war and for the diplomatic battle that would follow it. Chad had taken a dangerous step, but how would the French and the Africans there live? However, they knew their duty, and he was thankful for their loyalty.[15]

Thus there was no sign of change in his fundamental ideas about colonization at that time, or if there was, it was not expressed. If he was even thinking of the African peoples' side of colonial life, he did not mention it. Perhaps the great welcome at Douala and the other encouraging experiences he had had in Africa laid the foundation for his future thought and for his real devotion to the African states of the future. As 1940 faded into 1941 he was still immersed in the current problems of the Free French movement. The proof of that is seen in the communiqué he gave out over the Cairo radio in April 1941:

I am a Free Frenchman
I believe in God and the future of my country
I do not belong to any man
I have one mission and only one, to pursue the struggle for the liberation of my country.
I declare solemnly that I am not bound to any political party, nor tied to any politician, whoever he may be, neither of the Center nor of the Right nor of the Left.
I have only one purpose: to deliver France.[16]

So the Empire was still there, but it was for France and for France alone.

8

The Road to Brazzaville

Can thy soul know change?
                    —Browning

These are my politics: to change what we can; to better
what we can; but still to bear in mind that man is but a
devil weakly fettered by some generous beliefs and
impositions; and for no word, however sounding, and no
cause however just and pious, to relax the stricture of
these bonds.

                                        —Lyautey

The early part of the year 1941 did not bring any great change in de Gaulle's colonial policy. His speeches followed the same pattern as before. They dealt with the strength of the Empire and the way the "men of the Armistice" had failed to understand the power France still possessed after the great defeat.[1] Then suddenly, in the late spring of 1941, "independence" was discussed by the Free French for the first time; but it did not relate to independence for Black Africa, only to freedom for the states of the Levant—Syria and the Lebanon— then under mandate to France. It is of interest here chiefly in order to see what de Gaulle thought of as "independence" at that time.

   Political reforms and possible freedom for the states of the Levant had been considered before the war by the Popular Front government. Treaties concerning their future status had even been drawn up, but they lay unratified on the scrapheaps of French governmental archives, for the passing governments of France had not been willing or able to implement them.[2]

   General de Gaulle had discussed the matter with Prime Minister Churchill for some time after he had arrived in England. De Gaulle believed that after the war was over, some new plan for these states was inevitable because of the rising movements in Arab countries and the general international situation, though he did not explain—at least not in writing—what areas and circumstances he had in mind. The mandate could not go on indefinitely, but he felt the continued presence of France in the Near East must be safeguarded.[3]

   The Levant had been under the control of Vichy since the Armistice, though at first High Commissioner Gabriel Puaux and General Eugène Mittelhauser, commander of the French army of the Levant, had considered resistance.[4] For the greater part of a year Churchill did not seem impressed with the necessity of ending that control. Then, in the spring of 1941, it was reported, apparently with truth, that German planes were using the airports of Syria in order to reach Iraq, where pro-German nationalists were launching a revolt. British dander rose at once, for this would touch British interests; the great aerial route to the Far East via Baghdad and Mogul might be cut off.

Neither France nor Britain wanted the Near East controlled by anyone but their own governments; each was jealous of the other. So after considerable argument, it was decided to send out a joint expedition to the Levant to take Syria and the Lebanon away from Vichy and from her connivance with the enemy, Germany. The Free French wanted to terminate the mandate when permitted to do so by the League of Nations that had assigned it to them in 1924. Thereafter, they expected to conclude treaties with the new nations they would form there; though while the war continued, France would keep the supreme power in the Near East, together with her obligations to the countries there. Both Syria and the Lebanon, de Gaulle thought, would be aware that they needed a close alliance with France. Still, only one regime could be established there, and that was independence.[5]

The dreadful little war in which Frenchmen fought Frenchmen began in early June, but it lasted only a few weeks. De Gaulle had said at the beginning of his movement, in establishing a legal basis for Free France in Great Britain, that he would never use his military forces to fight Frenchmen; but he had to come to it, if he was going to get the Germans and their influence out of the Near East and keep it for France. Fortunately for him, there was a little "saving" secret clause in the letter he wrote to Churchill about their agreement of August 7, 1940, in which he had said his armies would never attack the "real France." Churchill had interpreted that as meaning a France free to choose its own path and in no way under the power of Germany. Obviously, from de Gaulle's point of view, Vichy was not the "real France," for it was not free to act except in a very limited way, and in the unoccupied section of the country.[6] The quibble passed at the time.

The expedition to the Near East began on June 8, 1941, with much fanfare, trumpets blowing as the British-French troops crossed the border into Syria on three roads. Over them waved the Tricolor, the Union Jack, and the white flag of peace. Leaflets dropped from the sky where tricolor planes were flying. The tracts promised independence on the part of both the French and the British, though they did not specify the date on which it would be granted. There were several battles, most of which were bloody. The war ended in early July, after several cities had fallen to the Free French, and the British navy had forced the Vichy ships to leave the Near East so that supplies could not reach the cities. Though some troops had rebelled against the idea, the Free French had been forced to fight other Frenchmen. Later, it was not much comfort for those who had lost relatives there to know that the dead soldiers of both camps were buried side by side in a little cemetery in Damascus, or that on one tombstone marked merely "A Soldier of France," someone had scribbled "So was the man who killed him!"[7]

After some time, an armistice was signed. It caused a "word war" with the British, for General de Gaulle's representative on the commission that drew up the text allowed some clauses that his superior did not like, but after a time an agreement was reached. However, restrictions were put by de Gaulle on the promised independence for Syria and the Lebanon. Their constitution was not reestablished; and the elections, which to the people of the country were the real sign of full sovereignty, were put off. Then why had both Free French and British promised independence—even though undated—on their entry into Syria? It was certainly an evasion.

In addition, the delegate-general of France was empowered to designate the chiefs of state, keeping for himself the control of defense, foreign affairs, the "common interests" of Syria and the Lebanon: national education, food, customs, railroads, etc.[8] When, soon after the end of the war, two chief executives were named who were both conservative and francophile, the Syrian and Lebanese nationalists felt they had been deluded and scoffed at again. They said independence would be real only after elections had taken place.[9]

An interesting question remains. How did either England or France have a right to convey independence, real or symbolic, to two states still under mandate of the League of Nations—even though that League was at the time in a state of decadence? A mandate could not end unilaterally or even bilaterally without the approval of the League—or later of its successor, the United Nations. And what, after all, is independence? Can one have it halfway? De Gaulle's reservations in this case seem similar to those he proposed in setting up the *Communauté* in 1958, for the powers reserved for the French delegate to the Levant were similar. In neither case do they appear to have been satisfactory for those who were expected to live under them. Still, the idea of independence, however limited, had begun to appear in connection with the French mandated territories.

De Gaulle's answer to these problems about independence was that the arrangements in the Near East had been established only as a means of transition. It would be better to wait for elections until the return of normal conditions at the end of the war, when French responsibilities as mandatories and defenders would be lightened. But the English pressured the French representative, General Catroux, for speed, and the French had to agree, though they delayed the accomplishment of the elections.[10]

On August 28, de Gaulle said independence had been the aim fixed for the French in the mandate—it was the task of France and France alone to institute it.[11] But had it been so understood at the beginning of the mandate? Or was he following where *les contingences* led? After all, when the mandate was decided on in 1924, de Gaulle was still occupied with military colleges and exercises.

When the battles in the Near East had ended and resultant troubles with Britain were at least partially settled, de Gaulle turned his attention to other matters, and one of the first of these was the progress of Africa.

On October 23, 1941, he spoke at a luncheon of the Royal African Society in London. He began by reminding his hearers of the civilizing work his "noble and unfortunate country" had done in Africa, and of the great contribution the countries of Equatorial Africa had made, and the hope that the rest of the African states would join the common effort. Africa was already in the war, and that gigantic effort must influence its evolution. Permeability and coherence were coming in the African countries, together with improvement in communication and economic unity and the revision of tariffs and customs. Moral solidarity was developing there. It was really a revolution. If liberty could break through the tyrannical ambitions of the enemy, Africa might be revealed to herself, and the road to a great future might open before her. The France of tomorrow could be counted on for cooperation.[12]

Was this speech the beginning of a change in de Gaulle's ideas? Certainly, from this time on, Africa and her problems occupied more and more of his thought. This was a first statement lighting the future of what had been the Dark Continent.[13]

On June 18, 1942, the second anniversary of de Gaulle's first appeal, he spoke of the "magnificent faithfulness" of the Empire, a homage to the French civilizing genius, and of all the Empire had given so far, saying, however, that any attack on her sovereignty would be hateful to France. Having employed this sovereignty for the benefit of the liberated territories, he claimed it for all the others. France was using the resources of the Empire to the full and clinging to her imperial integrity. The war had shown the nations everywhere their material solidarity and also the necessity of a moral community of purpose. From one end of the world to the other; above the fields of battle as inside the factories; among peoples both oppressed and free; in the minds of the men in the streets and those of their leaders; standing out beyond all interests, prejudices, rivalries; the wave of aspirations toward an international ideal was rising and spreading.[14]

These ideas—the necessity of the complete restoration of the Empire, the harsh terms that liberty required of men, the complete sovereignty of France— were central to de Gaulle's thought at the time and were often expressed. France must remain indivisible; the Empire belonged to no one if not to France; there could be only a single battle for a single country—France. For today, as always, ideas lead the world. Perhaps that summed up everything from the General's point of view. Certainly it indicated better possibilities for all humanity, for it is both the mind and heart that carry off victories.[15]

Reasons for reform, national and international, were felt even before the war.[16] One hundred thousand Africans fought in the Free French armies; at one time, they formed nearly half of them. Their aid in aerial traffic, technical progress, radio, etc., was important.[17] Then there were those troublesome Allies—Great Britain and the United States. Great Britain had already made two landings on Madagascar in 1942, though de Gaulle had managed to reassert control over the Great Island that France had thought for a long time was her own.[18] Would the English try to return there?

In the United States, anticolonial feeling was growing with a return to Wilsonian ideas under Franklin Roosevelt. De Gaulle was always nervous about his Allies and their projects. After World War I, only the defeated powers had lost their colonies, but "the Second World War called the very existence of colonialism into question."[19] The Atlantic Charter of 1941 had contained a phrase concerning "the right of all peoples to choose the form of government under which they live," and there must be restoration of sovereign rights to those deprived of them. Another phrase allowed all states access to raw materials and to whatever trade restrictions might be necessary for their economic prosperity. Of course, Churchill had said this applied only to Europe, but Roosevelt had contradicted that, saying that it applied to the whole world. To get the peoples of the world to help, it was necessary to promise them some advantage at the time of the common victory, and some reforms as well, but independence need not be immediate.[20]

There was also the Communist party to consider. In general, it was favorable to the emancipation of colonies, though the French Communists would restrict that privilege to states that were ready for self-government, those that had real economic independence.[21] The Communists were already setting up study groups in Africa to create national consciousness there. By 1943 such associations had begun in Dakar, Conakry, Abidjan, Bamako, and Bobo-Dioulasso. The Empire would have to clear itself of charges of "imperialist exploitation" if it wished to survive.[22] However, neither the Communists nor the anticolonialists appear to have thought of independence as immediate for colonial lands. As for the Christian churches, while they did not try to destroy colonial power directly, they nevertheless aided the forces of emancipation.[23]

Toward the end of 1941, there was another source of recognition of the need for reform. Félix Eboué had been made governor-general of Equatorial Africa by General de Gaulle in November 1940,[24] and within the next year, he issued a call to the leaders of the colonies under his charge to meet as a commission in November 1941 to consider policy toward the Africans. There were about fifty members in the group: the governors and representatives of the spiritual and economic values of French Equatorial Africa. After three days of hard work, they produced a text to be sent out to the administrators of all Equatorial Africa, giving the principles of the policies they thought should be adopted.[25] This was necessary, for one consequence of the war was that the Africans began to see the value of certain local means that had been used. They wanted more facilities and were making claims for economic as well as political and social reforms. They had made great sacrifices for the war, and the European leaders knew they had to listen.[26] All those in charge of Equatorial Africa, after it had rallied to de Gaulle, realized they must produce some evidence of the changes that would take place at war's end, and that these alterations must come as soon as possible.

At the meeting of the commission, Eboué made the statement that if France wished to work in depth with the Africans, she must take more account of their needs, the degrees of their evolution, the form of their civilization, and the physical and moral security she had agreed to bring them to better their lot. She must collaborate in all research and in the application of measures to that end. This policy, Eboué said, would be in effect a revolution, a renunciation of the errors and prejudices of the past. It would also be a starting point and would help the countries of Africa to serve France, as well as to be served by her.[27]

Certain conditions must be met before the new reforms could be put into effect. There must be an advance in prosperity, and the countries must be stable and peaceful. All must collaborate in the policy to make it the will of all. Traditions must be kept, or there would be no foundation for government. Chiefs must be designated in the old way, and sovereignty and authority, however stable, must not attempt to make a newer sovereignty in its own image—that of France. In this way, the African system would be valuable, and the inhabitants of the continent would be led toward the management of their own affairs.

Eboué went on to say that the colonies were menaced, as were granaries when they were being emptied. The great commercial companies, using the concessions made to them, were exploiting the colonies by awkward prose-lytism, by putting educational advance to sleep, by the forgetfulness and scorn shown to the political and social African *cadres*, the leaders. If the mass was disintegrating, without a new policy the evil could not be stemmed. To copy France would mean certain defeat. The Equatorial Federation must be itself to regain a profound sense of life and a desire to perpetuate it.[28]

To implement these ideas, Eboué said the Africans must be given a program of collective work, using the various *Societés de Prévoyance* (Provident Societies), the forward-looking organizations set up to prevent disaster, and other sport, civic, and health groups. Christianity could help, but the change could not be hurried. Education must be developed and the gaps filled. The African must not be uprooted or dealt with impatiently or without seriousness. Finally, he quoted Marshal Louis-Hubert Lyautey, the former colonizer of Morocco, who had said of a resident of Annam in Indochina, where he had served with Joseph Simon Gallieni: "He is very intelligent, but he will never do anything, because he lacks that little parcel of love without which no great human work is done."[29] So Eboué "put the essential colonial problem on social grounds, while the geographical manuals and the minutes of administrative councils put it solely on the material ground," said Michel Devèze, a thoughtful writer on colonialism.[30]

It is hard for us today to comprehend how revolutionary these ideas were in 1941.[31] According to Eboué, the African was a human personality who would one day govern himself. He was not a mere child with an adult frame, capable of hard work and of enduring hard conditions while he lived. These ideas were nearly unbelievable to many of the men who heard the governor-general speak. If they saw beneath the surface of the words, it meant that the policy of assimilation was dying, if not already dead. Only advanced thinkers had seen that up to this time, even though officially the policy was said to be association. However, it did not mean that France was to fade out of the picture—far from it! The reference to serving France shows that. To us today, it may seem that was what they had been doing—with little else—for a long time. Certainly, French influence would continue to be as strong as ever, partly because Eboué (and others, too) believed that France, better than any other country, knew how to apply Lyautey's "little parcel of love."[32]

The next attempt Eboué made to improve the African's lot was to ask General de Gaulle (now referred to as Chief of Fighting France, President of the National Committee [of London]), to approve certain decrees worked out in accordance with the ideas he had set forth. Eboué knew already that de Gaulle agreed with his chief ideas. The decrees concerned a code for forced labor, still actively used until after the war; a statute setting up rules to be adhered to in order to create a superior class of Africans, *notables évolués*; regulations to establish African "communes," or towns, as a beginning of municipal life for the African masses; an extension of native jurisdiction over criminal as well as civil cases in newly constituted courts; and finally, an African housing bureau to be created and the preeminence of the hereditary chiefs to be reinforced. All this was to lead to an Afro-European civilization in which Eboué believed very fervently. De Gaulle approved all Eboué's recommendations. Still, it is only fair to say that by some Africans Eboué was thought to be too close to the colonials and to be repressive in certain directions.[33]

Félix Eboué was undoubtedly one of the outstanding men of the last colonial period before decolonization. His effect was felt long before he exerted his influence on the Conference of Brazzaville, only a few months before his death. He was known not only for his spiritual qualities but for fiscal reform and advances in education, agriculture, and industry.[34] He left behind him a memory of a strong figure of a man, with a fine bearing, courteous, affable, expressing himself in French with elegance, a man who was thoughtful and who, in spite of severe deafness, gave every person with whom he spoke the impression of being heard and understood. He was an excellent administrator, surrounded by men who were devoted to him; and to de Gaulle he was a great aid and support.[35]

It is hard now to evaluate Eboué's relationship with General de Gaulle. Most people who have referred to it in the hearing of this author have felt that the ideas of the two men coincided, and that neither one influenced the other. They merely found out that they agreed. A few Gaullist opponents have felt that the ideas all came from Eboué, but no one really knows. What is certain is that at various times between 1940 and 1944 General de Gaulle and Governor-General Eboué had private interviews with no third person present, so there is no record of what passed between them. Gaston Palewski, a close associate of de Gaulle, later president of the Constitutional Council, notes in C.-R. Ageron's essay that Eboué's conversations with de Gaulle were psychologically very important. Nor can we overlook the close presence and influence of Henri Laurentie, though no one knows just what part of Eboué's famous circular may have been his.[36] Perhaps the best idea of what they might have said comes in a passage in de Gaulle's *Memoirs*, in which he praised the loyalty of the Africans to Free France. He said that it left nothing to be desired, noting that "at the same time a thrill of hope and liberation made these Africans tremble." The drama taking place in the world, the efforts of the war, the work of the Gaullists, were changing conditions and had already "led thousands of black men in cabins and forests, in the deserts and along the great rivers of their continent, men hitherto oppressed by ages of servitude, to raise their heads and question their destiny." Eboué, "that convinced humanist," said de Gaulle, was using his efforts to control this "inspired movement," to raise the people and to turn French authority to account. "He did not shrink at all before the material, moral and political transformation that was soon to penetrate the 'impenetrable' continent, but this revolution must bear the stamp of Africa herself, and the changes made in the life, customs and laws of her people, would be so constituted as to respect traditional institutions and forms." De Gaulle knew that Eboué felt that this was necessary for Africa's progress and for the glory of France as well. His view and Eboué's corresponded, he said, "and in this domain, as in others, the unity of Fighting France seemed solidly cemented." Still, it can be noted that General de Gaulle was speaking in terms of development, while Eboué's ideas were, probably in his own mind and certainly in those of many others, revolutionary.[37]

Thus de Gaulle's agreement to new advances in policy toward the Africans and his abandonment of the old belief that they must be made into Frenchmen indicate clearly that the interests of the colonized were taking a greater place in the General's mind. This may well have been a critical period in his thought on colonialism, when he foresaw possible developments in policy to the Africans but still wished to insist on the necessity of French sovereignty. France must maintain the fullness of her power within her Empire, but she must also grant reforms that would make that possible. He saw the approach of a different world but admitted no questioning as to its relationship to France. The war was still going on, and things could not be altered too quickly.

De Gaulle's friends and his opponents differ vastly as to the liberalism of his colonial ideas. Some feel that essentially he was a conservative and a colonialist, accepting change only when he must.[38] Others believe that he was ready for reform when it would be possible to make changes.[39] As we know, he was no *a priori* politician, basing all on prearranged rules. Naturally enough, he has often been pilloried by those who have resented his changes of position according to circumstances, especially by those who resented his changes with regard to Algeria. Yet, if opinions always remained the same in spite of change in the outside world, would not that limit the possibilities of advancement in the world at large? To sum up de Gaulle's attitude at this time, he was certainly accepting the possibility of changes in the overseas lands, though he believed that they must be carried out within the framework of the French Empire.

Even during most of the year 1943, General de Gaulle's references to the

Empire remained close to that pattern. The resources of the Empire, those "trump cards for the Metropole," now gathered almost entirely under de Gaulle's banner, represented unity in diversity. He summed it up in the *Memoirs:*

> But the same profound reasons that required great and immediate reforms in metropolitan France also demanded the transformation of the status of the overseas territories and the rights of their inhabitants. I was as convinced of this as anyone while I was fighting the war with the cooperation of the Empire's men and resources. How could I doubt, moreover, that on the morrow of the conflict that now enflamed the world, the passion for freedom would rise and swell universally? What was happening in Asia, in Africa, in Australia, would have its repercussions everywhere.

Then, in a new advance, after speaking of the events so prejudicial to the prestige of France, he said that the Africans had nevertheless been aware of the example of Fighting France, that they recognized that French recovery was beginning on their soil. It was "the point where everything must begin again, but on the formal condition of not maintaining these states and these territories at their former level." He would see to it that his government took the initiative in this direction without delay.[40]

So, willingly or unwillingly, he planned two further steps for his *France Combattante* in order to act on what he had said. The first of these was a declaration on Indochina made on December 8, 1943, in which he promised greater liberty to the Indochinese peoples in line with their own traditions. They were to have free access to the employment and functions of the state. A new economic statute would assure prosperity for the whole region of Indochina and its neighboring states, with France always pursuing her mission in close association with them.[41]

The second step de Gaulle made a few days later, in a speech at Constantine in Algeria on December 12, 1943. He began by saying that if the nation did not draw a lesson from its trials, in a world where everything was driving toward change, if France tried to remain fixed in her past, it would be useless to speak of recovery. Each nation must install a more just balance between its children—those who have done credit to France—in fraternity of races, the equality of opportunity, the maintenance of order. Reforms were now approved granting a large number of Muslims of certain categories the right to retain their personal status and still be part of the first electoral college represented in the French Parliament. The rest of the Muslims, voting in the second college (by far the greater majority) would have an equal proportion of representatives in the assemblies, "including the French Parliament." Many administrative posts would now be opened to them, and the conditions of life would be improved. The new France had taken note of her duties in Algeria.[42]

These proposed reforms in Indochina and Algeria were the first evidence of a major change in de Gaulle's attitudes. They showed a considerable alteration from the old colonial procedures and, in effect, they breached the wall of colonialism, giving greater freedom and more cooperation by the French government to the dominated peoples, no doubt increasing their already burgeoning hopes of greater liberty. The Muslims listening to his speech at Constantine, according to de Gaulle, wept with joy.[43]

Of course, there had been previous promises of reforms, but they had not been fulfilled.[44] The Algerians must have wondered whether the changes would be put through this time. The words "including the French Parliament" do not appear in the original speech but appear in the account of it in the *Mémoires*.[45] Was the intention different? There is no explanation of this. But it is to be remembered that in 1943 most people felt that the world would be different after the war. There would be a new deal.

How far did these ideas come from de Gaulle himself, and how far from others? The new Consultative Provisional Assembly of the Free French began its meetings in Algiers on November 3, 1943, a month before these declarations. The government of Free France, under which they served, was now called "The Committee of National Liberation." Not until June 1944 was the committee spoken of as "the provisional government of France." In the first meetings at Algiers, not a great deal was said that could be considered new in the doctrine of colonialism, except that more importance was given to the idea of assisting in the evolution of the masses. One man even remarked that the old idea that the colonies were made for the metropole was false. Others said that there must be a democratic spirit of service in the Empire. The France "which had educated Europe" could make a contribution of this sort, and the Empire would guarantee it with the blood of her children, but no bit of the Empire's lands would be given up! The Assembly could not quite admit that possiblity!

Thus it was the same old Assembly in the way it behaved; but now that it was sitting in one of the larger cities of the Empire, it had to have that Empire a little more in mind. Apparently, thus far at least, de Gaulle and Eboué had furnished the new ideas and the progress, except that on November 24, Pierre-Olivier Lapie, a distinguished Gaullist, had spoken in the Assembly of the "federal character" of France. The word *federal* would appear often in the discussions of the next few years.

On October 13, Commissioner of the Colonies Pleven announced over the radio the plans for the Conference of Brazzaville, and in November, he sent a program for it to the governors of the various colonies, so that they could prepare statements to be made during the sittings. It would be held at the end of January 1944.[46]

There was another meeting of the Assembly on January 14, 1944, at which the word *federation* was spoken again. The speaker, M. Bourguin, a deputy, felt that such an idea could not be implemented at the present time. There were no elections set up—no organism with real power, like the former High Council of the Colonies—so any organism would be born dead, since it would not be able to write laws or make decisions. No one could build a roof before there was a house to cover. Democratic freedom must come first, and that could not come until after the colonies had given up their very primitive economy and passed through agricultural to industrial economy.[47]

Another deputy took issue with this, conceiving the French role as one of protection and association with colonial peoples: living with other civilizations by loving them, like the missionary Charles de Foucauld.[48] He did not mention that Foucauld did not succeed too well in living with another tribal civilization, since a member of another tribe of the same civilization killed him!

René Pleven spoke of the fidelity of the colonies and then referred the question of federalism to the forthcoming Conference of Brazzaville.[49] Others urged no more exploitation, no racial differences; a real revolution was necessary. Political rights for the Africans were important, and with no change of status, just as de Gaulle had made possible for the Muslims in Algiers.

The debate, however, was important. By implication, it admitted French faults, upholding France as a humanitarian nation with the progress of the Africans at heart. All this was a signpost for the men who would go to Brazzaville at the end of the month. The word *Empire* was little used. There would be a Commission for Overseas France instead of a Commission for the Colonies. If the words Overseas France had come into use in the interwar period, it was now the only way in which the former colonies were referred to.[50] On the nineteenth, de Gaulle spoke, using, however, the term *Empire* and insisting on its value as a refuge, a base for departure. He was going to Africa, he said, "to confirm the new policy that was leading to the French Union."[51] Clearly, there would be something new at Brazzaville. They were all ready for it!

Such was the attitude of the Free French in January 1944, but, of course, looking back at the world situation just before that time, it is easy to see why steps to benefit the native populations of Africa seemed imperative to the Gaullists. First of all, the Free French were now in relatively secure possession of the greater part of the French Empire. This included much of North Africa, all of West and Equatorial Africa, and those Pacific and Atlantic islands that had belonged to them before the war.

In summary, the events that triggered the West African colonies' change of allegiance from Vichy to de Gaulle were the American landings in North Africa in November 1942 and the subsequent takeover by the Germans of the "unoccupied" part of France; the destruction of the French navy by the navy itself as the Germans approached the great naval base of Toulon; and the flight of General Pétain and his aides to Sigmarigen in Germany.[52]

After Pétain left France, the only man who could take authority was Admiral François-Xavier-Louis-Jean Darlan, commander-in-chief of the Land and Sea Armies, with whom the American general Mark Clark had negotiated the "Darlan Deal" in early December 1942. After Darlan was assassinated on December 24, 1942, the Vichy power was almost gone. The West African colonies, one by one, came under Free French domination.[53]

De Gaulle's Consultative Assembly now sat in Algiers. True, it was nominated and not elected, for France had been entirely occupied by the Germans since the Allied landings in North Africa at the end of 1942. Still, the new government represented France more completely than the Gaullist

"National Committee" had previously done. Furthermore, Free France was now back in the war in the eyes of the world, thanks to two expeditions to Koufra and the Fezzan that Colonel Leclerc led, in 1941, and also to General Marie-Pierre Koenig's brilliant defense of Bir Hakeim in 1942. Since the North African invasion of 1942, the Allies now held a firm foothold from which to attack the German forces in France itself, in Africa, and in the Mediterranean. The war in the Pacific was going well. The battles of the Coral Sea, of Midway, and of Guadacanal in 1942 and of the Bismarck Sea in 1943 had shown beyond a doubt that the turning point in the war against Japan had been reached. The German forces in Europe and Africa were weakening, and Italy had been forced out of the war. In short, the Axis had passed its zenith, though Germany was far from defeat as yet. However, the strength of the Allies was still growing.[54]

Still, the Allies did not recognize de Gaulle's followers as the new government of France. Franklin Roosevelt's hostility to de Gaulle had not diminished, and Winston Churchill was always eager to give in to the American president at the expense of the Free French. So the battle for control of postwar France was far from won. All the United States would admit, in the autumn of 1943, was that "General de Gaulle administered those overseas territories that recognized his authority," while Great Britain stated that de Gaulle "was functioning within specific limitations during the war. His group was not a government of France or of the French Empire."[55] And the Allies tried to install their own candidate, General Henri Giraud, at the head of the French army in Africa and of French public affairs as well. This venture never succeeded. Giraud, as even the Allies soon began to see, was a fine general, but he lacked political experience and acumen, and de Gaulle was able to cause him to fade out of the picture before the end of 1943.

All in all, it was a time to think ahead, and, clearly, it was of prime importance to the Gaullists to tie the overseas lands as closely as possible to the France that was to come. A conference of the kind that was envisaged at Brazzaville could give valuable assistance. And the final end of independence for the colonies would sometime have to be considered. De Gaulle had already said in a speech in Beirut on August 28, 1942:

> The liberty of a nation like that of a man, is a precious but costly possession, which is obtained and kept only by a great and continual expenditure of courage and wisdom.[56]

9

Nationalism in Africa—A Chain Reaction

> Martin Delany, the first Negro commissioned in the
> United States (by Lincoln), said at Philadelphia, in
> 1852, "The claims of no people are respected by any
> nation until they are presented in a national capacity."

George Orwell says that nationalism is "the habit of identifying oneself with a single nation or other unit, placing it beyond good or evil, and recognizing no other duty than that of advancing its interests."[1] These lines, though possibly somewhat exaggerated in maintaining that "no other duty" than the national one is recognized, still show more clearly than most other definitions of nationalism its importance among those personal emotions that have often caused wars and revolutions. Others have thought of it differently. For example, Robert Rotberg has said that nationalism has not meant only devotion to one's country, for the borders of the states—arbitrarily arranged by the conquerors—did not always correspond to the tribal limits. William J. Foltz has remarked that this question of frontiers was colonialism's most enduring legacy to Africa, for it made a policy based on independence bound to arise. It was more important to be independent than to attempt to achieve an international unity. Thus nationalism was a common protest against white or any other alien rule, and consequently all the African peoples have ascribed their ills to the oppression of colonial regimes. There is no doubt whatsoever that the roots of nationalism can easily be found in the "fertile soil of European conquests." "It is a truism that without colonialism there would have been no movements of protest." Sir Arthur Cohen agreed with this belief, saying that nationalism in West Africa owes its origin to the impact of the West. Still, it was Rotberg who summed up the whole question by saying, "The triumph of African nationalism is but the final coordination and intensification of all the tangled strands of an earlier, usually unrecognized disaffection."[2] Immanuel Wallerstein has added that "nationalism had to come in a sense," for "in the drive toward equality, nationalism provided the least difficult solution." Integration was really impossible.[3] James S. Coleman supported this by saying, "nationalism is the terminal point of colonial protest."[4] He also wrote that

> African nationalism is more than the activities of a few disgruntled journalists and frustrated intellectuals . . . it is the inevitable product of the impact of Western imperialism and modernity upon African societies; it is also the assertion by the Africans of their desire to shape their own destiny. Imperial systems are disintegrat-

ing, new nations are emerging, and new forms of political organization transcending the national states, are under experiment. These political aspects of African nationalism, however, are but the surface symptoms of a great ferment about which we know very little.[5]

Coleman analyzes nationalism further, pointing out the varying threads of the nationalistic movements: the spontaneous resistance, the nativistic, mahdistic, or messianic mass movements, all of them traditionalistic in origin. He mentions also the syncretistic groups that arose, including those of religious fervor, kinship, or tribal associations. Finally, he speaks of the modernistic movements: those of economic interest groups, those led by Western-educated élites to create modern states and achieve social and political equality, sometimes even transterritorial in their efforts to generate national unity and local autonomy. Still, he repeats that each one of them arose in response to alien rule.

If these movements were at first the product of tiny educated minorities, later they were popularized and energized until they became a nationalist crusade to emancipate the black race from the servile colonial mentality. They channeled all grievances into the drive to make nationalism the object of the people and to politicize or nationalize all groups and all thought.

Then Coleman points out the literary and cultural revival that has accompanied nationalism. It has touched the world outside, and, of recent years, it has pointed up the meaning of African revolt. Nationalism is the consciousness of belonging to a nation, existent or in the realm of aspiration.[6]

The world in general has recognized nationalism by now and has admitted its necessity, even its virtue; yet sometimes many of us in America are afraid of it, for its meaning has been so adverse to the achievements of the white past. Still, the Third World has become so important in the last three decades that we understand better what the opposition to the white race has done.

After this affirmation of all that nationalism has been, it is curious that Georges Hardy, once a respected writer on Africa, could state in 1953 that there was no nationalism in French West Africa, only "scattered instances of social unrest due to the propaganda of the RDA [The *Rassemblement Démocratique Africain*], which was a communist-inspired party," at least at that time.[7]

Still, apart from Hardy, the other specialists on the subject cause us to feel that nationalism was a many-textured thing, born in times of war, growing up in protest, and approaching maturity as independence arrived.

Of course, the movements of nationalism have had a history. Paul Alduy, a former councillor of the French Union, wrote in 1950 that events in the Balkans in the last century were the first episodes in a new phase of the history of the planet, for they contained the awakening and affirmation of nationalities all over the world. They increased slowly until the next aspect—their regroupment in larger combinations—should arrive. Equality, autonomy, and independence are only the successive waves of a deeper surge from the depths.

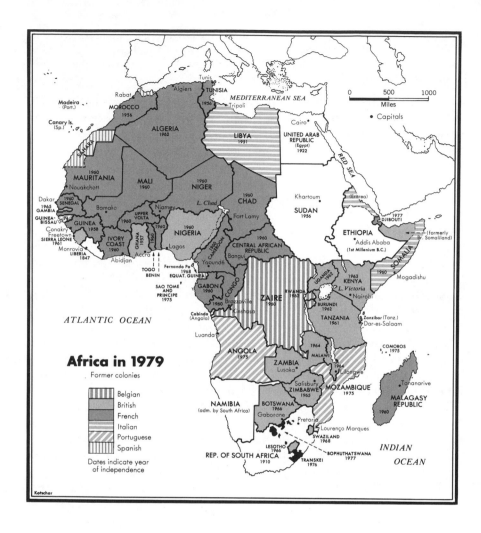

Africa in 1979

Former colonies

- Belgian
- British
- French
- Italian
- Portuguese
- Spanish

Dates indicate year
of independence

Kotschar

Map labels

MEDITERRANEAN SEA

Tunis
Rabat
Algiers
TUNISIA
1956
Tripoli

Madeira
(Port.)
MOROCCO
1956

Canary Is.
(Sp.)

ALGERIA
1962

LIBYA
1951

Cairo

UNITED ARAB
REPUBLIC
(Egypt)
1922

0   500   1000
Miles

• Capitals

RED SEA

1960
MAURITANIA
Nouakchott

MALI
1960

1960
NIGER

1960
CHAD

L. Chad

Fort Lamy

Khartoum

SUDAN
1956

(Eritrea)

1977
DJIBOUTI

Dakar
1960
SENEGAL
1965
GAMBIA
GUINEA-
BISSAU 74
Bamako

Niamey

Conakry
GUINEA 1958
Freetown
SIERRA LEONE
1961
Monrovia
LIBERIA
1847
Abidjan

UPPER
VOLTA
1960

1960
GHANA 1957

IVORY
COAST
1960

Accra

NIGERIA
1960

Lagos

1960
CAMEROON

CENTRAL AFRICAN
REPUBLIC
1960

Bangui

Yaoundé

ETHIOPIA
Addis Ababa
(1st Millenium B.C.)

(formerly
Br. Somaliland)

SOMALIA

1960
Mogadishu

TOGO
BENIN
Fernando Po
1968
EQUAT. GUINEA

SAO TOME
AND
PRINCIPE
1975

GABON
1960

CONGO
1960

Brazzaville

Cabinda
(Angola)

Kinshasa

ZAIRE
1960

RWANDA
1962

BURUNDI
1962

UGANDA
1962

1963
KENYA
Nairobi

L. Victoria

TANZANIA
1961

Zanzibar (Tanz.)
Dar-es-Salaam

ATLANTIC OCEAN

Luanda

ANGOLA
1975

1964

ZAMBIA
Lusaka

MALAWI
1964

Lilongwe

MOZAMBIQUE
1975

COMOROS
1975

Tananarive

MALAGASY
REPUBLIC
1960

Salisbury
ZIMBABWE
1965

NAMIBIA
(adm. by South Africa)

BOTSWANA
1966
Gaborone

Pretoria

Lourenço Marques

SWAZILAND
1968

BOPHUTHATSWANA
1977

LESOTHO
1966

REP. OF SOUTH AFRICA
1910

TRANSKEI
1976

INDIAN
OCEAN

Nationalism, he added, poses the problem of the survival of empires.[8]

Thus, looking back at the nineteenth century, we can easily see why the larger nations of Europe became nervous about any signs of nationalism anywhere. The Balkan principalities had so many wars that any threat there was enough to raise the blood pressure of the calmest European diplomat. Beginning with Serbia in 1804, and from then on to the Great War of 1914, each eastern Mediterranean state had from two to four wars or insurrections, in addition to major expeditions against the "Terrible Turk." The sultan of the Ottoman Empire had his troubles, too, for in that period he had three wars with Russia as well as the Crimean War. The Young Turks movement, in 1908, was too late to arrest the decomposition of that empire. The nationalist movement of Mustapha Kemal never really got under way, in spite of unrest and agitation in Turkey.[9] Two more important conflicts—the Balkan Wars— took place in 1912 and 1913, just before the initial grand march of the Kaiser's devastating army through "poor little Belgium" in August 1914. After that, empires were on the down grade. Germany threw off her imperial regime, the Austrian Empire was broken up and the "Sick Man of Europe" could no longer call his lands an empire.[10] Few of the people of the nineteenth century saw, as Paul Alduy realized later, that behind the wars, coups, pressures, protests, conferences, and treaties lay the beginnings of national consciousness in many of the smaller states of the world. That consciousness increased until it spelled the disintegration of the larger groups that we have come to call empires. Alduy was writing only a decade before the second largest empire, that of France, disintegrated; the British Empire had even preceded the French in its dissolution.

The signs of trouble for the colonizers developed slowly, becoming more menacing as the numbers of dissidents became larger. Such is the way with opposition movements. Geneviève Anthonioz-de Gaulle, a niece of General de Gaulle, who spent two years in the German concentration camp at Ravensbrück, once remarked to the author that when there were only one or two women in the camp who were interested in improving the lot of those incarcerated there, little could be done to help them. When additional well-disposed women entered the camp, it was possible for all of them together to have some influence on their captors.[11] So it has been with the nationalists in many countries, whose aims were sometimes ill-defined or not admitted at all. But as their numbers grew, their influence spread and their purpose became clear, even in surrounding countries, in the manner of a chain reaction. So it was with the antecedents of the final decolonizations.

Some of the events that should have acted as a warning to all the colonizing nations in this century began in 1904 with the defeat of Russia by the small islands of Japan. Young Asians saw the possibility of attacking great powers with some hope of success. Tokyo became a mecca for the youth of Asia, especially those of Indochina. The French, who dominated the states of Indochina, were at first unaware of this new movement toward freedom.[12] Then came the Russian revolution of 1905. Although it was abortive, all Europe knew about it,[13] and when it was followed by revolutions in China, India, and Indonesia some of the citizens of the countries involved learned, when in Europe, the hidden reasons for Western power, its organization, and its techniques. Feeling rose, too, in Islamic lands, whose people had not found the freedom they wanted in the peace and began to wish for a unity of their own. South Asia became solid against the Europeans, as the Europeans had been against them. So England had to give independence, in 1947, to her Far Eastern colonies—India, Pakistan, Burma, Ceylon, and Malaysia—all except Singapore.[14]

Nationalism was not as far advanced in Africa as in Asia or the East by the end of the Great War. However, Henri Brunschwig, a much respected French specialist on Africa, believes that Africa was in full evolution and had already begun "to move" by the time of the partition in the last decades of the nineteenth century. The European virus had already affected that continent. According to Brunschwig, Europe did not change the direction of the peoples of Africa; it only increased the speed of their development. He explains this by the new needs of modern trade, the people having been enriched by oil of palm, or armed with new guns, or centered around the many missions they had joined. Michael Crowder speaks, on the other hand, of "the immense upheaval of African society brought about by the partition and the African response to it." Much of this response lay in military resistance to European domination. Crowder observes that European diplomats and historians have paid little attention to that reaction, looking at it merely as "resistance to the enemy." They did not ask why it took a quarter century to subdue many parts of Africa, even though the Ivory Coast, Mali, Eastern and Northern Nigeria, and Mauritania were not "pacified" until the second decade of our century. Nevertheless, the battles fought by African tribes to retain their own lands were not thought to have been motivated by nationalistic instincts. Still, the Europeans did note that some of the African leaders were brilliant fighters, though without the Maxim gun they could not succeed in battle.[15]

Another stage of nationalism began in 1900, when the first African Conference opened in London under the leadership of a non-African barrister from Trinidad, H. Sylvester Williams. The idea of Pan-Africanism was mentioned there for the first time, but independence was not considered, though at the end of the conference there was a protest against the treatment of Africans in South Africa. That conference had little effect.[16]

After World War I, however, though revolts were localized and discontent repressed, the Africans had become a little more aware of Europe's waning power, and they were somewhat more vocal. Many peoples all around the globe had heard of Woodrow Wilson's policy of self-determination.

Still, the French were very confident about their Empire. Governor-General Sarraut, speaking at the Pagoda of Confucius in Hanoi in 1919, very soon after World War I, was able to insist that the question of French sovereignty could not be touched upon or dealt with, and that no member of the governing power must allow discussion of it in the colony, for "it is the law of progress."[17] Was

Sarraut afraid that it was being discussed too much, that he felt he must sound such a warning? Perhaps, knowing the colonies well, he sensed the latent discontent in them more than others would have done.

However, some time before 1922, the French announced a more liberal official policy on the colonies:

> Without attempting to assimilate the colonies to each other nor to the mother country . . . let us consider each colony as a native city which must evolve under our tutelage, and with our aid, proceed toward entire self-government, the bond which unites it to the mother country to be untied when the proper moment has come. . . . For our part we would wish in setting them free to remain associated with our former subjects. There are really many Englands, there will be only one France, a greater France.[18]

This official declaration was probably a public explanation of Albert Sarraut's philosophy, expressed in the same year of 1922, that one day the colonies would no longer be tied to the mother country, though neither Sarraut nor the government spokesman gave a possible date for the disengagement. Wallerstein has remarked that there was at least one Frenchman who thought in this way, and Sarraut's philosophy was essentially the one followed by the French in the interwar years.[19] Yet it did not seem to liberalize government actions toward the Asians or the Africans—at least not at that time.

One supposes, too, that the French declaration was a sort of answer to Woodrow Wilson's Fourteen Points. Certainly, the American president's freely expressed ideas about self-determination made Europeans clamp down and demonstrate their refusal to bend to the Wilsonian wind. But a new bone of contention soon arose to plague relations between the countries east and west of the Atlantic.

In 1919, W. E. Burghardt DuBois, an American black with some Dutch and French ancestry, founder and head for several years of the National Association for the Advancement of Colored People, had asked Prime Minister Georges Clemenceau for permission to hold a Pan-African Congress in Paris while the Peace Conference was in session. Clemenceau said to him, "Don't advertise it, but go ahead!" So DuBois, together with the first African to be elected deputy to the French Chamber, Blaise Diagne, went ahead, though only nine of the fifty-seven members of the congress came from Africa. Still, its founder believed the congress had an effect on its chief object, for it was "an appeal to give the Negro race of Africa a chance to develop unhindered by other races."[20]

Did President Wilson, seeing a menace to American policy, really try to countermand the congress, as Jean Suret-Canale, a recent historian of Black Africa, says? Possibly Wilson did, for George Padmore, a Jamaican who wrote on Pan-Africanism forty years later, says that DuBois tried to get an interview with the president to convince him that the meetings would not feature the black problem in America, a possibility feared in Washington. But DuBois got no further than the presidential adviser, Colonel Edward House. The State Department told the American people that the French government had informed them officially that no conference would be held. In spite of that denial, the Passport Office refused passports to those Americans who wished to attend the congress.[21] After all, the Department of State can hardly have been ignorant that it was going to take place.

DuBois persevered, the congress was convened, and out of it, according to its founder, came the idea of the mandates. The truth of that assertion seems more than doubtful, for Samuel Bemis, Henri Grimal, and other reliable authorities credit the authorship of the mandate idea to Prime Minister Jan Smuts of South Africa.[22] On the French side, Prime Minister Clemenceau is said to have supported the congress as a counterweight to American distrust of colonization. However, all in all, the success of having gathered together such a congress at that time was of real importance; it was there that DuBois spoke his famous line: "The problem of the Twentieth Century is the problem of the color line."[23]

However, the conference did not take up independence, any more than the conference of 1900 had. It asked only participation by blacks in the government of the various countries, as fast as their development would permit. It was not until a similar congress, sixth of its kind, was held in Manchester, England in 1945 that an outright demand for freedom was made. Colin Legum has said that there were no Africans in attendance at that congress, but that does not appear to be correct, for Ras Makonnen, an Indian living in England, who was there, noted the presence of Kwame Nkrumah—later the leader of Ghana—and of other Africans as well. He admits, however, that there was very little French African participation, partly because of the language barrier and partly because of the black association with French political parties, among them the Communist party; so they may not have felt comfortable in going to the conference. Thus the gathering became largely a conference of British and American blacks, including W. E. B. DuBois, who had sparked the previous conference. Makonnen adds that the old idea "that you could do more for African liberation outside of Africa" was being laid aside. It was, he said, "a more explicitly political conference" than the preceding ones (London, 1900; Paris, 1919; and elsewhere). It was a place where Africans like Nkrumah of the Gold Coast, Jomo Kenyatta of Kenya, and I. T. A. Wallace-Johnson of Belgium could be seen as professional rebels.[24] This rebellious aspect of such well-known Africans might easily stand out at a conference whose themes were "anti-imperialism, anti-colonialism, and national independence. It was openly asserted that independence would be the only valid solution for Africa's political aspirations."[25]

If no Africans actively demanded freedom in the congress of 1919, or in the next two decades until 1945, it is probably because they knew there was no hope of obtaining it at that time. We do not know that they really wanted it then, for as late as 1927, Blaise Diagne rejected the idea of independence in the French Chamber. He felt that his people were ill-prepared for complete freedom at that time.[26]

Another outsider became important in the twenties in French and African thinking. A Jamaican of African parentage, Marcus Aurelius Garvey—the "Black Moses," as he was called—preached a "Back to Africa" crusade to his race in the New World. It was referred to as "Sionisme Noir" (Black Zionism).[27] His movement "got into a frightful mess," however, and was dissolved in the twenties. His work never had the same success in Africa as in the United States. But some of the ideas contained in it reached African students in Europe, just when such republican beliefs began to seem dangerous to the French.[28] Garvey was a master propagandist,[29] and his anticolonialist beliefs were spread far and wide in Africa. Consequently, Governor-General Jules Carde of West Africa, annoyed, issued a decree forbidding the publication in his district of drawings, books, or periodicals that might lessen respect for French authority.[30] There was no break yet in the wall of French colonialism.

Europe's anxiety deepened with the publication, in 1918, of Oswald Spengler's *The Decline of the West*. He showed what he felt was the probable deterioration of the Western nations as they followed the down-curve of history. In addition, in 1920, Lothrop Stoddard wrote *The Rising Tide of Color*.[31] These impressive volumes were widely read, laying before Europe and America the most terrifying new ideas. The white nations were not invincible; they were on a descending path and might splash into the ocean shortly, just as the moon capsules splashed recently, only there would be no helicopter from a nearby carrier to pick them up. Even if they revived their aging peoples, they might have to face a yellow peril from the teeming masses of Asia, or a dark cloud of the black relatives of their former slaves. A tawny panther or black leopard, ready to spring on its prey, could not have been more frightening to white men, defenseless against such dangers.

However, in West Africa, nationalism did not get fully under way between the wars. The politicians there were only "protonationalists," as Crowder says. After all, they were asking only for an increasing share in government. Thomas Hodgkin believes that nationalism in Africa was always a "chain reaction," and toward the end it derived its ideas from the French Revolution's "Rights of Man," only now the Rights had become the "Rights of Nations."[32] The chain reaction went from country to country and from year to year. The beliefs of the colonized gathered strength unperceived. Still, as Walter Wallbank has said, the interwar period contained the formative years of African nationalism. Little was seen on the surface, but it "broke loose with astonishing force" at war's end.[33] Certainly, the antecedents and the build-up had been present long before 1939. The final phase came later than Wallbank suggests; for, except for an abortive request for freedom made by Madagascar to the Constitutional Convention in 1945–46, it was not until 1958 that an important African leader asked outright for independence.[34]

The interwar years were increasingly difficult for the French colonialists. While grateful for the help of the black soldiers in the war, they sensed an ever-present danger afterward. The same countries that had sent their men to fight in Europe might not always remain quiet and docile if given too much liberty of action or of thought.[35] So the French politicians, ministers, governors, and administrators were bound to be tense and repressive. Their charges must not win a freedom that would destroy their usefulness to the metropole. As Sarraut had insisted in 1919, there must be no diminution in French authority.

There is no doubt that the European colonizing nations continued to believe in the validity of their position. Gabriel Hanotaux, the former foreign minister of France, wrote, in the thirties, that colonizing was a need of society, for rising generations aspired to far-off lands; raw materials were needed by countries where they could not be obtained; and, he said, "These riches do not belong to African or Asiatic peoples, they are the common treasure of humanity." It seems certain that except for a few people influenced by Woodrow Wilson, or, later, by Franklin D. Roosevelt, most of the Western World peoples thought ideas of emancipation and evolution were unfortunate. As Lyautey said, such ideas could not be spread about the world with impunity.[36]

During the whole interwar period, the Communist party did not exert any great influence on the colonial question. Against colonialism in general, they had stressed the importance of revolutionary movements in the Far East, the Near East, and the Mediterranean, but during the thirties much of their effort was directed against fascism in Europe. Even the League against Imperialism, founded in Brussels in 1927 to coordinate movements of national independence, was hampered because of its inability to give independence priority over the fascist problem.[37]

In the early interwar years, the mandate system, established by the League of Nations, brought under French rule, at least temporarily, Syria, the Lebanon, Togo, and part of the Cameroons. It was intended as a safeguard for states not considered capable, as yet, of governing themselves; so they were put under control of certain of the greater, more "civilized" powers. These "mandatories" were to govern the territories allotted to them according to rules laid down by the Council of the League, aided by a Permanent Commission of Mandates. Categories of mandates—A, B, and C—were established, each with differing conditions based on the development of civilization in the country concerned, the A category being more liberal and closer to Wilson's ideas.[38] "Class A mandates included former communities attached to the Ottoman Empire, all of which would soon be able to stand alone; the Class B mandates included the former German possessions in Central Africa, still regarded as in need of governmental supervision; and the Class C mandates were German South West Africa and the German possessions in the Pacific, all to be best administered under the laws of the Mandatory as integral portions of its territory."[39]

Unfortunately, the League had a very "effaced" role, for it was unwilling to undermine authority anywhere. The rules for the mandated lands indicated they must establish an "open door" in trade, and freedom of conscience and religion. They must prohibit military training and the establishment of military bases in their countries. The abandonment of certain abuses was also required. Unfortunately, these rules were not obligatory, and the submitting of reports to the League was also taken lightly. Conflicts with the mandatory authorities in

Syria and Lebanon were continual, and in the French B mandates, Togo and the Cameroons, there was also opposition. Still, as Engelbert Mveng, the historian of the Cameroons, says, it was probably the best solution for the time. A little before this period, in 1918, small tribal groups, Pan-Douala and Pan-Ewe in the Cameroons and in Togo, had asked for republics in both these states. There was, of course, repression; in the Cameroons, suspects on their way to the North Cameroon town prison of Mokolo were forced to walk an incredible distance to reach there and died by dozens on the road. Mandate rule was not very popular.[40]

In time, the Africans learned of other movements far away. The National Vietnamese party was set up in 1927, on the model of the Chinese Kuomintang; and a little later, an Indochinese party began to function. Closer at hand, in Tunisia, the Young Tunisians had been involved in protests ever since 1906, and in 1919 they had asked for a constitutional state. Later, the Destour (Independence) party and the Neo-Destour said that limited reforms were not enough. In Morocco, the Young Moroccans and the Committee of Moroccan Action tried to transform the protectorate there into a kind of mandate, but the movement did not obtain the adhesion of the country. In Algeria, the Young Algerians had worked many years for liberal reform. In 1936 their leader, Ferhat Abbas, issued a "profession of faith," asking for the application of some of the principles taught by the French. Soon after, several Muslim religious movements demanded independence in violently nationalistic terms.[41]

In India, there was wide ferment, for limited reforms had not been enough. The uprisings were repelled with severity and sometimes with great mortality. Gandhi's noncooperation movement, begun in 1920, had spread, and by 1929 civil disobedience was all over India. In Nigeria, too, demands for at least some self-government were put forward. And the Dutch government's "moral policy" in Indonesia was not effective. The Dutch "foreigners" in the country united the people against the government until even the Islamic religion contained facets of nationalism. An Indonesian Communist party was active, and students set up a National Indonesian party as well.[42] All these movements around the world were based on nationalistic creeds.

The developing virus of nationalism had already touched French lands, too. A preliminary movement in Madagascar, in 1915, was not effective, and a repression followed. All gatherings were carefully watched. As there was no disobedience, the repression was not severe, but it left scars on the minds of the citizens. Direct administration was established; the old social structures changed; European thought and customs took their place. The newer method of government was called "association," but it was that only in appearance. The Council of Notables, now part of the administration in some of the French colonies, was of little value, and the Malagasy people were put on an inferior level, for they were refused admission to European schools and treated with conservatism. A movement for emancipation was the result, and the word "independence" was pronounced at last. The nationalists gained some power but not enough. Still, political conscience had been awakened.[43]

In other French countries there was open revolt between 1920 and 1940. The Tuareg tribes and the Mauritanians were always troublesome. As late as 1927 they were still raiding Port Etienne, since they had been under French rule only since 1910 and were not yet "pacified." In the Ivory Coast and the Upper Volta, hundreds of thousands left their homes because of the bitterness over forced labor. In 1934 there was a movement against the requisitioning of food and animals by African chiefs, who were permitted by the French government to despoil their people. In Dahomey, in 1923, there were riots against the forcible collection of taxes, and they were repeated in 1933–34.

The reasons for these revolts were clear. One great subject of discontent in the colonies was the *indigénat,* the system of penalties applied only to the African population. It had been installed in West Africa, Equatorial Africa, Madagascar, Somaliland, and the mandate countries of the Cameroons and Togo in 1924. Much of it existed before that time. Only *notables* with official posts, those who were known to be friendly to France or those who were citizens of the Four Communes of Senegal were exempt from these penalties.[44]

However, the chief grievance was the requirement of forced labor. The French saw this requirement as the method by which they might develop the countries under their control. Since all the colonies were intended to be self-supporting, with no deficits made up from Paris, it seemed that the way to procure the necessary work was by forcing it. The argument was used that the African was unwilling to work; therefore, it was the duty of the French to teach him that he must.[45] So, in addition to recruitment for war, there was also recruitment for governmental projects; and it was carried out often without regard for the need for men to work in their own fields. Frequently, too, it took them to far-off places, away from their families, with unhealthy conditions and inadequate food supplies. It was true that after 1930, forced labor was used—at least theoretically—only for public projects and could not be exacted by individual traders or *colons.* But the governor arranged the conditions and duration of work, and the press was limited in reporting infractions of these regulations by the colonizers; so they could not be forced to obey the laws.[46] Apparently the most severe system of forced labor was in the Ivory Coast where workers went to fell trees, or later to work on cocoa, coffee, or banana plantations. In 1927, men received 2 francs a day for three months and then 2.50, while women had 1 franc a day for three months and then 1.25. So that workers should not leave, only half of the wages were paid during the contract. If any man in the work force died, the climate or something similar was blamed, and the cost to the government was only 300 francs.[47]

The protests against this situation took many forms. In the twenties and thirties, a small beginning of political life took place. Some of the élite had been trained in French institutions, and they now held positions in schools and offices. They had seen much of European life and did not wish to submit to the controls of colonial governments. The more advanced were working in ports or on railroads, where they had at least the possibility of forming workmen's movements. Many were not in large cities where that could be done, but in the faraway bush, out of touch with protest. Thus the early efforts at forming unions were easily smothered by the government. The French feared the tendency of the more civilized African *évolués* to feel the contradiction between the laws of the *indigénat* and the French republican traditions. Those regulations, for the Africans only, did not resemble the French tradition. Claims for citizenship in the name of the well-known assimilation policy were growing, as was anger at the exactions of the government, of the chiefs, and of private societies.[48]

There was little freedom of association or of the press, except in Equatorial Africa, where the government was slightly more liberal. And when a law gave some leeway, those in power found means to thwart it. Missionaries, many "radicals," and freemasons, in addition to the administration, denounced the claims of the *évolués* and called those who made them "agents of Moscow" and "enemies of France."[49] Even in the Four Senegalese Communes of Dakar, Saint-Louis, Rufisque, and Gorée, where French citizenship had been granted in the nineteenth century and confirmed again in 1916, there were efforts to limit the power of the votes on the part of those who feared black citizenship in the Empire.[50] There was strong reaction to these efforts when the blacks could express it, for their grievances were now developing into national movements against imperialism.

Even before the Second World War there was some change. Blaise Diagne, a Senegalese who had been a customs official and temporarily a judge in Madagascar, was elected to the French Chamber of Deputies in 1914.[51] He managed to stay there until he died in 1934, by rallying to the French side of colonial policies—at least to a certain degree. This enraged some of his countrymen, but in the end they acknowledged the rather hidden patriotic character of his motives. After the recruiting for the French army that he had carried out in the First World War, he defended the big companies of Bordeaux in their trade with Africa, and at the Geneva International Labor Bureau he sponsored the position of the French government on forced labor. This is hard to understand, since he must have known of the abuses connected with it. In 1931 he became under-secretary of state for the colonies in the Laval government, and he was with Marshal Lyautey at the opening of the famous Colonial Exposition in Paris in 1931.[52] Diagne is remembered as the first of the courageous Africans who began the serious political development of their countries.

Lamine Guèye was another exceptional case. He was the first African admitted to the practice of law in Dakar, and he became famous as a lawyer and as a promoter of his race. He often opposed Diagne, but later he wrote that the two had agreed on the essential objects of Senegalese policy, as well as on the means of attaining them. He realized that Diagne had a wide political viewpoint.[53]

So two men had succeeded in the world of the colonies. They had attained posts in government and the legal profession, and they helped in social contests whenever they could. In addition, in the thirties, trade unions began to appear.

By 1937 they numbered 119 in West Africa, most of them connected with the developing railroads. With the unions came strikes, legal and illegal. Ideas could penetrate faster now because of the famous William Ponty School in Dakar, where students from various parts of Africa came together. In addition, there were many "voluntary associations," beginning as sport or cultural clubs and turning later to politics. Lamine Guèye speaks of a group to which he belonged in his youth. It was called *L'Aurore de Saint-Louis* (The Dawn of Saint-Louis), named for his own city in Senegal. The group was political in a sense, but it also discussed other ideas, learned the meaning of words, and studied anything that might be useful. One of its chief reasons for existence was the promotion of sports and recreations, such as hunting and fishing. At the same time, Guèye was a member of *La Lyre de Saint-Louis* (The Lyre of Saint-Louis), a musical organization that gave concerts. It is a little ironic that at one time the members sang—of all things—the national hymn of the Transvaal, under the illusion that it dealt with the freeing of South African peoples.[54]

Crowder speaks of an Association of Learned Soudan. It began in Bamako, but its political discussions alarmed the authorities, and they transferred its founder to a new post. Under the Popular Front government, there was a *Maison du Peuple* (House of the People) at Bamako, though it was partly controlled by the government and not by the people. Sometimes a newspaper was published here and there in French West Africa, and an Association of Friends of Popular Government existed. In spite of controls, all these groups advanced the growth of political consciousness to a certain degree.[55]

Yet these were only a few of the voluntary associations that were formed, and as time went on they became very important. They had begun early: in 1787 an African minister in Cape Coast Colony had tried this form of association when he founded a "Torridzonian Society," whose purposes were "to promote conviviality and to open a school to educate twelve mulatto children. It had twenty-six members including Europeans and it met twice weekly." There were small societies like this wherever there was colonial rule. The associations were voluntary, but sometimes they were encouraged by the colonials—verbally or financially.[56]

The societies had other purposes. Sometimes they helped in tribal unions, in urban groupings, in teaching, hygiene, and education, especially in the spreading of literacy in the colonies. Indeed, Wallerstein says their share in the development of change and in the increase of political consciousness was indispensable. Groups founded for religion, temperance, or dancing caused less anxiety to the government, though the religious ones—whether Christian or Muslim—sometimes had political overtones; yet they continued to exist. They were born sometimes of injustice, for example, the lack of fairness in the prices given the African farmers in comparison with what the French *colons* received. Sometimes they could diminish the extravagance of traditional funerals, or bride prices, or matriarchal inheritance. "They were unconscious nurseries of democratic life." As time advanced, they became more and more important, for there was "a great need for such independent secondary organizations in society. They could serve as a basis for the new democratic planning for the different countries, and the force of their new ideas was evident as the nationalist movement became successful."[57] As Crowder says, it is surprising that so much political feeling could be expressed, in view of the severity of the penalties of exile or imprisonment sometimes exacted from the critics of the administration.[58]

Real political parties were beginning, too. In 1938, a small Socialist Senegalese group fused with the French *Section Française de l'Internationale Ouvrière* (SFIO), the main French Socialist party, which still exists. These Socialists claimed certain improvements in colonialism, but they did not yet contest its main principle. The Popular Front government in Paris was less strict than previous governments, and the advances made while it was in power for two brief years enabled such movements to begin.[59]

In the thirties, there was increased taxation and much forced labor, and the *indigénat* was particularly galling. At times racism showed itself. Agriculture was neglected, and French reform in the colonies was paralyzed. Promised changes had not been put through. Yet reform had to come. More participation in the government and in the economy was essential. It could not be neglected for long.[60] By 1938, African parties were appearing everywhere. Weakness in France meant boldness in the colonies.[61] And weakness was seen in the government's inability to face changes necessary in the army, in foreign relations, and in the colonies.[62] In Africa, the black élite was becoming more and more critical. Michel Devèze wrote later that France should have been more liberal.[63] It was an understatement.

George Padmore summed it all up later from the point of view of the Africans and their Pan-African Congress:

> This period was one of the most stimulating and constructive in the history of Pan-Africanism. It was then that the Congress had to meet the ideological challenge from the *Communist Opportunists* on the one hand, and the racist doctrines of the Fascists on the other. Also it had to defend the programme of Pan-Africanism—namely the fundamental right of black men to be free and independent, and not be humbugged by those who preached acceptance of the *status quo* in the interest of power politics ... many Negro intellectuals ... later prominent ... in the colonial nationalist movements, began ... systematic study of European political theories and systems (Liberalism, Socialism, Communism, Anarchism, Fascism) and evaluation of these doctrines objectively, accepting those useful for the cause of Pan-Africanism, and rejecting the harmful.[64]

So the years between the wars were not empty of significance. Nationalism was on its way, and the chain reaction was doing its work. After all, this chain reaction, says Hodgkin, was just national consciousness developing; and in its last stage came the knowledge of the ideas of the French Revolution. The whole nationalist movement in Africa was a revolt against the European theory of colonization, which did not chime with the beliefs of the Africans. Georges

Balandier says that it was a reaction to the colonial situation and a claim for greater autonomy. And Ndabaningi Sithole, an African himself, has written that the basic ingredients of African nationalism are the African's desire to participate in the government of his country; the fight for the economic justice of equal pay for equal work regardless of skin color; the attainment of full political rights in his own country; the dislike of being treated as a stranger in the land of his birth; and the rejection of the laws that prescribed for him a permanent position of inferiority as a human being. The exclusive policy of white supremacy brought to the fore the African's "consciousness of kind."[65] However, in addition to these reasons, Ruth Morgenthau believes that "in the rear of the drive against colonialism, there was another issue, modernization." Thus "behind the struggle for power between Europeans and Africans there was a contest among the Africans, between modernizers who believed in social equality, and traditionalists, who believed in social distinctions based on heredity."[66]

The effect of these attitudes became more and more important as World War II began and General de Gaulle came into the picture. From June 1940 on, Africa and all that went on within it was vital to him, because it furnished his first real support apart from that given to Free France by the approval and help of Winston Churchill. It was vital, too, for Africans, since they quickly perceived the possibility that General de Gaulle would aid in what soon began to be called their "liberation."

The stage Black Africa had reached on the eve of the Second World War meant a harsh life for the peasant in the French states of the "Dark Continent." The farming Africans had to give the French government 175 million francs in annual taxes and 21 million days of *prestations* (required labor on government projects), and they had to furnish 12,000 men for the army. Governor-General Robert Delavignette, whose deep devotion to Africa and the Africans we have seen in connection with the *broussards,* must have realized that this was a large requirement, but he does not mention that. Jean Suret-Canale points out that these statistics do not include amounts given to the chiefs, or food that was requisitioned or paid for at prices below the current rates. Nor did it include the additional labor the chiefs had to procure for necessary public and private works. In times of famine, when taxes could not be paid, household goods often had to be sold to get money. Occasionally, children were pawned. And the soil was so worn out with lack of fertilizer and the speeding up of crop rotation that it could not renew itself. Such facts were not mentioned until after the war.

Suret-Canale, always hostile to colonialism, believes that the repressive measures of the colonial system were largely responsible for these miseries.[67] All government reports are not yet available, so this statement cannot be checked easily. It is generally true, however, that many government officials in any country are loath to report all the troubles of their areas, and sometimes investigations must be held before the truth comes out. However, a few statements can be made with some security; first, that forced labor was certainly an accepted policy of the French administration in Africa for a long time, and that its use brought much anguish of mind and body to the populations there. This stain on the French government's record was not entirely wiped out until after the Second World War; and Suret-Canale says it took ten years to enforce its abolition in far-off places, though the law of April 11, 1946, seemed to be a liberation from this requirement.[68]

French General Hilaire, chief in command of troops in French Equatorial Africa, is quoted as saying that the best of the tribes were decimated, if not destroyed, by the "prison of the machine," by which is meant the murderous work on the railroads of Equatorial Africa. The men came to their work by barge or on foot, sometimes for 600 kilometers through uneven territory, with no food provided. Albert Londres, writing of the same district, tells of one contingent of 1,250 men reduced to 429 by the journey and by the unimaginable conditions of life to which they were subjected—conditions that promoted epidemics. Governor-General Raphael-Valentin-Marcus Antonetti is reported to have said the French must accept the sacrifice of 6,000 to 8,000 men or give up building the Congo-Océan railroad. But, according to Gilles Sautter's article, 16,000 men, at least, died to make that railroad. They died of disease, of conditions of work and clothing, of crowding in the camps. Yet, says Sautter, the project was justified in principle![69] But, one wonders, was it the French who "accepted" this sacrifice? Wasn't it rather the African men who made that costly payment?

This situation led to a general insurrection on the Sangha River, a tributary of the Congo, as far as the Oubangui River. It took several years to repress the uprising. When the work was done, there was little for the railroad to transport except a few civil servants on mission. Many people were afraid of that rail line—too many accidents occured on it. Road making in those regions was just as bad as work on the railroad, for there were no tools—or almost none—and the work had to be done with bare hands.[70]

The interwar period, even though it was the zenith of colonization, may well have included the worst of its abuses, though Ruth Morgenthau thinks the mistreatment was worse after the Second World War because the number of workers had decreased.[71] It is hard to know. Excesses in Africa were protested by some voices in France, especially that of André Gide, who went to the Congo and to Chad in 1926 to see what conditions were really like there. His report, widely publicized, wakened public opinion in France to a considerable extent, for it was dotted with horrible scenes. He saw a group of women roadmenders, who were more like cattle, working in the streaming rain, some with babies at the breast. Every twenty yards there were huge pits, generally about ten feet deep. Out of these

the poor wretches had dug the sandy earth with which to bank the road, and this *without proper tools*. It has happened more than once that the loose earth has given way and buried the women and children who were working at the bottom of the pit . . . the poor women have built themselves temporary huts in the forest, wretched shelters of branches and reeds, useless against the rain . . . their overseer had made them work all night to repair the damage of a recent storm and to enable us to pass.[72]

Another day Gide met a group of eleven prisoners tied together with a rope (though it was, in reality, nothing but a string).

> They carried a load of manioc on their heads—heavy no doubt, but not excessive for a man in good health; but these men seemed hardly capable of carrying themselves. Only one among them had no load: a little boy of about eleven or twelve, frightfully thin, and exhausted with misery, hunger and fatigue; at moments he trembled all over and his stomach quivered spasmodically. The top of his head looked as if it had been scraped and as if his scalp had been replaced in parts by the kind of skin that forms over scalds. He seemed incapable of ever smiling again.[73]

Gide wrote that the "first-class" guard had been keeping indentured laborers on starvation diets, as well as the porters who carried millet for the railway gangs. "These porters," he said, "have had nothing to live on for the last six days but the grass and roots they could manage to pick up, or what they have been able to steal."[74]

But, since there is another side to everything, there was another kind of life at times in far-off villages. Gide has reported that, too:

> The native town consists of rectangular enclosures, fenced around with palisades made of rushes (seccos). Behind these are the saras' (soldiers') huts, where they live with their families. . . . This is the quintessence of the exotic. The beauty of the huts with their trellised roofs, edged by a sort of mosaic made with straw, is very great— like the work of insects. In these enclosures, the few trees preserved from the annual burnings become very fine. The ground is of level white sand. There are quantities of little hanging granaries, so placed as to be out of reach of the goats, that make these minute settlements look like a Lilliputian village, built on piles. The climbing plants . . . enhance one's sensation of long-drawn-out hours, of slowness, of idleness, of sinking into a delicious dream. The atmosphere is one of peace, forgetfulness, happiness; the people here are all smiling; yes, even the suffering, even the sick. I remember an epileptic child in the first village of Bosoum; he had fallen into the fire and one whole side of his handsome face was frightfully burnt; the other side of his face smiled—an angelic smile.[75]

So even in the depths of the Congo or Chad, there could be an almost idyllic life, except, perhaps, for that child!

Other interwar protests came from Albert Londres in *Terre d'Ebène* in 1929, and from Denise Moran, a French teacher in a school in Chad in 1934. Both of these writers were struggling against the unjust situation of the blacks.[76] The French colonials have always admitted that there were abuses in French colonization, as indeed there have been in the same processes carried out by other countries. No one knows the exact extent of these wrongs. Many who have loved the colonies feel that the excessive cruelties to Africans were not frequent, and that they were due to certain unfit characters sent out to the colonies by recruiting forces in France. It would be hard to prove the statements on either side of the question, now that French African colonization is no more.

However, as we have seen, some anticolonialism was expressed in France throughout the centuries. The French public, in general, had been reluctant to support colonial ventures—even during the inspiring times when the Empire was being acquired.[77]

It is clear, too, that through the last years before World War II, and even during the war itself, the colonial system had made very evident improvements. It had done much for communications, for Africa's slow development was due, in part, to the relative isolation of the various countries. Paths through tropical forests could be overgrown in a few months; rivers with sandbanks and rapids could not always be utilized, and those with insufficient water at certain seasons could not always be expected not to flood at other times. Deserts, as we have seen, were hard to cross at any time. But now there were new roads in the forests, improved and lengthened railways, and a few more modern ones. One of the new lines in Madagascar had used part of the military contingent for its construction, and had done its work well; another, from Brazzaville to Pointe Noire on the coast, had used forced labor and done it badly. In any case, such railroads connected administrative centers and had ended much of the isolation of the bush. Human porterage was nearly done away with. It had been a necessity, but a grievous one for the Africans. Deep-water ports had been constructed in the largest cities of Madagascar, Somaliland, the Cameroons, the Congo, Guinea, and Senegal. A canal to alter the lagoon at Abidjan in the Ivory Coast, and make it into a usable port, had been begun. The Sahara could now be crossed by automobile, and from 1930 on, airlines began to join various parts of the continent and to make the crossing to Europe more speedy and more comfortable.[78]

This is a good list—if one can forget the suffering involved in forced labor and the repressions that followed recruitments, sometimes forced, or exactions from the Africans. However, life in West Africa was still based on a subsistence economy, each family raising only what was necessary to maintain life, with a few old tools and minus the new technology in agriculture. But in some places new policies of exchange came in, with the use of money and with modern crops of bananas, coffee, cocoa, and groundnuts. Madagascar seems to have been relatively fortunate, for it had varied crops: rice, manioc, meat, vanilla, etc. European methods of import and export had some effect, though accompanied by a protectionist involvement with France, which was, in a way, a form of assimilation. It certainly benefited France far more than it did the Africans. Still, it was an advance toward a more modern world.[79] But the way to the modern world was hard for the Africans. Ruth Morgenthau reports that many in Africa who wanted to modernize their countries "believed that the colonial administration, by making use of cooperating African traditionalists, 'grafted modern abuses on ancient injustice', and combined being anti-colonial with being anti-chief."[80]

During this period between wars, European medical institutions were established in West Africa, mostly around administrative centers. There were 152 medical establishments and 258 dispensaries in West and Equatorial Africa, and a medical school in Dakar and one in Madagascar. The few doctors worked on vaccines for the plague and yellow fever, and attempted to conquer sleeping sickness.[81]

Finally, with improved communications and money economy, the trend toward the cities began. This meant a great change in social attitudes. Old people lost some of their influence, and the ancestors lost power. Islam secured new converts, and so did Christianity. The number of government schools increased, though the percentage usually in school was small. Madagascar did best, with 20 percent of their young in some sort of school, and then came the Cameroons with 15 percent; but the percentage dwindled to 6 percent in Equatorial Africa and to 4 percent in Senegal.[82]

The French regime showed no change, though by the time of the opening of the war, "pacification" was complete. France still felt that the African colonies and Madagascar belonged entirely to her. The agitation in them was not menacing, since only French citizenship was asked.[83] But there was some understanding in France that new policies toward the Africans were becoming necessary. This realization was the cause of three great new loans in the interwar period. The additional money obtained stimulated constructions, and gave a more industrialized character to agricultural efforts by irrigation and other new methods. Numbers of people were transported to areas near their work. The big concessionary companies were aided by the great banks of Paris and the Low Countries, among them the Crédit Lyonnais and the Rothschild banks. The world crisis was subsiding and conditions were better.[84]

Some of the statements by the ablest of the French administrators in Africa help in assessing the situation in the African colonies. Maurice Delafosse wrote on the subject several times in the era of 1919–22. He pointed out, after the congress of 1919, that the blacks asked only justice, secured by certain international laws. What the French had done in Africa was good, but more was needed. In 1921, he sent out a clarion call for Europeans to consult their consciences and to change their methods of dealing with the Africans and other colonized races. They must respect other peoples and their civilizations and act for their happiness. There must be progress and testing of the efficacy of the programs for the colonies. He pointed out the brilliant prospects for West Africa, if diseases there were conquered and local traditions were respected. The black army was a necessary part of the picture.[85]

Delafosse had recognized some of the important aspects of the problem; but, though much was done for physical improvement, there had been little attention given to the psychological health of the colonial races. Little evolution had taken place in French thought.[86]

Albert Sarraut, as discussed earlier, had conceived that the end of colonialism was possible if no change was made in the methods of control. Later, in his *Grandeur et Servitude Coloniale* of 1931, he wondered whether Europe would be able to federate and keep the structure she had created. Attentive observers had been pointing out the difficulties, but it was not yet clear whether they had been heard. The technical advance of colonization had outdistanced its moral side, and any sense of humanity and its spirituality had waned. But Sarraut showed no sign of wanting to give up the colonies; he only wanted to control the spirit by which they had been dealt with. Later, in 1947, as *président d'âge*, or presiding officer at the opening session of the Assembly of the French Union, Sarraut spoke of the transformation the Empire had undergone by its change into the Union, and of the great hope it now gave to humanity. But Governor Sarraut, now full of years, never lost his essential belief in colonization and in some form of empire—whether one called it that or gave it the new name of Union.[87]

Other governors spoke of the necessity of study of the African problem. Governor Jules Brévié, in his September circular to his administrators, once pointed out the necessity of considering the wishes of the population in the matter of selecting chiefs, and in the study of village life.[88] Had no one thought about that before?

Two brief paragraphs were written in 1931 by one of the men sent by France to Africa, whose lives and affections were closely involved with the Africans and their future. Such men thought of what the Africans could do for themselves with French aid, in addition to what they could do for the metropole. Governor-General Delavignette wrote the following lines in a book called *Les Paysans Noirs (The Black Peasants)*, as he reflected on the people whose lives he had to administer and whom he loved:

> He paused suddenly in his reverie. Were they really black, these peasants? Yes, indeed, evidently black. But as a fact, that did not impress him any more.
>
> He smiled at them. The beauty of one of their men or of one of their women, sometimes magnified the distinctive signs that came from the shining quality of their race. But that was not what the White Man was now mindful of this evening, any more than he was of the somewhat feverish singularity of his own covering of pale flesh. What counted was the indefinable and melancholy understanding that existed between them and himself.[89]

Sometimes, with the right individuals, there was such understanding by one race of the other.

However, there was bitterness, too, not only among the Africans, but also among the whites. Often they lived alone, without their families, suffering the heat, the streaming rain, or even the cold, and ofttimes in real danger. But at least they were in control, while the blacks had to undergo the many indignities of a race held inferior, as well as its actual sufferings. These facts came out not only in what the white men wrote home, but in the prose and poetry that began to pour forth from the blacks, as they developed in learning and could express themselves. As early as 1927, at the foundation of the League against Imperialism and Colonial Oppression, an African, Lamine Senghor, had warned the Europeans:

> The Blacks have slept too long. But take care, Europe! Those who have slept too long, when they waken, they will not go back to sleep. Today the Blacks are awakening![90]

In the thirties another black man, Léon Damas of Guyana, put his feelings into poems in a little book that became famous, *Pigments:*

The Negro's Complaint

They have made my life more heavy, wearier,
My todays, each one, look back at my former time
With great eyes rolling from side to side with bitterness
With shame.

Days inexorably
sad have
never ceased being
in my memory
what my life cut off was like.

My dullness about
the former time
still goes on
with blows of knotted cord
of burned bodies
from toe to back
of dead flesh
of fire brands
or red iron
of arms broken under the whip let loose
under the whip that keeps the plantation going
and the sugar factory slakes its thirst with blood,
with my blood
and the commander's pipe swaggers skyward.

So Often

So often my feeling of rage frightens me
as much as a dog barking at night
death close at hand
of someone
I feel myself ready always to foam with rage
against what surrounds me
against what keeps me
from ever being
a man.

And nothing
nothing would do so much to calm my hate
as a fine pool
of blood
made by those
sharp cutlasses
that lay bare
those little hills of rum.[91]

And a third African, David Diop, a Senegalese, wrote the following poems:

Waves
The wild breakers of freedom
Lash, lash the maddened Beast
From yesterday's slave springs a soldier
The Suez docker, the Hanoi coolie
All those poisoned with fatal creeds
Fling their huge song into the breakers
The wild breakers of Freedom
Lashing, lashing the maddened Beast.

Defiance against Force
You, bowing, you, crying
You dying, like that, one day without knowing why.
You, struggling, you watching over another's rest
You, looking no longer with laughter in your eyes
You, my brother, your face full of fear and suffering
Stand up and shout No![92]

The violence, the abrupt style of these verses speaks for itself. How many blacks felt this deep bitterness, almost impossible to express in measured language, we cannot know. The strange work of Aimé Césaire, a Martiniquais, different but equally bitter, would come a little later, but it belongs with these other words that seem almost torn from the speakers:

Listen to the white world
horribly tired from its enormous effort
its unwilling joints creaking beneath the hard stars
its steel blue stiffnesses piercing the mystic flesh
listen to its predatory triumphs trumpeting its defeats
listen to its wretched stumbling among pompous alibis.
Pity on our conquerors omniscient and naive![93]

These poets, others, and the prose writing of Léopold Senghor's *L'Etudiant Noir (The Black Student)*, which began publication in 1934, were the forerunners of a burst of African literature. Yet not all of them had the sort of feeling and attitude these examples show. Gaston Monnerville, a mulatto from Guiana and later president of the French Senate, could still say in 1955, when nationalism had grown even stronger:

There is no doubt that the masses as well as the élite of the Overseas peoples persist in recognizing that they are French. The perception of France is clear overseas, its incomparable contribution to the perfecting of man, and the value of its methods. People know the work of France on the intellectual level with regard to civilization.[94]

So France still had a deep hold on the Africans.

10

Brazzaville—An Uncertain Step into the Future

He will not go far who knows from the first whither he
is going.
                                                —Napoleon

There is need for a rendezvous with the future.
                                    —Maurice Schumann

De Gaulle had taken one step into the unknown when he flew to England in
June 1940. Now, in 1944, at Brazzaville in the Middle Congo, he would take
another of a different sort. He cannot have known then that the path on which
he was entering would lead to independence for nearly all of the French
colonies within sixteen years. True, he had said that it was not possible to make
Frenchmen of those people when he spoke about North Africans (apparently)
in 1944.[1] Evidently he was rejecting the old French policy of assimilation, but
he can scarcely have thought emancipation from French control for any of the
colonies would come so soon. Possibly he had been thinking about the future of
the colonies ever since he found himself at the head of the Free French
Movement, as some of those close to him believe.[2] At any rate, we now know
through Governor-General Laurentie that the idea of a Franco-African
Conference came to birth in London between Charles de Gaulle and René
Pleven.[3] The General had been aware since 1940 of the need for a Franco-
African Conference, so that after the war there might be the creation of a great
French group of countries, which in "the age of Empires" that the General
believed was coming could constitute a renewed imperial ensemble compara-
ble to those of the Soviet and American giants.

René Pleven, then de Gaulle's commissioner of colonies, agreed with him in
this, adding that there must also be a long-considered and thought-out colonial
policy for France, though no one at that time thought of remaking the entire
French colonial system. The suggestion did not, however, awaken any very
considerable interest in the French Committee of National Liberation in
London at that time. After all, the Committee had only been instituted in
September of 1941, and it had had little time to consider the many weighty
problems that had come before it.[4] Still, there must certainly have been a desire
for change in the management of the colonies among those members of the
committee who considered the question.

When Henri Laurentie, then chief of political affairs for the commissioner of colonies, reached Algiers in August 1943, his chief requested him to set up a program that would set forth the basis of a new colonial policy. The idea of summoning all governors of the colonies was considered but abandoned because of the difficulties due to the war, so it was decided that the conference would be limited to part of the single continent of Africa—Black Africa— though the governors of Madagascar and Réunion would also be invited, as well as observers from North Africa and a few other personalities.

Finally, on October 13, 1943, the conference to be held at Brazzaville was announced over Radio-Alger. The program was completed by November 10 and was sent out to those who would be invited on November 22, 1943.[5]

It is notable that in de Gaulle's statements about the need France had for her Empire, in his promise to return her colonies to France at the end of the war, and in his words recognizing differences between people there was nothing about independence from France. Nor was there in his words of gratitude for the 80,000 blacks who had fought in the French army in World War II.[6] There would be many stations on the road to that freedom. Independence was on a far blue horizon; but necessary reform of colonial institutions was much closer, for that could not wait. The sadness that the General spoke of later, in feeling that he must deliberately put an end to the colonial domination of France, had not come upon him so far. He did not yet have "to close a great book of History."[7] He had believed the Algerians were happy when he eased their burdens a couple of months before he went south of the Sahara, though that was denied later.[8] But Brazzaville would be a turning point. What had been a glorious past would be ruinous in the future, if the same situations continued.[9]

In late January 1944, as he flew to Brazzaville, de Gaulle paused "with deliberate solemnity" at the other African cities that had shown themselves favorable to him: Dakar, Conakry, Abidjan, Lomé, Cotonou, Douala, and Libreville. In all of them he received "demonstrations that revealed the vibrant certainty of victory." Even in Dakar, where three years before he had been greeted with gunfire, he now had a "moving welcome" offered him by the army, the fleet, the French *colons* and indeed the whole population. They gave evidence of "an indescribable enthusiasm."[10]

The reasons for de Gaulle's circuitous route to Brazzaville go back to the less evident purposes of the proposed conference. Charles-Robert Ageron notes that there was a "menace of American plans hanging over imperial France." Pleven, who had been in Washington for some time shortly before, had felt the sharpness of the American criticisms of French colonialism, its character of exploitation, and its tendencies to provoke wars. The great army of American churches were talking of working out a series of points to assure a just peace that would provide for the autonomy of colonized peoples, and the need for common responsibility for their care. "Trusteeship" was the new word for the solution of their problems, and it was clear that the United Nations must exercise guardianship over them. Thus it was essential for France to provide an alternative answer to these ideas, an answer that would enable her to maintain her own Empire.[11]

There was another matter, too, in the minds of the members of the Committee of National Liberation: the fact that Indochina, such an important part of the French Empire, was still under the Japanese yoke; so the whole group of countries that had been under France could not be considered as gathered together. A recent declaration had prescribed a liberal statute for the Indochinese states that would allow them to dispose of their own institutions. It would be necessary to send a speedy message to captive Indochina.

Thus it was important to be not only speedy but inclusive and foresighted in what was said and done, and since Algiers would be difficult because of the various currents of nationalistic opinion there, it would be better to hold the conference on the great Congo River at Brazzaville. By his trips to the other African capitals, de Gaulle would make the announcements of the conference seem more important. It would be the real response of France to the world situation, and greater knowledge of it would emphasize the importance of the recommendations to be made there. Other African conferences had been held in the past, but they had been forgotten.[12] This one would hold a place in history.

Arriving in Brazzaville, de Gaulle was received by Governor-General Eboué and the twenty other governors-general and governors who had come for the conference. Others present included Monseigneur Biéchy, bishop of Brazzaville, certain presidents of chambers of commerce, and a few observers from other African colonies. In addition, there was a delegation of six men from the French Consultative Assembly, the outgrowth of de Gaulle's London Committee, that had been sitting at Algiers since November 1943. There were also members of French commissions on social, economic, administrative, and educational matters; and finally, there were a few observers from the diplomatic services of other nations. Because of war conditions, difficulties of management, and travel problems, the states of the French Empire outside of Black Africa—except for Réunion, Madagascar, and Somaliland—were not invited to attend.[13]

This assemblage greeted the General, and he reviewed the European and African troops.[14] In the city, General de Gaulle then took up his residence in the "Case de Gaulle," which the city, "in its generous devotion" had built for his use. The distinguished guests were given a superb dinner by Governor-General Eboué, and next day there were soccer games between Europeans and Africans in the new "Eboué Stadium." De Gaulle gave Eboué a special tribute, calling him a "great Frenchman," and then he led them in singing "The Marseillaise." The following day, he welcomed all the guests and dedicated a monument to Savorgnan de Brazza, and the conference could begin.[15]

Another reason why Brazzaville had been chosen for the conference was because it was already de Gaulle's capital. It was the city from which he had sent out the "manifesto" and the "declaration" in the autumn of 1940, thus giving a constitutional base to Free France and adding the appointments to the Council of the Empire. Dakar was, of course, larger and more important than Brazzaville, since it represented the 18 million inhabitants of French West

Governor General Eboué, Commissioner of Colonies
Pleven, and General de Gaulle at Brazzaville.

Africa, while Brazzaville, as the capital of French Equatorial Africa, had only
3.5 millions in its hinterland. But Dakar, now Free French, had been under
Vichy in 1940, and it would have been hard to forget the defeat there, the firing
on the Gaullists under the flag of truce, and the worldwide scorn that had
followed the General's first attempt to secure a foothold in the French colonies.
Léopoldville, too, was a larger city, but it was Belgian and therefore unusable.
And, finally, the National Committee wanted to honor Eboué, now governor-
general of French Equatorial Africa. Since de Gaulle had a cabinet and a
Consultative Assembly in Algiers, he could go to Brazzaville as the head of a
"legitimate government," for it was legitimate—at least in his own mind—even
if the Free French Committee of National Liberation would have to wait four
months more before it could declare itself the provisional government of
France.[16]

   Brazzaville was already a large city for the Africa of 1944, even though some
still thought of it as a village.[17] It had banks, some large buildings, an army post,
and an airport. A few of its streets were not yet paved, but there were electric

lights and telephones, stores and trading stations. A visitor in 1942 spoke of scantily clothed Africans, of the tiny wheeled chairs (*pousse-pousses*) pushed by "boys,"[18] and, above all, of the difficult climate. One of the most difficult in the world, said another writer, adding that it was not too bad in the "good" season when the humidity was not so great.[19]

Brazzaville had its picturesque side, too. There was the European district with its pastel-colored bungalows, their concrete bases striped pink and white, with purple and red bougainvilleas spilling their luxurious growth over porches and roofs. The city also possessed entirely African subcities: Lower Congo (Bakongo) and Potopoto, on or near the plateaus over the river, their compounds surrounded by conical straw-built huts. A good place to live? Perhaps, though many diseases were rife there and everywhere else in the district. There was malaria, dysentery, scabies, guinea-worms, and other ailments with names not included in large French-English dictionaries. Nor should one forget that there are many poisonous snakes in the vicinity.[20]

But the chief magnet that drew people to the city then—and even now—is the great, wide, dull green Congo River, rushing swiftly and inexorably between its banks after it leaves the Stanley Pool to foam into rapids barely visible downstream from the cities on its banks. On its way to the sea, the Congo carries on its breast little bunched islands of river reeds and grasses, "contemptible trophies," Jacques Lorraine called them when he wrote a couple of months after the conference.[21]

Most of the men going to the Brazzaville Conference took the little railroad that runs to the capital city of the Middle Congo from the coast at Pointe Noire, though Henri Laurentie, the secretary-general of the conference, claims that no one came by sea. But some of them undoubtedly crossed the Stanley Pool from Léopoldville, on the other bank, where the water bulges to a width of several miles, only narrowing into a river again after it has passed the cities of Brazzaville and Léopoldville—now Kinshasa. Some came by air in old Douglas Farman or Dewoitine planes. Even these names are unfamiliar now.[22] One group tried to take a plane at Gao, on the Niger River, but it could not be made to take to the air. Finally, they found an old outmoded Latécoére of the "Emerald" type whose wings flap up and down. The little plane flapped as far as Brazzaville, but slowly, so its occupants were a day late, thereby missing the ceremonies planned for the dedication by de Gaulle of the new statue to Savorgnan de Brazza, the founder of the French colony of the Congo.[23] The routes by which they came had of necessity to be varied, for the participants in the conference arrived from all parts of Africa, from Madagascar and the island of Réunion, from Somaliland and Chad, from places closer at hand such as Mauritania, Senegal, the Ivory Coast, and the Cameroons, and from many others; and, arriving, they found the entire city decorated with the Tricolor.

René Pleven, commissioner for the colonies, presided over the conference, with his director of political affairs, Henri Laurentie, doing the secretarial work assisted by Georges Peter, director of economic affairs for the commission.[24] Only one African had been included among them—Félix Eboué. Eboué would be there because he was a governor-general, not because he was an African by race, though at the conference he would think and speak both as a governor and as an African, and it must be remembered that he was culturally French. There were no other black men present. No one seems to have thought it strange that the indigenous peoples of Africa were not represented. Except for a report given by Governor Eboué from groups near Brazzaville, no opinions of black Africans were heard.[25]

The Brazzaville meeting was the first gathering on African soil of the French chiefs of the African colonies and the first to take place in the presence of members of the Provisional Consultative Assembly, now meeting in Algiers, or, indeed, of any other assembly. Prior to arriving in Algiers in November (1943), the French National Committee had given little thought to changes in the colonies, a reason for deciding to hold a French-African conference in Brazzaville. They wanted the conference to formulate suggestions for reforms and then submit them to Algiers. General de Gaulle knew that change was necessary. He said he had intended to have his government "take the initiative without delay." The subjects to be discussed were native policy, the *évolués,* economic development, and administrative reorganization. A new project of political change was to come up.[26] The conference had no powers of decision, for its members had not been elected by the people of the metropole, Paris being still in enemy hands. But its recommendations could be valuable.[27]

The working proceedings began with a message to still-captive Indochina, assuring that country that it would return to the Empire at war's end. Wires were also sent to uninvited colonies, explaining the reasons for their omission as due to distance and logistic difficulties. Another wire went to France with promises of liberation and continued faithfulness.[28]

Next in order came the speech of the presiding officer, René Pleven. Pleven, says Georgette Elgey, one of the historians of the Fourth Republic, "was a man without history and his career had been without any sudden jars." In private business before the war, then with Jean Monnet on the French Supply Commission, he had joined de Gaulle in London and had been one of the chief actors in Africa's "Three Glorious Days" in 1940. After that he became for a time commissioner of the colonies. Elgey goes on to say that this "tall, robust Breton, with a phlegmatic British quality, had a certain humor, a belief in his own rôle and a sense of the State, with respect for its functions." She adds that he appeared sure of himself, had "an aristocratic concept of democracy"; and that, faced with a difficulty, he went around it, modifying its data.[29]

Perhaps Georgette Elgey, in saying Pleven has no history, is hard on a man who has done such good work in occupying many of the most important posts of his country, among them prime minister and minister of justice. He seems able, but essentially conservative. He agreed with what was done at Braz-zaville, though it seems to have been some advance on his previous ideas. Perhaps that was because his father had trained him in the belief that if France fell, she could still fight on from her colonies. General Georges-Albert-Julien Catroux said of him later that he never progressed any further in his ideas than

General de Gaulle opening the Brazzaville Conference, January 1944.

he had at Brazzaville, for it was said that Pleven thought even at that time that possibly de Gaulle had gone too far toward the blacks.[30]

Still, Pleven, the presiding officer at the conference, was always loyal to de Gaulle through all the early years; and another of de Gaulle's faithful followers, the deputy Claudius Petit, said of him that neither he nor Pleven had forsworn that allegiance.[31] Of course, Pleven had enemies. He had done too well not to have them. They say he is hollow and uses occasions for personal propaganda, but it is to his credit that he supported the findings of the Brazzaville Conference at the time when it took place, and when it was most needed. He was a worthy official at the conference.

Speaking there at Brazzaville, Pleven's first words concerned General de Gaulle, so solitary a man in June 1940, followed only by a handful of the faithful. He had set his feet now on a path trodden by an entire nation. His coming to Brazzaville was the crowning of his effort to use the human and material resources of the Empire in the struggle against the enemy. Yet the real significance of the conference in the minds of its promoters lay in the desire to share the advantages of France with the peoples of the Empire. Other imperial conferences had only considered economic questions, but at Brazzaville the chief subject would be the African as an individual and as a member of a group, and his closer incorporation into the French world. The ascent of the African peoples toward the development of political personality was the important part of the work the conference would promote. Thus the great colonial tradition of France, begun by discoverers and administrators, would be continued. Policy toward the Africans, duties of non-Africans, representation of all the integral portions of the Empire in the new French constitution would be considered. In a half-century, France had brought peace; she had built institutions of education, assistance, and technology. She had done much for the propagation of the Christian faith in these countries. De Gaulle's presence would reaffirm faith in the mission of France and in her will to carry out that mission. The conference would confirm its own desire to carry out such immense, exalting responsibilities. "No anonymous institutions must share in this work. . . . In Colonial France," said Pleven, "there are no peoples to free, no racial discriminations to abolish. There are populations who feel French and who wish to take a larger part in French life. . . . They should be led toward political personality and franchise step by step, not wishing to know any other independence than that of France."[32] The blacks would not have agreed with some of those statements.

In the phrase about "anonymous institutions," was Pleven referring to the possibility of the international trusteeship of all colonial countries to be taken over by the United Nations? Such subjects were already under discussion, even though the United Nations held its organizational meetings in San Francisco only a year later. There is no doubt that rumors of what they had decided had alerted the French to possible future difficulties.[33] But the indication that there was no need for independence in French Africa seems both naive and almost intentionally blind, in spite of the fact that Black Africa below the Sahara had not yet demanded autonomy, much less independence from France.

Pleven's speech must, of course, be considered in relation to the Free French position in the world at the time. By the end of July 1943, when he had suggested to General de Gaulle the holding of an African conference, Vichy had disintegrated. The Americans had now landed in North Africa; the Italians had surrendered in Tunisia and Libya; and all of the former Empire had been taken over by the Free French except Indochina, which the Japanese still held. In addition, General Catroux, in treaties of December 1943, had turned over French power in Syria and the Lebanon to the authorities of those countries. If France did not want to lose Black Africa, there must be no confusion between that situation and what was going on in Algeria, where independence had already been demanded.[34] The turning point in the war had now arrived, and the Allies held the initiative.

De Gaulle had by this time managed to exclude General Henri Giraud from his governing committee and had put him in charge of the Free French Army; and de Gaulle was in full command of the policies of Free France. During the previous winter, René Pleven, as his representative, had met in London with the members of the allied governments-in-exile. There, and elsewhere, no doubt, Pleven had heard much of the American pressure for international institutions, as well as of the growing anticolonialism throughout the world.

The Declaration of the United Nations of January 1942 had reaffirmed the principles of the Atlantic Charter, and the United States was entirely committed to the construction of an international organization for peace. As Thomas A. Bailey wrote soon after, "the winds of public opinion were setting in strongly for world cooperation."[35]

Evidently, Pleven and de Gaulle had shared the fear that the Allies would try to keep them from reinstalling themselves in all parts of the Empire. The Allied governments might even try to get some of them for themselves.[36] Certainly, Pleven's phrase concerning not sharing the responsibilities with anyone, not needing any "anonymous institution" to help them, confirms this idea.[37] It was early in the day to think of these things.

Additional reasons within the African continent required the meeting on the Congo. As de Gaulle said, France would rather give a reform than have it forced from her.[38] The territories of West Africa, particularly, had had a hard time during the war, for both Vichy and the Gaullists had made "exorbitant demands" on the countries there for the products needed by the armies in Africa and elsewhere. Districts had to forward supplies they did not have, which they had to buy at a high price and sell at a lower one in order to be able to furnish them. [Hence the famous story of the administrator who was required to send honey to the government and who wired, "Honey agreed Stop Send bees."] During this time, little had been done, even after the Gaullist takeover, to conciliate the inhabitants of Free French Africa, especially Equatorial Africa—then known as the "African Cinderella." Instead, there were often arrests and reprisals. If Equatorial Africa and the Cameroons were prosperous because some of their products boomed, West Africa was not. A worldwide price collapse did not help. In order to acquire the necessary labor force, the harsh practices of the great companies were reestablished.[39] So Brazzaville was a natural place for the conference.

Certainly, all these reasons influenced Pleven. And if Churchill could claim, as he had in 1942, that he had not become prime minister to preside over the dissolution of the British Empire, then France, too, could hope to maintain her worldwide power. Brazzaville would be able to say no to the Atlantic Charter.[40]

After Pleven's speech, Félix Gouin, president of the Consultative Assembly at Algiers, greeted the conference, giving thanks for the assistance of the colonies during the war, and mentioning the possibility of more modern and humane colonial policies for the future.[41] Then General de Gaulle rose.

By 1944, most writers on General de Gaulle had stopped describing his physical appearance. Perhaps by then he had become too familiar a figure, whereas in England in 1940 he was surprising in his personal as well as in his political aspect. Time after time writers noted his height, his stork legs, his large nose and long arms, his glacial air—which, one of his family quipped, came from the lasting effects of his having fallen into a refrigerator in his early days.[42] But they spoke also of the sheer power of will, the sense of personal dignity, as well as the undercover kindness that he displayed.[43] Perhaps André Weil-Curiel gave one of the best descriptions of him at that time:

> This enormous man with the small head and the disciplined but ungainly body, had such an upright stance that the position seemed to be part of him. His unruly black hair was plastered close to attain the neatness his meticulous standard required. It acted as a frame for dark eyes that did not seem to focus on the world around him but were rather turned inward upon some vision hidden from those with whom he talked. Leaders are generally thought of as more compact and better coordinated than de Gaulle, with the awkward uplifting gestures of his long arms to which the small hands hardly seemed to be attached.
>
> . . . Yet the impression de Gaulle made on those who saw him in this early period of Free France was one of extraordinary power and ability. . . . He was made to command obedience and respect.[44]

A crueler critic spoke of the "lifeless body which lacked all animal warmth," the gestures "slow and heavy like his nose."[45]

But somehow, by 1944, the body had grown up to the man inside. The nose had begun to fit his face, and those seeing him later on scarcely noticed it because of the strong impression of a tall, large, imposing man, one who meant much to both friends and enemies. Georgette Elgey speaks of him some little time after the Brazzaville Conference: "As a person, he seems unalterable," she said, adding that his mission was anchored in him, and yet "he seems to have hesitated at times to get or to retain power—contrary to the legend of his security in himself and his destiny."[46]

But the official picture of him in the book on the conference does not indicate any hesitation. It shows him standing tall and erect in his uniform without any of the heaviness of later years. Behind him was the flag of France with the Cross of Lorraine sewed on it, and before him, another table also covered with the flag. A large audience, its members all bent on his words, was seated before him.[47]

De Gaulle said that world events did not permit any delay in the acceptance by France of her duties and her rights. From the beginning of the war, the necessity of new bases for the development of Africa, for its human progress, and for the exercise of French sovereignty had been evident. The great men of France had opened so much of Africa to civilization that it was only necessary to pass through it to understand the great work that France had done there. But this very work imposed still greater tasks, which the war had made more urgent. If any power knew how to lead the 60 million associated peoples of the colonies, together with France's own 42 million children, it would be France herself, with her immortal genius for raising men to dignity and fraternity. The metropole was now burning with eagerness for the renovation of an Empire that had followed her unwaveringly. Autarchy for tomorrow was neither to be wished nor was it possible; but there could be no progress in Africa if its inhabitants could not profit morally and materially by raising themselves to the level at which they could govern their own affairs. The stages to that end would be long. The French nation, in its sovereignty, must decide on the necessary reforms of structure. The conditions would be studied at the conference—which he then declared open.[48]

There is no mistaking de Gaulle's attitude at that time. He looked forward to some autonomy but not to autarchy. In his view, the Empire would never be without the guiding hand of France.

The conference was held in a large white-columned building that opened on a terrace facing the river. In the main room, the white-clad governors sat around a long green table with René Pleven at its end. The observers were at another table. Jacques Lorraine, writing a month later, described the scene:

> At the right of the Commissioner [Pleven] sat Governor [Henri] Laurentie, his Political Director, as Secretary General of the Conference—smiling shrewdly, his head bent, thinking his inner thoughts. Beside him was Governor-General Eboué listening. His deep black color showed startlingly against the delicate pallor of his neighbor. Soon he was to charm his colleagues, his comrades he called them, by the precision of his thought, the elegance of his expression, the harmony and softness of his voice, all of it surprising because of the contrast between his black person and his marvellously pure French. Opposite sat M. [Governor Pierre-Marie] de St. Mart, who had been for thirty years in AEF and then in Madagascar [as governor-general], closer to Asia than to the Black Continent . . . Often he had to differ from his colleagues, and as a man of good will he suffered from it. Beside him was [Governor-General Pierre-Charles-Albert] Cournarie of the AOF, Mauritania and Ivory Coast, his powerful neck and grey hair standing up like a bit of the Bush. He was collecting himself, head lowered.[49]

The conference must have been aware of the possibility of inconvenient talk about such matters as independence; so, even before it worked out its recommendations, it nailed down the coffin lid on such ideas by a phrase that soon became famous:

> The purposes of the work of civilization accomplished by France in the colonies removes every idea of autonomy, every possibility of evolution outside of the French Empire bloc; even the establishment at a distant time of *self-governments* [in English] in the colonies is to be ruled out. . . .[50]

René Viard, writing later of the conference, remarked that "no one ever formulated with a force equally deprived of nuances, the principle of the subjection of colonized peoples to their metropole."[51]

The report of the conference, however, a few lines later, went on to say:

> The desire is that the political power of France shall be exercised meticulously and with strictness over the lands of her Empire. The desire is also that the colonies should enjoy great administrative and economic freedom. It is also desired that the colonial peoples should experience this liberty and that their sense of responsibility should be developed little by little so that they may find themselves associated in the management of public affairs in their countries.[52]

With no indication that its authors had seen any contradiction in the foregoing sentences, the report went on to give recommendations. The colonies must be fully represented in the metropole. Rules for the regime would be determined when the new central government of France was established. The word *federation* was mentioned, but it was thought that its powers should be carefully defined. Already, the Overseas Commission, presided over by Pierre-Olivier Lapie, had indicated its preference for a federation, and even a Communist, Mercier, had spoken of it in the Assembly as possibly replacing the Senate. Partly, this was due to the American influence (the book of Jean de Laroche and Jean Gottmann, *The French Federation*, appeared in Montreal in 1945), and partly to the government of Queen Wilhelmina, which had declared in 1942 that the Dutch realm would be reconstituted on a federative basis.[53]

Assemblies of Europeans and Africans would be established, though they could vote only on the budget and on new programs of work. The number of African representatives was not mentioned. Principles drawn up by committees of experts would see to it that the colonies were represented in the metropolitan Assembly that would draw up the new constitution for France. Later, the Africans would also have better representation in France than in the past. The old system of administration was outdated, and more patching up of its antiquated laws would not suffice. But it was clear the new organism that would be created, whether it be a colonial parliament, or "preferably a Federal Assembly," must guarantee the unbreakable unity of the French world, respecting the local liberties of the "French Federation," if it was possible to use the term. The governors would search for good advisers on all these points. Decisions on the roles of the central powers and on those of the territories would have to wait—but it is desired that the territories must proceed by steps from administrative decentralization to political personality. There were questions as to who should be consulted on representation of Europeans and Africans and as to whether there could be a common representation.[54]

The old councils now were evidently useless. New subdivision councils and regional councils of *notables évolués* and representative assemblies of Europeans and Africans would take their place, designated, where possible, by universal suffrage, or, if not, by the assemblies or by qualified "native Europeans." The councils would be only consultative, but the assemblies could vote on the budget or on new programs of work.[55]

So ended the political recommendations. The conference turned next to social problems. With a view to the progress of Africans, it was recommended that more professions should be opened to them, with wages equal to those of Europeans. They would be chosen by competition but could not hold posts of command. Methods of assimilation to the principles of French civilization must be studied and directed toward political responsibility.[56]

Then they considered African grievances. *At the end of the war*, the *indigénat* must be progressively suppressed. There must be *a school in every district with fifty children of school age* (when?), but *all the instruction must be in French*. Women would be trained as well as men, though they could not hold positions of command. *After a five-year delay* forced labor would be abolished.

(All italics added.) However, all men of 21–25 must give a year of service, except for those in the first military contingent. Laborers would have a weekly day off and an eight-hour day. Their pay must not be withheld when due, and there would be inspectors of labor (indications of what must have been grievances). A record would be kept to assure the African of some money for his "retreat"—his retirement. Professional associations or unions would assure better conditions, and a man could be accompanied by his wife to his place of work. Medical services and plans for medical training and social hygiene were laid down. Religious customs would be respected. The judicial system would be revised, with native judges for commerce and civil affairs. In family matters, polygamy would be combated, and attempts would be made to liberalize the dowry system and assure the bride's consent before marriage.[57]

In the economic sector, rather vague plans were suggested for promoting the prosperity of the colonies by a customs service, industrialization, agriculture, public works, and communications. There was to be a better administrative system, with pensions. Most of the rest of the section was devoted to the preservation of the European position of privilege in the colonies. The French *colons* must be protected. The plans suggested were to be carried out in accordance with the principles suggested by Governor-General Eboué in his circular of November 1941, though that was not a rigid rule.[58]

In addition to the first contradictory statements, there was another interesting section in the official report. On the fifth day of the conference, February 3, Eboué read to the delegates several reports submitted to him by some of the black *évolués* of Brazzaville. The first pages were moderate in tone. Assimilation to French civilization ought to be done in two stages, the first being a grant of "citizenship of the Empire" to those who qualified according to Eboué's decree of 1942, creating the status of *notables évolués*. In the second stage, full and complete French citizenship, with voting rights in France and the colonies as well, would be given those who had led particularly meritorious lives.[59] These ideas were certainly an expression of the strictest meaning of the policy of assimilation.

Other statements came from Fily Dabo Sissoko, a teacher and chief of the canton of Niamba in West Africa. They consisted in two articles on evolution and colonization and were read by Eboué to the conference on the same day. Sissoko spoke first of the fact that Rome had foundered under the domination of the vast numbers of barbarians she had tried to assimilate. Colonizers, he said, had better beware of assimilation, for it would never work. "The zebra does not lose his stripes," said Sissoko, quoting from Maurice Delafosse.[60] But few except Edward Mortimer[61] have spoken of the latter part of Sissoko's statement. He had said that to apply to the colonial blacks the cultural methods of the whites, without taking into account their levels of evolution, could only end in a hybridization that would run counter to the end pursued. The black remains black in life and in evolution, and the whites should try to make the blacks evolve along their own black lines. One cannot reconcile unreconcilables.

Association would constitute a much more possible policy, and Sissoko ended by saying that "it is adaptation and not assimilation that we need."[62]

These ideas that seem so reasonable to us now have been observed— apparently—by few writers, and, though they were published in the official report, no comment was made on them there. It is interesting that, though the conference lasted from January 30 through February 8, there was a full account of the first day (apparently), extracts from the third of February, minutes of the sixth, and extracts of Pleven's speech on the closing day and of his report to the Assembly in Paris on March 15. What happened on the other days we do not know. There was only one stenographer there, and as she has now gone to her fathers, there seems to be no way to recapture the remainder of the proceedings. The rest of the papers of the conference lie enclosed in the dark depths of the National Archives, from which no fishhook can retrieve them until the usual fifty years of oblivion have passed. Recently, there was a report that the termination of the closure at the Archives had been altered to thirty years instead of fifty. The latest information on this point was procured in March 1978 by this author, who was told that the thirty-year idea was pure fiction. Nothing after 1940 is visible at the Archives or at the former Ministry of Colonies (the Rue Oudinot) except by special permission from the director of the Archives. In the case of the papers of General de Gaulle, this permission must be obtained first from his son, Admiral Phillippe de Gaulle. However, it is thought highly unlikely that he would grant it, except, possibly, in the case of certain specific papers already known to exist; and there was doubt whether even those could be seen.

In his closing address, Commissioner Pleven indicated that there had been entire homogeneity of views at the sessions of the conference. It is certainly true that there was no open conflict, no disagreeable confrontation. Still, there certainly was difference of opinion, and that difference might have caused some contention in the outside world; so it may have been better not to refer to it. It is like one of those questions about open diplomacy, with which Woodrow Wilson had so much trouble, for certainly it could not have been insisted on at all times. Clearly, the ideas contained in the report were liberal in comparison with the ideas of most French people at the time, and they were undoubtedly grandiose for a France worn out by war and occupation. As Thomas Hodgkin wrote later, the conference was "torn between two principles"; it was a "succession of uneasy compromises" between the essential control of the colonies by France and the aim of assisting those colonies to learn to control themselves.[63]

But Pleven made no reference to the conflict of ideas. He was right, at least, in saying that the conference "was the indispensable preface of a work whose chapters must be edited one by one to be submitted to the government and the Assemblies." A special committee would work out the details of these great human problems—problems that make French presence on the continent legitimate—for France would exhibit there the products of her genius rather than mere material products. On the shoulders of the members present, he said, would depend in great measure the future of the motherland.[64] On that note, the conference closed. The meetings were over, but the consequences of the sessions by the Congo would continue far into the future. The conferees got into their various conveyances and disappeared over the Stanley Pool, down the roads, or into the blue of the sky. De Gaulle wrote later that the spirit given breath there

> had the possibility of making this reform a national undertaking on a universal scale. . . . This conference had taken place by France's own choice at the moment when her reviving power and her reanimated confidence put her in a position to bestow what no one would yet dare claim to tear from her.[65]

He might have added what many people have observed since: that no other leader of the time would have dared to sponsor and hold a conference that, for the time, was daring in both its implications and its contradictions.

11

Post Mortem on Brazzaville

> The brutal colonial fact, the imposition by force of a
> foreign country that has occupied a less developed one,
> belongs today, from the point of view of civilization to
> a past age.
>
> —Marius Moutet

Were the delegates to the Conference at Brazzaville, as they left the city and its great river behind them, satisfied for the most part with what they had done? Or did they see what might be called "the Great Inconsistency"? A month passed before Commissioner Pleven gave his report to the Consultative Assembly at Algiers, and during that time there must have been discussion. How could anyone deny the possibility of autonomy, of evolution outside of the Empire—and forever—and still say that the colonies must enjoy great administrative and economic freedom and be trained up to be associated with the management of public affairs in their own country? What is the management of public business except a form of autonomy? Is the refusal of autonomy not the very antithesis of administrative and economic freedom? And what does "political personality" indicate, if not the ability to participate in political matters?

At first, some people thought they saw de Gaulle's hand in the first restrictive paragraph of recommendations adopted by the conference; in fact, says Teresa Hayter, the phrase "was generally attributed to General de Gaulle."[1] General de Gaulle was not present at the conference after the first day of opening speeches, having flown back to Algiers, where the Consultative Assembly was in full swing. Still, undoubtedly, his shadow remained in the wings of the hall at Brazzaville, for while he lived, his force was such that a vast number of people were always aware of him, even when he was not with them. But there is no evidence that he had any connection with the later phases of the conference. Henri Laurentie had set up the working papers for the meetings and was present through all of them. He has said that de Gaulle did not try to influence the proceedings after his departure.[2] If Pleven and General de Gaulle had been in communication with each other later concerning instructions, etc., it would be curious if the commissioner had not informed his secretary-general about the matter.

De Gaulle's analytical brain must have observed the contradiction, though he made no written comment about it. Perhaps he thought a little incongruity was useful in dealing with the men on both sides of the question! The tracing of the route to be followed seemed enough to him for the moment.[3] Or perhaps, as Ageron says, the fact that the governors at Brazzaville had been brought closer to the National Committee and its purpose meant something to the General, even though those governors had not dared to really enter into the future of the colonies. So de Gaulle allowed his commissioner of colonies, René Pleven, and his director of political affairs, Henri Laurentie, to deal with any necessary publicity about the colonies for the time being.[4]

René Viard, an expert on the subject who worked ten years on a journal about the French Union before writing a most valuable book about Brazzaville and its aftermath, discussed the controversial phrases.[5] They were surprising, he said, and had caused anxiety in circles used to more discretion. Among other things, he remarked that Louis Mérat, formerly director of political affairs at the Ministry of Colonies in the rue Oudinot in Paris, had said that the sentence must have been inserted by someone little versed in politics, for it was so very categorical. After all, those who had known liberty (for example, the peoples of Madagascar, Morocco, Tunisia, and Cambodia) must necessarily wish to return to their former freedom some day.[6] Thus there was discussion on various occasions as to how this contradiction was allowed to occur in a group of persons gathered together to plan, as de Gaulle had said, the renewal of an empire, and "to study the reforms that would make it possible."

The text of the document of the Ministry of Colonies certainly meant that any self-government of the African colonies would be ruled out, even in the distant future. On the other hand, great administrative freedom would develop the responsibility of the various populations of Africa, so that they might be associated in the management of public affairs. It was evident that some representation of the black peoples would be allowed in the various assemblies that would be set up, but no one said how large that representation would be. If the word *federation* was mentioned during the meetings, it would need to be defined. A vote might be allowed in the colonies on limited subjects, or in a "colonial parliament," if that existed, and that would guarantee the unity of the French world. The whole complex would thus proceed from the administrative decentralization to "political personality." The new councils would be only consultative, and the assemblies to be created in the territories could only vote on budgets or on new programs of work. There was no time limit on anything, and little assurance that any of these reforms would take place. After all, it was stated at the beginning that the conference held no actual political power. It could talk and hope to influence people, but it did not have the power of decision.

Such was the situation when the conference turned from political problems and began to deal with those that were social. We know, very certainly, that there were two definite points of view at Brazzaville about the whole colonial question. There were assimilationists who wanted Africans made into Frenchmen; the colonies would thus become an integral part of France. C.-R. Ageron, writing for a colloquium that took place at the Institut de Gaulle in Paris in June 1978, says that Governor Raphael Saller, a member of the conference, asked for a large representation of the colonies in the new National Assembly in Paris.[7] That was apparently as far as he would go toward autonomy.[*]

There was another element, however, in the conference, one that was more liberal toward the black peoples. Henri Laurentie, Governor Eboué's chief aide, represented this group and shared with Eboué the belief that the evolution of the Africans must take place within the limits of their own customs and civilizations—it must not be restricted to imitation of French civilization. The result of this division of opinion was the contradiction so evident to many people later. One can only suppose that time was not allowed in the meetings to smooth out these differences, before the page was turned and a discussion of social matters was taken up. Pleven's closing speech, indicating that there was homogeneity of views in the assemblage, can only be viewed as an attempt to gloss over these divergencies and leave their solution to a later time.[8]

Another important factor in the situation should be noted. By this time Governor-General Eboué was very deaf. He had no hearing in one ear, and he heard only with difficulty with the other. Henri Laurentie, sitting beside him, did his best to convey all that was being said, but Eboué's poor hearing was obviously a great handicap. Laurentie thinks that the outcome of the conference might well have been different had Eboué been as acute as he was formerly; the delegates would not then have been satisfied with such a monster of contradiction. But who can tell? Many people have felt, in any case, that Eboué was the predominant influence of the conference.[9] Since there was such a definite difference of opinion there, it is hard to believe that an adequate solution could have been worked out at that time. Still, concessions might have led to a less evident contradiction. The conference was quiet; there was no open conflict evident in its report; and Eboué's sudden death three months later put a definitive end to discussions about what might have happened.

The consequence of the failure to find a compromise solution for policy toward the Africans would plague French colonial administration for almost another generation. Possibly, most of the actors in the drama of 1944 did not look at it in that way, and did not realize what a heavy mortgage had been put upon the work that they had done. Opposing underwater currents meeting at a sandbar in a harbor may create a raging barrier that is almost impossible to cross. The first constitution drawn up in 1945, implementing some of the recommendations of Brazzaville, appeared to satisfy the Africans, but it was rejected. The second one, which was finally approved, was the work of those who held other opinions. So the Africans felt cheated.[10] And some Frenchmen even thought the conference had gone too far in the direction of the Africans, so they attempted to counteract the original intentions. The result was the

---

[*] A statement exists that a member of the conference proposed making all natives of Black Africa citizens of the French Republic with all the rights of citizens. This had been done in Senegal's four communes and in the Antilles. If it were done, it would eliminate all future ideas of self-government. This suggestion is said to have been rejected by the conference as assimilationist and belonging to the past. The accuracy of the statement has not been confirmed.

"French Union," a "deceptive federation with its powerless assembly and false colonial parliament." Its power was illusory. Still, Viard admits, the men at the conference had realized that the old form of domination and administration was already outmoded; so, in a certain sense, the essential meaning of the conference remained clear. The meeting at Brazzaville stands as the beginning of the end of the French Empire, even though that was the opposite of what the promoters of the gathering had intended it to be.[11]

The first repercussions to the actions of the conference took place in the Consultative Assembly at Algiers, on March 15, 1944, when Commissioner Pleven made his report to that body. He referred to the conference as a program to develop the Africans and to increase European activities in Africa. By this sop to the Cerberus of the European position, he wanted evidently to placate the deputies, who would have to approve or disapprove his recommendations. Still, strict control of the colonies, all higher posts, and other advantages had been kept for the French, according to the text of the report. Pleven said the Africans looked to France for help and were much drawn to her civilization, "so Africa could and should assimilate to herself our civilization, adding to the means that we give her, those that are her own." Perhaps Pleven took that from some of the *évolués'* opinions that Governor-General Eboué had quoted. The commissioner said he hoped the French African would become an African Frenchman. People might be upset with the "negrophile" tendencies of the conference when, at the present time, all energies should be kept for the war that was still in progress. Nevertheless, he pointed out, the colony that had been best prepared for what must be done for the war, a colony on which all others could be modeled, was that governed by a black man, Félix Eboué. The commissioner said that the conference had been unanimous in its conclusions. More prosperity in Africa would be for the benefit of both blacks and whites. He was sure that now the Africans had more confidence in France.[12]

Obviously, this speech was pure assimilation policy. It must have been well received by its listeners, for there was little objection to it in the debate that followed. One or two deputies, indeed, said that the administration had not been sufficiently heard. They also noted that neither French *colons* nor any of the colonial peoples had been admitted to the sittings. Some tendency toward democracy ought to be shown in the colonies. And there had been no reference to supplies or food provisions that ought to come from the overseas lands. But, on the whole, there was little objection to what had happened down on the Congo, and Marc Rucart, a deputy, summed it all up by saying, "The net result is that the Conference is a great date in French Colonial Policy."[13]

Well, indeed it was a great date, even though it was then looked on as something that it really was not—a guarantee of a free passage to the future for the promoters of great African prosperity, education, emancipation, and lasting freedom. But it was great because people thought it was, without considering its contradictions, its vagueness, its imprecisions, and its refusal to allow an opening for what the Africans would surely want in the future.[14]

It was, on the whole, a psychological victory. It satisfied the Europeans, who thought the conference had been liberal, and it gave the Africans a hope that the colonial government would be more liberal as time went on.

Other European voices soon commented less favorably on what had happened. Louis Mérat wrote that giving representation, and then limiting the power of the assemblies to be created, was in itself a contradiction.[15] Some writers blamed de Gaulle, saying that the conference was only the fruit of the necessity of responding to the hopes raised up by the Atlantic Charter. The conference, they thought, was at once a concession and a refusal. Yes, the reforms were progressive; but they had little relation to the needs and legitimate hopes of the Africans.[16] Another said de Gaulle had merely used the ideas of others. What he had done was opportunism or expedience, merely intended to get the support of the populations.[17]

There were others, however, who supported the honesty of de Gaulle's intention and believed he was sincere. The General had thought about decolonization even as far back as 1940, they believed. Still, at the time of Brazzaville, and afterward, General de Gaulle did not have the means or the opportunity necessary to carry it through. For that, he needed a stronger government than the one projected by the first suggested constitution; when the Fourth Republic finally got under way at the end of 1946, with a second constitution that the people approved, de Gaulle had left office. Even the new constitution did not have the necessary strength to enable decolonization to proceed further at that time; nor, as Foreign Minister Maurice Schumann remarked later, did France have the powerful international position that a general freeing of the colonies would have required. As the vice president of the Senate, Maurice Bayrou, said in a later year, "Brazzaville began things!" "Brazzaville awakened hopes," wrote Devèze. "The important fact was Brazzaville; action began there," said General Pierre Rondot, a military man well versed in the affairs of the Empire. That point—that the conference was a beginning—was the one heard most. People ignored its failings, remembering only that it initiated the long series of actions that ended in the decolonization of all the French African states. No doubt, Jean-Hilaire Aubame, a Gabonese, was right when he wrote later that many misunderstandings would have been avoided if Africans had been admitted to the deliberations. Nevertheless, he thought, the conference had been a "guide" in deciding on measures to be taken—a beginning, not an end, of which the most important section was the admission of black Africans as deputies to the Constituent Assembly.[18]

Henri Laurentie did his best to make the results of the conference known. He was undoubtedly disappointed at not having been able to push through a more unified and liberal statement of the government position. He spoke, as Aubame did, of the admission of the blacks to the French Assembly as being the main consequence of the new policy, the beginning of which went back as far as 1942.[19] In saying that, was he referring to the policy enunciated by Eboué in his Circular of 1941, or to de Gaulle's decrees of 1945, or to the beginning of the implementation of the policies of the Atlantic Charter? It is noticeable that Laurentie, writing a year after the conference, presented the conference as "the first term of an action whose crowning point would occur in the first Assembly of the Fourth Republic." Also, on the first anniversary of the conference, in 1945, he spoke of it as in the image of the "Fête de la Fédération" of July 14, 1790.[20] In his mind, it was a historical event of great importance, with overtones that referred back to the French Revolution.

Laurentie also said that there Eboué had defined the principles of a policy for the *indigènes*. The élite that Eboué had promoted had evolved swiftly, and it had to have its place. Brazzaville had shown "in its bold wisdom" how much the Empire now wanted to be heard in the place of France . . . "the great new fact was the colonial initiative exhibited by all the populations. The struggle had speeded up the maturity of the colonized peoples."[21]

A few days later, on February 9, 1945, Laurentie said that the idea of transforming Africans into French citizens was practically impossible. The best solution would be a juridical innovation which would assure to each part of the Empire, in accordance with its political evolution, the freedom or the stage of freedom that was fitting. Links with the metropole would be tightened or loosened without compromising the bond uniting the parts of the Empire. The indigenous peoples would no longer accept tutelage as they had formerly. They expected the French to grant a reform in a spirit of wide and generous comprehension.[22]

Others helped too. Jean Mialet, a judge of the *Cour des Comptes* and a long-time worker for de Gaulle, said once that de Gaulle had always been between two fires: those who wanted him to stay close to the colonies, and those who wished him to remain further from them. Jacques Lorraine, writing soon after the end of the conference, said that Brazzaville was one of the first to show the Empire the road of honor and reason, and that by its actions it had turned men's eyes to the future. An article even appeared in *Bingo* twenty-four years later saying again that Brazzaville had pointed to the conditions of development and integration in the Community, and that de Gaulle's influence had been preponderant in the breaking up of the colonial system, though the governors at the meetings on the Congo had not really dared to enter into the future with all its possibilities.[23]

Furthermore, the word *federation* did not die. If it had not been used to any extent at Brazzaville, at least a commission at the Consultative Assembly at Algiers continued to study the problem, though its work has never been published. When General de Gaulle was in Washington on July 10, 1944, he spoke of the future of the Empire which would be prepared in a "federal form." Apparently Pleven, his commissioner of colonies, did not agree with this use of the term, for he said on October 12 of that year that he thought the term *political personality* adopted at Brazzaville was preferable. A few days later, on October 25, de Gaulle remarked that the colonial policy of France had been determined by the work done at the Brazzaville Conference, though at that time he did not use the word *federation*, but instead, "a French system in which each would play his part." To which Pleven replied again on November 15, insisting on the use of the term *political personality* but adding, according to

Henri Laurentie, a new component to his statement, namely, that the colonial countries had the right to govern themselves. So the General and his commissioner may have agreed in principle but not in the use of the terms to describe their projects. But the discussion of federalism survived for some time, for when the new commissioner of colonies, Paul Giacobbi (soon to be "minister" under the Provisional Government of France) published, on March 25, 1945, the declaration that was the "birth certificate of the French Union," he used the term *federal organisms*. [24]

After this time, clearly, thought was developing more liberally than it had at Brazzaville. The conference had been bypassed, and Laurentie, writing in May 1945, could state that the world now knew that the old colonialism of France was dead and that the French Union had substituted new laws in place of the old ones. [25]

Thus, at the conference, while the government appeared to have taken its stance, it had admitted needs far greater than it would have been prepared to acknowledge before the war. But, of course, French sovereignty could not be assailed. Some thought that the recommendations of the conference were revolutionary. All decisions, however, must wait until the end of the war. Still, after even a year had passed, a storm of criticism wreathed the heads of those who had been at Brazzaville. In a session of March 19, 1945, after the Assembly had returned to Paris, Hettier de Boislambert, *rapporteur* (reporter) for the Commission of the Colonies, defended Brazzaville against the assertion that all sides had not been heard there. Blacks needed more responsibility and more knowledge, he said, but all must be in accordance with the maintenance of French sovereignty. A ten-year plan for the development of the colonies was necessary. Gaston Monnerville, a mulatto from Guinea, then president of the Overseas Commission of the Assembly, followed him with a plan for decentralization and popular expression, to which he felt the colonies had a right. Federation should be considered along with plans for the colonies' economic advancement. Others said that the plans made at Brazzaville had not been implemented. The colonial spirit was still there, and that was the reason for some of the hatred of the recommendations of which one heard. The old Colonial Pact and the subordination to the metropole must go. France had talked too long without doing anything. The governors had been made too powerful; autonomy had all been for them and not for the people. A year had gone by, and what had happened? Why wait five years to get rid of the *indigénat* (the special regulations for Africans alone) and of forced labor? Abuses and injustices should be eliminated quickly. And so they went on "about it and about"! [26]

The new commissioner of the colonies, Paul Giacobbi—René Pleven now had another post—was very defensive. Inspectors of work had been installed, he said, and a work code would be published. Judicial practices had been reformed, councils set up, and local committees studied. There were offices for the production and sale of certain products now; and a commission would be named to arrange native representation for the Constituent Assembly. But there could be no international control—France was the only sovereign, and, indeed, the list of new laws was really impressive.[27]

Yet all had not been done, and there were other problems. Few councils had been established, few teachers prepared and sent to the schools.[28] Still, even then, enough had been achieved so that the social recommendations could be called the greatest success of the conference. A door had come ajar and black voices could be heard through the opening.

There was a more unified feeling about the conference among the Africans, though news of what had happened penetrated slowly to them. After all, they still felt the need of a French presence in Africa.[29] As Lamine Guèye says, there was so little possibility of political expression among them that the news had to seep through by bits and tatters. Guèye wrote later, in agreement with Laurentie and Aubame, that de Gaulle's admission by decree of black representatives to the French Assembly was one of the chief practical results of the conference. It was, wrote Guèye, "a gesture which appeared to be an essential contribution to the work of African emancipation and we have never ceased being grateful to him."[30]

Another African, who has served his country of the Cameroons since that time as ambassador to the United States, Jacques Kuoh-Moukouri, has written a moving account of what Brazzaville, and the events that followed it, meant to him and to his race. In the brief autobiographical volume, Moukouri refers to himself as "the Writer," a title used because he had more education than the rest of the men in the village. Hearing of the conference, he was told General de Gaulle was going to put "black on white." There would be better posts for Africans, and the conference would be under the aegis of a black man, Governor-General Eboué. When Moukouri was told what Commissioner Pleven and Félix Gouin, president of the Provisional Consultative Assembly, had said there, "the Writer" wept tears of joy and admiration for France. Then he heard what de Gaulle had added. "What comfort! What hope!" he applauded. So, replenished in spirit, he redoubled his efforts in his work. He was not well prepared for the clerical work he was given, but with self-sacrifice, he even accepted responsibilities for which he received no fair return. He did this with dignity, reaching up nearly as high as the real "nobility" of his functions required. When it was over, even if no promises had been kept, how could he regret defending his world against the madness of those who tried to enslave it? No! Once more pushing ahead, he publicized the exploits of the troops, supplied needs of soldiers, and contributed to war work—work such as "Aid for Black Soldiers" and "Aid for Soldiers' Families." Then the war ended. It was won. "The Writer" breathed again . . . the coach had reached the top of the mountain.

Soon, he said, the reforms of Brazzaville were instituted . . . now there were professional unions—syndicates! Had he not begged for such things in 1931? And the Europeans who yesterday had been harsh exploiters were freely offering to organize these unions. Would "the Writer" now be able to see the true face of France? Still, he knew all men too well: the devotion and the sudden solidarity of the whites demanded caution.

He wanted the young people of his country to separate their professional and political purposes, but they called him a coward—one who had sold himself—because he wanted their combined claims presented loyally, objectively. So he withdrew quietly. Then one day he heard that the Youth Congress of the French Cameroons was to meet. It meant a chance to work openly on political matters. Everyone was interested.

The French *colons* who still supported colonialism had met recently as the "Estates General of Colonization." The Youth Congress rose up against them, and in the last days of September 1945, there was a general strike of the workers in Douala. There were casualties. It was an overflowing of anger, of hatred, of reaction to the cynical slavery long endured. During the strike, the movement took issue with the employer rather than with the administration. Yet a month later the Cameroons had their delegates in the Constituent Assembly.

And so victory had come! Politics were now carried on in the daylight. "The Writer's" clandestine role was ended. . . . What a relief!

He concluded, "My children, you are one and all the fruits of my efforts, of my sweat, of my tears, even of my blood, in my clandestinity and my anonymous life. I am the 'Writer-Interpreter' of the first days, I am both great and small. I am the proven metal of colonization. I defy anyone to prove the contrary." So, when our protagonist resigned himself to what seemed an unalterable lot, everything had changed. The phenomenon so permanent, so irreversible, was loosened from the height of the slope. As days passed, its downward speed grew overpowering. "War," as General de Gaulle had said, "speeds up evolution."[31]

And at the beginning of it all lay Brazzaville.

12

Promises, Dreams, and First Fruits

> If, after the war, whose stake is the human condition,
> every nation is to have the obligation of establishing
> within itself a more just balance among its children,
> then still greater duties will be imposed on countries
> which, like our own, ever since the age of the great
> discoveries, have been associated with other races and
> other peoples. It is for France to honor her contract.
> —de Gaulle

For almost two years after the close of the Conference of Brazzaville, de Gaulle continued at the helm of what was first called the French Committee of National Liberation, and later, after June 1944, when the Allied landing in France took place, the Provisional Government of France. Dreams and promises flowered during that period, but many of them were premature and could not be fulfilled at that time. De Gaulle told some of his plans to President Roosevelt when he saw him in Washington on July 10, 1944. One or two points about colonization emerged as he spoke with the president:

> If it is true, as I am the first to think and to say, that the colonial powers must renounce direct administration of the peoples they rule, and form with them a regime of association, then it is also true that this enfranchisement cannot be accomplished against [the will of] those powers under penalty of unleashing in the unorganized masses a detestation of foreigners and an anarchy dangerous for the entire world.[1]

Before he left Washington, de Gaulle held a press conference on July 10. France, he said, expected to find her Empire intact after the war, but the form of it would be different in different countries, especially in Indochina, where it would take a federal form. The policy of the Brazzaville Conference had been to make the countries of the Empire capable of governing themselves. Every territory in the French system ought to be represented in a federal organization in which everyone could be heard; this is what he had meant by the term *federal form*. This policy could be seen in the gift of citizenship that had been made to many Arabs.[2]

Most of the European colonizers felt then that colonial peoples had seized upon and used apparent promises in the Atlantic Charter, from the writings of the Institute of Pacific Relations, and other statements of those who wanted the colonies internationalized to damage the colonial cause. All the colonizers now feared the depth of the growing movements among dependent peoples. They were promising reform, yet they always insisted on the maintenance of the supremacy of the metropoles and the safeguarding of their own interests.[3] They opposed anticolonial attitudes on the part of the United States.

De Gaulle made another reference to the Empire at a press conference in Paris on October 25, 1944. He told newsmen that his policy had found its path at Brazzaville. The plan laid out there would lead a state toward a development that would permit it to administer itself and later to govern itself. He would not use the term *Fédération Française*, he said, for it might open discussion, but the system would be arranged so that each country could play its part. And it must be remembered, he added, that even during the war, France had done much for the development of Black Africa. In 1935, the blacks of the Congo had lived in a manner that could not be compared with their way of life in 1944.[4] Evidently, by that time the General feared the exact term *French Federation*. No doubt he had heard comments.

Toward the end of 1944, in a discussion of foreign affairs in the Consultative Assembly, a reference was made to the fact that France must not renounce her century-old position as the ideological guide of humanity. By now, Paris was liberated, and the end of the war was, at least, foreseeable. There was a truly human international law based on justice and fraternity, and France must insist on that before men could think of recovering their political and economic power. After that, France must show the way for in her greater aspect, she had 110 million inhabitants and limitless resources; so ran the speeches by several representatives: Gaston Tessier, Louis Sailland, and Florimond Bonte.[5] Did they think as far as independence? Possibly, because de Gaulle told President Truman, in August 1945, that the new epoch would mark the colonies' accession to independence according to the means which must be varied and progressive. "We have decided, I told the President, to work towards the free disposition of themselves of the countries that are dependent on our own." So he used the idea if not the term of *independence*, though he enclosed it that time within the word *federation*.[6]

Thus the grandiose dream of continuing empire was not all of de Gaulle's making. It still held for some time at least. It is curious and noteworthy that de Gaulle could point to the Brazzaville Conference as the path of the future, whereas the ideas expressed had been so contradictory and so narrow that the men there could refuse the possibility of future freedom to the peoples of Africa—indeed, to all the Third World. Was General de Gaulle thinking of the conference as perhaps he had intended it to be: a promise to be executed at a time so far off that its difficulties did not seem like real obstacles? Or was he trying to make it what it was not? He wrote of future developments as having been foreshadowed at Brazzaville,[7] and yet they were really blocked there for an indefinite time.

Looking at the cold words of the recommendations of the Brazzaville Conference, it seems Governor-General Delavignette was right in saying the general impression in the long run was that it was an event leading toward independence. Still, by its own terms, it had really closed off the path to independence, at least for a time. Delavignette asks whether, since de Gaulle, Pleven, and Eboué really wanted to keep the Empire, Brazzaville might not have been intended to serve as strong opposition to the meaning of that series of international conferences: the Atlantic Charter, the United Nations Declaration, and the Moscow and Teheran meetings. All of these public issuances and events had menaced the position of the French Empire—indeed, of all the Empires. Delavignette notes that

> the third principle of the Atlantic Charter . . . to which France had adhered respected the right of all peoples to choose the form of government under which they would live. . . . The founders of the United Nations hoped equally to assist the colonial peoples in acquiring home rule . . . independence was the inevitable and the the only morally desirable goal of colonization.[8]

Of course, the three men Delavignette mentions—de Gaulle, Pleven, and Eboué—might have had opposition to these world events in their minds, but certainly they had other motives as well. The quieting of the nationalistic spirit of revolt that they had begun to observe as it developed in the colonies was certainly one motive. Brazzaville had value, however, and Delavignette thinks that it was the Africans themselves who had breathed into it the spirit that they wanted it to have, for from 1944 on the growth of its influence was mythical, and the legend created around it was important all the way up to 1960. The French public, exaggerating its effect, even thought that Brazzaville had brought about all the necessary changes. The Empire would now be secure.[9] Such wishful thinking made it into something that some people, at least, had wished it to be!

But, in addition to the practical results of the conference noted by Paul Giacobbi (minister of foreign affairs in the Provisional Government and formerly commissioner of France Overseas), and the optimistic feeling that it had brought to many blacks, there were more specific and practical results that followed in the next year or two. An educational conference was held at Dakar in Senegal at the end of July 1944, at which a twenty-year educational plan was set up, providing for 50,000 primary schools, 200 upper primaries, and 75 normal schools for teachers, of whom 50,000 would be needed.[10] How much of this vast program was ever accomplished is not clear.

During 1945 the scene changed a little. There was a beginning of the fulfillment of promises when de Gaulle's government issued a statement on Indochina, on March 24, carrying out some of the pledges made to the Indochinese on December 8, 1943. The French now had their territories in their own hands; they were reestablished in Indochina, even though their control there did not last many years.[11] The Free French leaders, alerted in part by the recent Japanese attacks there, knew the Indochinese peoples would no longer tolerate complete subordination to France. Giacobbi made the declaration, using the term *Union Française* for the first time publicly, though both *union* and *federation* had been used in referring to Indochina even before the war.[12]

Giacobbi said Indochina would hold a special place in the Empire, since it was more evolved than some of the other colonies. The Indochinese Federation would form, with France, a French Union, whose external interests would be represented by France. Citizens there would be Indochinese citizens as well as citizens of the French Union, without distinction of race or religion on a basis of equality. All government posts in Indochina and the Union were to be opened to the population. There was to be a governor-general and responsible ministers chosen from the Indochinese and the French living there. A council of state would make laws and rulings, and there would be an assembly, elected by the most appropriate method of each country, with French interests represented. Freedom of the press, of association, and of beliefs must be supported. Democratic liberties would be the basis of its laws. There would be economic autonomy and compulsory education, inspection of work, and development of syndicates. This declaration gave the reforms the Indochinese had been asking, though it was criticized in Indochina because it did not give universal suffrage or parliamentary control.[13]

Also, because of Brazzaville, a Franco-Malagasy Commission composed of twenty-six Malagasy and twenty-six Europeans was established in 1944. The commission now ended the *corvées,* or work requirements for government purposes, and gave new rules for workers. This was in accordance with some previous happenings, for in the Cameroons, even before the conference, a Bureau of Labor had provided inspection to prevent accidents and to see that inferior goods were not sold to workers. The *indigénat,* the code for punishment by decree of the administration, was made easier. The commission was only consultative, however, while the Malagasy wanted it to be deliberative— like a real assembly. In 1945, it was fused with the financial delegations in Madagascar to form a Representative Council of sixty members—thirty French and thirty local noncitizens. But only a third of it was elected by the population, so it could easily be controlled by the French.

Other government regulations abolished forced labor (April 1, 1944), set forth a single penal code for all Africa (July 17, 1944), and authorized professional syndicates (August 7, 1944). On the other hand, the conference had not condemned the exploitation of Malagasy labor by the great concessionary companies, which were still thought to be necessary.[14]

There were changes, too, in countries other than those south of the Sahara. On March 7, 1944, it was decreed by de Gaulle's Committee of National Liberation that the Muslim Algerians should have the same rights as non-Muslim Frenchmen, though they must still vote in two colleges. In the first electoral college the French far outnumbered the Muslims, and in the second, the majority of Muslims were allowed to fill only two-fifths of the seats in local and municipal councils. As in Madagascar, this gave the French complete control of these bodies.

Obviously, all this could not happen without awakening the hopes of the black race and the Arabs, as well as the Indochinese people. Things were moving all over the Empire. It may have seemed to the colonizers like a good haul of the net, but the Africans wanted more fish.

The year 1945 brought more changes. General de Gaulle had proclaimed, from June 1940 on, his wish to return republican legality in France. In 1942 he had said that the French would have to choose a new regime by electing a constituent assembly. This had seemed important to him after "the terrible lightning of disaster" in June 1940 had shown "the abyss on one side of his country and on the other the way the French must take." That way was the admission of the African blacks to the path leading to self-government, the path foreshadowed at Brazzaville. France, with her colonies in hand, could look at her work as ended.[15]

So General de Gaulle had foreseen a constitutional assembly, not only for the metropole but for the Empire as well.[16] To this end, a commission was set up on February 20, 1945—even before the final battles of the war had taken place—to plan for a constituent assembly and for the work it must do. Gaston Monnerville, a mulatto from Guiana, who had been in the Chamber of Deputies before 1940, would head the commission. Two of the members would be Léopold Sédar Senghor, a Senegalese, resident in France since 1928 and very thoroughly educated in the French manner, who had served as a professor in French schools; and Sourou-Migan Apithy of Dahomey, who had also studied in France and was an accountant, economist, and lawyer. Both were in France, represented no one, and were out of touch with Africa; but they reacted against any arrangement by which Africa would be dominated by France. They were against the double college of voting, one for Frenchmen, the other for Africans; the time had come for equal rights. They wanted the commission to recommend a single college and more African deputies in the Constituent Assembly, though they did not ask for that number to exceed one-fifth of the whole. Thus the seats of the assembly would not be proportionately distributed.[17]

In March 1945 this early Constitutional Commission sent the Consultative Assembly proposals outlining two possibilities for the future constitution: autonomy within a union freely agreed to with the metropole, and the old Jacobin plan of a republic, one and indivisible. In other words, this new plan would create a form of federalism or the old assimilation project. But the proposals also contained new principles. The first was that the Africans should no longer be subjects but citizens. In addition, local assemblies would be installed in the territories. Finally, they suggested that a different terminology should be employed in speaking of French overseas possessions. The word *territories* should be used in place of *colonies,* and the whole project should be called the French Union.[18]

De Gaulle preferred a plan he had suggested: to consult the country on the basis of a free constituent assembly. He did not doubt the referendum would abolish the Constitution of 1875, but he wished to hold in check the powers of the Constituent Assembly. The Socialists and the Communists insisted that the assembly be elected the same day as the referendum; it was decided that this referendum should take place on October 21, 1945. Two questions would be posed: whether the assembly to be elected that day should be constituent, and, if so, whether the people would agree to limit the sitting of the constituent to seven months. This plan would give it only the power of making the constitution; in this way it would not be able to overthrow the government.[19]

In late August and in September 1945, de Gaulle's government had issued ordinances organizing the electoral colleges—one for citizens, one for non-citizens. The noncitizen, or native, college was bound to be small, as only less than 1 percent of the population was qualified to vote. This group included the *notables évolués,* as Eboué had suggested calling them: members of certain associations, holders of decorations or certificates of education, ministers, former servicemen, tradesmen registered by chambers of commerce, and elected or tribal rulers—many of these categories overlapping.[20]

But the great innovation was that the local people, without counting those of Indochina, would have 63 representatives in the Constituent Assembly of France, though most of them would be white men.[21] While this was not a great number out of a total of 586 seats, it was some progress, for before the war, the only colonial representatives were those elected by the "old colonies" (the Antilles, Réunion and Cochinchina).[22] "For the first time since the beginning of colonization he, the 'subject'—now a citizen, though a minor one—was going to participate through his elected representatives in the fashioning of texts that would rule his destiny: for the first time he was going to make his voice heard."[23] Another interesting point was that everywhere, except in Oubangui-Chari, the government candidates were *not* elected; those who would be the new leaders of Africa were preferred. They included Lamine Guèye, Senghor, Apithy, F. D. Sissoko, Yacine Diallo, Félix Tchicaya, Gabriel d'Arboussier, and Douala Manga Bell—all prominent black men. Thus, in the First Constituent Assembly, when the votes were finally counted, there were 158 Communists and Progressives, 142 Socialists. They could have governed alone, but the Socialists chose to ally themselves with the new tripartite policy of the MRP (*Mouvement Républican Populaire*), with 152 members, thus becoming a brake on the more radical leftists. In one territory—Guinea—there was a riot during elections, with a cost of five dead and nine wounded.[24]

This great change dated back to Brazzaville and its conference, for de Gaulle's government, in setting up the Assembly, had adhered to the principle laid down there. And it was, said Lamine Guèye, a Senegalese lawyer, whose great repute gave him authority, "a decisive turning that was thus realized in the destiny of the peoples of the French Union in the promulgation of this ordinance which had a considerable importance."[25] Probably no one knew exactly how great its influence would be, but the leaders of France cannot long have been in doubt after this that their world had changed.

The Assembly met first on November 6, 1945, and after eight days of "somewhat offensive words," they elected de Gaulle president of the Provisional Government. At one point, he resigned, when the Communists tried hard to get one of the most important portfolios in the government (Foreign Affairs, Interior, or Defense). De Gaulle denied them a post of such value. But he reversed his decision to resign and stayed on, though he undoubtedly realized from that time forward that the going would be difficult.[26] Elie Chetrit and Jean-Pierre Timsit, in their thesis on the General's thought while in the Desert, have said that de Gaulle had no illusions after August 1945, and that he had decided to leave his post toward the end of that autumn. France was "on the point of providing herself with institutions of which he did not approve. He had not been able to conclude his task of renewal satisfactorily." The Battle of Peace, fought by the men of the war, was the one in which Clemenceau, Wilson, and Churchill had failed. "People would become hostile as the danger faded," but, the General added, "the loyalty and adherence of the people would steel me to my task."[27]

13

Two Constituent Assemblies
Create a Union

> At this time [1946], France, in spite of the
> terrible blows that she and her Empire had
> received during the war, had in her charge
> unmortgaged and without exception, all the
> territories of which she was the sovereign or
> protectress. She was in a position to build with
> them a French Union.
> —de Gaulle

Soon after his initial difficulties with the new Constituent Assembly, on January 20, 1946, de Gaulle tendered his ministers his resignation as president of the Council. A recent writer says: "If the Government was taken aback, the public was indeed stupified."[1] But the reasons for his action were clear, at least in General de Gaulle's mind. He wrote later: "Despite the accord achieved, I could not doubt that my power hung by a thread." Then he spoke of the financial measures his government had taken and the final prohibition of a strike of civil servants that took place because he felt he could not give them more than his finance minister, Pleven, had promised. He had won, but a debate in the Assembly over the budget had shown his power was precarious because of that of the parties. After the budget discussions, the Socialists had asked a 20 percent reduction in the credits for national defense. He felt that request was inspired by "electoral demagogy and hostility toward me," but that evening, "probing hearts and hopes," he had realized the matter was already decided; that it would be vain and even unworthy to presume to govern when the parties had resumed their old tricks; "in short, that I must now prepare my own departure from the scene." He had warned the Assembly on January 1 that "if they do not take account of the necessities of governmental authority, dignity, and responsibility, they will be in a situation that will cause them bitter regret." The bill passed, but the fact that defeat had been possible produced a profound effect. De Gaulle knew that his prestige would decline and "the parties would no longer tolerate him or they would relegate him to a harmless decorative function."[2] De Gaulle was speaking then of the political parties in France, for those in Africa had not yet become established institutions.

He noted that the first draft of the Constitution gave all control to a single sovereign assembly. The executive could only apply what was prescribed. The president, if one existed, would have no political role, and he, de Gaulle, would bring upon himself impotence and insult if he stayed, for he was not considered to be a member of the committee to shape the future government of France. He ended by saying that he would absent himself for a while; and during his eight days in the south, he determined his fashion of withdrawal. "To the people," says Jean Chauvel, "the shock appeared as abandonment."[3]

As we look back on it, we see that an era of Charles de Gaulle's life had closed. What he could do for the Empire in that first period of power he considered he had done. Probably the two most important colonial events in it were the Brazzaville Conference and the admission of black Africans to the Constituent Assembly. There is every reason to suppose that in that latter measure he was aware of the importance of what he was doing, even though Suret-Canale suggests that he and his councillors had not realized the probable effects.[4] De Gaulle wrote of the rise of nationalism, and he had spoken to the sultan of Morocco, the bey of Tunis, and the president of the United States, Harry Truman, of the changes that must come.[5] He had seen "the path" France must take. Did this mean, as yet, any radical change in his ideas? Probably not. If he had spoken all through the forties of independence and decolonization, as some members of his family have told the author, such a resolution of the difficulties must still have seemed very far off from the point of view of 1946. Even later, it would have been political suicide for him to speak of such matters in public. So, even though de Gaulle always had a habit of looking into the future,[6] when he took his first steps "into the Desert"—as his followers have called his years far from power—it seems probable that he could not have thought of the probable change as at all imminent.

Suret-Canale believes that de Gaulle's departure may have helped the rise of the popular democratic movement in France and her Empire, for the Leftist majority in the First Constituent Assembly was able to carry through a program of reforms. Would he not have wished for some reforms, at least, after what he had learned on his trips to Africa in 1940, 1942, and 1944? Suret-Canale's conclusion seems uncertain. Strikes by European professors began in Africa in December 1945, and were continued by African workmen, metallurgists, commercial employees, postal workers, and auxiliaries. They may have helped to make reform a necessity. By the end of March 1945 they had reached beyond their starting place at Dakar, into Guinea, the Ivory Coast, the Cameroons, and the Middle Congo.[7]

When the Assembly gathered itself together after the shock of de Gaulle's departure, it elected Félix Gouin, a Socialist, president of the Provisional Government of the Republic and Vincent Auriol, also a Socialist, president of the Constituent Assembly. This was in January 1946, during the constitution-making process. The new Constitutional Commission, already named, was composed of forty-two members, some from overseas; of those, only one or two were men of the black race. The commission began its task in earnest on January 18. The Overseas Commission, on which there were more Africans, was given a hearing on January 25.[8] On April 9, the Constitutional Commission presented its report to the Assembly. It was accepted, though by a narrow margin, because of the deep division between the MRP—the Popular Republicans (*Mouvement Républicain Populaire*)—and the Socialist-Communist groups. The vital points for the overseas world were that the preamble to the document of the Constitution contained a real Declaration of the Rights of Man. The declaration was longer than those of 1789 or 1795 and was divided into a section on liberties and one on social and economic rights, among them the rights to work and to aid, to enjoy culture and leisure, and to strike. The Constitution itself described a "regime of assembly." The Assembly would elect the president of the Republic, the prime minister, and the ministers. It would vote the laws and the budget. In short, it would manage the government. The powers of the president would be much reduced. He would preside over the Council meetings, and those of the Defense Council and the High Court, but he would not direct the government; nor would he have the right of pardon. There would be a Council of the French Union, but it would only examine laws sent to it, and the Assembly would have the last word.[9]

On May 5, 1946, the Constitution was put to the people and rejected. Apparently this was not because of the rather liberal articles on the French Union.[10] The reason for its defeat appeared to lie in French hatred for a regime of assembly, for such an arrangement appeared to the average Frenchman to give the Communists a possibility of seizing power. Its rejection made necessary the holding of another election to try again to set up a constitution that could pass the electorate. A date was set for June 2 to begin the new process.

However, the First Constituent Assembly was important, in spite of its failure to please the French people, for it gave relative satisfaction to the Africans. In an entirely constitutional form, by a law of April 11, 1946, promoted by Houphouet-Boigny of the Ivory Coast, now a delegate to the Constituent Assembly, it abolished forced labor and the *indigénat*. A law of April 13, 1946, stated that all overseas territories were to be represented in the national Assembly, and there would be a single college, including both sexes (and both races), for voting. Its Declaration of Rights was particularly important in clarifying what the Africans wanted: equal rights with the French, so that the civil status of a man could not bar him from his due powers. The speedy rejection of this Constitution was followed almost immediately, on May 7, by the "Lamine Guèye law"—named after the celebrated black lawyer and deputy from Senegal—that made all "subjects" into citizens. Of course, there was still omission of ordinances the overseas peoples would have liked to see included. No right of separation from France was mentioned; the Senate, as outlined, would apparently be controlled by colonialists, and the Assembly of the Union was only consultative. Above all, voting would still be by the double college system, giving far more power to the French *colons* in the first college than to the Africans in the second. Article 41 said that the Union must be "freely consented," and the fact that no definite structure was prescribed for the Union made evolution seem possible. Local assemblies in the different countries were to be elected by universal suffrage, and the French government would be represented in the Union by ministers resident, rather than by governors.[11]

It was, all in all, a centralist constitutional plan, for Article 40 proclaimed the French Republic "one and indivisible," and it made no specific plans for the colonies. Still, the French government had realized that something must be done. Marius Moutet, now minister of Overseas France, said late in March:

> It is the hour of decision. Either we give satisfaction to the legitimate aspirations of the peoples, or we must resign ourselves to seeing them pull away from us.
>
> They no longer want to be treated as minors, even by a benevolent but authoritative guide; they want to be treated as equals.

Then, says Suret-Canale, Moutet told the racist *colons* that by the restrictions they were digging their own graves, and he added:

> The brutal colonial fact, the fact of conquest, the imposition of one nation on other nations, the maintenance of sovereignty that rests only on force, is impossible today. The historic period of colonization has passed by.

The minister went on to point out that the "free consent" of the peoples to their association with France is indispensable, not only as a law of history but as a contractual obligation, to which France had already subscribed by signing the United Nations Charter in San Francisco.[12]

However, the attempt to carry all these advantages at once had failed by a margin of 10.6 million to 5.5 million. It makes one wonder whether the failure was not due to other factors besides the dislike of assembly government. Did General de Gaulle, now retired but still tremendously influential, have an effect on the people even before he had made his important speeches on the subject? The speeches would come in June, August, and September 1946, before the proposal for the second Constitution was voted on, but perhaps his ideas were known already in the spring. Suret-Canale, for example, says de Gaulle had already come out against the plan for the Constitution before he spoke in June, but it is not indicated where or when he did so.[13]

De Gaulle did not like the plan for the Constitution. He did not like a regime of power for an assembly, and he did not want presidential authority reduced to a merely "decorative function." He had said as early as September 1945, speaking at the seventy-fifth anniversary of the Republic, that the Third Republic's uncertainty and powerlessness to carry out executive and legislative action had created a state of political agitation, of party rivalry, of parliamentary groups, of personalities, by which the essential interests of the country tended to be clouded. That was one of the vices of the Third Republic.[14]

Of course, at this point de Gaulle may not have been too secure about the future of the French Union, for one of its states had already undergone a change of status. The "Republic of Vietnam," on March 6, 1946, after demanding independence, had finally signed a convention with the French authorities which recognized it as a free state, with its own government, parliament, army, and finances. It would be a part of an Indochinese Federation and of the French

Union. Negotiations would follow. When this instrument was signed, it seemed a logical consequence of the governmental declaration of March 24, 1945, concerning Indochina. To Lamine Guèye, an African delegate to the Assembly, the agreements of March 6, 1946, indicated additional difficulties rather than fewer. Rights and duties, meaning, and application were controversial. The Conference at Fontainebleau that summer of 1946 ended in failure, closing on September 10. Soon there were bloody confrontations at Hanoi and Haiphong, and, after that there seemed no way out. Many date the French disaster in Vietnam from that conference. [15]

The connection was close, for the struggle that began in 1945, when de Gaulle sent Leclerc, now a general, to Indochina to see that the country remained within the French community, had great influence on the formation of the French Union. The French government overestimated its power to control political change in Indochina, and to this was added the "frustrating confrontations" between the delegation of the Vietminh and France at the time of their conference at Fontainebleau. That meeting coincided with the reconsideration of the articles on the French Union by the Second Constituent Assembly in the summer and autumn of 1946. The failure of the conference made the French feel that the future of their country as a great power was at stake. General de Gaulle insisted on French authority—on imposing unity with Vietnam from above, for the "shrinking" of the French world must be halted. The presence of the Vietminh delegation forced the African deputies to take a more radical view of their relationship with France, and the fact of the presence of the conference so close at hand, and so fraught with danger for the future, forced the Assembly as a whole to confront the problem of the French Union more realistically than they had before those last days, when it became time to present the completed constitution to the French nation. [16]

Others beside General de Gaulle were worried about what was happening in the constitution-making process, especially the French *colons* in the Ivory Coast and the Cameroons, although they viewed the events from a different standpoint. They called their committee the "Estates General" after the body so named that dealt with grievances during the French Revolution. They proclaimed themselves in favor of a federal French Union with a president, a high council, and an assembly. Representatives from the Associated States and from the French government met with them. In their plans there was no mention of native representation in the French Parliament, and they claimed, too, that it would be impossible to mix French citizenship with citizenship of the Union. French citizenship must not be extended to all the inhabitants of the Empire, most of whom would not understand the meaning of it or its greatness. It must be restricted to those who could understand it. Then they protested against the "Intergroup" of the Second Constituent Assembly, formed by the Africans to protect their rights. French sovereignty was still necessary, and the higher interests of the various countries must not be forgotten, nor the aspirations of the Africans for a "French peace." The government should see that such things were remembered.

Meantime, in Paris, other critical groups—the Colonial Union and the

Colonial Institute—merged into a *Comité Centrale de l'Empire Français*, becoming the *Comité Centrale de la France d'Outre-Mer*, by the end of 1946. Even in 1945, they were complaining that the *colons* had developed the countries of Africa, and therefore they should be the only groups allowed to give opinions on questions of the colonies. Apparently, this outburst was due to alarm caused by the preparatory commission of the Assembly. Others joined in, notably the editorial personnel of a new magazine, the *Marchés Coloniaux*. They tried to make some concessions to safeguard the vital interests of the big French business firms in Africa. But as time went on and the first Constitution was rejected, the magazine became more open in its opposition to liberal change, and René Moreux, the chief editor of *Marchés Coloniaux,* remarked that the same voting bulletin was given to a negress carrying a tray as to a Parisian working woman, and the same bulletin went to a Soudanese sorcerer as to Joliot-Curie, the celebrated scientist. A colonial manifesto was published under the joint signature of the Committee of the French Empire, the Academy of Colonial Sciences, the Maritime and Colonial League, the Committees of French Africa, French Asia and French Oceania, the *Marchés Coloniaux,* and the *Merchant Marine Journal.* The manifesto said that the Constitution made the French people second-class citizens, and the white race inferior to the black races. It also objected to the UN Charter for putting into practice integration instead of autonomy. The groups involved did not mind secession if they could control the governments of those who seceded (!). They claimed that the populations overseas were completely satisfied with their lot and did not want citizenship or universal suffrage, and that all the trouble came from international revolutionaries. Finally, they set forth their own ideas of a constitution. They would provide ways in which people could become citizens; there would be autonomy in the territories, elections by double colleges, and an electoral law which would take into account the degree of evolution of the Africans. Only French citizens would be eligible for election to posts. Suret-Canale says that those holding these opinions were greatly aided by de Gaulle's speech at Bayeux.[17]

General de Gaulle made this, his first public speech of any importance since his resignation, at Bayeux on June 16, 1946. It was given before discussions on the second plan for the Constitution had really begun. At Bayeux, he said the new Constitution must provide for three balanced powers: a National Assembly, a Second Chamber "to give a chance for the great activities of the country to be heard," and a Grand Council of the Union, composed of the Second Chamber and of delegates elected from the membership of overseas assemblies. The Council of the Union would be qualified to discuss laws and problems of the countries of the Union, such as budgets, reports on national defense, economy, communications. The holder of the executive power would be president of France and of the Union as well, and he would be elected by a much enlarged college. His influence must be preponderant, for he would be an arbiter to maintain the continuity of political action, and he would help in political difficulties. He would name the ministers, especially the premier, who were to direct the policy and work of the government. The president would act in moments of grave confusion to aid the public in making known its will.[18]

In these proposals, de Gaulle was clearly intent on preserving French sovereignty. However, he did not mention other points in the colonialist manifesto, such as secession—and subsequent control of the country that seceded—or autonomy, or the electoral laws. Thus it is hard to find in the Bayeux speech a close parallel or any great help to the conservative cause such as Suret-Canale suggests. At another time, de Gaulle attacked the famous *Titre* VIII, the colonial section of the new Constitution, and also the principle of self-determination, since the Constitution ought to put the rights of France beyond question. Perhaps Suret-Canale was thinking of the objectives General de Gaulle set later, for apparently de Gaulle's Bayeux speech worried the Africans. In it he had proposed federalism for the more advanced colonies but merely rule by presidential decree for the colonies of tropical Africa. By midsummer the Africans had formed an "Intergroup," with Lamine Guèye as president, because of the *Etats Generaux* and their rigid requirements. They knew the era of good feeling was over and that the Estates General wanted to "save the Empire." They wanted to lose as little as possible of what the first plan for the Constitution had promised them, and they were much aware of their danger from the colonial lobby.[19]

The chief subjects of discussion at the Second Constituent Assembly were the single or double college for elections, the methods of election, federalism, citizenship and representation, freedom of choice in joining the Union, and the possibility of permitting the various states to change their status from territory to associated state. On every one of these questions the Africans had strong feelings.[20] Yet, to sum it all up, for the first time in history the native section of a great colonial empire was allowed to express itself freely, even though the black delegates were not allowed to obtain all the advantages they had been promised in the first draft of the Constitution. Finally, the enabling laws were so arranged that the single college was permitted only in West Africa and Togo. The African element, however, was able to obtain adoption of the project for *Titre* VIII, the section dealing with the overseas territories. It condemned systems of colonization based on annexation, conquest, or domination of the overseas countries. It rejected unilateral sovereignty over colonized peoples and recognized their liberty to govern themselves democratically. Since the French Union must be "freely consented" by the states involved, in twenty years its members should have the option of keeping or giving up their bonds with France. The territories also demanded that the Constitution of the Union should be referred to a special assembly of states, where they would have representation proportional to their populations. They claimed the right within twenty years to decide among three alternatives: independence; federation with France; or integration with the French Republic. They called for a third constituent assembly with deputies elected by universal suffrage, who would represent an equal number of votes. This project called forth a violent outburst in the Assembly.[21]

There were other criticisms. Edouard Herriot had become fearful of what might happen. He was now far to the Right, though in the Third Republic he had begun as a Radical Socialist, then belonged to a middle of the road party. On August 27, 1946, Herriot said in the Constituent Assembly that if French citizenship were given to all the nationals of the overseas territories, it would make France the colony of her colonies.[22] He also made a reference to the Brazzaville Conference, but Félix Tchicaya, a black delegate of the Middle Congo and Gabon, countered his remarks by saying that Brazzaville had now been outdistanced. The French government was becoming worried, too. They had promised not to interfere with the work of the Commission on the Constitution, but apparently that promise was tucked away in a file where it could easily be forgotten, and at one point the minister of France Overseas, Marius Moutet, came before the Constitutional Commission with a text considerably different from the one the commission had proposed.[23]

A long discussion followed, in which the African delegates in the commission pointed out the contradictions and complications of the government's project, and how it would affect their countries. The new text implied that there would be a double college for elections, an extremely sore point. It reduced their representation to almost nothing, since the first college elected most of the representatives. The result would make them second-class citizens. Moutet replied that the government would not go back on its decision as to the single college.[24] This was scarcely satisfactory to the black representatives. They thought the change was due to the Estates General's propaganda.[25]

A little later, Ferhat Abbas, the Algerian leader, said that colonialism must not be constitutionalized, and another deputy, Bétolaud, of the Republican party of the Liberation, replied by defending the colonial work of the Third Republic, for which he said he would not ask forgiveness. The African delegates "rose against" the government's text, protesting that all men were equal before God, and the blood of a black or yellow man was equivalent to that of a white man. They held that the Republic was one and indivisible. It was composed of territories where the same law was applicable everywhere and for all—let no one speak of a French Union that did not abide by that principle. The *rapporteur,* Paul Coste-Floret, urged that the text of the government be used in order to make the metropole respected in the Union. He threatened to bring the various questions to a public debate if the government's text was not followed. He would accept only editing.[26] While the government's project for *Titre* VIII, the colonial section, was discussed, the African delegates walked out of the Chamber and sent in their resignation, returning only after a concession had been made. The concession took out of the Constitution the question of the double or single college, though it left it in the electoral law, except for legislative elections. This maintained the double college everywhere, except in Senegal, for local elections. When Tchicaya, the deputy of the Middle Congo and Gabon, managed to get the single college approved for Equatorial Africa, the colonial minister, Moutet, got the Assembly to withdraw its permission. Yet, when the wordy battle in the Assembly was over, most of the overseas deputies either abstained from voting or voted to accept the Constitution as it was. "They were angry and disappointed, resenting the part played by the Socialist Overseas minister." It was better than that under which they had previously lived. Refusing it might lead downhill instead of up. They said from the beginning that the plan of the Constitution was only a starting point.[27]

While the argument was going on, de Gaulle made two other statements about the Constitution before it came up for a vote. On August 27, 1946, on the same day that Herriot spoke, and in answer to the Intergroup's project, de Gaulle made a declaration to the press, saying:

> The Constitution should affirm and impose the solidarity with France of all the overseas territories. In particular it should put beyond question the pre-eminent responsibility and consequently the rights of France in that which concerns the foreign policy of all the French Union, the defense of all its territories, the common communications, and the economic measures that concerned all of it. . . . every really national territorial entity must be organized so that it would develop according to its own character, whether it was already a State bound to France by a Treaty, whether it might become a territory that would enjoy an autonomy proportionate to its development, whether it might be incorporated in the French Republic. Finally institutions of a federal character should be created, common to the Metropole and to the Overseas Territories: a President of the French Union, and a Council of the Union, and Ministers whose activities would be federal.
>
> No doubt the Constitution would not be able to regulate immediately in detail the situation of each territory or the organization of federal power. But it should give the power to an institution which after a fixed period of time could set up projects of laws for the necessary organization.
>
> This would naturally be a Council of the French Union, consisting of the Council of the Republic in addition to delegates elected by local overseas assemblies, except, naturally for those already bound to France by a Treaty.[28]

In addition to this explanation of Herriot's constitutional ideas, de Gaulle said that, with the territories which she had opened up to civilization, France was a great power. Without them, she would risk not having that power. So a new and precise plan must arrange for the relations between the metropole and all the races to which she was bound. But the Constitution as proposed did not do this, he said. It would lead to agitation, dislocation, and finally domination by foreign countries. There was nothing constructive in it.[29]

Again, at Epinal on September 29, he gave voice to much the same ideas, pointing out that "to us it seems necessary that the French Union should be a Union and should be French," and again insisting that the overseas peoples must develop according to their own national characters and should have the opportunity of sharing in the administration of their own affairs "to whatever degree their social progress permits."[30]

For de Gaulle, if the second effort was no better than the first, it was checkmate for a Constitution that he would approve. He predicted a rudderless Union. There would be no central federal agency, no supreme arbiter, no guardian—only a chief of state "for show" who was not destined to preside over a useful organization. Certainly, he wanted the sovereignty of France secure in the Empire. Even later than this, he was saying that the authority of France must be maintained.[31] But General de Gaulle had approved the granting of far more autonomy to Indochina, though he may have wanted it to come more slowly. After all, what does autonomy mean? *Larousse* says it is the freedom to govern oneself by one's own laws.[32] But, in de Gaulle's parlance, it meant self-rule in a federation, where the federating power retained authority over foreign affairs, economy, defense, and communications—a rather large slice out of the freedom pie. The two ideas are not the same. If de Gaulle had been in power, would he have found a way to safeguard the sovereignty of France and still give more freedom and authority to the native populations? As things were—*selon les contingences*—he wanted, above all, to keep French authority safe. So he went on fighting the Constitution as it was planned. On October 9, just before the referendum that would ratify the Constitution, he announced that if the project were adopted, people would see the present system as an illusion; the parties would dispose of everything as they wished, and without any counterweight from all the powers of the state. "The consequences would be powerlessness, anarchy, and, soon, dictatorship." After its adoption, he called the system "absurd and out of date."[33] He was opposed to "this parody of a republic and this rising day of servitude to which certain people were leading France."[34] So he came out of his silence to bear witness uselessly to his opposition to the plan.

Of course, much of de Gaulle's fire and fury was directed not only at the overseas plans but at the general framework of government provided by the Constitution. It was approved in spite of him on October 13 and promulgated on October 27, 1946. It had no Declaration of Rights such as the first plan had had, only a short *préambule* giving certain principles of the French Republic, which was to be "indivisible, secular, democratic and social." It would give equality to men and women in the vote; right of asylum for the persecuted; the rights to work, to form unions, to strike, and to participate in management of enterprises; the right of the state to nationalize monopolistic enterprises; the rights to instruction and to leisure. It declared the establishment of a French Union with its overseas peoples. Its ruling power was to be a Parliament made up of two chambers—an Assembly and a Council. It would be elected by proportional representation—which was later seen to be one of the causes of its failure. It would have a Second Chamber elected by indirect vote of local bodies—really nothing but a "chamber of reflection." The Assembly was the source of executive power for the president, who was there only to preside over certain bodies and to exercise the right of pardon. There were strict and complicated rules about ministerial crises, in an attempt to make them rare—in which, of course, the writers of the Constitution did not succeed.[35]

The Constitution embodied certain of de Gaulle's ideas for the organization of the French Union, but it did not really create a federal state, for there was no upper organ of decision. The Assembly would be merely consultative, and the

High Council only a diplomatic meeting with very little power. So, the changes of 1946 were mostly indefinite and not federative; indeed, as Chetrit and Timsit said, "The Constitution was a tendency towards assimilation with a window open on independence." *Titre* VIII, the section devoted to the Union, said France would maintain its sovereignty over the Union countries within the Republic, although the preamble had given them the possibility of reaching independence. It said:

> Faithful to her traditional mission, France proposes to lead the peoples of whom she has assumed charge to a state of freedom in which they administer themselves and conduct their own affairs democratically; rejecting any form of rule based on arbitrary power, she guarantees to all equal access to the public service, and the individual or collective exercise of the rights and liberties proclaimed or confirmed above.[36]

This section was "the window on independence," but it gave no date for reaching freedom and no suggestion as to how to open the window. Could the countries concerned have confidence that the opening would be possible? The Africans said from the beginning that the plan was only a starting point.

After one more blast, on November 1, dealing with the subject of elections, in which de Gaulle said the Constitution was absurd and out of date, he was silent about the new government until March of 1947. He had said his say on "the parody of a Republic" and the dawn of servitude "to which the leaders were exposing France."[37] Hope for France must have died within him for a time; or was he merely feeling his own lack of power?

While de Gaulle did not mention the word *federation* publicly at this time, the question of federalism or a federation was becoming more and more important. Such words had been in many peoples' minds for a considerable time. In 1945, Jean de La Roche and Jean Gottmann had written a long book about *La Fédération Française: Contacts et Civilisations d'Outre-Mer.* The authors had hoped that the metropole would even then "give colonial peoples their chances in spite of many obstructions." They saw an opportunity then to pursue the *mission civilisatrice* by giving the colonial populations the famous freedoms to a degree that other nations had not yet attained for their metropolitan populations. After all, the colonies had shown comprehension in the war and had given proof of national unity. France, they said, was nothing other than a federation that had attained its apogee. But, they added, there is no formula for what ought to be done.[38] They did not trouble to write out a detailed version of what the *federation* ought to be in the future; nor did they define the word *federation*.

A little later (1946), Léopold Senghor asked for a federation on the scale of the French Union, to last until complete independence could come, and he pursued the idea of a plan that would give equality to the overseas citizens. The French politicians were not interested, and he abandoned the project for the time, together with the hope for independence, thinking that his wish for a "French Imperial Community" was not a practical possibility. Senghor always had a distinct ability to adapt himself to political realities. Still, he continued to think of a "closely knit federation, Eurafrica." Thus until May 1958 Senghor advocated Africa as part of a Federal French Republic. Then, however, seeing the changes planned for the new Fifth Republic, he began to speak again of independence, and decided that only a *confederation* could solve African problems. He advocated this as a member of the Constitutional Committee, but the committee remained federalist.[39]

Perhaps the best definition of a *federation* is given by *Petit Larousse,* which says that it is "a political system in which several independent states each abandon part of their sovereignty to the profit of a superior authority," also noting that in the French Revolution a *federation* was an association formed "to struggle against the enemies of Liberty."[40] The *Larousse Universel* says that a *federation* might be made up of societies that allied themselves together, working for a common end.[41] But was the dominant state in such an association able to withdraw some of the privileges granted to the composing states, as some had suggested, or was the federation to be more akin to the American type, in which only a revision of the Constitution by the representatives of all the states could alter the initial form? It is not easy to be sure how different nations thought of it.

The word *confederation* has varied definitions. *Petit Larousse* thinks it is a "transitory form" ending in dissolution or transformation into a federal state.[42] But the *Larousse Universel* says that a *confederation* is a group of states with an organ that decides common interests, leaving a certain sovereignty to its members.[43] And Webster says that a *confederacy* is a compact for mutual support, while a *confederation* is merely a league or state of being confederated.[44] So these three language authorities do not agree on what the powers of such a group must be—and everything about a federation or a confederation is vague. We are therefore thrown back on what we already believe—namely, that a *federation* groups together states of which the central member has considerable powers of direction and action, whereas a *confederation* is a looser organization in which the dominant power is less important. We have seen that de Gaulle did not like the Constitution because it had no supreme arbiter, no guardian, and no federal agency, so he must have been thinking then, in 1946, of a federation on his own rather authoritarian terms.

De Gaulle, however, spoke of a federal union several times between 1946 and 1948, saying that the French Union was not right in its present form and must be a whole, federal in character, and constituted around France, which would assume its responsibilities, especially for public order, foreign affairs, defense, communications, and economic policies. It was clear that such a federal union would remain under the direction of the French government. It was to restrain the growing forces of nationalism, said Chetrit and Timsit, that the General thought a revision of the bonds between the French State and the territories was necessary. There should be an attempt to satisfy the desires of the territories, but there was no allusion to complete independence, only the idea that the countries of Africa must learn to administer themselves. In 1953, the words *association* and *federation* were key words, but after 1953, until his return to power, the General did not refer again to either *federation* or *association*.[45]

However we may analyze the differing ideas about federalism, it is clear that General de Gaulle had the strictest idea about it of anyone. The Community that he set up in 1958 was essentially a federal government in his mind, and it claimed the right of the federal state to control the Community through the intermediary of an executive council of prime ministers, and one other minister from each state. This control included all that related to currency, foreign affairs, defense, diplomacy, common economic and financial policy, justice, higher education, strategic raw materials, transport, and telecommunications—though who would be on the executive council for these powers was left undetermined. In view of the lack of definition and of allocation of functions, this constituted a massive collection of powers for the French government to exercise if it so chose. There seems to this author to have been such tight control and such constraints on the part of the federalist central state, now called the Community (by Philibert Tsiranana's suggestion), that it could scarcely hope to succeed in its plans as then specified, or at least, not for long. Almost at once, during de Gaulle's trip around Africa at the end of August, only a few weeks after the first draft of the *Communauté* was written, the network of the restraints began to give way.

14

In the Desert

> The period following his departure is that in which, no
> longer exercising political power, he expressed with
> clarity and intransigence the deepest currents of
> Gaullism.
>
> —Chetrit and Timsit

Early in March 1947 de Gaulle told some of his intimates that he wanted to
throw himself again into the struggle and create a new movement. Possibly, as
Paul-Marie de La Gorce suggests, the real break with the Fourth Republic had
come in the previous September,[1] after the declaration to the press of August
27, 1946, and the speech at Epinay on September 29 in the same year. On these
occasions de Gaulle had denounced the principles of the new Constitution.
The bone of his relationship with the Fourth Republic had been broken clear
through by the speech at Bruneval on March 30, 1947. He had spoken then of
the "voices of decision, of decadence" that "had been able to cover for a time
the voice of national interest." He added, "The tide rises and falls
back. Perhaps it is in the nature of things that a clear and great effort should
be followed by dark gropings." It was no time "to vegetate in the shadows";
the day would come when "throwing aside the sterile games and reforming
the badly built frame in which the nation has lost its way and the state
has disqualified itself, the immense mass of the French will reassemble for
France."[2] Two days later, an emissary in the shape of Premier Jean Ramadier
came to see General de Gaulle, telling him he would henceforth be deprived of
military honors whenever he took part in a nonofficial occasion, and that what
he said would not be broadcast over the state radio. The parties evidently
thought the General was threatening a *coup d'état*. From that time forward, de
Gaulle's new movement, the *Rassemblement du Peuple Français* (the Assemblage of the French People), was in existence in fact, if not in law. Indeed, in
his speeches that spring, the General predicted the catastrophe of the Fourth
Republic, the ruin of the French Union, and the coming of social disorders.[3] He
had begun to prophesy the future again. Jacques Fauvet notes that in advance
of history, the General said, "The French will react when they become afraid of
losing Algeria."[4] Small wonder that, given this open scorn of what they had
done and were doing, the government would try to limit the General's
activities. The tact required to tell him this must have been enormous!

From now on, General de Gaulle used the words *unity* or *national unity*
more and more frequently. Sometimes it was in connection with the Commu-

nists, who he believed were "separatists" and therefore not really a part of the national community. France could not be France with such cancers in her heart. Thus the keystone of the arch of Gaullism became national unity.[5]

To explain what he proposed to do with his new movement, and to set up its structure, de Gaulle spoke at Strasbourg on April 7, 1947. The *Rassemblement*, he said, is composed of "companions" who have freely responded to the appeal made to the French people to insure common action. It ought to extend to the metropole and to the French Union as well. He said that the French Union was

> to lead each one of the entities that yesterday composed our Empire to develop on its own account, in its own frame, for its own profit, to cause it to benefit economically, socially, morally, intellectually as far as its capacities would permit. The Union was to associate each member state with the Metropole, in conditions conforming to the degree of its development and in accordance with the treaties concluded with France; but, in keeping with the experience, the wisdom, the authority of France, should care for public order, external defense and the economic activities that concerned all the communities. Such was the task that must be accomplished.[6]

De Gaulle noted, too, that Africa was becoming conscious of her condition and emerging from her lethargy. The political parties, he remarked, do not agree on anything; nor do they agree on colonial policy. Of course, he referred only to the political parties in France. Unity, he thought, had to be the way to proceed to national renewal. He wanted to restore to France her independence, so that she could play her role on the international scene and point out the path of liberty again—for France, restored within herself, could recover her greatness. She would serve as an element of equilibrium and stability to reduce the pretensions of the great powers and to bring back peace. For this purpose, she must keep the French Union. "To lose it would be a humiliation that could even cost France its independence," for she would lose her rank as a great power. So it was necessary to be united and strong and to keep the Union.[7] The RPF was the force to make the new France.

During the year of 1947, de Gaulle made two speeches on Algeria. In Paris, he spoke of what had been done there and what was still needed. But the most interesting point was that the fact that Algeria belonged to France must not be questioned.[8]

On October 12, 1947, in Algiers, he spoke of better conditions for the future; the separation of Algeria from France would lead to decadence. The RPF, a great new movement, was essential for the renewal of France, and it would constitute a geographic bond between France and the African territories. Algeria was considered to be an integral part of France, with a relationship closer than those of the other African colonies.[9]

For the first few months of 1948, the *Rassemblement* rose fast. Had there been elections then, its membership would have been in the majority. But suddenly it began to decline, possibly because of the hostility of the Socialists and Popular Republicans to de Gaulle. The trade unions were also against the movement, and there were some conflicts within it, as well as bad management in letting important committee chairmanships escape to the already existing parties. The apogee of the whole great effort came at a meeting in Marseilles in April 1948. After that, there were manifestations during the year, but gradually the current that had been flowing toward the RPF diminished, and by 1949 it was in full retreat. From 1952, de Gaulle's representatives waned in loyalty to the cause. By 1955, de Gaulle was saying goodbye to the journalists. "Such was the bitter end of a great hope."[10]

De Gaulle had said at Marseilles that the French Union must be a whole, federal in character, and constituted around France, which would assume its responsibilities, especially for foreign affairs, defense, communications, and economic policies. The system already set up was not really an organization of a French Union.[11]

As year followed year without the smallest chance of a return to power, General de Gaulle seemed to sink deeper and deeper into the Desert of Hopelessness. He rarely spoke in public, though in a press conference on March 16, 1950, he told the soldiers of France fighting for Vietnam that what they were doing was necessary to maintain the presence of France in the Union.[12] In the Bois de Boulogne, on May 1, 1952, he added some phrases about the irreversible character of the movement toward self-determination and independence that was growing in the Empire, and he pointed out that France should help it to unroll. The renewal of the French Union would bring France back among the great powers; but the Union must be organized in such a manner that the territories would find it to their interest to be a part of the plan. Every country must have its own statute, its own character, and its own traditions. It must appear as an entity among the states.[13]

But if de Gaulle remained firm about requiring in his planning a very supple federal system for those countries that were merely "waiting for their independence," he nevertheless felt, too, that a continuing evolution was imposed by present conditions. The French government must see to it that the changes were wrought by France, so that they might not be carried out in defiance of her.[14] He did not speak of complete independence, only of leading the overseas countries to administer themselves. That was all that was necessary. France would continue to take care of defense and diplomacy for the Union. After all, at that time, the only country asking for complete independence was Indochina; the others wanted only internal autonomy. It was a preparatory stage, so France must see that the situation did not grow worse. In any case, it was clear that the continuing evolution was irreversible. Destiny had been marked out, and by accepting its requirements, the effects could be controlled. Each territory must have the reforms that would enable it to take a growing part in its own affairs. On his trip through Africa, in March 1953, de Gaulle spoke again of binding the territories to France as part of an eager and powerful union on the scale of the world of today. The two words *association* and *federation* were key words. He held to that idea, though with the new circumstances that happened frequently, he had to change the means that should be used.[15]

It was really in 1953, after the demise of the RPF, that the "Crossing of the Desert" (as André Malraux has called it) began. After that time, de Gaulle did not mention the Union in his public speeches.[16]

De Gaulle did not arrive openly, in speech or in writing, at the idea of complete independence for the countries of the Empire while he walked in the Desert. He saw Indochina force her way out of the Union and both Tunisia and Morocco become independent between 1954 and 1956, after short terms of autonomy; and in the British section of Africa, Ghana became both self-governing and entirely free from Great Britain in 1957. Was it true that this was "the most important event in modern African history," as Aristide Zolberg says? No doubt it seemed so to the Africans, for it was the first state in Africa to achieve complete independence. For the Europeans, after the granting of freedom to the Far Eastern countries and the North African ones, it may only have seemed another warning straw in the wind. It was clear, however, almost immediately after General de Gaulle's return to power, at the end of May 1958, that he had done a great deal of thinking during his exile regarding what should be done about the Empire. This would be the final stage in the progression of his thought. The presence of the Union could enlarge Europe and would bring about a sort of equilibrium between France and Germany—the neighbor that had overrun her three times within a century. And France, because of her geographical position, would act as a pivot between Africa and Europe. He still would prefer to retain the Empire. What he said then, however, was significant: "Politics is nothing other than the art of realities." Time and events would do the rest. Chetrit and Timsit, writing in 1962, were at that time almost the only chroniclers of the period as far as de Gaulle's thought is concerned. They end their consideration of de Gaulle's mental processes in the Desert by saying that all through his solitude he was rethinking his conceptions and his principles—and it was always done in view of the interests of France.[17] France would have to come before Africa in his mind.

How many conclusions de Gaulle arrived at during his years in the Desert cannot be known. Whom did he see and what did he say to them? No secretary was present—in general—and the houses of important people were not "bugged" in those days. At first, there was a belief that he saw but few people—except, perhaps, on his weekly trips to Paris, where he kept an office at 5, rue de Solférino, close to the French political center, the *Chambre des Députés,* now called the *Assemblée Nationale.* The bare little room at number 5, all tan and dark wood with dull reddish curtains, the plain brown wooden table-desk, with two chairs in front of it and two in front of the mantelpiece, give no hint of what went on there, though it has been kept as he left it when he returned to power. But the author has met so many people that he saw during those years, and they refer to so many others, that it appears to be correct to say that while there were only a favored few whom he saw regularly, those whom he saw in Paris, or even at Colombey, once or twice during those long dry years were very many indeed.

In early June 1958, immediately after his accession to power as prime minister of France, General de Gaulle flew to Algeria, which, because of the war in progress there since 1954, had to be dealt with first. Having begun what he hoped to do there, he then speedily took up the question of Black Africa. This leads one to believe that his thinking had been done before the threatened putsch of the "paras," on May 13, 1958, sparked his return to political life. Indeed, in the twelve years of his absence from power, de Gaulle must have followed the events taking place in the world with acute interest, and sometimes with agony of mind. Of those concerned with the overseas territories and associated states after his retirement in 1946, one of the first of which he heard was doubtless the great rebellion of 1947 on the island of Madagascar. We have good evidence that he was well informed. None other than Germaine Tillion, that remarkable observer of customs and events in Algeria, who went to Colombey to see General de Gaulle at various times, has borne witness to the fact that he was exceedingly well briefed on many subjects, and not only on Algeria.[18] So, undoubtedly, he knew about the holocaust on the Great Red Island of Madagascar.

Who planned and gave the signal for the outbreak of the revolt there, on March 29, 1947? What were its causes? There are a good many people, French and Malagasy, who think they know. Some of them probably do, but a definite statement by a historian does not seem possible, for the accounts about the dreadful happenings there that year differ widely, and many documents are still unavailable.

The Great Red Island, so named from the color of its soil (also sometimes called the Polynesian Island from the origin of its people, or the Island of the Moon from its legends) contains such a variety of peoples and of opinions that you can hear nearly anything about it. Some liken the land to the "imprint of a giant's left foot in the sand" and will tell you that it has a harsh, bitter terrain, for over 40 percent of its surface has been denuded by erosion that has caused great gullies nearly everywhere. These desert spaces were created by too much burning over by the inhabitants, and grazing by too many cattle has added to them.[19] The island's crops were varied: coffee, vanilla, rice, sugar, manioc, corn, potatoes, and many others. Yet in spite of its devastated conditon, it was still largely dependent on agricultural production. The island had been definitively under France since 1896 and was a member of the French Union.

The people of Madagascar are as varied as the country. There are about 52,000 French, 7,000 other non-Asiatics, 13,250 Indians, 8,900 Chinese, 40,000 from the Comoro Islands. The rest, 5,536,000, are native Malagasy, divided into about 20 ethnic groups. Of these, the Hovas, or Merinas (Merne to the French)—about 1,424,000 of them—are the ruling class, living in the highlands and dominating the island before the coming of the French.[20] The people on the coast resented the Hovas. They still do. All of these divisions may have influenced the rebellion.

Claude Bourdet, a journalist of lands, peoples, and opinions, wrote a long preface to Maître Pierre Stibbe's book on the rebellion of 1947. He defends those imprisoned or executed for their share in the rebellion, giving a long list of causes, divided into those that were immediate and those that were more permanent.[21] The permanent causes of trouble, according to Bourdet, were economic. Referring to the bulletin of a missionary group, he says that the rebellion began on the east coast, a region that had suffered from exactions by the Vichy government, and later, too, there was trouble, for it is said that some of the Gaullist authorities exacted even more from the people than Vichy had done. On the east coast, in the coffee region, abuse by the *colons* had been worse because plantation managers economized on the workers' wages to reduce their own costs. The Europeans of the big companies there seemed unable to see that the interests of the people did not always coincide with their own. For example, peasants who sold rice had to buy back enough for their own consumption at black-market prices. The Europeans knew little of the Malagasy people, in proof of which Bourdet quotes Gide, who said that the less intelligent the Europeans were, the more they thought the Africans stupid; and, says Bourdet, the lighter the African skins, the more racist were the Europeans. In Madagascar, as elsewhere, these conditions in the twentieth century produced, in 1915, a movement of nationalism, abortive and possibly merely a student exploit, though it was repressed with excessive thoroughness. After 1945, there were intensive difficulties, for the aspiration toward independence was everywhere.[22]

The immediate cause of the rebellion, Bourdet thinks, was the existence of several radical secret societies, among them the PA.NA.MA. (*Parti National Malgache*) and the JINA, both of these nationalist movements planning to transform the political condition of the island by force. The JINA was a term used as a password and for a secret network which evoked the irreversible and sacred character of the promise given in religious traditional rituals to pursue the goal of liberation. The exact meaning is not understood even by Jacques Tronchon, a specialist on the subject of the revolt of 1947. However, the society appears to have had the purpose of training the young from an ideological standpoint. There is no proof that foreigners were involved in the rebellion, nor is there proof that these societies had started the revolt, as was rumored at the time. The police did nothing to prevent violence. Did they know about it and let it begin on purpose? One of the leaders of a secret society, Samuel Rakotondrabé, was put to death in haste before the trial of the others, those accused of starting the rebellion, took place. Some people thought that it was done to prevent the real origin of the rebellion from being known, but there is no proof of that either.[23]

There were also new political parties to reckon with. On January 2, 1946, a group of Malagasy met in a restaurant in Paris, on the street of the Montagne-Sainte-Geneviève. They swore on a handful of earth from Madagascar that they would consecrate their lives to the independence of their "Great Island." The name chosen for the group was the *Mouvement Démocratique de la Rénovation Malgache* (Democratic Movement for the Renewal of Madagascar). The movement took an office in Tananarive a month later, and Jacques Rabemananjara drew up its statutes. He was later foreign minister of the

The palace of the last Merina rulers of Madagascar. It
stands on a hill dominating the city of Tanarive.

country, from independence to the recent changeover of 1973. His manifesto of
1946, however, was an indictment of the white man:

> We do not pardon the White Man for utilizing the art of dialectics with such a
> strange subtlety that he finds it natural for another man in love with liberty and
> independence to live submissively, even with gratitude, under a regime that he, the
> White Man, abhors with all his soul, not precisely because he is a White Man, but
> simply because of the dignity of man.

The manifesto also asked independence for the country, adding:

> Because they have been beaten once, must the Malagasy be judged unworthy of
> recovering their sovereignty? To exact of a people that it must renounce the idea of
> independence, is, to speak true, to exact of it that it must resign itself to suicide. It is
> to exact that it must dry up the sap of its nobility, the source of its strength: its soul.[24]

The program of the MDRM demanded equality for all the Malagasy people,
and claimed that it was the defender of the poor and the Malagasy workers
against foreign capitalism. In a short time, the party had 200,000 adherents. It
became a mass party, well organized. It had attempted to gain its freedom,

during the First Constituent Assembly in Paris in 1945, but it was not successful. There were some violent attacks in the Malagasy press against France at that time. Some of the Malagasy wanted to remain in the French Union; some did not. Vietnam helped them by pointing the way toward independence. The leaders looked to the Anglo-Saxon countries for help and even to the Communists,[25] though except perhaps for one member of their group, they were not Marxists or Stalinists. They merely needed help. Still, by the violence of their anti-French position, seen in the speeches of their representatives and in their extremist writings, they managed to create an atmosphere of hate around them, unknown hitherto in Madagascar. The differences between the separatists and the parties who wanted a more moderate evolution led to a fratricidal rebellion.

The French tried to organize the country in political districts so as to prevent the Hova, the inland aristocrats, from controlling everything. The party opposed to the MDRM, the PADESM (*Parti des Déshérités de Madagascar—*The Disinherited of Madagascar), was supported by the French, who trusted in the loyalty of the coastal people who composed it. So they played the card of the PADESM, which did not ask immediate independence and showed gratitude to France.

At midnight on March 29, 1947, the rebellion burst forth "like a thunder-clap."[26] A camp of riflemen at Moramanga was attacked by 2,000 men armed with light spears, axes, and long knives.[27] In other places administration buildings were set on fire, and a few French people were tortured and murdered. At Diego Suarez, in the north, an armed band captured all the automatic arms in a depot and then fled. About 150 French died there. Most of the trouble was between the east coast and the high plateau that runs the length of the island, though some say it was also in the south.[28] In all, the rebellion covered about one-sixth of the island.[29] On April 2 a state of siege was proclaimed in a dozen districts. In May the rebels took the post of Vohilava, massacring all the garrison; and even up to September, the rebels encircled several of the important Malgache cities of the island. By October the French, with reinforcements, used Gallieni's "spot of oil" technique to contain the rebellion. The chiefs were taken, and the remaining rebels fled into the Great Eastern Forest, carrying with them some of the terrorized population—who presently died for lack of nourishment. Even the sorcerers, of whom Madagascar had many, were used in that war. They told their flocks that the spirits of the ancestors wanted the war, and had promised them that they would be invulnerable.

A great number of atrocities were committed on both sides.[30] Deschamps says that the rebels cut French *colons* in pieces, violated the women and put them to the sword, and massacred the children. The government used harsh repressive measures; they put to death prisoners in a train at Moramanga, as well as in some of the prisons, and executed some in the bush without trial.[31]

There had been warnings of trouble, but, of course, no one believed them. The overseas minister of France, Marius Moutet, in September 1946, had wired his staff on the island about the MDRM. One account of this wire says that it told the administrators to fight the party in every possible way.[32] But Alain Spacensky, a recent historian, says that Moutet's telegram merely told them to watch the party.[33] Perhaps it was not by chance that the revolt broke out on the eve of the elections of the Council of the Republic, and a few days before the first congress of the MDRM. Edwin S. Munger, writing five years after the congress, notes that the return of the Malagasy soldiers from the war provided a nucleus of leaders for the revolt.[34] Deschamps believes that there were 100,000 of the returned soldiers, who were much embittered by delays and the disorganization of the homeland after the war.[35] Nevertheless, no one really credited the possibility of such a revolt.

The burial of the many bodies of the victims did not end the contention on the island. An inquest began in the capital, Tananarive, apparently to prove the guilt of the Malagasy deputies in the French Parliament and the other leaders of the MDRM. They were all presumed in advance to be guilty. Many curious facts came out in the next months. On March 27 the leaders of the MDRM had wired all their sections to keep calm in the face of efforts to sabotage their pacific policy. Was this the real meaning of the wire, or was it rather a signal to set off the revolt? Spacensky thinks it was a signal and that the leaders later admitted it was.[36] But in the 1954 book of Maître Stibbe, the lawyer who went to Madagascar to defend the accused, there are a number of stories, seemingly well authenticated, that indicate this was not the case. They state that the rebellion's leaders, arrested for attempts against the security of the state, were tortured with great severity by their guards. Was the confession that they made extorted from them by blows, whips, water torture, or other forms of maltreatment such as being kept in stinking cells with no food or water? Stibbe was horrified by the results that he saw of the ill-treatment of the prisoners. After their release, several of them had to be hospitalized. In addition, the usual immunity of parliamentarians was denied them, and they were not allowed to use the radio, though apparently by then they were doing their best to keep the people quiet.[37] The accused claimed later that the confession had indeed been obtained from them by torture. But their innocence was never established, nor was their guilt of direct participation in the crimes committed made certain, though it seems clear that their responsibility was great.[38]

Nevertheless, the famous telegram served as a basis for the director of security to proceed against all the leaders of the rebellion. The man suspected of being the most guilty, Rakotondrabé, was condemned to death on April 16. He is said to have acted at the instigation of the deputies, and so it is especially odd that he should be executed just three days before their trial began. The president of the Republic asked a stay of execution, if the presence of the man would be useful at the trial. But the magistrate at Tananarive said that this was not the case, and Rakotondrabé was not even permitted the presence of his lawyer. When an attempt was made to transfer the trial, the high commissioner, questioned about the matter, gave no information or approval. In spite of that, he was retained in his post. In 1949, the minister of France Overseas, then Paul Coste-Floret, remarked that while justice should be applied, when it was necessary authority should be shown![39] That statement could be a cover for nearly anything! Also, Rakotondrabé was the only man whose guilt, as one of the two heads of the military system in the revolt, had really been proven. Consequently, he was the person who would have known most about what went on. So, one might ask, did the government aid the cause of truth by killing him just before the trial began?

The rebel leaders, especially Raseta, Ravoahangy, and Rabemananjara, tried to get out of the difficulties by condemning the insurrection formally. But it was too late.[40] The French did not believe them. In France, people spoke of the rebellion as a plot against the sovereignty of France, pointing out that it was the tradition of the Republic to be merciless to those who plotted against its indivisibility. On May 30 the MDRM and the secret societies, JINA and PA.NA.MA., were dissolved, and the effort to suppress all dissidence continued. There were six condemnations to death, and a number to varying lengths of forced labor. Appeals were forbidden, but, in 1949, the condemnations were commuted. To the Europeans, it appeared that the guilty had escaped, but to the Malagasy people, the men had become martyrs. Such a civil war left many hatreds behind it, and it was clear that reconciliation would take a long time.[41] Did it ever seem to the French that "battle for independence" would have been a better term to use than "plot against the sovereignty of France"?

What emerges from these statements and counterstatements is that whether the men were guilty or not, illegal methods had been used to convict them and to keep them imprisoned for a considerable time, though nearly all were released later. Certainly, Stibbe and many others thought at the time when Bourdet wrote his preface, in 1954, that the men were innocent.[42] But René Moreux, the conservative editor of *Marchés Coloniaux*, wrote on December 31, 1949, that no one doubted that they were guilty. Several men consulted by the author who were in a position to know a good deal—though their names had better not be mentioned since proof is lacking—felt that the accused men had been guilty.

Five years later, Edwin S. Munger, writing apparently in 1952, said that the Hovas were the main planners of the attack, and had the revolt gone as planned, France might have lost control of the island. Whether or not that was true, it is certain that news of the "greatest rebellion Africa had seen in the Twentieth Century" was slow to reach beyond the Great Island. Yet it left behind it not only hundreds of prisoners in the jails of the island, but an appalling number of graves. Apparently—and understandably—the French government desired to keep it quiet. Any government would want to.[43]

In the repression and during the rebellion, the Foreign Legion and the Senegalese troops went wild: estimates of the casualties range from 100,000 (given by a lawyer who said he had statistics); 80,000 (given by a South African army officer who thought his figure conservative); 40,000 (figure given by Munger); 12,000 (given by the American consul at Tananarive); to 5,000 (given by a Lutheran missionary). Finally, a figure of 11,342 is given by Deschamps, who had seen lists in many towns. This last estimate, from a careful historian, would seem to be the most reliable one, though figures as far apart as these do not lead one to give credence to any of them. But, obviously, many people died—only about 200 of them being Frenchmen. Part of the reason for that was the lack of arms among the insurgents. They charged machine guns with mere spears in their hands, having been told that bullets would not harm their enemies. But, after all, did they have other arms? In a few months order was restored, and it is a grim touch that the Foreign Legion paraded daily in Tananarive with kepis that had white cloths blowing behind them, pantaloons gathered at the ankle, red sashes, and automatic weapons on their shoulders. This was certainly a show of force and preparedness to impress the citizens of a territory in revolt.[44]

After the rebellion and the trials and repressions were over, there was silence for a time in Madagascar. Most of the deputies, after their release and the coming of independence, became ministers in the new state until the government was taken over by the military, in 1973. But several accused men, says Joseph Ki-Zerbo, the African historian, had died mysteriously, the political parties were dissolved, and political life was banned for quite a while. Yet the nationalist ideas continued, though Madagascar was in a state of "political prostration" so serious that 80 percent had failed to vote in the municipal elections.[45]

It has seemed necessary to go into this Madagascar situation in considerable detail, partly because it *was* the greatest revolt of the century; and it *must* have made a deep impact on General de Gaulle, for it meant a future danger to the French Union and its connection with France. When news of it finally reached France, there was quite a storm over it, led, at least in part, by André Philip, a prominent Socialist in Paris. He had been a member of de Gaulle's first London Committee, called the French National Committee. Previously, he had gone with Adrien Tixier, the Free French representative in Washington, to see Roosevelt in November 1942.[46] (That interview was an unhappy one. Philip and Tixier were said not to have been the type to deal with the president of the United States.) Also, the Madagascar revolt certainly increased the fears for the Empire. René Moreux expressed it in *Marchés Coloniaux*, in May 1946, quoting both an article of his own and one of Henri Laurentie's:

> One would have to be blind to deny that the Empire is in peril. A free breath is blowing through it from one part to another, so much the more dangerous that the hurricane of revolt is universal. It is a fact that the colonial peoples' general desire is for freedom and equality. . . . The universality of the war, the unanimity of suffering, the lack of balance between the powers, the renewal in discussion of all values, especially the moral ones, the unsettled present, the uncertainty of the future, push them [the colonial peoples] into demanding freedon and equality. They feel they must persist until these demands are satisfied.[47]

Today there is not much (public) reference to the revolt; but the writer, speaking to a very high government official in October 1969, wanted to find out how close it seemed to those now living in independent Madagascar. At her question, the minister looked out of the window for a moment and then said quietly, "Madame, my people have made a great effort to forget the past." Such a magnanimous response from such a source makes one wonder whether the recent turnover in power in the Great Island, in the spring of 1973, and the intensity in securing new articles of cooperation with France, stemmed, at least subconsciously, from the dreadful events of 1947. Marianne Cornevin notes that "the length and severity of the repression, as well as the rigorous censorship imposed on the press, was to mark profoundly and durably all Malagasy nationalism."[48]

Parties had begun to spring up in Africa immediately after de Gaulle's retreat from power in 1946. Of course, France had been "the prime deterrent" of political parties in Africa. The decisions always lay in Paris, for the colonial minister could rule by decree. So the parties, in beginning, formed "a precise response to the challenge of colonialism."[49] There were two main types, the first being those organized around an individual or a small group of leaders, who derived their influence from outside of the party, from the remaining traditional systems, religions, or the economy. These parties were called Patron Parties, and they often had a regional or territorial base. They made particular appeals to the people, rewarded great leaders, and had few or no members; the only obligations of those few was to vote for the party's candidates. A good example of these was the Senegalese branch of the French Socialist SFIO (*Section Française de l'Internationale Ouvrière*). It was based on the Senegalese urban élite, and in time it became the *Parti Socialiste Sénégalais* when its links with France were broken. There were also the Mass Parties, led by those who had some experience in politics. They tried to develop political principles and to diffuse appeals to their countries. They wanted a new structure of society and were more evolved than the Patron Parties.[50] They gave rewards to their members rather than to their leaders and served those members by integrating groups by their structure or by means of other groups. Their following had certain political duties: attendance at meetings, the spreading of propaganda, the collection of funds, etc.; and they covered wide areas, often entire territories, stressing allegiance to the territory and asking for radical changes. The French administration approved less of them than it did of the more moderate Patron Parties, for they worked for African unity and were opposed to the colonial powers. Each territory was different, and no one of them had a single ethnic base, though the dominant ethnic group gave a cast to territorial policy.[51]

The Africans needed pressure on Paris to acquire the rights they felt were due them,[52] and after the end of the Second Constituent Assembly, the Intergroup that had been formed during the summer of 1946 to resist the work of the Estates General wanted to reorganize against the reaction of the Second Constituent Assembly in comparison with what the first one had given the Africans. They called together an interparty Tropical African Congress in Bamako, in the Soudan, to work for African emancipation. That group became the *Rassemblement Démocratique Africain* (RDA). Many of its ideas at first came from Socialist and Communist leaders in France. Overseas Minister Moutet thought it dangerous, so his influence prevented all French parties except the Communist from attending. This influence also prevented two important Africans from attending the meetings: Lamine Guèye, head of the SFIO, which was still French and had not yet broken away to be the *Parti Socialist Africain;* and Léopold Senghor, who was then associated with Guèye, and who later regretted his nonattendance. The result of these abstentions from the conference threw the congress into the hands of the Communists with a clear field in which to work. Consequently, the RDA began by taking the Communist line and working directly against the French government. In its turn, the government took a strong position at the time against the RDA. The real repression of the RDA began, apparently, in 1948, when a "tough" man succeeded a mild one, with the specific task of suppressing that group. Soon after, there were incidents of revolt in the Ivory Coast, where the president of the RDA, Félix Houphouet-Boigny, resided.

Houphouet-Boigny had founded the *Syndicat Agricole Africain* (African Agricultural Union) among the Baoulé cocoa farmers to eliminate unequal treatment of its members and to help all the peasants of the Ivory Coast who were suffering from forced labor laws and the *indigénat.* The RDA, which he also helped to found, finally included people from nearly every African country in its work for complete freedom. A large mimeographed copy of the manifesto and report, prepared in 1946, came into the hands of the author a few years ago. It explains the intentions of the movement, and it also throws light on why the French tried for some time to repress the organization.

The first page of the RDA report, called "Birth and Death of the RDA," contains three lists of colonies. One list mentioned the French territories that "had certain democratic liberties," such as those in the Americas, the Indian Ocean, and on the horn of Africa. Even those in Senegal could be considered in this category because of the Four Communes and their representation in the French Parliament, and because of New Caledonia's having a local assembly. In the second group were those entirely under an "arbitrary regime," such as Madagascar, AEF, AOF (except Senegal), the Somalis, and the French islands in Oceania; and in the final list, the two under mandate, or trusteeship, Togo and the Cameroons, were named. These were called "associated territories." In addition, there were the protectorates—Tunisia, Morocco, Annam, Tonkin, Cambodia, and Laos—and also the special departments, such as Algeria. Those under arbitrary rule, said the manifesto, lived in a sort of coexistence, based on juridical lines of possession and subordination of contractual origin, but the element of force behind the arrangement could always be seen. The explanation was given that possessions were necessary to obtain markets, but underneath this necessity lay exploitation. Forced labor was only a form of slavery, said the founders of the RDA, pointing out that an African with a high degree could earn only half as much as a Frenchman; that a government employee with the same job as a European received only one-quarter as much; that products such as coffee, paid at a certain level, would be resold in France for four times that level; and that a pensioner received emoluments that could not be compared to those handed out to Europeans.[53]

The report of the RDA went on to discuss the special political and legal statutes for Africans in penal justice and in the *indigénat*, adding that there was no political liberty for the individual African, either in speech or association, and that every cultural expression by the inhabitants of the countries was forbidden. The victory in the war had had an influence, said the writers, naming the Atlantic Charter, the agreements in Teheran and Yalta, and the United Nations Charter. All these events and declarations had inspired a growing democratic nationalism, and the colonizing nations would have to revise their bonds with the colonized. That was why overseas representatives had been sent to the Constituent Assembly, for de Gaulle and the military reactionaries had thought they could thereby defeat the democratic thrust of the French peoples overseas; but those peoples would undo the plans of the colonialists.[54]

The report pointed out that owing to the two democratic influences in France and overseas, the more progressive measures had been adopted by the First Constituent Assembly and, unfortunately, refused by the second. In the elections, nearly all the more progressive candidates opposed to the administration had been chosen—a result of the oppression that had gone before. That same reaction could be seen in the first constitutional project, the one that had been so unfortunately rejected (in May 1946), but the later pressures of the Estates General of Colonization had continued the reaction against the liberalizing trend all during the Second Constituent Assembly. Nevertheless, a "serious breach" had been made in the colonial system, and the following principles had been established: no war or other force must be used in any country against the desired liberty; and union must be made on the basis of equality and without distinction of race or religion. The French Union is composed of peoples who will coordinate their resources and efforts to develop their civilization, increase their well-being, and assure their security. Finally, the combined efforts of the overseas civilizations must lead to self-administration and the democratic management of their own affairs.[55]

However, in the Union as planned by the Second Constitution, said the report, there would be associated territories and states, and overseas territories and departments. The overseas departments would be parts of the metropole, and the overseas territories would have a special statute. The Africans in the overseas departments and territories would have representatives in the French Parliament (55 deputies, 44 councillors, and 75 councillors of the French Union). There would be deliberative local assemblies, elected by universal suffrage for the general or representative councils and the representative assemblies. Those for the Grand Councils would be elected by second-degree suffrage. Political liberty would be assured by representation in Parliament and in the Assembly of the French Union, and by locally elected councils. All of the colonial populations would be citizens, and there would be no *indigénat* or forced labor. Thus they would have freedom of speech and of meeting and association, both forced labor and inequalities of pay due to racial reasons being suppressed. However, the report adds, these rights had not been given freely; they had been conquered. Pay was still not aligned on metropolitan bases, and there is a long distance between desires and realities: in addition, many repressive measures had survived the war in Vietnam—bloody provocations in Madagascar and electoral fraud in Algeria. In Black Africa there had been injuries, provocations, frauds, and violations. Consequently, what the overseas groups now fought was this contradiction between what the preamble to the Constitution had said, and the inequalities that were still permitted. There followed a list of such provocations and inequalities: imprisonment in the Soudan, and small offenses heavily penalized; sometimes the Africans in Niger had been forced to walk naked in public for small offenses; and there had been terrorism in the Upper Volta. Also word had gone out that the Africans were anti-French, because they spoke out against these abuses that were so contrary to the Declaration of the Rights of Man. This section of the report ends with "We will not fall into your traps, Gentlemen Calumniators . . . we will make the great French tradition our own."[56] The anti-French people, says the report, are those who sabotage the possibility of a "Union freely consented. A great hope has been born in the heart of the Africans that nothing can disappoint. We maintain our position. We send out word for union and organization in the struggle against colonialism and imperialism, whose defeat is the first condition of our freedom.

> Long live Black Africa
> Long live the Union of the Africans
> Long live the French Union of Democratic Peoples."[57]

It was signed by Houphouet-Boigny, Lamine Guèye, Félix Tchicaya, S. M. Apithy, F. D. Sissoko, Yacine Diallo, and Gabriel d'Arboussier, as eminent a group of African leaders as existed at that time. One important name was missing, that of Léopold Senghor, who had not yet joined the movement but agreed to do so later.[58]

This RDA report was sent out from Bamako in 1946. It was as good a statement as one could wish of the African position. Obviously, many of the French did not like it, for though it gave surface support to the Union, there was a hidden menace. Marius Moutet, minister of colonies, had ordered local administrators to oppose the meeting at Bamako. Fily Dabo Sissoko, a prominent African, then said to be the puppet of the French government at the United Nations, put all his influence against the congress, but he was forced to attend and to take the chair. But the meeting of 15,000 at Bamako on October 18, 1946, could not be stopped, and when held, it was well managed.[59] That meeting, and a later congress held at Bobo-Diolasso in January 1949, had the double objective, the Africans said, of union and of an alliance with democratic France. But reaction against it made it into a sort of scarecrow. The reviews *Marchés Coloniaux* and *L'Epoque* wrote calumnies about it, they said, and the middle-of-the-road party in France, the Movement of the Popular Republicans (*Mouvement Républicain Populaire*) showed itself as essentially reactionary, too. But the RDA kept demanding equal political and social rights, individual and cultural freedom, democratic assemblies, and a freely consented Union between the peoples of Africa and France. Dozens of thousands of Africans, they said, were fraternally united to France in large groups everywhere, and this Union must be completed.[60]

Having thus expressed their intentions, the founders drew up some rules for themselves. They would never fight any religion—only social and economic injustice—for there was need of massive resistance as the peoples awoke to conscious struggle. Their claims continued to be the right of peoples to dispose of themselves. They set up sections in the various countries; they founded papers: a weekly called *Réveil*, another, *The Voice of the RDA*, and several more. They had a good slogan: "To struggle so as to Learn, To Learn so as to Struggle." Soon they had about a million adherents. They were allied with the Communist party, but they said that they did not consider this the reason for the government's opposition to them; the cause was rather their fundamental principle of struggle against colonialism. They were not against the French government, they claimed; only against the constant violations of the Constitution that were taking place. Those who thought they could not act without permission of the Communist party did not understand their frank and loyal relationship with it. They proclaimed that the RDA based its sections "on alliances of democratic forces." "The History of Humanity was sown with obstacles, and no progress ever came without a constant struggle." Their Union was not a proletarian movement but an organic democracy with a single front. Their crisis was one of growth. Everything must be done in the interests of the mass of the people. Today, the privileged people felt themselves menaced by the rise of such popular movements. In several places—Vietnam, Madagascar, North Africa, and the metropole—there had been bloody struggles. The first thing needed was to change governmental policy and then take up again the march toward liberty and progress.[61]

In October 1948, the Committee of Coordination of the RDA at Dakar reaffirmed these principles and rules and urged all Africans to rejoin their ranks. They ended their remarks again with the same "long lives," adding, "Long live the active solidarity of the forces of progress of the world, and long live the French Union, fraternal and democratic."[62]

There are several interesting things about this long document (it contains 114 mimeographed pages, double spaced). There was a sort of "sop to Cerberus" to the French at the end. It contained a kind of threat under a promise. The Africans wanted to be a part of France, but France had better be the kind of France they wanted. There was also that terrible bogey of their relationship with the Communists. In 1947 the French had managed to get the Communists out of the government places de Gaulle had given them, since he had had to recognize their help in the Resistance. He had done it rather gingerly, of course, for he refused to allot to them any of the important ministries (Foreign Affairs, National Defense, and Interior), fobbing them off with three economic ministries, where he thought they could do no harm.[63] But the Communist connection was, in truth, only a part of the reason for the government opposition. The meaning that shone through the manifesto was that even if the Africans were not demanding complete freedom at that time, they were certainly going beyond the governmental position—and going a long way! That could be seen in their comments on "force" and "arbitrary rule," and because of their interest in the Atlantic Charter and the United Nations. They were scornful of the position of the overseas independents in the Parliament, to which Senghor belonged. They thought the group was without "national principles" because it contained not only Africans but Malagasy and Algerian people. They said [Léopold] Senghor was under the influence of J.-P. Sartre and that he thought the racial fact was a sufficient cement to bind Africans together. Later, they excluded from the RDA two men—Aku and Apithy—because they had benefited by the "scandalous support" of the administration and were its accomplices in repression.[64] Somehow, it is always surprising to find such internecine strife in a movement that needs unity against a strong opponent.

Some time after this, the RDA, realizing the handicap the Communist alliance caused them, found it better to retreat from their "loyal" relationship with the Communist party. Houphouet-Boigny had left that party after the Ivory Coast troubles of 1949.[65] It seemed to be no longer necessary to the groups of the RDA. The Africans must have known it was causing real trouble with the French on the government side, so they were willing to break with it.

Perhaps this retreat from communism was due to the fact that the Communists had sent an important delegation to the Second Congress of RDA, at Treichville, a suburb of Abidjan, in January 1949. This seemed to confirm the fact of the close relationship of the RDA with the Communist party. A month later, repression by the French occurred again, and 383 Africans were arrested for crimes of which a majority of them were said to be innocent. In March and October of the same year, there were further troubles, and in December, women of the Ivory Coast surrounded the Bassani prison where some of the arrested were held and where some of the conditons were extremely bad. It was even said that they lay down there on the pavement and undressed and had to be dispersed with firehoses. Next day, there were strikes and a boycott of the railroads. Meantime, they abused the Europeans. The troubles continued, even in Houphouet-Boigny's village, and a warrant for arrest was issued for Houphouet-Boigny himself. He refused to obey it, however, for, being a deputy, he could claim parliamentary immunity. At Dimbokro, on January 29, 1950, there was a great demonstration in Houphouet's favor. The white population was anguished, having heard the rumor that all the whites in Abidjan were to be assassinated, and, in the general excitement, the French troops fired on the crowd, killing thirteen and wounding fifty Africans. Then the Assembly of the Union, well warned, recommended appeasing the rebels, and the prisoners of January were freed. Houphouet-Boigny then renounced the relationship of the

RDA of the Ivory Coast with the Communist party of France and opened a period of understanding with the French government.[66] Other sections of the RDA, except those of the Cameroons, soon followed suit.

In part, this was due to the fact that the low wage policy of the European merchants and planters was bitterly resented; and while this took place elsewhere, too, it was particularly accentuated in the Ivory Coast. It should be noted that in spite of government efforts to build up an opposition party in the Ivory Coast, the strength of the RDA in that state was very real.[67] All this increased the government's belief that something had to be done about the former colonies.

To Charles de Gaulle, watching from Colombey-les-deux-églises, or from 5, rue de Solférino, the rebellion in Madagascar, the rise of African parties such as the RDA, and the failures of the Fourth Republic to solve these colonial problems, not to mention Britain's agreements to allow her Far Eastern territories their freedom, were all events that must have affected him deeply. It can scarcely be doubted that they led him to begin, at least, to take a more liberal—less possessive—line toward the colonies. Of course, as all Frenchmen know, de Gaulle had never approved of parties even in France. He thought they only represented particular interests and could not therefore represent the general interest. They did not understand each other on anything, and not, certainly, on colonial problems.[68]

It was clear now that the old policies of assimilation and association had been replaced by the slogans of *federation, unity,* and *independence.* After de Gaulle's Bayeux speech in June of 1946, even "federation now" seemed reactionary, for de Gaulle had proposed a federation from the top, and that, the Africans felt, was an entirely reactionary idea. For a time, the idea of any federation faded entirely. It was, however, revived in 1948 by the African *Indépendants Outre-Mer* (IOM) in the French Assembly.[69]

15

The World from Colombey

> You cannot know what the opposition was like to any
> evolution in the French Union. Its violence seems
> inconceivable. It came at least as much from the
> Radicals as from the Gaullists. . . . Let us not allow it
> to be believed that France only undertakes reforms
> when blood begins to flow.
> —Defferre

If, as people say, coming events cast their shadows before them, certainly there were plenty of shadows looming over the Empire at the beginning of the fifties. However, the colonizing nations of Europe tried to ignore them. De Gaulle, of all the French, was probably most likely to be affected by these shadows. But he saw most of them only from Colombey.

A labor code for Black Africa had been formulated in 1949 and was promulgated in December 1952, but there was not much equality yet in French Africa, except that in the western states they did have the single college for voting. The RDA was well on its way by 1950, having broken with the Communists, and asking only autonomy in the bosom of the French Union. In 1953, a Constituent Congress of the Independents in the French Chamber was asking for the revision (in the direction of an active federalism) of the much-contested *Titre* VIII of the Constitution. But, more important than these signs of the times, was the Conference of the Afro-Asiatic Nations at Bandoung in April 1955.

Arthur Conte calls his book on that conference *Bandoung: de l'Histoire,* possibly because it was the first great international conference in which not a single white man took part, or because Jawaharlal Nehru, prime minister of India, remarked of it that its importance lay in its having taken place. It was a historic event. Jean Rous, a writer well versed in African affairs, said that it was the death of an inferiority complex. Everything about it was unusual. It was the event of the century, people thought, and they commented on it everywhere. The setting was worthy of it. And the men were worthy of it, too, for among them were such eminent personalities as Chou En-lai, Nehru, Nasser, U Nu, Sukarno, Sihanouk, Romulo, and Mohammed Ali.[1]

The agenda contained five points: economic cooperation, cultural coopera-tion, the Rights of Man (including the self-determination of peoples), the problems of countries not yet independent, and worldwide unified action for peace. At the end of the week of working meetings, the conference issued a final communiqué. Regarding colonialism, its most important decisions were:

Colonialism in all its manifestations is an evil to which a speedy end must be put. Subjection to, and exploitation of, a country by a stranger country is a negation of the fundamental rights of man, is contrary to the United Nations [principles], and prevents work for peace and world cooperation.

It [the conference] supports the liberty and independence of such peoples.

It calls on the interested Powers to grant liberty and independence to them.[2]

The effects of the gathering were very considerable. It embarrassed the Western powers, who could not decide what to do about it. The nations of Southeast Asia were entering into forceful positions just as Europe, weakened by two wars, had ceased to command the destinies of Asia. The conference supported Algeria, Tunisia, and Morocco in their desire for independence. It hastened the progress of neutralism and pacifism, and it created solidarity among the races. Other concrete influences were the stimulation of certain international agreements, the growing rupture between China and Russia, and the holding of more such conferences and meetings. Léopold Senghor summed it all up by saying, "It is the greatest thunderclap of History since the Renaissance."[3]

At long last, the French, who had begun to perceive in the early fifties that something must be done about their overseas territories, were galvanized into action—action that would lead to some degree of autonomy.[4] Bandoung had a good deal to do with that.

Other events of the fifties were important for the French, and vital for their neighbors to the south. As Georgette Elgey has noted, nationalism was reinforced by that time; for Libya, Syria, Egypt, India, Pakistan, Indonesia, and several other countries had gained their independence.[5] In the Maghreb, nationalism had developed long before it began to any extent in Black Africa, and it was in full swing after the close of World War II.

In Tunisia in 1937 there had been riots, arrests, and imprisonments, and the Neo-Destour party that was fighting for independence had gone underground. The French made certain inadequate concessions and reforms, but the party nevertheless constructed a trade union of 100,000 members by 1949, and the party itself numbered half a million individuals. Plans for Tunisian executives, assembly, and constitution were made, but they were defeated by the French *colons* and their friends in the French Assembly. There were incidents of violence, and reforms, as usual, came too little and too late. The United Nations was asked to put Tunisia on its agenda, but new arrests followed, dialogue with France stopped, and there was widespread terror and counterterror in the land.[6]

In Morocco, the nationalist leader Allal el Fassi began a reform movement in 1937, but, after massive demonstrations, he was exiled for nine years to Gabon. In 1944, from Gabon, his party, the Istiqlal, issued a manifesto, but the Free French rejected its proposals. Cables were sent to the United Nations, but the *colons* in North Africa, their groups in Morocco, and the North African lobby in Paris were too strong for them. The Arab League, founded in 1945, helped, but could only act as a sounding board. The new resident-general, Marshal

Alphonse Juin, was severe, increasing his demands on the sultan, Mohammed V, and thus bringing many Moroccans over to the Istiqlal party. By 1951, there was a united front in Morocco behind that party's program. Some of the Tunisians managed to appeal to the Security Council; when they refused to withdraw their appeal at the request of the resident-general, he arrested and exiled them. Riots and bloodshed followed with repression and loss of life. The sultan was deposed by the French, and a puppet was put in his place. There was resistance of various sorts: fires, trains derailed, etc. By the early fifties, both Tunisia and Morocco were aflame.[7]

Then in 1954 came Dien Bien Phu and the defeat of France in Indochina. The premier of France, Pierre Mendès-France, saw that something must be done, and on July 31 he agreed to internal autonomy for Tunisia.[8] Rebellion now broke out in Algeria in November 1954, for nationalism had grown there in the interwar years. The leader of the Algerians, Ferhat Abbas, had issued a manifesto in 1943, asking liberty and equality—in short, demanding abolition of colonial rule, though the word *independence* was not mentioned.[9]

There had been manifestations in Algeria in 1945, for the more extreme groups thought that de Gaulle's effort, in 1943, to give more Muslims the vote was inadequate, and tension had mounted. The reforms were not enough. The uprising in 1945 became violent and the French repression even more so. This had a direct effect on the revolt that began in 1954. In 1945 de Gaulle had still been in power, but it is probable that he looked on the events as just another in the long series of colonial wars. He did not refer to that revolt in his *Memoirs*. It was to be forgotten. However, in 1947, the French Chamber promised to set up an Algerian Assembly, and suggested special regulations allowing the Muslims their religious ceremonies and the teaching of Arabic, and giving the vote to Muslim women. Still, the Muslims felt the statute did not open the way to true autonomy. It was inoperable as the Muslims became more and more violent. The French rigged the elections and suppressed opinion. The *colons*, the governor-general, and the administration in Algeria together made the statute fail of its purpose.[10] The Algerian Assembly was dissolved in 1956, and the promised statute of 1947 went down with it, if indeed it had ever existed in practice. Still, the beginning of the Algerian War on November 1, 1954, was a surprise. No one seems to have been warned by the many incidents that had taken place. The minister of the interior in France, François Mitterand, said that Algeria was France, and she would recognize no authority but her own. The citizens of Algeria had only one hope, he thought, and that was France.[11] The years passed, and Pierre Viansson-Ponté wrote, "Algeria, bloody and torn, plunged deeper every day into the shadows, dragging with her the flower of the youth of the country, upsetting the conscience of the nation, and, as a side issue, managing to destroy a regime that was already no more than a phantom."[12]

By 1956, then, Tunisia and Morocco had both become entirely free, and Indochina was no longer in the French Union. General de Gaulle, watching the war and the loss of a great part of the Empire, saw that the final stage was at hand. If Brazzaville had marked out a path, as he said, there was a point where that path divided; and the troubles in the Maghreb were like a red hand pointing to the branch of the road that France must take thereafter.[13]

As in the old days of colonization and colonial wars, it was Great Britain who sparked the development in the trusteeship state of Togo, that little strip of land running north and inland from the ocean under the great bulge of West Africa, some of which was under British control and some under French. In the neighboring Gold Coast, soon to be renamed Ghana, Kwame Nkrumah had risen to great power through his party, the Convention People's party, and the British were trying to persuade the people of the Ewe tribe—half in French land, half in British—to join with Nkrumah's party and become a section of the proposed new state of Ghana. "France," says Mortimer, "saw a chance to show that her section of Togo was getting a better deal." Thus, he added, Togo became the "shop-window of the French Union," a showplace for the reform of French colonialism. In 1954, the British presented their report as trustees to the United Nations Trusteeship Council, for Togo was a trust territory in the hands of both Britain and France, and France hurried to do the same. A Togo statute, piloted through the French Assembly by a new and liberal minister of France Overseas, Robert Buron, became law on April 16, 1955. Togo was given a "Council of Government," but the council still lacked any real executive power. Meantime, previously set up *Conseils de Circonscription* were given some decision over local budgets. Buron was soon out of power, and an African party under a leader named Nicolas Grunitzky, who favored membership in the French Union, agreed to accept the statute. The new Territorial Assembly called for full autonomy, rejecting Britain's effort to unite the two Togos. The United Nations sent a mission to Togo, and the men of that mission realized the division in the country and came to the conclusion that the trusteeship should not be terminated until a plebiscite had been held.[14]

In 1956, a new statute was drafted by Overseas Minister Gaston Defferre, together with Nicolas Grunitzky, and according to the will of the Territorial Assembly, the country was declared to be an autonomous republic, even though it would be under a form of only limited autonomy. Still, the door for change was left open, and the French promised to allow certain FIDES (*Fonds d'Investissement de Développement Economique et Sociale*—Investment Fund for Economic and Social Development) credits to go to Togoland.[15] On August 30, 1956, the Autonomous Republic of Togo was proclaimed, and Grunitzky became its first prime minister. On October 28 a referendum was held, but since it had been carried out without UN supervision, the United Nations sent a new fact-finding mission to Togo in 1957 to check whether all had been properly done. It appeared that the referendum had been held without universal suffrage, and the new statute did not give full autonomy, the mission said. So France had to agree to making over to the Togolese government all powers except currency, defense, and foreign policy. They arranged a universal suffrage referendum. All was now in order, and the trusteeship could be ended.[16]

The speed and the near completeness of the Togolese march to independence cannot fail to have impressed General de Gaulle. The final arrangements were made on February 22, 1958, less than three months before he returned to power. Events in Togo were still another warning for de Gaulle.

Apparently, everyone knew that the Cameroons would be a difficult problem to solve. They were full of regional, tribal, and ethnic divisions, and, like Togo, were partly under British control. The minister of Overseas France, Gaston Defferre, sent out Pierre Messmer who, together with Paul Soppo Priso, then head of a national union, attempted to find a solution. But the union split over the question of amnesty for those who had been involved in terrorist activity and the refusal to lift the ban on the opposing UPC (Union of Cameroonian Populations). It finally broke up in November 1956. Elections were held at long last on November 18, a year after the new statute, similar to that given to Togo, had been passed. According to Edward Mortimer, Messmer was "over-trustful," and a new terrorist campaign broke out before the end of the year. The government responded with severe repression in which hundreds of Africans, some of them undoubtedly innocent, were killed. But the new Assembly, elected in November, started work in the next year, with Ahmadou Ahidjo, the man who is now president of the republic, at its head. Soppo Priso and others were now demanding complete independence, but Ahidjo and his party produced a moderate program, asking only autonomy and a transitional period before independence.

Finally, a compromise was reached with Prime Minister André-Marie Mbida, who had been on various sides in the whole controversy. Both groups asked the French to name their Cameroons a state under trusteeship, rather than a territory. This was accepted by all except a new group—the "Eight"— now under Soppo Priso, and the French government made it law on April 16, 1957. The French high commissioner was still responsible for defense and relations with France and other countries, and he was also given the power to choose the prime minister, who would then be invested by the Assembly. Mbida was made prime minister, with Ahidjo as his deputy and minister of the interior. In June the statute was inaugurated, and though the Cameroons was now a "state under trusteeship," it was outside the French Union, though still represented in the French Parliament—a very curious arrangement.[17]

Unfortunately, this was not the end of the trouble. The UPG, the local African party, continued its campaign of terrorism, asking for amnesty, a new election, and immediate independence. But the prime minister merely threatened "severe measures," and guerrilla warfare continued, especially by night when the terrorists were supreme. The French refused Mbida's request for troops, and, hoping that new men could settle things, they sent a new high commissioner, Jean Ramadier, to see whether he could calm the country. He did not succeed, and a more orthodox man, Xavier Torré, was sent to succeed him. Mbida resigned, Ahidjo became prime minister, and on June 12, 1958, the new Assembly voted to ask de Gaulle, now prime minister, for real autonomy, with an option for independence at the end of the trusteeship. De Gaulle replied favorably, and soon negotiations began.[18]

The remaining step to independence was begun in October 1958, when the

Cameroons Legislative Assembly asked reunification of the French and British zones of the Cameroons and complete independence by January 1960. They asked the French government to request of the United Nations the abrogation of the trusteeship agreement, to be timed to coincide with independence. In the transitional period, they acquired complete autonomy and took over all internal affairs except currency, foreign policy, and defense. The federal state of Cameroon came into existence on February 11–12, 1961, together with reunification of the different parts, except for sections of the north which joined Northern Nigeria.[19]

This abbreviated report of what happened in the Cameroons after 1956 gives little indication of the many troubles gone through in that very disturbed country, but it was important for de Gaulle because it showed a different aspect of what might happen if the divisions in the new federal state could not be brought together. It is a sad fact that it did not stop the burnings and the attacks. It was very clear, even by June 1958, that the Empire was rapidly disintegrating.

By the mid-fifties, de Gaulle was not the only one to see the direction signs. There were those in France, besides Mendès-France and Edgar Faure, who saw them too. And, at long last, those in power began to act. Immobilism, that characteristic of the Fourth Republic, was dead.

Under Prime Minister Guy Mollet's government, in 1956, Gaston Defferre, minister of France Overseas (later better known when he opposed de Gaulle in the presidential election of 1965), became the official sponsor of a new bill in the Parliament that concerned territories. Defferre was aided by Houphouet-Boigny, then *Ministre-Délégué à la Présidence du Conseil*, the first African to be a full minister in a French cabinet.[20] Together they pushed through the *Loi-Cadre*, an Enabling Act or Framework Law, the text of which had already been worked out by the previous government of Edgar Faure. The final version of the texts was now drawn up by Gaston Espinasse, director of political affairs for the premier. They hastened, for, as Defferre said:

> By acting quickly we will not be at the mercy of events. There exists presently in the Overseas Territories a certain malaise, and it is necessary to dissipate it by efficacious action to restore a climate of confidence.[21]

Considering what was going on in the three states of the Maghreb and elsewhere, these declarations of intention, however good, sound like understatement and wishful thinking. It is never easy to restore confidence. However, the proposed law was in many ways a good and interesting one.

Rudolph von Albertini has given a good summary of the contents of the *Loi-Cadre:* It provided universal franchise and a single college for elections in all the states or territories. This had been one of the chief bones of contention. Africans would now control a great deal of political decision making. Territorial assemblies with wider powers would exist in every state. A ministerial executive council would be elected by each assembly. A French governor would be its chairman, so control would be held by Paris. However, the vice president of the council would be an African. The distinction between the state services (*services d'état*) and the local affairs (*matières locales*) preserved a good deal of power for France, for such affairs included foreign policy, the army, general security, currency and tariff questions, economic planning, supraterritorial communications, higher education, and radio stations; and, says von Albertini, Paris "indirectly reserved for itself further powers," though he does not indicate what these powers were. It did mean greater control of the budget and of the other ministries such as public works, civil service, and primary education. After all, what did internal autonomy mean under these conditions? In any case, it was certainly a step in the right direction, even though it was not clear whether at the end of the road there would be a federal republic or complete independence for all the states of Black Africa. The law gave power to the states rather than to any federation.[22]

Defferre told the author that the project was motivated by the ideal goal of future independence, and that decolonization would have come in five years in any case. The *Loi-Cadre* was the next step—autonomy—after what had been begun at Brazzaville. It was not possible to halt the movement leading to independence. Perhaps, Defferre thought, General de Gaulle might have carried out something like decolonization in 1944, when he could, it seemed, have done almost anything; but at that time he was not ready for even the single college in Algeria. Then, for a long time, he said nothing about it, though when he came back to power, he was primed for change.[23]

Gaston Espinasse, the political officer who had drawn up the texts for the *Loi-Cadre*, felt that the moment had come to take a step in advance. At that time, in 1956, independence was still unthinkable. The real difficulty in working out the law lay in the Constitution, which would not permit the grant of real powers. And there were those who were not favorable, among them some of the leaders of General de Gaulle's *Rassemblement du Peuple Français*, as well as some of the traditional African chiefs, who were often extremely conservative. Those who wanted such a law had to work out a policy that would change the whole situation, so that blood would not be shed as it had been in Algeria. His superior officer (Defferre), Espinasse said, wanted to keep ahead of events, and, together with the aid of Pierre Messmer, Félix Houphouet-Boigny (then minister of state), and others, they managed to push the law through.[24]

Others closely connected with the government agreed with the project. Martial de La Fournières, then *chef de cabinet* (chief of staff) for the minister of the army, felt it was what needed to be done, and Bernard Tricot, then in a high position in Algerian affairs, looked upon it as a point of departure for what would be accomplished in the future for the overseas territories.[25]

Pierre Messmer, then *chef de cabinet* for Defferre, who was responsible for a considerable part of the law, believes that it was a step that pointed toward independence. Under that law, there would have been real autonomy in all the states of the former Empire, for they would have been able to govern themselves just as they wished (though, of course, the law stopped short of granting independence). The Fourth Republic was never able to make final decisions. Others were even more definite about it. Former Governor-General

Laurentie said that it came at the last possible moment of time to prevent a revolt in Black Africa. The *Loi-Cadre* gave hope without shedding blood, though it came, indeed, too late. Nevertheless, it had a considerable impact. Geoffroy de Courcel, then ambassador to England and one of de Gaulle's earliest adherents, said the law was in the right direction. A number of important people supported the law.[26]

Of course, there were those who felt that the law's purpose was other than the obvious one. Among these was Edouard Sablier, in 1967 the head of the television network, who said that Pierre Mendès-France, then prime minister, had begun the decolonization process by setting Tunisia on the road to freedom, and that the *Loi-Cadre* was an effort to arrest that process. Others, such as Governor-General Robert Delavignette, did not feel that this was the case.[27]

Indeed, most of the Africans to whom the author spoke about the *Loi-Cadre* did not feel it went far enough. The net result was that when the law was voted on in the National Assembly, Léopold Senghor and his supporters abstained, though they specified that they wanted the reforms carried out.[28] Only the Poujadists, grouped together, voted solidly against the decrees of the *Loi-Cadre*. The African politicians, however, agreed to work with it for the time being, though they pressed for its reform even before the measures contained in it were carried out. Senghor, always full of similes, as befitted the literary man he was, said that France's attitude was "a kind of hesitation waltz, in which you move two steps forward to go one step back, and in which the left hand takes back half of what the right hand gave." The African Labor Unions, meeting at Cotonou in Dahomey, were even more stringent in their comments. They saw the law as "a mystification, a façade, which fools no one. Its sole object is to divide us, to mask and to perpetuate the colonial regime." Even Houphouet-Boigny, who had worked on its development and had to supervise its execution, admitted that the decrees "were not an end in themselves . . . they were only one step in a momentous turn in African history."[29] Part of the Africans' resentment, naturally enough, was due to the fact that most of them, at least, had not been consulted during the preparation of the decrees.[30]

Summing up the matter with regard to the National Assembly, the French deputies, as well as the Colonial Administration, did not want to see executive power in the hands of a united group of Africans, so they would probably have voted against anything that led in that direction. In addition, French commercial men wanted to weaken administrative control in Black Africa so as to play on African inexperience. Luc Durand-Reville, "the ultra-reactionary first college senator from Gabon,"[31] said the *Loi-Cadre* was "a bastard tarred from birth as an unsuccessful hybrid, which experience will show to be impotent." African students summarized their feeling about it by making a cartoon of Africa "chained hand and foot" by the *Loi-Cadre*.[32] Thus it was, on the whole, rather remarkable that the law passed at all.

Thus the law and its decrees did not please many groups, French or African. It did not give full territorial self-government to Africans and therefore did not relieve the pressures for unity that were coming from the various countries, chief among them being, of course, the pressure on France to permit that unity. But change was in the air. In 1956, the debates in the African organizations dealt with territorial government and autonomy, whereas in 1957 they dealt with federation and independence.[33] But there were always divisions among them. The "territorialists," led by Apithy of Dahomey and Houphouet-Boigny, wanted the states separately to join in an equal federation with France, while the federalists, led by Senghor, wanted a responsible federation of the African states, which would later join France in a loose confederation.

One more point about the *Loi-Cadre* should be noted. The controversies in the Assembly over the law, and the general publicity regarding it, contrasted with the privacy of the decisions of the British constitutional conference that same year. Knowledge of what was going on was undoubtedly helpful to the Africans. They took such definite united stands in the debates that the sessions on the *Loi-Cadre* came to be known as "the revolt of the African deputies." These deputies were less clear about the powers of the AOF federation, which the European deputies wanted minimized and centered in Paris, not in Dakar. Later, in 1957, the debates concerning federalism developed further, and Senghor and his party tried to get more and more power for the federation, while Houphouet-Boigny opposed both independence and federation, calling only for a federation of France with the separate African territories.[34]

Looking back over the beginnings of decolonization, there was a long space of a whole decade when little seemed to happen between the Conference of Brazzaville and the dreadful defeat of France at Dien Bien Phu, when France lost Vietnam, one of her most prized colonies, for good. In 1954 and 1955, the Mendès-France and Edgar Faure governments had set in motion the liberation of Morocco and Tunisia from the French. These were momentous events for de Gaulle, watching from Colombey. It seems probable that, with his intense feeling for France and for her Empire, he felt these three occurrences even more keenly than he did England's action in giving self-government and then independence to Ghana in 1957, though Aristide Zolberg characterizes that as "the most important event in modern African history."[35]

Philip Williams and Martin Harrison, both of them authoritative writers, have said that "the Africans were satisfied for the moment," though they admit that their differences mounted steadily after the publication of the *Loi-Cadre*. African opinions, however, were certainly more varied than that about the *Loi-Cadre*. Léopold Senghor of Senegal recognized the law as an instrument of emancipation, but criticized the fact that it gave power to so many small states. Boubakar Guèye, then vice-president of the Senegal Assembly, said in December 1969 that the law did not go far enough, though it was a step toward independence, with which Onambélé, Secretary General of the National School of Administration, agreed. Jacques Rabemananjara, then minister of foreign affairs in Madagascar, topped it off by saying that, after all, the law was only a framework—and any frame was an empty thing that had to be filled in. Minister Houphouet-Boigny was quieter about it, though those approving the law thought it was a triumph for him and for his country. Perhaps that was not only because he had been instrumental in getting it into shape and passed, but also because, when the author saw him on March 28, 1972, the *Loi-Cadre* had been dead and buried for a good while and other changes had intervened. The promoters of the *Loi-Cadre* no doubt look back on it as a step forward, though it was soon outdistanced. Thus recollections of it were very different, and have become dim in the minds even of those who fathered it. Clearly, however, some of the formerly "colonized peoples" felt that the *Loi-Cadre* was not a straightforward step toward what they wanted.[36]

In reviewing what was said about all of these happenings, the frequent refusal of the human race to heed warnings and its desire to cling to old and worn-out traditions and regulations must be remembered. All the races seem to have this trait; it does not belong to the French alone. The refusal to be warned goes on century after century. Galileo saw that the earth still moved—no matter what the people of his time thought. A few people may see in advance of their time and work for reform, but for the many, perception of change comes slowly, and they refuse to admit the possibility until they are forced to accept it.

There was a certain skepticism about reforms among all the Africans. President Habib Bourguiba of Tunisia wrote in 1954:

> Don't let yourself be hypnotized by this French Union. For it seems today like the supreme manoeuver of a colonialism at bay, a kind of gold-beater's skin in rabbit fur. With events it could evolve. The question could then be put in a more valuable way. And given new data, we will see it more clearly. We can reconsider the whole matter, for I remain a convinced partisan of a close cooperation with France if France renounces its policy of domination.[37]

What did General de Gaulle, still walking through the Desert, think of this, the first great effort at reform since the Fourth Republic, after it had come into existence? It was, no doubt, as Williams and Harrison say, "the most hopeful achievement of the dying years of the Fourth Republic." Pierre Viansson-Ponté says that the *Loi-Cadre* began an evolution that de Gaulle "understood and approved"; on the other hand, André Givisiez, writing in *Afrique Contemporaine*, complains that de Gaulle, in his *Mémoires d'Espoir*, is unjust to the Defferre law "which gives the African and Malagasy Territories a large autonomy that will prepare them usefully for the practice of public life." Givisiez says the reform showed progress and marked an important step in advance, facilitating the later evolution toward independence. De Gaulle said, however, that

> in the territories of Black Africa and Madagascar, after having resisted a movement that led them to claim the right of disposing of themselves, and notably repressing a bloody revolt in the Great Island of the Indian Ocean, on the initiative of Gaston Defferre, they [the government] had applied the *Loi-Cadre* which created governments and native parliaments with important legislative and administrative capacities, without accepting the need of going further than this beginning; the reform remaining incomplete and beside the point.[38]

Still, General de Gaulle apparently did approve "the intentions" of the *Loi-Cadre*, though it was arranged for Algeria differently, because of the "federative orientation" of the law and its distinctions between the two communities

involved. Algeria, after all, was singular—not like other countries. But de
Gaulle thought it all came ten years too late, and he said that the regime,
which, after all, was incapable of transposing the law into fact, would not in
any way arrest the movement of the Arab demands; no one, indeed, could stop
that movement. Another regime, however, that would restore her youth to
France and make her attractive, could try an entirely new type of association.[39]

The General's opinions about the regime come out again in his remarks to
Louis Terrenoire, who later became his minister of information, and who has
given us perhaps the best idea of de Gaulle's thoughts during the Crossing of
the Desert:

> It was the eighteenth of May, 1955, when the General spoke to me for the first time of
> the future of Algeria.
> "We are in the presence," he said, "of a wave in the world that carries all the
> peoples towards emancipation. There are imbeciles who do not wish to understand
> it; talking to them is not worth while. But it is certain that if we wish to maintain our
> position in North Africa, we will have to do vast spectacular things, and create the
> conditions of a new association. Well, it is not the [present] regime that can do it. I
> myself would not be sure of succeeding" and, as I made a gesture of protest . . . "but
> certainly I would try to do it. . . . The [present] regime is entirely capable," he said,
> "of accustoming itself to successive abandonments and of absorbing them."

And again:

> Without a new regime that would restore its proper significance to the State, made
> of authority, continuity and efficacity, no righting of the situation could be
> accomplished.

Again, apparently later:

> Often the General feigned pessimism for the short run, and great optimism for the
> future:
> "The decadence can last fifty years more but the recovery will be all the more
> vigorous . . . but come on! France will bury us all!"[40]

Though de Gaulle had been partisan of a great federation in 1945 or even in
1950, henceforth he admitted that legal bonds had deceptive appearances.
Terrenoire quotes the words of Bourguiba:

> To end the current trial by a reasonable solution would enable France to save what
> ought to be saved, and even to increase her potential and her influence by turning
> her back on colonialism; the General could reconquer Africa by reconquering the
> heart of the Africans, such is the rôle that General de Gaulle could play today in
> saving the vocation of his country.[41]

Terrenoire also speaks of de Gaulle's comment to an Algerian writer, Jean
Amrouche, in an interview of April 1955:

> The Algerian affair is too large for this regime. Algeria will be emancipated. It will
> be long. There will be trouble. A great deal of trouble. You will have to suffer a great
> deal. As for me, I will only talk on the day when I am in a situation such that I can do
> what I will have said I would do.[42]

Raymond Offroi (a former French ambassador, later president of foreign affairs in the *Communauté*, and later deputy of the Department of Seine Maritime) has also made very interesting comments on the attitudes of de Gaulle during the Desert period, when he saw him a number of times. He points out that the defeat at Dien Bien Phu was a warning sign for the General. After France's subjects had beaten her, General de Gaulle felt that she could no longer keep her colonies. In 1952 and 1953, de Gaulle was the only one in the RPF who was for independence for the former colonies; the others were still colonialist in their attitudes. But de Gaulle wanted complete independence and cooperation, especially for Indochina, and he once said in the presence of Mendès-France that peace must be made on the basis of independence.[43]

Finally, Louis Terrenoire has given us a glimpse of de Gaulle's last days in the Desert:

> At the approach of the decisive weeks of 1958, General de Gaulle appears to me like a watcher in the night, with a cluster of light-rays in his hands whose illumination leaves immense patches of shadow between his face and the line of the horizon, between what he thinks is truth for the future and all that separates him from it. He is silent, he listens, and, in spite of appearances he prepares himself. If, again, History beckons to him, above all he will avoid binding himself.[44]

16

The Climax of Decolonization

> Decolonization is not only the struggle of people for
> their independence, it is also a mixture of the ideal and
> of interest. It is a drama, with innocent victims on one
> side or the other, it is the faith of some and the passivity
> of the many. It is a moment of History in the Twentieth
> Century.
>
> —Elgey

> You don't go to the banks of the Rubicon to go fishing.
> —Delbecque

The story of the steps in General de Gaulle's return to power after the crisis of
May 13, 1958, in Algiers—carried out with the menace of a military takeover
there or in France—is too well known to recount here. Besides, there is so much
in that story that has not yet been made clear that it would be folly to attempt
it. Invested as prime minister by the National Assembly in Paris on June 1,
1958, de Gaulle turned his attention first to the burning question of Algeria. As
he said later, it was a time when, with mediocrity assailing him from all sides,
his task was to seek greatness. At that time he wondered, too, whether it would
be possible to solve the vital problem of decolonization.[1] His only reference to
the overseas lands before coming to power was at his first press conference at
the Palais d'Orsay on May 19, when he said that the party system had not
solved the problems of the association of France with the African countries, nor
that of coexistence with the communities in Algeria.[2]

De Gaulle was, of course, different himself when he returned. After all, the
twelve years out of power would have had an effect on anyone. Jean Ferniot
has written of him at the time of that first meeting with the press:

> The General has aged. His figure is heavier, the planes of his face have disappeared,
> the great nose has become a huge nose, in his hands he holds—stylishly—the folded
> spectacles with the thick glasses that protect his sore eyes. But he keeps all his
> authority and his voice remains firm. It has even gained a new charm by becoming
> more muted. He establishes himself behind a small table covered with a green cloth,
> equipped with loud-speakers, his interminable legs folded back under the chair. The
> familiar gestures come back to him, arms that separate like wings, an index finger
> that points.[3]

Of course, a number of people in France had been working on the African
problem for some time. The Africans had proposed a very considerable
revision of the 1946 Constitution; Professor François Luchaire had suggested

excising *Titre* VIII, the offending article about the former colonies. A constituent assembly of the French Union had also been suggested by the constitutional specialist Maurice Duverger, and François Mitterand wanted a conference of the government and of African representatives to create a Franco-African community. Marc Jaquet, who had been minister of France Overseas for some time, was working on plans for such a meeting. But the French politicians were unwilling to accept either partial sacrifice of French sovereignty in a federal egalitarian constitution or practical independence of the territories in a loose confederation. The Africans had more hope in de Gaulle. Senghor saw him soon after his return and reported him as favorable to the plans of his PRA.[4]

On June 13 an interministerial committee was set up, and Houphouet-Boigny and former Prime Minister Pierre Pflimlin were entrusted with the problem of *Titre* VIII. Preparations were beginning for the great change. But, previous to his return, had de Gaulle known what a different Black Africa he would find when he went there again—or even when he dealt with its representatives in Paris? A good many of his private remarks about Algeria while he was in the Desert have been repeated, but almost nothing about Africa south of the Sahara. As he said in 1958, he had made no declaration on the subject for three years.[5] Alexander Werth remarks that "De Gaulle was fully conscious of the Awakening of Africa," that he took the reasonably progressive view of "enlightened capitalism," and that he thought the independence of the Black African countries (with the possible exception of South Africa) was only a matter of years. Thus in the long run Europe's best chance in Africa was "to leave in order to stay."[6]

We know, on the other hand, a great deal of what was going on in the minds of the blacks. They had formed parties, now that suppression of political activity in Black Africa had diminished somewhat, and those parties now stood for definite policies for their countries. But they had not made real and vocal demands for independence before the time of de Gaulle's return. Indeed, only the student organizations, the important UGTAN (*Union Générale des Travailleurs de l'Afrique Noire*—the Central Union of Workers of Black Africa) and a small Marxist party of African Independence (*Parti Africain de l'Indépendance*) were the only open partisans of independence so far.[7] However, the Africans were now divided one group from the other to a very considerable extent. And this division, or "quarrel," was passed on to the French through contact with their very able group of leaders.

Among these leaders, there were three whose names, already referred to, are now known all over the world and who were destined to be known as closely connected with General de Gaulle. He would have to reckon with all these in the process of decolonization: Léopold Sédar Senghor, Félix Houphouet-Boigny and Sékou Touré. Senghor comes to mind first, perhaps because he began in a different career (that of poet), and his works had been widely read before Houphouet-Boigny came into general view at the time of World War II. Coming from a well-to-do family in the country of Senegal, young Léopold studied at Dakar, and then went on scholarship to Paris, where he received first the *Licencié ès Lettres,* so honored in France, and later the diploma of the *Etudes Supérieures;* still later, in 1935, the *Agrégation.* One can go no higher in the French academic world, and Senghor was the first African to receive that degree. Later, as a naturalized Frenchman, he taught in French schools. Senghor wished, he said, "to assimilate not be assimilated," for though he was a product of French education, he nevertheless prized his African culture. Later, he called that heritage *négritude.* He illumined his race and its future by his literary work before he came to politics. In contact with Aimé Césaire very early, in 1934, he helped him to found the magazine *L'Etudiant Noir (The Black Student),* which brought to general knowledge the word and the theory of *négritude.* He says, "Thus we discovered, between the years 1930 and 1940, the marvels of desire, the vital force of African Negroes." After mobilization, Senghor was in a prison camp for two years during the war, and when he emerged and went back to teaching, he joined the Resistance. The poem he wrote to de Gaulle, in September 1940, is worth recording:

To Guélowar (the Noble One)

Guélowar!
We have listened to you, we have heard you with the ears of our hearts.
Luminous, your voice burst into the night of our prison . . .
Guélowar!
Your voice speaks of honor, of hope and of the combat, and its wings flutter
    in our breasts.
Your voice tells us of the Republic, that we will build in the City in the
    blue day.
In the equality of fraternal peoples and we tell ourselves "We are present,
    O Guélowar!"[8]

Senghor continued to write later, and a book of his poetry was published in 1945. Two of his poems appeared in the first and famous issue of the magazine *Présence Africaine* in November–December 1947. A biographer said that "the liberation of France marked a turning-point in his life," and though the Brazzaville Conference was timid in its reforms, still it set off a movement, as we have seen, that affected the Africans as a whole very deeply.[9] He was converted to socialism in 1945, oddly enough by the recent president of France, Georges Pompidou, a school friend. Also in 1945, he was elected by the Socialist party to be one of the two Senegalese deputies to the Constituent Assembly following de Gaulle's decision to admit African representatives to that body. His companion at the Assembly, the other deputy from Senegal, was the elder statesman of African socialism, Lamine Guèye. Thinking Africans were much affected in the next years by Vietnam's effort to do away with colonialism, and also by the excessive repression in Madagascar after the abortive uprising in 1947. Senghor was soon divided from Lamine Guèye, for Guèye wanted to adhere always to the French branch of SFIO (*Section Française de l'Internationale Ouvrière*), and Senghor felt that an entirely African party was necessary. Nor did he care for the RDA of Houphouet-

Boigny, for it was still allied with the Communist party, so, amid all sorts of protests, he founded a different African party: the *Bloc Démocratique Sénégalais* (Senegalese Democratic Group). The party was very successful, and it placed him at the head of the political work going on in Senegal, thereby assuring him of the presidency when the country became independent. In the fifties, Senghor was secretary of state to the Presidency of the Council in Edgar Faure's administration. He tried to warn the French government of the importance of the conference at Bandoung, and he did not agree with it in its Algerian policy. After 1956, his party was called the *Bloc Populaire Sénégalais*, and when the *Loi-Cadre* was passed, he protested against what he felt was the "balkanization" of the African states.

The issue of federalism was the essential reason for the division between the groups of politically minded Africans. Senghor and his party wanted a federal government in Africa, with some connection to France, but an arrangement that would not be subject to France. Africa, they felt, must be united within itself by one or more federations, before attaching itself to the metropole. The African states would thus be protected better in their new independence. They did not want abrupt secession, though the followers of the party were crying out for independence.[10]

Another of the important Africans with whom de Gaulle would deal was the head of the largest African party, the RDA (*Rassemblement Démocratique Africain*), Félix Houphouet-Boigny, who later became president of the Ivory Coast. Houphouet-Boigny was born in 1905 at Yamoussoukro in the Ivory Coast, the son of a prosperous planter said to be descended from one of the Ashanti kings. Some say, however, that he was born a peasant (no doubt because of his family's occupation). Studying first in the Medical School at Dakar, he became a medical assistant—the highest medical grade Africans were allowed then to attain. By 1940 he was chief in his own district and a planter in his own right. He first came into public notice when he started an agricultural union in 1944. Finally, outraged by the discriminatory tactics of the colonial commercial regime, which did not grant Africans fair prices for their products, he set out in 1946 to form a new party, the RDA, whose purpose was the emancipation of the overseas peoples. By 1948, the party controlled a majority of the votes in five of the eight territories of French West Africa. In 1945, Houphouet-Boigny was elected deputy from the Ivory Coast to the French Constituent Assembly, at the same time as Senghor, remaining there until 1959. Early in his work there, he helped in the Assembly adoption of the Houphouet-Boigny Bill abolishing forced labor in West Africa.[11] His fame in his own country has been based on this achievement ever since.

Houphouet-Boigny was disliked by the French government during the time that his RDA was allied with the Communist party of France. He has told people since that he was never really a Communist, but that this affiliation was necessary in the early years of his party, for no other group would help in his work. Still, he appeared to be Communist then, and the French were very wary of him.

In 1949, there were instances of revolt in the Ivory Coast, generally arising

Léopold Sédar Senghor, President of Senegal since 1958.

from the RDA's opponents and used by the government as excuses to arrest local RDA leaders. The administration's dislike of Houphouet-Boigny stemmed partly, also, from the suspicion that he controlled the territory more effectively than they did; the party had its own judicial system with law enforcement officers.[12]

At an inaugural meeting of an opposition party on January 30, 1949, Houphouet-Boigny was denounced and not permitted to defend himself. At another meeting, in February, there was a riot and houses were attacked. One person was killed, four injured, and forty-six arrested. Other incidents occurred around Dimbokro in the Baule district, and the administration began a campaign against the RDA party and Houphouet-Boigny's union, the *Syndicat Agricole Africain*. Several people were shot, including a small child on its mother's back, and the village was plundered and burned. By the end of the year, there was trouble everywhere in the territory; some leaders were imprisoned, and it all ended, as we have seen, in a mass march by the women on the prison. The RDA claimed, however, that it was loyal to the French Union, and it managed to survive until, in 1950, the ties with the Communists were cut. After that, Houphouet-Boigny gained in favor with the French.

Houphouet-Boigny's group in the Assembly tried to form an alliance with the *Indépendants d'Outre-Mer*, a small section of mostly black deputies, among them Senghor, Apithy, and Louis-Paul Aujoulat, a white representative of the

President Félix Houphouet-Boigny of the
Ivory Coast.

Africans, who had banded together to increase their power in the Assembly by
forming a parliamentary section independent of the metropolitan groups.
Negotiations broke down, but as the RDA came closer to the government, that
group became respectable in spite of the fact that Houphouet-Boigny had
previously denounced the government and its policy. But the closeness to the
more conservative side of the Assembly did not last for long, and soon
Houphouet-Boigny was considered almost treasonable again. In 1952 the
Union Démocratique et Sociale de la Résistance (UDSR) joined what was left of
the RDA, since neither had the necessary fourteen to sixteen members to make
it possible to form a group according to the Assembly rules. After that, the
attacks ceased.[13]

The Africans were slowly acquiring some sort of status with the French
government in the fifties. Even laws concerning them were improving. In 1950,
the Second Lamine Guèye Law was passed, requiring equal pay, recruitment
possibilities, and promotion for African civil servants in accordance with
European standards. Times were still hard, but after the funeral of the victims
at Dimbokro, a black deputy was heard to say, "It is no longer a time to insult
each other when fifteen inhabitants of the Ivory Coast have just been buried.
For us Africans, there is a simple but tragic question to be answered. Twice we
have been ready to die for France. For whom are these men dying now?"[14]

Houphouet-Boigny was in the middle of the disturbance, but, claiming parliamentary immunity as a deputy, he refused to go with the officers who came to arrest him. It is rumored that on one occasion, there was an attack on his life. Mortimer says that it was just as well that he did withdraw when the troops came to arrest him, for crowds had gathered to protect him, and he was only just able to quiet them. [15]

Over the years President Houphouet-Boigny has become much loved in his country, and he certainly gives the impression of being a powerful man and a statesman in thought. Though he is not the literary man that Senghor has always been, he is well able to express himself when he wishes to do so. He wrote a paragraph, in 1946, that is a challenge to those who promoted forced labor:

> One has to have seen these worn-out workers, skeletons covered with sores, wandering or in the fields; one has to have seen assembled for recruitment these thousands of men, their whole bodies trembling before the medical inspectors; one has to have watched the distracted flights from the *chefs de village* or *chefs de canton* into the bush; one has to have seen the long lines of men, women, and children, brows furrowed, march silently along the road to the fields; one has to have seen the recruiting agents, the modern slave traders, crowd people heedlessly in trucks, exposed to all climates or lock them into baggage cars like animals; one must have lived, as chief, through the poignant heart-rending scenes, when old women ask for their sons, their only source of support, orphans ask for their fathers, women weighed down by children for their husbands, their only providers, in order to understand the drama of forced labor in Ivory Coast. [16]

Sékou Touré, the new young Guinean leader who had now come on the scene, is of rougher temper than Senghor or Houphouet-Boigny. After all, he claims to be a descendant of Samori-Touré, [17] the great Soudanese warrior of the late nineteenth century. He did not have the classical schooling that both Senghor and Houphouet-Boigny received in Paris or Dakar. He made his way through the labor unions—the *syndicats*. Born in 1922, he began to work in the French Company of the Niger at the age of eighteen, and by 1945 he had become secretary-general of the postal syndicate of the CGT (*Confédération Générale du Travail*—the General Confederation of Workers, or labor union). Politically, he was a member of the RDA and one of its founders. In 1956 he was elected deputy and mayor of Conakry, the capital of Guinea, and after a year he had become president of the UGTAN (the *Union Générale des Travailleurs d'Afrique Noire*—the General Union of Workers of Black Africa). After the *Loi-Cadre* began to be applied, he had reached the post of vice president of the government of Guinea. He was rigid in applying the party regulations, and soon he began attempts to break the hold of the traditional chiefs of the country. Though he was a newcomer, he had enormous influence and was willing to use it. Few men in the world have reached the summit of their country's power so quickly. Both Senghor and Houphouet-Boigny must have known they would have to get on with him, and that it might be difficult. [18]

In 1957 Senghor founded the party of the African Convention. Its goals were African unity, political autonomy, and the right to self-determination. In

March 1958 some African Socialist deputies who had left the French SFIO (*Section Française de l'Internationale Ouvrière*) joined the Convention, and it took the name of the *Parti du Regroupement Africain* (PRA, Party of African Regroupment). The new party planned to hold its first congress at Cotonou, the capital of Dahomey, on July 25, 1958.[19]

Meantime, the RDA, after a congress at Bamako in what is now Mali in September 1957, had been talking of an egalitarian federation with France, with no idea of secession. The federating executive power would be in France, and the African territories would be autonomous, except for certain designated powers held by France. Thus Houphouet-Boigny proposed a definite federation, while Senghor wanted a confederation similar to that of the British Commonwealth.

Obviously there was deep division in the thought of the two groups, and controversy causing tension developed. Sékou Touré belonged to the RDA; nevertheless, in October 1957 he came out publicly for federal executives to be established at both Dakar and Brazzaville, a solution quite different from the RDA's plans. Ruth Morgenthau has noted that African debates had centered in 1956 around the problems of territorial government and autonomy, while the discussions of 1957 and 1958 centered on federation and independence. These questions brought out in both parties the difference in thought between the generations in Africa and the great difference in opinion of the parties and of some African peoples. Houphouet-Boigny and the RDA wanted the power and the ideas to start from the territories, ending up with a federation, with France at the summit. Senghor and his group (the PRA—*Parti Republicain Africain*) talked of federations that would begin in the African states and be related rather loosely to France after they had been set up. Sékou Touré was not close to either group after he left the RDA. No one, in 1957 and early 1958, seems to have thought of severing all ties with France, though they were beginning to discuss French institutions and culture and their value. African unity, the chief subject of discussion, concerned not only French links to Africa but also the new responsibilities coming under the *Loi-Cadre*.[20]

Five days after de Gaulle came to power, at the beginning of June 1958, the *Parti Démocratique de Guinée* (The PDG—Democratic Party of Guinea) held a congress at Conakry, the waterbound capital of the territory of Guinea. The statements and demands put forth were very clear. They said that France remained the nation with which they intended to ally their destinies, but she must realize that such a political option was the fruit of neither fear nor opportunism—only the correct expression of a deliberate and enlightened will. Then they went on to make a series of demands. The new constitutional revisions must be dominated by this dynamic spirit:

> Recognition of internal autonomy.
> Constitution of a Federal Executive.
> Transformation of the Grand Council into a Legislative Assembly with full powers in the matters reserved for the Territories now possessed by the High Commissioner and the Ministry of France Overseas—this last to be suppressed.

> Creation of a Franco-African Community of the French West African States and Madagascar, with a Federal Parliament and Government. This means the transformation of the present Assembly of the French Union, which would act on matters belonging to the Federal Community.

The PDG added that the recognition of the right to independence of Algeria would help in enabling the other Maghrebin states, and Togo and the Cameroons, to join the Federal Community.[21]

This was certainly straight talking. What they wanted was spelled out, except, perhaps, for whatever small portion of power or usefulness would be left to France. Some report of this must have reached General de Gaulle at the Elysée.

The next event of importance in this African dispute was the prearranged meeting of the PRA (*Parti du Regroupement Africain* under the leadership of Senghor) at Cotonou on July 25–27. Michael Crowder says of it:

> The demand for immediate and total independence was carried by the Congress and even acclaimed by conservative leaders like Lamine Guèye, who was either carried away by the enthusiasm of the moment, or, perhaps, wanted to place his cautious colleague and former rival, Senghor, in an embarrassing position. Only Senghor, with considerable courage, in view of the conservative nature of his views on the subject, sounded a note of warning about total independence at the close of the conference.[22]

Apparently, the PRA leaders did realize the problems that would be raised by these demands, and they attempted to think out possible solutions such as that of linking France directly with territories transformed into republics. (This was the idea ultimately adopted by de Gaulle.) There might be a confederation of the two existing federations to be joined by France; or they might declare their independence first, and then join with France as sovereign states. Of course, there was also the possibility of complete independence. Senghor must have put himself in a bad corner at one point in the conference when he cried out, "Independence by September!"[23] Of course, the French would be hostile to this anyway, for the federations might soon be strong enough to demand independence, and France might then be dominated by her former colonies.[24]

The Guinean party (PDG) held a Territorial Assembly on July 28, 1958, and Touré told his adherents of all that had been done in Guinea thus far, adding that his government had informed the French people that any constitution that did not end the old and impossible policy of assimilation and did not recognize the right of independence of the former colonies, as well as the principle of equality of peoples, would be firmly rejected by his government. He added again the Guineans' wish that France would speedily construct a federation of states.[25]

Such was the situation in West Africa in the two months after de Gaulle came to power. The General spent those months in dealing with governmental problems at home and in going twice to Algeria, where the situation was going from bad to worse. But to improve matters in Africa, he received the black

A delegation of Africans at the Elysée, 1959.

leaders on July 14 and gave the Africans a first taste of something new. The vice-presidents of their *conseils de gouvernement* would now be presidents of the Councils of Ministers and would thus have as real authority as prime ministers for the countries they represented.[26] By July 29, the Consultative Constitutional Committee de Gaulle had named came together for its first meeting and was given the report of the Interministerial Committee. The Africans on it were Senghor and Lamine Guèye for the PRA, Gabriel Lisette of Chad for the RDA, and Philibert Tsiranana, head of the government of Madagascar. But before this committee met, the French government, now in the person of de Gaulle, had already begun to act. By July 30, when the preliminary draft of the new Constitution of the Fifth Republic was published, a good deal of it had already leaked out. It contained no recognition of the territories as states, though they would dispose of their own affairs, and there would be representation of the Africans in the Senate; but the Constitution did not indicate that it would permit self-determination or the right to independence.

This had happened when the delegates were still at Cotonou, and a resolution condemning de Gaulle's draft was published, together with the demand for the calling of a National Constituent Assembly. This Assembly would organize a federation based on equality and the sacrifice of some sovereignty by the territories who were demanding immediate autonomy. It would consider negotiation after the Constituent Assembly had met, without abandoning the will to unify the African states into a "United States of Africa."

Their password would be "immediate independence," and they would mobilize all Africans around those words. Senghor was the author of this plan, but he had worded it to mitigate its roughness by saying, "Immediate Independence but not in the immediate future." His second in command, Mamadou Dia, said that the PRA did not believe in the de Gaulle government which led the party by its inadequate proposals to pose the problem of independence. Independence should come first—the rest later. He added: "In colonial matters France is always one reform behind." The delegates were, all of them, for independence—even Lamine Guèye, who for so long had not wanted it.[27]

Senghor, and possibly Sékou Touré, had a chance to see General de Gaulle after this, but the interviews must have been trying in the extreme, for de Gaulle was not pleased. As far as one can understand his mind, he was for autonomy and possibly for real independence in the future, but the future was not now. The blue haze on the horizon of the future had not cleared away. General de Gaulle expected to grant independence, not to have it forced from him.[28] Cotonou made him speak in an acid manner: "A leader," he pointed out, "should lead his troops, not follow them." As for the anticolonial polemics that were now in fashion, he did not think much of them. Why could Africans not admit that French colonialism had done them good? After all, had it not been for Roman colonialism, "who would have taught us Gauls to wash?"[29] Senghor left somewhat chastened. There is no word about how Sékou Touré felt about that interview, or whether he was really there, for Mortimer, who wrote of it, is uncertain whether Touré and de Gaulle ever met before their fateful confrontation at Conakry at the end of August.[30] Apparently Sékou Touré did see de Gaulle on August 8, though he was not a member of the Constitutional Committee; nor was he with Senghor when he saw the General.[31]

On August 8, de Gaulle attended a meeting of the group of the Constitutional Committee that was dealing with overseas problems. At that meeting he made an important announcement, saying that the referendum in September was for the purpose of finding out whether or not the idea of secession was uppermost everywhere in the overseas territories. He added that the rejection of the Constitution suggested would mean "independence with all that it carried of charges, responsibilities and dangers." Approval of the Constitution meant the desire to build a new ensemble on the basis of spontaneous acceptance. After this, he worked on a new imaginative scheme of his own. Tsiranana of Madagascar gave it the name of *Community*. A few powers would be held in common; the institutions would be related to a federation; but every five years its members, all autonomous, would choose between independence and a confederation. This text he would take with him when he made his dramatic trip around Africa, as a solid basis for the future of France linked with the territories.[32]

The same day that the Constitutional Committee met (August 8), de Gaulle, says Georges Chaffard, made a speech over the radio, saying: "Of course one might want secession, but it held duties. It carried with it dangers. Independence had its cost. The referendum would test whether the idea of secession would carry the day." And he referred again to the consequences the French government would draw from the manifestation of such a desire, whereas an affirmative answer would mean the rejection of secession.[33] The Africans reacted "in sorrow and in anger" at de Gaulle's policy. Forgetting, at least in part, about what he had said at Cotonou, Lamine Guèye urged: "I implore you, do not put weapons in the hands of those who really favor secession. We can only be Frenchmen like you if you are willing to be Frenchmen with us. . . . Since you are creating an association of free peoples, at least leave us the right to enter it one day: we will never do so without your consent, only by unanimous agreement." Senghor said that "for Africans, the recognition of their right to independence is a question of dignity. . . . If you do not give us the option which we demand, certainly we shall remain French in our civilization, but nonetheless we shall vote against the Constitution. Have the Bretons been told that if *they* vote 'No', they will be Separatists? Why then should that be said to us? . . . If I refuse a federal association and pronounce for a confederal one, the alternative stated by General de Gaulle means that confederation equals secession."[34]

It was apparently at this point that Tsiranana's suggestion of the word *Community* instead of *Federation* came into the picture. Also, the "Community of Free Peoples" became an "Association of Free (i.e., independent) States." There would be an Assembly which delegates from all the countries would attend. It would have some powers over economic and foreign policy. An Executive Council of Prime Ministers and one other minister from each state would manage Community affairs. These included currency, foreign affairs, defense, diplomacy, common economic and financial policy, justice, higher education, strategic raw materials, transport, and telecommunications. But who would be the executive for these powers? The text was unclear on this point.[35] But this Constitutional Committee report reached the Elysée, and changes were made:

> The option to change status every five years disappeared and it was merely stated that change could happen in the future, but, if independent, a State would no longer be in the Community.
> The Assembly would be a "Senate" with only those powers relegated to it by the Legislative Assemblies of the States.
> The executive powers fell somewhere between the Executive Council and the President of the Republic, who was also President of the Community. He would be elected by a college including overseas representatives.[36]

As it emerged from the Elysée, this was really the first draft of the Community. Since independence was conceded only "grudgingly" and meant leaving the Community, and "secession" with its "consequences" indicated being considered as "foreign countries" with economic penalties, the Africans felt exasperated.[37] However, the final text changed considerably during de Gaulle's trip around Africa. It was not published until September 4.

De Gaulle's much publicized trip began at Orly on August 21, 1958, and ended in Algiers on August 26, as far as the sub-Saharan countries were concerned. His first stop was at Fort Lamy in Chad, where the acting premier, Jules Toura Gaba, greeted him. He made no public speech there, but his reception by the people was "triumphant."[38] Next he flew to Tananarive, the capital of Madagascar, where he began the task of winning the African people over to his plans for them. Obviously, convincing the leaders would not be enough. He must reach the masses.[39]

At Tananarive, de Gaulle spoke in the sports arena down by the central lake of the town, a lake encircled by purple jacaranda trees, gorgeous at the blooming season. Above, on the hill, stands the elaborate stone mass of the palace of Queen Ranavalo, the last queen of Madagascar. It is so magnificent and yet so gingerbready that it looks as if it had been built by the architects Queen Victoria sent down there during the ninteenth-century years when Madagascar was essentially British.

De Gaulle told the vast crowd gathered there, "Tomorrow you will again be a State, as when this palace was inhabited." The crowd applauded wildly. But Tsiranana, later that day, said to a newsman, "When I let my heart talk, I am a partisan of total and immediate independence; when I let my reason speak, I realize that it is impossible."[40] The crowd continued to be enthusiastic, though they did not know what de Gaulle's plans would mean in the future. Would independence come? And, if so, when?

The next stop was Brazzaville in the Middle Congo, where de Gaulle had set up his first capital at the end of 1940. De Gaulle was immensely popular there, as demonstrated by the many children in the district named "N'Gol" after him.[41] Before he spoke, General de Gaulle saw Barthélémy Boganda, the leader of Oubangui-Chari. Boganda had been for some time a deputy in the National Assembly at Paris. He had a great deal of personal beauty and charisma, and the people of Oubangui-Chari were devoted to him. He must, indeed, have had charm and an active mind and persuasive speech, for he was able to make a real effect on de Gaulle. He told him that the territories of Oubangui-Chari, Guinea, Senegal, Dahomey, and Niger would vote no in the referendum of September 28, if they were convinced that they had to renounce all idea of independence by a yes vote. Indeed, a further step in the decolonizing process was necessary, and de Gaulle's speech there at Brazzaville showed that it was on the way.[42]

After referring to the past, when he, General de Gaulle, had been among them, and to French pride in what had been accomplished in Africa, he told the people of the Middle Congo of his plans for the Community. It would be based on two main principles: the entire responsibility of the peoples of a country for their own affairs, and their right to group themselves in large ensembles within the Community. "But," he said, "people think also 'We have a right to independence.' Yes, certainly! Indeed, independence, whoever wishes to take it may act immediately. The Metropole will not oppose it. A certain Territory may have it at once if it votes 'No' in the Referendum on September 28. That will mean that it does not wish to be in the Community, and that, in effect, it secedes. In doing so, it follows an isolated road at its own risks and perils. The Metropole will draw the consequences, and I guarantee she will not oppose it."

De Gaulle then went on to clarify how the Community would evolve. But if the electoral body voted yes of its own free will; then the Community of which he had spoken would be constructed now; and he was sure that would be to everyone's advantage. Even better, if, at the end of a certain time (which he would not specify), a territory felt it could undertake the duties of independence, its elected assembly could so decide by a referendum of the inhabitants. The Community would receive notice of that, and would settle all affairs by agreement between the country that wanted independence and the Community itself. Again, the metropole would not oppose this arrangement. But the metropole, too, would keep its right to sever the bonds between the Community and the territory, for it is evident to everyone that the Community will impose heavy charges on the metropole. He hoped, with all his heart, that the metropole would continue to bear these expenses, but she must keep, too, her own power of decision. He believed, he said, that this work was essential for the common political power, for economic and cultural development, and, if it was necessary, for the common defense. No one is unaware today, he said, that great dangers are latent in the world; great menaces hang over our heads, especially in Africa. Under the ideological shield lies the imperialism of the interests and the desire for a bridgehead which might facilitate invasion. It was not possible to conceal that, and it was the reason why France offered the Africans this common ensemble which would permit them, together with her, to ward off this menace. "It is for the Africans to choose," he went on, "and with my whole soul I hope that they will choose what I propose. I wish it for them, for there are enough bonds between them and me so that I can speak frankly. I wish for France that her work may continue in spite of the heavy expenses. She must feel called to this effort by the sympathy and friendship of those who live in Africa. Also, I wish this project for a world that needs so much to see cooperation established on firm bases by those who desire to be and to remain free. Long live the Republic, long live France!"[43]

This was as full an explanation as one can find anywhere of General de Gaulle's policy for the Community, and it was a great advance, for it gave real hope of independence and told how it could be obtained, although it did not give the time a state must wait to apply for it. This speech and the one on August 25 at Abidjan, where he was "hailed as a bringer of friendship and freedom," marked the high point of de Gaulle's hopes for the Community, and his belief that it would come into being in the form he desired.[44] It was his brainchild, and in proposing it, he had two trump cards that would work for him: the economic aid that France would give young states, and the feeling for de Gaulle himself that had grown up in most of Africa. Perhaps he could win the gamble. The two speeches in Guinea and Dakar that followed, however, would show the dangers to which his project was exposed.[45] Nothing would seem so sure, so safe, after that speech in Brazzaville.

The pictures of Ahmed Sékou Touré show a rather heavy-set man with a round head, broad features, and extraordinarily brilliant black eyes. When he smiles in a photograph his face has a rather strong appeal, winning in character, but there is little solidity or direction in it. He appears to be a man of force and will, but where will he go? In any case, de Gaulle was firmly opposed to African federations loosely tied to France, and Sékou Touré had been somewhat violent in desiring independence at the *Parti Démocratique de Guinée* congress in early June. Furthermore, de Gaulle had been very much irritated by the Congress of Cotonou; and the Territorial Assembly meeting on July 28, which had rejected his Constitution, was also unpleasing to him. Still, the explosion that occurred was not expected.

Meantime, a group headed by Lamine Guèye was at work on another project. It suggested an assimilated Department of the French Republic as an independent state within the "Community of Free Peoples" or within a confederation linked to France by agreement; but de Gaulle was not interested in such a project, for if a confederation was permitted, a possible federation would soon disappear. Those in the confederation would have more advantages and much more independence; and others would copy them. De Gaulle remarked, " 'Federation' or 'Confederation,' these are only words. I, de Gaulle, say 'Federation' and there we stop." The Africans thought that such an arrangement might give them both independence and a Community, but it was not to be, at least not in that form. We know, however, that Sékou Touré was outraged by the policy de Gaulle was following in ruling that a country voting no in the referendum would have seceded, and that he said, "Charles de Gaulle has said that we can take independence with all its consequences. I shall reply for my part, that the consequences are not exclusively African but may be French as well."[46]

Trouble began on the way back to town from the Conakry airport where Sékou Touré met de Gaulle on August 25. The Guinean leader was given a place in the fifth car instead of the first—in which he thought he ought to have been at de Gaulle's side. He was insulted, and so were his followers. Who it was who made that mistake no one has told. On the way to the city, the crowds hailed "Silly," the Guinean name for elephant. It was also Sékou's own symbol. The placards put up everywhere had the Cross of Lorraine marked on the elephant, but that did not conceal the fact that the cheers of the crowd were directed toward their own leader instead of his guest. De Gaulle was not used to that. Then, at some point, a copy of Touré's speech had been given Governor Jean Mauberna of Guinea, as was customary. He showed it to Overseas Minister Bernard Cornut-Gentil, who accompanied de Gaulle. The minister looked at it and then showed it to Pierre Messmer, the French high commissioner. These gentlemen are said to have seen little or nothing wrong in it. They are reported as saying something like, "That's the way Sékou Touré talks." Mauberna told de Gaulle that the speech had nothing in it about the referendum; so de Gaulle paid no attention to it, and, some say, stuffed it into his pocket. Others say it was pocketed by Cornut-Gentil or Mauberna. The accounts vary. What is certain is that the General was taken by surprise by Sékou Touré's speech. His aides had not taken into account General de Gaulle's intense pride in France and her now-disappearing Empire, and his rather oversensitive attitudes on such subjects. Otherwise, they would have seen to it that he read the speech.[47] However, all seemed to go well until after the arrival of the cortège in Conakry and the walk to the old white Assembly Hall on one of the tree-shaded streets of the town. De Gaulle found a chance on the way to invite Sékou Touré to fly into Dakar in his plane next day when he was due there.

When the Guinean leader rose to speak, he forgot the softer words with which one addresses a superior officer, and his voice grew harsh and cold as he turned rather toward the large excited crowd than toward de Gaulle. Sometimes the rhythm of loud applause accented what he said, and General de Gaulle seemed bothered more by these frantic, noisy gusts of approval than by the words of the speaker. De Gaulle looked pale and tired. There was an outdoor loudspeaker, too, shouting away. The whole atmosphere was dramatic in the extreme.[48]

The formation of Sékou Touré's beliefs about Guinea had begun when he joined in the *Confédération Générale du Travail* (CGT—the French labor union). While Senghor and Houphouet-Boigny had been thoroughly trained in the French manner, he had arrived at his position as spokesman for Guinea only through his union training. He always chose the most radical alternative, and this affected what he said at Conakry on August 25, 1958. His ideology was expressed in public speeches rather than in thought-out philosophies. There was more desire for action than thought in his words. His basic concern was to beat colonialism. He believed that there was a natural trend toward unity, though African societies were divided, not as a healthy pluralism, but as contradictory forces. Unity must be shown by support of the dominant party, the *Parti Démocratique de Guinée*, of which he was the leader. Sékou Touré felt he must eliminate regionalism and racism in order to reinforce the nation, and failure in unity could stem only from those "who willfully interfere with the natural course of history." Political support for the party meant participation in the Community by Guinea.[49] With ideas such as these, it is easy to see why he would oppose membership in any such Community as de Gaulle suggested.

The Guinean leader began by blaming the retarded conditon of his country on colonialism. A poor man, he said, wishes to efface the inequalities and injustices, and since the Guineans had been subjected to much of those lacks of liberality, they felt it deeply. Their first need was dignity, which does not come without liberty, and Guinea would prefer poverty in freedom to riches in slavery. The fundamental object of the Guineans lay in the complete decolonization of Africa to make it possible to build a solid Franco-African Community. We are Africans, and our territory cannot be a part of France. We will be citizens of our African states, members of the Franco-African Community. He spoke also of the sum of new possibilities that emancipation contained. They—the Guineans—required the complete disappearance of the colonial phenomenon and the establishment of an era of true liberty, of equality, and of active fraternity.[50]

There was more—much more—but the bare words do not seem so violent today. Still, those present in the old Assembly building say they were spoken in a harsh, rather offensive tone.[51] Jean Lacouture writes about the scene:

> This text, which had not moved the Frenchmen who had seen it . . . pronounced in the face of an old man, heavy with glory and filled with generous ideas, who represented France and was the guest of Guinea, did not fail to provoke a heavy uneasiness in the least jingoistic of the French listeners.
>
> Lying back in his arm-chair, his strange face furrowed and asymmetrical, and covered with a veil of deep fatigue, General de Gaulle listened to the harangue which the public presentation had made into a prosecution. . . .
>
> A man was heard, already old, full of knowledge and experience, irrefutably proud of the past of his country but lucid enough to perceive the rise on the horizon of peoples lacking in modern science as well as in material means . . . [and] "A young African, vehement, vigorous, and peremptory, standard-bearer of peoples too long forgotten and struggling to emerge from the night" was answered by an old white man, full of history and still yearning to prolong by grandeur, ruse, and generosity altogether, the brilliance of his country and his own glory.[52]

When de Gaulle rose, he spoke of the work of France in Africa; there was nothing in it for which France should blush. He had believed for years that the African peoples were called to the running of their own countries; he had proved that when it was necessary. The question was whether the French and the Africans wanted to engage each other in a Community for an uncertain length of time—a Community that would aid in development and would defend their common liberties. Guinea was free to choose independence, but she would suffer the consequences. The road would not be easy. The lack of dignity had already been conquered in part. That conquest must be completed to give an example to the world, and if they (the French) did not do it, imperialistic influences would descend upon them all. We must keep together, for it is our human duty. "I have spoken. You must reflect. The feeling that I have of Conakry is that it is on the side that I would wish, and I will wait now to see you come together with us to celebrate the founding of our Community. And, if I do not see you again, you may know that I will not lose the memory of my visit in this great, beautiful, hard-working, noble town, a town of the future. Long live Guinea, long live the Republic, long live France!"[53]

And then, says Lacouture, he went away with the uncertain step of a weary giant, turning his eyes elsewhere.[54]

But, however weary, de Gaulle reacted quickly, saying to his companions that they could never get on with that man. He evidently retained only the vehemence, the snarling tone of the leader, not the words, which, as Lacouture says, would today seem moderate. The French leader had no more hope. France would leave Guinea on August 29, the morning after the referendum. The "consequences" he had spoken of would begin at once.[55] Sékou Touré should not go with him in his private plane to Dakar as had been suggested, and some of the most usual farewell courtesies to Sékou Touré were omitted. The Guinean, angry, did not want to accompany General de Gaulle to the airport. Governor Mauberna persuaded the leader to go, but the ride was grim, with the two men sitting tight-lipped enclosed in a car. At the airport, de Gaulle shook Sékou Touré's hand for the last time and wished Guinea good luck. The incident was closed, but its effects continued for long months and years. The moment, as Chaffard says, was historic.[56]

Naturally, there was much talk about the incident on both sides. Cornut-Gentil, the overseas minister, had persuaded General de Gaulle to include Conakry in his itinerary. Was he upset that he had done so? His reason had been that Touré had been left out of the Constitutional Committee and was probably offended; so oil had better be poured on the sore spot.[57] De Gaulle was angry and used rather strong words with those who were supposed to have prepared his trip.[58] He would not allow Mauberna to give Sékou Touré a period of reflection. There was nothing to do now but break with the arrogant leader of Guinea. You could not talk with him; he was an agitator. De Gaulle thought a trap had been laid for him. When he reached Dakar, he was in a murderous humor.[59]

If Houphouet-Boigny thought of Sékou Touré as a "turbulent younger brother," this must have seemed the high point of his turbulence. Houphouet-Boigny himself, now minister of state in France, had done all he could to have good relations with de Gaulle, including a courtesy call at the General's office, 5, rue de Solférino, before the investiture and the subsequent move to the Matignon Palace, the home of prime ministers. Houphouet-Boigny's own office was close to the rue de Solférino, and it seemed a good thing to visit de Gaulle. But Houphouet-Boigny had apparently not helped to get Touré a place on the Constitutional Committee.[60] Now, however, he must try to bring the Guinean to reason. He tried, but Sékou Touré was adamant. He had *his* pride, too.

Gabriel d'Arboussier, a former officer of the RDA and later holder of many important posts in Africa, had also seen Touré's speech, and had suggested to him that he had better not say anything about independence before General de Gaulle; after all, independence had been conceded at Brazzaville. But Touré did not listen and was apparently unaware of the Brazzaville promise, with its statement that independence at term did not mean secession.[61] He answered merely that independence was not in de Gaulle's final text.

In a statement made soon after to the press, Sékou Touré announced that if Guinea was to approve the Constitution, the document must state in both preamble and text the right to unrestricted independence of the overseas peoples. He thought there was a lack of frankness on the French side.[62]

The visit to Dakar produced other forms of difficulty for de Gaulle. There were a good many militants there from extremist organizations such as the PAI (*Parti Africain d'Indépendance*), the *Unité Africaine,* the *Nation Fédérale Africaine.* They were mostly intellectuals, young students, and a few Communists from the *bidonvilles,* the ghettos of Dakar.[63] They carried red flags with black stars and violent placards, even on the great central square of Dakar, the Place Protêt, where the ceremonies attending de Gaulle's speech would take place. They shouted, "Down with de Gaulle!" and their banners demanded immediate independence, African unity, or a Federal African Nation.[64]

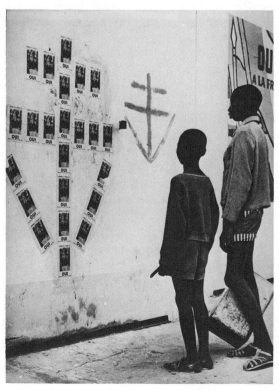

Campaign for the Referendum. Senegal, 1958.

There were many notables there, but it is a curious fact that the two most important men in Senegal—President of the Council Senghor and its vice-president, Mamadou Dia—were absent. Visiting his family in Normandy does not seem a very valid excuse for Senghor's missing a meeting that might mean so much for Senegal, and Mamadou Dia's doctor's appointment in Geneva does not sound so very important either. Of course, Senghor had made some fairly strong statements at the Congress of Cotonou, and he probably thought it better not to face de Gaulle just then. At Conakry, too, the loudspeaker had played a tape of the Cotonou congress in which Senghor had called for "independence by September."[65] All in all, it was probably just as well the two men in power in Senegal at that time were not there.

The hostile slogans had begun to be heard even on the way into Dakar from the Yof Airport, and de Gaulle remained sitting in the car, his teeth clenched. When they reached the city, a strike of the African trade union was in progress. The palace of Pierre Messmer, the high commissioner, was surrounded with parachutists wearing red berets. It was not a calm town when the General arrived. At one point, de Gaulle turned to Cornut-Gentil, the overseas minister, and asked him what he thought of the whole situation. The minister said he found it very disagreeable, but de Gaulle said it amused him.[66] It seems legitimate to wonder why.

Reaching the place of the ceremony, de Gaulle remarked sarcastically to the crowd that those who carried the banners and shouted the slogans were perfectly free to vote no.[67] In the speech he made in the Place Protêt, he spoke of the hope that the Dakar citizens would vote yes and take the road with the French like brothers. Then, he added, "The way is clear and the light is before us." And he took leave of Dakar with the hope that there would be an expression of confidence in France, and that the answer on September 28 would be yes![68]

There was a reception later that day, with apologies for the behavior of the *Dakarois,* the people of Dakar. Then the General flew to Algiers, and the *périple,* the tour around Black Africa, was over. At that time, de Gaulle thought all was lost at Dakar as well as at Conakry.[69] The great question now was whether the battle to install the Community was won. The referendum was yet to come. Still, the journey had been marked by rapid evolution toward an increasingly generous solution of the African problem.[70]

De Gaulle evidently felt that he was offering the territories freedom when he spoke to the people on September 4, 1958, after his return to Paris, telling them, as he had the Africans, about the Community and his plans for it, and adding:

> Thus this vast organization will renovate the human complex grouped around France. This will be effected by virtue of the free determination of all. In fact, every Territory will have an opportunity through its vote in the referendum, either to accept France's proposal or refuse it and, by so doing, to break every tie with her. Once a member of the Community, it can in the future, after coming to an agreement with the common organs, assume its destiny independently of the others.

De Gaulle said later that it was to be a "free Community of Peoples" that would be established between metropolitan France and the overseas territories.[71]

Did General de Gaulle really think that the segments of power that he named as being retained by the Community (and who knew then who would control its various organs?) would mean so little? They seem to have been a fairly large slice of the governmental pie. And the possible freedom for the future in this proposal would not give any certainty to all the former dependent nations. They wanted liberty in *all* their dealings, and they wanted it now. Would they even be consulted by the president, the Executive Council, the Senate, or the Court of Arbitration? They did not know.

Evidently, at this period, in spite of having gone beyond his previous positions, de Gaulle was not ready to give full and immediate independence to the territories, at least not openly. Even if the final necessity had been in his mind for a long time, he did not feel free to state it publicly, especially in the case of Algeria, which, to so many, belonged body and soul to France. De Gaulle said once that "a constitutional regime applied to African territories might serve as a framework for the solution of the Algerian problem."[72] Terrenoire wrote that "it is understood, it must be always understood, that General de Gaulle had completely modified his views on the future of Algeria between May, 1958, and the declaration of September 16, 1959, offering self-determination to the Algerians and what followed."[73] Raymond Offroi thought on June 5, 1958, that de Gaulle knew it would be necessary to give independence to Algeria.[74] And in the summer of 1958, Paul-Marie de la Gorce wrote "Algeria dominated French policy, so the destiny of French Africa could not be without influence on that of Algeria."[75]

Not all the Africans were in accord with de Gaulle's speech of September 4, or with that of September 26 either. Perhaps the most antagonistic of these was Bakary Djibo, then president of the Council of Niger, formerly general secretary of the PRA—*Parti Républicain Africain* (Senghor's party), and leader of the majority party of Niger.[76] Djibo was an ardent supporter of federalism in Africa. He had been upset by General de Gaulle's stand before his trip, and Cornut-Gentil had tried to calm him: "Look, Little One, don't get your blood up! If necessary we will screw them tighter!"[77] How this was to be done was not indicated.

But Djibo evidently paid no heed to that remark or to the Brazzaville speech permitting the taking of freedom. He announced that his party, the Niger group of the PRA, called the *Sawaba* (homeland, in the Haussa language), would vote no. Touré, Djibo, two politicians from Senegal and one from the Soudan met in Dakar the day after de Gaulle's speech there and decided for the no, subject to a conference to be held at Bamako on September 10. They knew that the trade unions would be with them, as well as the unionized teachers. They did not wait for the rest of AOF, though this would mean a break-up of the federation there, as the Ivory Coast under Houphouet-Boigny would vote yes. Houphouet-Boigny had even said, "All Territories will vote 'Yes'. . . .

Africans are not madmen." Houphouet-Boigny and d'Arboussier did not think
Touré would vote no. The Democratic party of Guinea was to decide on
September 14. In the Soudan, there was some feeling for the no, but they did
not want the Dakar-Niger railroad to be cut off from them if Senegal voted yes.
So their leader, Modibo Keita, accepted Houphouet-Boigny's lead.[78]

Three small parties in Senegal wanted to reject the Constitution, but
Senghor prevented it. He was a recent convert to independence, but France
meant much to him, and so would the new Community. He wanted the door
left open for federalism, and did not want to cut Senegal off from France.
Among other reasons, his country was a one-crop land—and the French paid a
high price for his ground-nuts. So he said: "Independence will have to be paid
for. That is no reason to renounce it, but it is a reason to see that it is well-
organized. . . . My 'Yes' will be a stage on the road to independence." And he
ordered a yes vote in the Senegal section of the PRA. That vote would carry the
day in Senegal, for the opposition parties were small, and Senghor had for him
the French administration, the religious leaders, and the experienced politicians. Also, the AEF was safe for France. But Niger held to its no, and Sékou
Touré was obstinate in Guinea.[79]

Of course, Sékou Touré, in speaking as he did, had wished to show his people
that he was not afraid; he as a man could "talk up" to the chief of the French,
the colonizer. This right was claimed with so much fire that he seemed to make
a grab for the honor of Africa. But he had turned the speech into a prosecution
of France, and in a half hour he had put Franco-Guinean relations on the block.
Governor Mauberna worked with him half the night to change his attitude,
with no results. He would not attend the subsequent meeting of the RDA,
whose position he did not approve. Others tried to change his mind and failed.
Touré said, "We will vote 'No' to a Community that is nothing but a French
Union rebaptized—old merchandise with a new ticket. We vote 'No' to ine-
quality, 'No' to irresponsibility. From September 29 we will be an independent
country."[80] The Guineans did not believe that economic sanctions would be
used against them. Yet before the referendum took place, Sékou Touré made an
informal application for association with the Community—as Djibo hoped to
do for Niger.[81] They still wanted some relationship with France. When
Mauberna warned of the cessation of aid, the Guineans laughed. Even newspapers warned them that de Gaulle could not change because of Algeria.[82] It
has been said that Sékou Touré wanted to give a yes vote up to September 15.[83]

As opinions in Africa solidified, it appeared that it might be possible to gain
Niger for the Community, since the chiefs were for a yes vote, and so were the
RDA, the French governor, Ignace-Jean-Aristide Colombani, and the administrators. And French troops were not far away in southern Algeria. There was
a growing impulse, except in Guinea, to vote yes. And so the referendum
approached, and the outlook was good for the French, though according to
rumor the French had used "blatant electoral and pre-electoral manoeuvres"
in their campaign in Niger. Finally, on September 28, the Senegalese voted yes
by 97.6 percent; Niger by 78 percent; the upper Voltaians by 99.1 percent; and

everywhere else in AOF they voted yes, except in Guinea where the vote was 95.2 percent no.[84] It was a real victory for de Gaulle.

After that, the territories chose to be states, members of the Community individually; and the Community was constituted. But Guinea was not in it nor likely to be. A few days after the vote, a note was sent to Sékou Touré cutting off the aid of the French administration, the French state, and the equipment credits, and transferring the French civil service within two months. The army also would leave. In the future, relations between the two countries would be according to the principles of international law. That the states of the Community did not rely on the Guinean example and maintained bonds of cooperation with France justified French policy.[85]

By this time, Sékou Touré realized that it might be hard to remain close to France, as he had claimed he wished to do after independence. Then there began, says Georges Chaffard, "an unbelievable merry-go-round of notes that were diplomatic, verbal, written, semi-official, a game of cross-purposes, of declarations, of press conferences in which the Guinean government could be seen clinging to the idea of associating itself with France and the Community, and Paris hesitating with a disdain that was scarcely polite."[86]

During this time, Sékou Touré gave the impression of being a nervous, tense man, a little uneasy, perhaps, but adopting neither an attitude of defiance nor a mask of despair. The cards were down, "he would have to play a difficult game."[87] At last, in January 1959, three brief protocols were signed for financial agreements and technical and cultural arrangements. They implied recognition of Guinea, who sent an ambassador to Paris, and Paris sent a chargé d'affaires to Guinea. But France let Guinea feel the hard experience of independence without her aid. This policy was much criticized abroad and in France, too, for many feared it would open the door to communism, and because its harshness showed resentment to Guinea; yet it had seemed necessary to the French to make a distinction between those who had voted for the Community and those who had not. A different attitude would not have been understood at that time. Also, Touré did not utilize the French protocols after they were made, and he engaged at once in relations with the East, among other states with Russia and Czechoslovakia. France had to sustain her African policy as well as her dignity. But Guinea survived, and her example gnawed at the body of the Community.[88]

Sékou Touré became an international personality and something of a hero. Young men in Nigeria were wearing "Sékou Touré" hats, and those who had voted for the Community were put into the shadow. There were other repercussions. When Sékou Touré moved into the governor's palace, after he was sure there would be no weakening of French policy, Edward Mortimer says:

> He found an absurd scene of desolation: furniture and pictures had all been removed, the cellars emptied, the crockery smashed. The safe was intact—but no one knew the combination. Even the telephones had gone. It was the same all over Guinea . . . this involved the departure of all the army doctors, who had been largely responsible for

the health of the civilian population. They left abruptly, taking their medical supplies with them. The police force left after smashing the furniture and windows of its barrack. Officials took with them anything portable that belonged (by the *Loi-Cadre* division) to the French State, and fouled or broke anything that was too cumbersome to take. At the same time Guinean students in Paris and Dakar lost their French government scholarships, French public investment in Guinea ceased altogether, and the French government tried to get private firms to stop investing there too (on the whole unsuccessfully).[89]

Could these orders have been given without de Gaulle's sanction? Probably not. Yet Mortimer says that "de Gaulle's attitude was not the result of pure pique," though others, like Crowder, thought it was. He "was anxious about two things"—whether Guinea could survive as an independent state or whether it would need French aid on a larger scale.[90] What, after all, would be the result on the other nations if Guinea was treated as a fatted calf and feasted almost before it had left home? Houphouet-Boigny counseled de Gaulle that he should give a demonstration of the advantages of being inside of the Community rather than outside it. If Guinea was preferred ahead of the others, it would be like an oil spot that spreads.[91] A few weeks after the referendum, de Gaulle said that Guinea had not been obstructed by the metropole, but no one knew where it was headed or what it would do. The future would determine French relations with it. France could not furnish what she would have furnished if Guinea had not opted for the "so-called independence system"— the world understood why "such assistance had to cease."[92] So it seems as if he thought, as some of his aides believed, that other nations would follow Sékou Touré's line, and that then there would be no France outside of the metropole.[93] But the procedure of the lesson de Gaulle gave Sékou Touré left scars on the office walls and on the minds of those who had worked for France in Guinea. It was an unnecessarily exaggerated action that could not and would not be forgotten—a black mark on the Gaullist record. He had taken away, as a Guinean official told the author, all the things that would have made independence possible.[94]

17

The Life and Death of a Community

> By virtue of these principles and that of the free
> determination of peoples, the Republic offers the
> Territories Overseas, who express the wish to adhere to
> it, new institutions founded on the common ideal of
> liberty, equality and fraternity, and conceived with the
> view of their democratic evolution.
> —Preamble to the Constitution of 1958

On the twenty-eighth of September, by evening, the metropole and the overseas territories knew that the Community had been born, though without Guinea. "It was," as Gilles Néra said, "the first time an old colonizing nation had submitted its constitution to the sanction of its overseas territories, giving them the free choice of their destinies and the possibility of immediate unconditional independence."[1] Others looked at it differently. Philippe Decraene, an excellent writer on Africa, called it "the last gasp of the policy of assimilation."[2]

Five territories chose to stay under the old *statut*, or status, "in the bosom of the Republic": the French Coast of the Somalis, the Comoro Islands, New Caledonia, Polynesia, and Saint Pierre-Miquelon. In addition, there were a few small islands in the southern ocean that decided later to do the same, among them Wallis and Fortuna in the Polynesians. At the time of the referendum in September 1958, all the others chose the statute of "Member of the Community," transforming their territories into states and entering singly. Their former Assemblies voted their transformation into states and proclaimed new organization of public powers. They would be republics governed by constitutions in the old Republican tradition. They would take up the question of regroupment as allowed by the Constitution later: in political groups like the Federation of Mali; or economic assemblages like the Entente. The last state to join, Niger, came in on December 18, 1958.[3] There had been a delay there on account of the need of a new election after the resignation of Bakary Djibo; he had opposed joining the Community, but the electors had not followed him. In addition, the new French governor had set in motion all possible propaganda resources in favor of the Community; so the chiefs as well as the electors had deserted Djibo. It might have seemed that France had rigged the elections had it not been for the counterproof of what happened in Guinea, and for some better balanced results, such as those in Niger, the Somalis, and Madagascar. The elections, in fact, were carried by the local African leaders.[4] The African territories had voted for the new Constitution, which was put into final form when de Gaulle reached Paris. Only the French Republic would be an entirely independent state. The other states would have their own institutions with internal autonomy, but they would not have complete sovereignty, for certain domains would be beyond their competence: foreign policy, defense, money, common economic and financial policy, raw materials, control of justice, higher education, organization of common exterior transportation, and telecommunication. Many points of these restrictions, however, were not made clear, nor was it evident who would exercise the common powers. The institutions of the Community would include a president, who would be the president of France, elected by the states as well as by the French, and an Executive Council constituted by the prime minister of France under the president of the Community. The states would have chiefs and ministers of common affairs and a Senate of delegates from the Parliament of the Republic and from the legislative assemblies of the states, with powers only sketched in; finally, there would be a Court of Arbitration.[5]

Thus by September 1958 de Gaulle had revised the entire Constitution. Zolberg has written that "as the man of Brazzaville, the General enjoyed almost unlimited trust among African political leaders, and was a mythical figure among the masses," even though his intentions concerning the future of tropical Africa were not clear. The Overseas (African) subcommittee of the Constitutional Consultative Committee had added "confederation" to the three choices that territories might take, already included in the draft of the Constitution. This was "unacceptable" to de Gaulle. He said in personal appearance before the subcommittee that "those who rejected the government's three choices demonstrated for outright secession." This was in a certain sense "the first acknowledgement of the existence of the ultimate solution, independence," for territories that seceded would do so "at their own risk," and it was deduced that that meant recall of the French administration and of economic and financial aid as well. It might even be more drastic than that.[6]

Ruth Morgenthau states that several points were apparent among the Africans in 1958. There must be African unity, always at the expense of France and in relation to the right for the acquisition of independence, and they were already questioning other matters, such as revision of frontiers. Evidently the African leaders had influence in France, though there was some dissatisfaction there with all three of the most prominent ones: Senghor, Houphouet-Boigny, and Lamine Guèye.

On the other hand, the majority reaction in France was that it all expressed the policy of de Gaulle—the giving of more subsidies when the Constitution was put in place, in the hope of preventing independence. That hope, says Ruth Morgenthau, was disappointed.[7] This statement may be somewhat too categorical. De Gaulle had already admitted the possibility of future independence. It might be better to say "immediate independence." Certainly, de Gaulle would have prevented that solution of the problem had he been able to do so. He did not expect to agree so soon to the liberation of all Black Africa, but he certainly saw the handwriting on the wall. It is interesting that the word *independence* did not appear in the Constitution. By this new statute, France "broke the federalist forces, giving power to the territories." The old federations of AOF and AEF (*Afrique de l'Ouest Française* and *Afrique Equatoriale Française*), the trade unions, the youth political parties, the civil service, and the Grand Council would all disappear in the new regime. The territorialists had won.[8]

The next stage of the decolonization was the passing of three ordinances on December 19, 1958. By these acts, the Executive Council of the Community was declared to be the supreme organ of cooperation for the member states on the governmental and administrative plane. The president of the Community was to have the chief role in formulating and notifying all members of necessary measures and seeing to their execution. The Senate would have an entirely consultative role, considering projects on economic and financial policy, and, when requested by the president, examining treaties and international agreements concerning the Community or on declarations of war. Finally, it would make decisions necessary in order to implement the orders passed by the legislative assemblies of the states.

The Senate did not meet until July 15, 1959, at a time when the future of the Community was being considered again. There were only five full sessions, of which the last was held a year later. The Court of Arbitration was planned in order to deal with suits concerning the interpretation or application of the rules of law imposed on the states, especially constitutional affairs, organic laws, and agreements. Its decrees would concern internal matters of the Community rather than international affairs. The court disappeared before any case was heard.[9]

The Executive Council had the task of orienting the Community. It met in February, March, and May of 1959 in Paris, and in July at Tananarive, but already independence was coming into question. After a session at Saint-Louis in Senegal in December 1959, one last meeting was held in Paris in March 1960. The Senate and the court did not outlast it.[10] The Community, now dying, was soon dead.[11]

At first, the Executive Council had something of a federal aspect insofar as the Constitution permitted. Its debates were secret, and no votes were taken, for the president of the Community, having heard various tendencies expressed, would decide for the rest of the members. This made the Council "almost like a government." It was a central institution deciding for everyone. It is interesting that the language was to be French; the hymn would be "The Marseillaise"; the motto, "Liberty, Equality and Fraternity"; the flag, the Tricolor with a distinctive sign for the Community; for the only nationality was to be that of the French Republic and the Community. Only the president could pardon. There would be an Official Journal, and the fete days were designated as July 14, November 11, and May 8, exactly as in France. A budget would be set up; the contributions of the states would be decided by the president in Executive Council. Decisions must be signed by the president.[12]

The common competences were those of the Constitution, with the widest possible interpretation of matters of interest to all. Naturally, this would limit the autonomy of the states. Army and foreign affairs would be dealt with in common with France. The authorities of the Community would decide on rules of grades, diplomas, and titles of higher education.[13]

The federal aspect of the organization began to disappear very soon, for it tended toward the federalism rejected by the Constitution. In accepting this arrangement over a long period of time, France would have alienated her independence to the profit of an organism *without real existence*—the Community—for it had no real executive, no representation of France, no diplomatic organization. She would be on the same footing as her partners, and the budget could reach higher figures than those decided by the French Parliament. The decisions now required a visa by each minister involved, instead of a countersignature only. No common diplomatic corps was established. And there was a serious fault in the planning. The French Republic had no representation in the other states of the Community: only the president of the Community was represented; the French government was not. So the high commissioners of France in the various states could only maintain relations and give information between the president of the Community and the heads of government of the states. Local governments saw to it that the commissioners kept to this role and could not represent France with them. The Community secretariats and administrations acted like a federal administration. So the French government saw reason to pause in its planning.[14]

The other members of the Community outside of France were not happy either. There were contradictions and impossibilities in their situation, too. For example, their delegations at the International Labor Bureau were only observers, and their problems were different from those of France. This seemed unbearable to them. Nationality belonged to the French Republic, for the Community was not internationally recognized; so the passports were issued to their citizens as being of French nationality. That was not pleasing either. Nationalism in the states appeared again. They wanted flags of their own, and Madagascar wanted Tsiranana to be president and not merely head of state. The other states followed that lead. Since there were no diplomats, the states began to send "delegations" to Paris. And the ministers of the Community appointed in common began to get mixed up with the ministers of the French Republic. Federalists like Houphouet-Boigny did not like the bureaucracy in the arrangements for the Community. They wanted a kind of personal federalism, with each state possessing real autonomy and its chiefs of government dealing directly with the president concerning common affairs, with no intermediary. Also, the ministers in common were all French, and what African would like that? The new autonomy at home, and certain eddies of feeling, made Houphouet-Boigny finally resign as secretary of state in the French cabinet. He returned home to the Ivory Coast to be prime minister there. Also, he lost interest in the Community after Mali was allowed to be independent and yet remain in the Community. The new states would discuss only with the president the aid they would receive.[15] The idea of the Community was already onerous to the Africans. It seemed to work out in such a way that common affairs were largely reserved for the French Republic.[16]

To coordinate the aid to be given to the new states, previously arranged by FIDES, a new organization came into being—FAC (*Fonds d'Aide et de Coopération*—Fund for Aid and Cooperation)—but it lacked unity and was much criticized. After trying pure bilaterism for a while, it was decided to use for aid an ensemble plan agreed to in common. But all this was frustrating and it caused bad feeling. Nevertheless, the Community services played an effective role while they lasted.[17]

The net results of the Community's organization were not what had been expected. "The Senate of the Community turned out to be nothing but an abortive successor to the ill-fated Assembly of the French Union." The lack of a Community legislative body "enhanced the power of the Executive." The ministers appointed were all French. Consequently, the Africans interpreted the Constitution "in accordance with their predispositions." Senghor, Tsiranana, and other leaders thought it was "a tolerable transitional framework" but Houphouet-Boigny endorsed it lock, stock, and barrel. He urged his men in the Ivory Coast to forget narrowing nationalism. Naturally, his devotion to the idea of a Franco-African Community entered into his beliefs, for the Ivory Coast was dependent on France for its prosperity. His officials were not so certain, but they followed him, for his choice seemed necessary at the moment.[18]

Africans, however, had not given up their ideas of regroupment, and at Bamako, on December 29 and 30, 1958, they held a congress. The Africans who were federalists thought they could count on Senegal, the Soudan, Upper Volta, and Dahomey. There was a later meeting at Dakar in January 1959, at which a new federation, that of Mali, was constructed. Mali (the name came from an old African empire) was not hostile to France, and discussed independence only under the cloak of unity. But only Senegal and the Soudan were really ardent about a new federation, and the two others dropped out quickly. The new Federation of Mali lasted only until independence was attained.[19]

De Gaulle hoped, at about the time when Mali was being formed in early 1959, that the Community would hold together long enough to be a model for Algeria. Though, in general, he agreed with what the African leaders of Senegal and the Soudan were planning to do, he realized the danger to the Community if other states broke off. He did not want to intervene personally, but he was aware that the moment of independence for all was fast approaching.[20]

Equatorial Africa also made an effort at unity—a customs unity, begun in a meeting at Paris in January 1959. It continued at Brazzaville in June, those voting being Gabon, Congo, Chad, and the Central African Republic. At first, the latter wanted federation, but after the death of its leader, Barthélémy Boganda, the Central African Republic did not pursue the project it had proposed of the "United States of Latin Africa." The states would coordinate their customs services, and each country would make a contribution. This would take the place of the old government general. The states of West Africa that had not joined Mali (the Ivory Coast, Dahomey, Niger, Upper Volta) came together in an Entente Council—a supple union with no loss of sovereignty and with the purpose of harmonizing internal taxation and plans of development.[21]

In the summer of 1959, at Dakar, Mali announced that it would seek independence in confederation with France. Houphouet-Boigny and the Entente were against this, but France in the person of de Gaulle yielded to independence at the sixth meeting of the Executive Committee at Saint-Louis in Senegal in December of 1959. It was confirmed at a meeting at Nouakchott, Mauritania, on December 13, 1959. Thus Mali became independent on June 20, 1960, by means of a transfer of competences provided for in the Constitution. De Gaulle evidently felt that the use of the other method allowed by the Constitution—referendum—would mean a rupture, and to avoid it, France chose the means of transfer of competences.[22] Further agreements stated reciprocal obligations, and the Constitution was changed on June 4, 1960, to permit Mali to remain within the Community and yet to become independent.

Obviously, the other states would follow in a chain reaction. First came Madagascar, proclaimed independent in a similar manner on June 20, 1960.[23]

The states of Equatorial Africa wanted to do likewise, but Houphouet-Boigny suggested that they wait until the agreements with Mali were signed. They felt extremely weak in facing the demands of independence, though they were encouraged in regrouping by the French government; and in a short time, they continued on that path. But their efforts to unite did not succeed; so each requested separately its complete sovereignty, and four series of agreements were set up for them.[24]

The Entente tried to work together, but they requested their independence separately, as the others did. Eventually they asked the transfer of competences but did not sign agreements with France until after they had been admitted to the United Nations, thus satisfying the rule that they be entirely independent. This requirement was made by Houphouet-Boigny, possibly, says Yves Guéna, because he, who had been first in planning, did not wish to follow so closely after Mali and Madagascar.[25]

Some few points about the final process of the first stage of decolonization should be noted. The arrangements differed with the states. The Entente left the Community after they took their independence, without asking permission. Obviously, Houphouet-Boigny did not like the disappearance of the Community he had promoted.[26] And the Mali Federation burst wide open in the summer of 1960. There were several reasons for this. The former Soudan wanted a more centralized federation, which Senegal did not approve. Senegal thought that it was paying the lion's share of the expenses of the Mali federation and that there were too many Soudanais in the federal government. "Federation is a far-off ideal," said Senghor. Senegal was intransigent when de

Gaulle tried to conciliate the two parties to the federation. Mali thus disappeared from the federation on September 22, 1960, and both entered the United Nations singly. Still, there was no brusque rupture. In January 1962 technical agreements with France were worked out by Mali (the old Soudan kept that name).[27]

Mauritania asked the same conditions as the Entente—independence before cooperation. That independence came in November 1960, and Mauritania entered the United Nations in October 1961. Equatorial Africa (formerly Oubangui-Chari, Chad, the Middle Congo, and Gabon), Senegal, and Madagascar remained technically in the Community and arranged a common defense. A tendency to unity still existed among them. Even Togo and the Cameroon were now on their way to freedom. On both sides there has existed an ineffable feeling for each other.

There has been no actual balkanization of French Africa, though the Community had no real life after 1959. The military presence of France remained everywhere, except in Guinea and Mali, after the demise of the Community. France still had other obligations in Black Africa, too—cooperation in finance and cultural and technical assistance—but the states gave her political advantages and used the French language. The wages of the French assistants came back to France, and the larger public works were done by French firms. Aid was the cement that held the former territories to the mother country. All in all, the balance sheet of colonization in Black Africa and Madagascar at the time was positive in a certain sense. It had furnished an apprenticeship to modern life. The continuity and authority of de Gaulle gave conditions that assisted the passage to independence.[28] When the final peace came in Algeria, in February and March 1962, French decolonization was complete as people thought of it then.

How did General de Gaulle view these changes and counterchanges? What did he say or write about them? His purposes and attitudes toward decolonization are very clear in his speeches during the decolonization period and also in the later *Mémoires d'Espoir*, published in 1970. On November 10, 1959, he said at his press conference that there were two facts with regard to the peoples with which France had linked herself that were "as large as the earth itself." The first was the idea of self-determination: that the peoples should be free to decide their own destiny. "It is the kind of elementary psychological state of mind which is all the more active as it finds the support of the entire world, including the countries that yesterday were colonizers." He thought that to open the way for civilization, it had been necessary for Western Europe to penetrate the lands of those who had been so long isolated due to natural obstacles or to their own characters. "Where would the various continents be if this [penetration] had not been made? But these countries were now revealed and reawakened, and each people wanted to decide its own fate."[29]

The second fact was that these countries now had a growing desire to see their standards of living rise, for they resigned themselves with more and more difficulty to the idea of hunger, disease, and ignorance; and they wanted mechanical civilization and the education that would develop it. They could not have that without the administrative, economic, and technical aid of others. There were plenty of people who did not want to accept this situation, but their opinions did not agree with the idea that France had of herself or with the idea the world had of France, and of her continuing humane mission. Such attitudes would lead France into difficulties. The people who need assistance must have it if they want it. "France must . . . respect their free disposal of themselves and . . . form a whole with them in which they would have her support and she would have their participation."[30]

"This was already the basis of the agreement between France and the eleven new states and the Malagasy Republic," though if they wished to leave France, they must do so. Revisions are possible, but there must be a foundation. This Community, freely joined, means independence and guaranteed cooperation for everyone. The next year, two states for which France had been trustee, the Cameroon and Togo, would be free to join the Community if they wished. As for Guinea, it was, in effect, a totalitarian regime under a single party, and its leader had rejected the Community, dreaming of a "springboard to dominate Africa." In this century, a policy to be valid must have as one of its aims the good of man. The relationship of France and the Community would satisfy this aim.[31]

Did de Gaulle already foresee the breaking up of his new, cherished Community? Since September 28, 1959, he had known that Mali wanted independence. Only about a month later, on December 13, 1959, he added to what he had said in Paris, saying that he preferred to use the term "international sovereignty" instead of "independence," for "it means that a people takes up its responsibilities in the world." While independence indicates an intention, the world is so small that no one really has that independence. No state can get on without the others; there is no policy without cooperation. That is what Mali is doing with the agreement of France. "Combat is the destiny of man—the law of our species"—and today it concerns the actions of those who ask for or renounce liberty. "Liberty is as old as man, and it is always the stake, so when a state takes liberty . . . all the world watches to see whether its choice will really be liberty or the opposite."[32]

Then, speaking of the necessity for a new country like Mali to choose its direction and constitute a state by itself, he noted that all the inhabitants of such a state must work toward the progress indicated by modern civilization. France knows that Mali wishes this responsibility and is ready to help because of her humane vocation. Speaking the same language, with the same disciplines, orientations, dreams, and ideals as their own state, Mali could count on France, and the two should stay together for the best service for themselves and humanity.[33]

Many of de Gaulle's speeches in 1960 dealt with Algeria. Then referring, no doubt, to his offer of self-determination for Algeria on September 16, 1959, he spoke of self-determination—he would not change his decision about Algeria.[34] If he did change the decision—and he used a telling simile—"France would be a poor broken toy adrift on the sea of hazards."[35] In these speeches he referred often to the events in Black Africa that proved that France had done well to act as she had. The Community was not a system of domination or exploitation, but a union of free states who wished to belong together. His main theme, as always, was France, what she was doing, had done, and could do. On February 26, 1960, at Castres, he said:

> Our country wants to marry the times in which it lives. We must be different with the countries we colonized formerly. They want freedom. France takes the consequences in a new manner—in the Community in which everyone has his place, freely working for the common good.[36]

During 1960, nevertheless, it became clear that the Community would not continue in the way in which it had been organized originally. De Gaulle acknowledged this in general terms in a speech on June 14, 1960. He spoke again of the great movement stirring Africa, the spirit of the century, saying that it would be useless to enumerate the causes of the evolution which had led France to put an end to colonization. Because of the progress made, France had granted self-determination, for to refuse it would be to contradict the French ideal, to start endless struggles, and to draw down on France the censure of the world. It would all be to gain a reward "which would inevitably have crumpled in our hands. It was unavoidable that one should feel nostalgia for the Empire," he went on, "just as one can miss the glow of oil lamps, the splendor of sailing ships, the charm of the carriage era." It was in taking the all-important realities as a foundation that eleven African republics and the Malagasy Republic were building with France "a free and friendly whole" of close relationships. "In the midst of the vast eddies in which Africa is caught, and of the currents that divide the world, our Community strengthens us while it serves the cause of reason and brotherhood."[37]

Implicitly, de Gaulle had at last accepted independence, but he still wanted closeness and cooperation with the former dependent countries. By the time of his next press conference, in September 1960, his mental crisis was over. He was almost nostalgic about decolonization, for he saw it as in the past. He had followed the same course from the beginning of his public life, he said, and "it was consistent with the aims of France and of its great colonizers, Gallieni and Lyautey" and also "with the irresistible movement set in motion by World War II and its aftermath, according to which he had directed the policy of France." Confirming this, he told Terrenoire that in his soul he had decided on decolonization ever since Brazzaville.[38] This statement agrees, also, with those made to the author by several members of General de Gaulle's family and close companions. They all felt he had decolonization in his mind soon after he came to power the first time; yet the author cannot but feel that he always thought of it with the haze of distant time and space spread over it. It never seemed to be in the present.

De Gaulle did not repudiate what colonization by the Western powers, including France, had done for the colonies, but he thought it was necessary to know when the time had come—and it had come now—to recognize the right of all to self-determination, to trust them in principle, and to expect all of them to contribute to the welfare of humanity. The old dominations could not continue; still, it might be possible to transform dependence into cooperation. It is to the interest of the new states to undertake their own development, "though it would be lamentable to see their ties with France broken—their new power must not be used against the former colonizer." And he pointed out that only one had refused cooperation, and its gain by so doing was not apparent.[39]

Some months later, on April 11, 1961, again in a press conference, he looked back to the past, mentioning the freeing of Syria and Lebanon; the giving of the right to vote to the Africans in 1945; his approval of the Statute for Algeria of 1947, though that had never been really applied; the making of the protectorate treaties for Tunisia and Morocco (though that had not been his work); and then the creation of the Community, which *was* his work; the proclamation of self-determination for Algeria. Finally, he spoke of the recognition of the independence of the young states of Black Africa and Madagascar. All of this, he said, dated back to Brazzaville and its small beginnings. Later that same day, he added: "What does this add up to? Decolonization."[40]

His policy, he said, was not only because of the "vast movement towards freedom" unleashed by the war, for it was not to France's interest, or valuable for her future ambitions, to be bound by obligations no longer in keeping with French strength and influence. The "itching for independence of erstwhile dominated peoples," the incitement of demagogues, were only part of the picture. Another factor, often concealed, was that the reasons for colonization were disappearing. Nations saw that their possibilities depended on their own development and on the cooperation of the formerly colonized countries, rather than on the domination of dissimilar peoples. France, with fixed trade, financial and agricultural ceilings, had been forced by the European situation to seek a new role. She did not regret the great advances she had accomplished in her overseas territories—in spite of her abuses and errors—but today she must use all her means to insure her defense and that of her neighbors to succeed in the economic, technical, and social struggle. So her policy must lie in decolonization to rid herself of unnecessary burdens. But, finding cooperation, she would give aid to her former dependencies and also to Algeria. "Yes," he said, "it is a matter of exchange, because of what is due us, but also because of the dignity of those with whom we are dealing."[41] This task of decolonization overseas is being completed, he said, in a speech on September 5, 1961.[42] Then, when it was definitely all over in 1962, and peace had come in Algeria, he spoke of the "outrageous" insults to France in calling her "colonialist." On the contrary, he said, she is an example for the world.[43] Certainly, in the matter of war, it was an example *not* to follow. It was all over now. Colonization had lived and died. It was merely a poignant memory, not only in de Gaulle's mind, but in the spirits of the peoples of Africa. Beyond that, he thought, it was a great turning point for the whole world of the twentieth century.

18

The Trial of the Spirit

> What a trial of the spirit it would be for me to give
> over our power, to fold our flag, to close there a great
> book of History.
>
> —de Gaulle

> In the context of that period, the gesture of General de
> Gaulle appeared to be an essential contribution to the
> work of African emancipation and we have never
> ceased being extremely grateful to him for it.
>
> —Lamine Guèye

There seems to be no doubt that General de Gaulle did not *want* to give up the French Empire. He had studied its growth. From his many references to the statesmen and generals of the early centuries of colonization, to the great French colonial heroes of the nineteenth century, as well as to the French army and its soldiers, the instruments of all their power, we know he had a detailed idea of the colonies. He knew how the first Empire was established and then lost. He knew, too, that France had consoled herself for those losses in the treaties of 1763 and 1815, and he had learned how the second Empire was gathered into an even larger whole by the time he came to power in 1940.[1] He was proud of that imperial record. The Empire had helped in the First World War, and, in the second, it had been the mainstay of Free France. He knew what it had cost his country over the years. As Edmond Pognon says, General de Gaulle knew history and was aware of its "great wind" and of the direction toward which it would blow in the end.[2] Accepting that verdict of time, de Gaulle said he would not see the Empire go "with a light heart."[3] And if, as a number of those close to him say, he had had decolonization in his mind ever since a short time after he came to power in 1940, that does not necessarily mean that he wanted to see the Empire broken up. The time for such an eventuality undoubtedly seemed far off to him, something that would have to be faced in the distant future.

In the *Mémoires d'Espoir* (1970) de Gaulle reviewed again what he had done or tried to do for decolonization. Curiously enough, however, he omitted from that account a number of the steps he had taken. He did not mention his first contacts with Africa; the giving of the vote, in 1943, to more Muslims than those who had had it previously; his approval of Eboué's new and more liberal decrees; the admission of the Africans as deputies in the French National Assembly. He told, however, how he had traced the path at Brazzaville and given the vote to the colonies. Then others had put through independence for Tunisia and Morocco and created the *Loi-Cadre* for the other territories. Later, he recounted that when he had reappeared at the center of the stage, he had built the Community and given the promise of self-determination to Algeria. Ultimately, he had freed all the states of French Africa up to and including Algeria. It was a lengthy list.[4]

He said nothing in this last book, naturally enough, of the influences of his early life that had made his later actions seem possible: his early training—the discipline and love of history in his family and the acquisition of his own deep knowledge of it; his early military achievements; the unusual fact of his having spent years in meditation, first in prison when he was elaborating his philosophy of life and later in the Desert while he was living at Colombey, after the first period of his active public life was over. There he considered at length what he could or should do for France and the Empire in the future. Even at an earlier stage, his perception of what life was like in the Near East was important—his understanding that those Arabs could never be Frenchmen—for that was probably the end of any belief he may have had in the old policy of assimilation. When he first came to power, the experiences he had in Africa, the contact with Governor Eboué and other thoughtful Africans, could not have failed to affect him strongly. Finally, in his second tour of duty, when he spoke as chief of all Frenchmen "wherever they might be," as he had said in his first broadcast from London in 1940—then, at last, he took his most important steps for Africa. At first, the advances in his thinking were uncertain and restrictive, but gradually they became more and more liberal. He sensed the changes that had already taken place in the Africans and accepted the necessity of change in his own beliefs. All these influences had formed him for what he must do between 1958 and 1960.

In analyzing the reasons for General de Gaulle's actions in all this series of events, we must remember, of course, that with a man of his almost unique strength of character, there are, and always were, many people who believed neither in what Charles de Gaulle did nor in his intellectual honesty. Often they were gifted and important people, and their estimates of him and of his actions should be recorded and considered. One influential businessman with an unusual knowledge of Africa told the author several years ago that de Gaulle's essential motive was to justify himself so that he could be declared chief of the government. According to this interlocutor, de Gaulle was never a liberal; he utilized liberal ideas only to obtain a hold on the African populations. Eboué was the great man at the Brazzaville Conference, and that conference was not very important in any case. Furthermore, this man thought, General de Gaulle did not want the blacks admitted to the National Assembly, and all the Gaullists were against the *Loi-Cadre*. In the long run, de Gaulle had not been able to refuse to carry out decolonization.[5]

This is a clear statement of the point of view of those who were opposed to de Gaulle. Most of these assertions are not credited by those persons whom the author has met who were close to him. But there were many dissenters from his views in France, among them other writers, men like Jacques Arnault, who agreed with the anti-de Gaulle attitude. Arnault wrote "to pretend to offer what one can no longer refuse was the soul of [General de Gaulle's] policy."[6]

Some of Charles de Gaulle's opponents were persons—*pieds noirs* (French settlers in Algeria)—who had been dispossessed in Algeria, or who had relatives who had lost everything there. Their feeling against de Gaulle was deep and bitter. This is, and was, perhaps the most logical and understandable reason for hatred of the then President de Gaulle, for he was the man who, more than any other, had accomplished their dispossession. It is indeed hard to give up lands and other property that have been one's own, or have belonged to one's family for a hundred years or more. After all, how long does possession have to continue before it can be an accepted fact? In addition, there were cases in which de Gaulle had refused pardon to those who had been convicted of crimes against the State. There is real hatred even today on the part of those connected with such cases. Finally, there are still many who do not believe in decolonization. They feel that the reasons why France felt it important to give up her conquests were insufficient. A military victory for France in Algeria appeared to them to be close at hand at the moment when that "integral part of France" was given up. Some of these people still feel that neither Africans nor Arabs are capable of self-government. Obviously, they do not approve of General de Gaulle's action in decolonizing the African states.

Some of this criticism and disbelief was natural enough. De Gaulle was, as he admitted, a "Man of the Tempests." Such human beings are full of many passions, and, in their turn, they arouse great passion and emotion for them or against them. Frequently they are also equipped with highly unusual capacities, and are apt to be not only oversensitive but also full of wrath. They are seldom easy to get on with. If they live on the summits, they pay for it. Among the many people around de Gaulle, there were always those who were very hostile to him, and no doubt they increased his sensitivity. The strains engendered by such enmity must have been very great. It was all the harder because he could not talk openly about many of his problems, even after he became premier and then president of France. He was continually criticized and shot at, as few men have been, both literally and figuratively, for there were thirty attempts on his life and innumerable diatribes against him. Nevertheless, he seldom let his critics influence him when he was sure of his position, though he certainly felt the difficulty of being himself. When Malraux asked him what it was like to be the "Man of June 18th," the day of his celebrated appeal to the French in 1940, de Gaulle replied, "But Malraux, it was terrible!" Jean Lacouture wrote of the incident at Conakry in Guinea, in August 1958, that de Gaulle was "like a man carrying on his shoulders the heavy burdens of a long destiny."[7]

On the other hand, there were, as there always are for a public man who has charisma for many people, some individuals or groups who thought all he did was right, and who put him on a pedestal. Pedestals are risky things, and generally they do not last very long, possibly because they are unreal. No man can be a hero all the time, for not everything he has done has been right. Failings have a way of coming to the surface in the course of time, just as undue criticism no longer moves people when it has become exaggerated. General de Gaulle wrote in *Le Fil de l'Epée*, in 1932, that "a chief was distant for authority did not come to a man without prestige, nor prestige without distance."[8] That distance that many felt in him added to the strength of his detractors and of his partisans as well. It has, no doubt, increased what one might call the decibels of feeling about him. Thus it seems more reasonable and more in accordance with historical fact to restrain both our adulation and our criticisms, and try to shed a more reasonable light on General de Gaulle's character and actions, for the time is short since he walked among us, and little that we can say can be considered definitive.

It seems possible to make one statement: He affected more people in his time, for good or for ill, than all others of his period except a very few such as Churchill, Roosevelt, Hitler, Stalin. For that reason, it is of great importance for historians to study what he was and what he did, and to keep their temperatures as low as possible while they do it.

It is evident that a man as many-sided as General de Gaulle could not reasonably be credited with only one motive in decolonizing Black Africa, whether that motive was merely self-interest, as his critics believe, or the more admirable characteristics of understanding and generosity, as his supporters thought. We know that by the twenties he had decided that the contingencies (*les contingences*) of the case were the most essential matter that a chief had to consider, for every case was different, and that idea, he had said, held for other situations besides those of war. That was his chief principle of action, and, as far as we know, he always applied it, though at times it gave rise to harsh statements about him, for it caused many to think of him as a mere opportunist. Perhaps in a sense he was, for he seized occasions when an opportunity was offered. Looking at his own century, he realized that it was the century in which the colonized nations would obtain their freedom. As early as 1934, he had seen that the peoples of Africa were looking forward to their independence. Later, after the Second World War, he had believed the conflict had brought renewed loyalty to France from the African peoples in spite of their discontent, and that very fact had laid a debt on France's shoulders that she must repay. His agreement with Pleven in organizing the Brazzaville Conference was an acceptance of that duty.

Marianne Cornevin, in her recent book on contemporary Africa, has come to the conclusion that Cartierism, the belief that France should stay within her own borders, was at the bottom of de Gaulle's motives. France must not expend her resources in foreign climes with little tangible gain. That theory, she thinks, was at the base of de Gaulle's interest in decolonization. She derives this conviction, undoubtedly, from brief paragraphs in the recent volume of de Gaulle's *Mémoires d'Espoir*, published in 1970. She cites his belief that he must extricate France from the bonds the Empire had imposed upon her, the bonds of expense in which France would have everything to lose and nothing to gain.

De Gaulle also said, in the same chapter, that he "had to surmount a heartrending emotion in putting an end to a colonial domination, formerly glorious, but henceforth ruinous."[9]

Of course, Marianne Cornevin was right in calling our attention to this passage, and de Gaulle was right in considering the restrictive and costly aspect of decolonization. He had often been blamed for not having paid enough attention to the economic affairs of France. Yet that could scarcely have been the only consideration in his mind in determining his policy toward Black Africa. There were other important motives.

De Gaulle said at Madagascar on July 8 and 10, 1959, that the Community was intended to develop the African countries, preserve freedom, and provide the security of common defense, as well as to give an example to the world. National cohesion and vigilance were more necessary than ever. De Gaulle had lived through two world wars. To him, defense was vital.[10]

Again, General de Gaulle had had a very close relationship with Africa during most of his public career. He certainly felt near to the land and its people, and his closeness to them was another reason for his acting as he did. The "Three Glorious Days" (Les Trois Glorieuses) in 1940 had given him his first opportunity of establishing the Free French Movement on the French soil of Africa. Some say those days lay behind all that he later accomplished with Free France. Without the support of the African territories, he would not have had "the independent base upon which its [the Free French Movement's] success depended."[11] It was his first real support in addition to that offered by Prime Minister Churchill and by the relatively few Frenchmen who had joined him in London. Perhaps the deep effect made on him by the almost unexpected aid caused him to be more willing in the final moments of decolonization to liberalize his formerly conservative ideas. It was from Africa that he undertook the "slow reconquest" of occupied France, and it was from there that the first public demand for his return to power came in May 1958.[12] According to his friends, de Gaulle has always appeared to be deeply attached to the land of Africa and its people.

Finally, and perhaps the most deep-lying motive of all, was the interaction between events in Black Africa and the increasingly terrible war in Algeria. In André Passeron's book, De Gaulle Parle, there is the statement: "Everywhere he cites African Decolonization as an example to show that a similar decolonization ought to take place in Algeria."[13] There is no doubt that Algeria was continually in his mind both before and after his return to Paris in 1958.

Certainly there were enough problems in Africa south of the Sahara to keep anyone busy, but the war in Algeria had worsened to such an extent that the entire population of France was absorbed in the accounts of it that reached the metropole. The murders, the terrorism, and the actual battles that took place so frequently, in a department that had been considered an integral part of France, were so dreadful that they seemed to exceed the horrors of other wars. De Gaulle, more than almost anyone, was immersed in that nearly insoluble problem. Paul-Marie de La Gorce has summed it up very completely: "The History of the Community begins, then, with the year 1959. One could not understand it without referring continually to Algeria." And again, he wrote, "Algeria dominated French policy," or, "The Algerian affair was in the background of French African policy; it was never lost to view by its artisans." And de Gaulle himself told Viansson-Ponté, "It is for Algeria that I made the Community."[14]

So the freeing of the black states was to be a pattern for Algeria, applied at the proper moment. De La Gorce adds that for de Gaulle, it was important that the Community should remain as it was, with the particular autonomy of each member state still existing, so that it could be a good example for the still resisting Algerian Department. Other men have stressed the idea that the problems of Algeria and Black Africa were interrelated. Governor-General Delavignette noted that Black Africa owed its decolonization to the fact that no one wanted another Algeria. Jean Mialet, judge of the *Cour des Comptes* (the Financial Court) in Paris, a long-time Gaullist, said that the speeding up of decolonization was due to Algeria.[15]

Most people seem to agree, however, that no one but de Gaulle could have put through decolonization with the possibility of transforming the old relationships of dependence into the modern bonds of political, economic, and social cooperation.[16] General Catroux remarked that de Gaulle could carry out the steps of decolonization for two reasons: one, that he respected the Africans so much, and two, that he had acquired such an outstanding position in his own country that he could impose his will on the opposition.[17] Marianne Cornevin, evidently agreeing with this statement, points out that General de Gaulle overrode the Council of State at one time to force through the law allowing the states to stay in the Community after they had become independent.[18] Probably no one else could have carried out that illegal action, which ran counter to the new constitution of the Community that he himself had set up. Many others, among them two Africans of great consequence, a French general, and the head of a television network, all agreed in talks with the author that de Gaulle was the only statesman able to take the necessary steps to free the former French states of Africa.[19] A high government official, who worked long and closely with General de Gaulle, has said that if de Gaulle had not done it, others might have carried it through in opposition to the Gaullists. Of course, he added, the loss of French prestige had precipitated the spirit of revolt in Black Africa, and, naturally, it had spurred things on.[20] So the time in which decolonization occurred had something to do with the matter, too.

But if, as René Viard says, de Gaulle was the first to make colonial peoples glimpse their future freedom, it is equally clear that he did not want that freedom to come as quickly as it did.[21] His policy had evolved gradually.[22] As General Catroux said, he wanted emancipation to arrive by stages, though the vice-president of the Senegal Assembly, Boubakar Guèye, felt the war brought it on, and that de Gaulle, having "the sense of the event," had let it come when it would.[23]

Thus in Africa, as time passed, for the masses and for the leaders, too, de Gaulle became first the "Man of Brazzaville," and later the "Man of Cooperation."[24] He enjoyed immense popularity in Africa. One has only to ask about him, and the emotion with which his name is mentioned is patent. Some of the leaders there have even called him "Father," and there is a rumor around Paris that one is known to have tried to use "Papa"; but de Gaulle would have none of it.

De Gaulle always treated the blacks as equals.[25] President Senghor of Senegal has said a number of times that General de Gaulle was the least racist of men.[26] Senghor went further, saying that he was "pleased to express the gratitude of the Senegalese people to General Charles de Gaulle. He was not only the greatest Decolonizer of the History of France. Under his firm, lucid direction, France was the nation that brought the most efficacious aid to our young independence."[27] That statement expressed the favorable point of view very well.

The adaptations of General de Gaulle's ideas had changed, as his niece noted, and by 1958 he had come to the point of understanding that, within the Community or outside of it, the freedom of the colonies must be completed; and this was in accordance with his belief in *les contingences*. Thus his essential principles had not changed. In 1934 he wrote in *Vers l'Armée de Métier* that "the effort of raising oneself above oneself to dominate others and thus to dominate events does not vary in essence." He had held to that belief all his life, and so he kept both his purpose and his promise to himself. Viansson-Ponté stated this another way: "One cannot reproach de Gaulle with change in the vision of himself and of the others in the world, and of History."[28]

In reviewing the whole situation of the colonies, due credit must be given to the many other men who had helped to set decolonization on its path. There were men like Pierre Mendès-France and Edgar Faure, who had carried out the freeing of Morocco and Tunisia, and Pierre Messmer and Gaston Defferre, who had done most to create the *Loi-Cadre*, to name only a few. They certainly prepared the way for Black African emancipation by taking those important steps. Perhaps, in reality, decolonization, as Defferre told the author, was on its way in any case.[29] De Gaulle, however, was one of the initiators of the process at Brazzaville in 1944. Without his support at that time, the conference could not have been held, and though it was inconclusive in its actions and contradictory in its statements, still, as we have seen, it had a tremendous psychological effect on Africa. The final liberation between 1958 and 1960 was carried out by General de Gaulle as president of France. That seems to be a fact, and it does not matter whether one approves or disapproves his actions. Louis Terrenoire, an old follower of de Gaulle's, has reported some of the General's final comments on his work of decolonization. After the summer of 1960, when the Algerian affair seemed "a whirlwind with no way out," de Gaulle told him that decolonization was coming everywhere and it was the task of France to lead it to a good conclusion, where she had control.[30] Still later, after the agreements about Algeria were terminated at Evian (as nearly as Terrenoire could remember), de Gaulle said:

> The era of the Empire is closed. . . . We had given up our European ambitions and this empire gave us riches and the soldiers that we lacked. It has largely contributed during a century to keep our country in the first rank. But that time has passed for us

General de Gaulle, President of the Republic, greeting
His Excellency Léopold Sédar Senghor, President of
the Republic of Senegal, July 30, 1968

as for others. Alone in the world we cannot oppose decolonization. And, besides, we
no longer have the same interest in colonization. The industrial era changed
everything. Our strength is within us. Before all else we must convince ourselves that
we have no more need of the peoples that we formerly subjected, but to the degree
that we reinforce ourselves within, we have a chance of keeping them with us. . . .
At the bottom of the affair we stick to self-determination: with France or without
her. . . .

I do not disagree that the rebellion might have confirmed and affirmed in my mind
what was already in my thoughts long before it was expressed . . . that the events
that happened and are happening in Algeria should have confirmed me in what I
have thought and demonstrated in more than twenty years, with no pleasure
certainly—and one can easily see why—but with the certainty of serving France wel
in this way.[31]

Thus, gradually, his policy became adapted to a decolonizing process. His
mind, said Claudius-Petit, a long-time collaborator of de Gaulle's, was always
turned toward decolonization, but he took account of realities.[32] He carried on
until the goal of freedom was reached, and he put the finishing touches on the
whole affair, even though many journalists, said Edouard Sablier of the
televison network, had a way of saying that he had done nothing.[33] The states of

the Levant had attained freedom after the Second World War, managing to force the troops of both Britain and France outside of their borders. The protectorates of Morocco and Tunisia had attained their freedom aided by Pierre Mendès-France and Edgar Faure. A foretaste of freedom was given Black Africa by the *Loi-Cadre* of Gaston Defferre, and then, in the grand finale of decolonization between the years of 1958 and 1960, in the second era of Charles de Gaulle's power, thirteen colonies became independent without the firing of a shot. Later, a legacy of friendly feeling remained in most of the new states.[34] Two years later, as Algeria fought herself to the edge of freedom, General de Gaulle granted her the independence he knew she had to have. The whole process was extraordinary in speed and completeness. Such are the facts, and only in the future will it be possible to judge them.

We must remember, too, that de Gaulle, during all this period, did not forget to mention the benefits that French colonization had conferred upon the overseas territories. He never repudiated the enormous work he believed France had done in Africa. In the last complete book he wrote, he spoke of the public works, the roads, bridges, and ports; the schools that had begun to teach the Africans the elements of Western European civilization; the health care; and the increased security that colonization had brought to Africa.[35] Both Manuela Semidei and Melville Herskovits have spoken of these improvements in recent works. Herskovits also referred to the higher standard of living the African had begun to enjoy under colonialism, and the wider horizons, adding that only freedom was lacking.[36] Also, Guéna, writing of the Community, felt that the Africans had actually profited from the much-discussed policy of assimilation, for it had furnished them with an apprenticeship to modern life. Finally, the passage to independence under de Gaulle had been achieved under unhoped-for conditions.[37] De la Gorce was optimistic, in his article of 1970, that some of the past of colonialism had been forgotten under the new policy of cooperation, for he believed that France was now a liberating state with prestige and freedom of action.[38]

Some of these words about colonization, decolonization, and colonialism may be wishful thinking. Some of the humiliations, hardships, and injustices suffered before 1958 certainly remain in the minds of a great many Africans; they speak of it at times. Nevertheless, a few generations in the future, many more of the evils of colonization will have been pushed back into the recesses of African minds. Thus they may both forget the benefits conferred and fail to realize the isolation of colonized peoples in the past. Held apart from the stream of life in the world before freedom came to them, they could not help to settle the world's problems; they could not even settle their own; nor could they exploit their own natural resources. So, says Arthur Conte, they remained economically underdeveloped.[39] But now they can go at their own pace.

Colonization, for those born long enough before World War II to remember life in a different period, seemed a natural phenomenon, one that was questioned only by those brought into intimate contact with it and forced to think about it more clearly. Yet with all the pros and cons, when all the good and the evil are weighed, we may see that as a result of the colonization of Africa by France "something ineffaceable has developed between the peoples of the two countries." And it gives some promise of enduring.[40] General de Gaulle, some believe, increased that feeling, for he "married with passion the cause of the transformation of human relations in modern society."[41] The Africans' great love for him is, at least, a partial proof of that. He touched many of them deeply, even though in the forties, as we can see in the 1948 report of the RDA, some of them then classed him with the conservatives who were trying to defeat the democratic forces in France.[42] What one might have expected from de Gaulle was a certain rigidity toward other human beings, due to his military training and also to something in his character that froze others in his early days. He seemed to cling to old ideologies, at least until he became interested in modernizing the methods of the French army. After that, for a time, he seemed bent on forwarding the cause of steadfastness in relations with dependent peoples rather than in developing any more sensitive quality. There was little humanity in his judgment of the Arabs when he first went to the Near East. What one did not and could not expect was his turning toward a more liberal and understanding creed in his effort to bridge the gap of nationalities and to understand the changes and the future needs of the various peoples with whom he had to deal. His gradual change in permitting the independence that he at first denied was unexpected to many who followed his life and actions. No doubt it was partly due to his always having had in mind the circumstances (*les contingences*) of the world at large; for, by the end of the fifties, many British colonies were free. Perhaps Eboué and other thoughtful Africans, or men from the French islands, gave him a different perception of the possibilities of the black race.

It is too soon to know whether General de Gaulle was right in all the methods he used. All we can see is that a major conviction of our century lies in the belief that the peoples of the earth have a basic right to determine their own destinies. Charles de Gaulle admitted that, and he acted in accordance with this new belief in allowing the states of French Africa to take their freedom and walk into independence, ready or no. Some were evidently not ready, at least in terms of managing their countries in the Western manner. Some did not like the situation they found on the farther side when the barriers went down. One African man, a person of great ability (not a politician), in speaking to the author, called the new independence "a poisoned gift" because of its many difficulties and problems. Possibly he was thinking of the Africans of certain states, who believed that when they had independence there would be no taxes.

Yet even if all the colonists did not like or approve the new independence, think of the joy of newfound freedom that came to some, even though that joy may have been short-lived as they found out the difficulties and responsibilities that awaited them. De Gaulle's face in their memory must be something of a Janus face. In the brightness of its high moments, it seemed to glow, and when the reverse side came into view, it had a grimmer appearance. Yet both remain in the memory, for General de Gaulle made an impression on his time that cannot be forgotten—whether it was for good or bad. One of the strongest reasons for this was his great influence in the colonial world. The Community was his "personal achievement,"[43] and though it did not last as an institution, through the promotion of the cooperation it has supplied came a more hopeful ideal for future communities of nations. The League of Nations has disappeared; the United Nations has many weaknesses; but does anyone doubt that it will be followed by other experiments in international communities?

A little-known Englishman wrote in 1841:

> Dim through the night of these tempestuous years
> A Sabbath dawn o'er Africa appears;
> Then shall her neck from Europe's yoke be freed,
> And healing arts to hideous arms succeed;
> At home fraternal bonds her tribes shall bind,
> Commerce abroad espouse them with mankind.[44]

The verses are not of great value in themselves. Basil Davidson, quoting them in 1964, said that Africa was still far from realizing this vision.[45] Nevertheless, Africa has brought to life at least a part of that dream, and General de Gaulle was an instrument in making that possible. President Senghor wrote some years since: "General de Gaulle is the great African of our time."[46] It is a real claim to remembrance.

19

After the Climax

It is nearly two decades since General de Gaulle completed, in 1960, the granting of political independence to the former African colonies of France south of the Sahara.[1] To the interested observer today, it is clear that this decolonization had to mean something more than that first great effort of tearing the Empire apart and—apparently—of giving it up altogether.[2] Was the independence of the new states then complete, and, if so, why has there been so much criticism of the continued influence of France in Africa, in political, military, economic, and cultural affairs? The feeling is now widespread that, no matter how much the young states need the aid and the assurance that the French government still provides, someday they must be able to carry on alone without it. This problem requires an understanding of General de Gaulle's policies in the years after 1960 until he retired in 1969, and a review of his government's actions in making that policy effective. Following that, there must be some indication of changes in policy since the General left the Elysée, and of what hopes exist for the future.

The first steps taken by the French government in its relations with Black Africa were probably the most important of the last eighteen years. It must be remembered that the first plans for the Community, in 1958, were strict in allocating great powers to the government of France. On this point Ligot said that if the Constitution of 1958, like that of 1946, announced the principle of equality, nevertheless it did not apply it immediately.

> The Organic Laws which dictated the application of the Constitution practically speaking reserved the direction of common affairs to the organs of the French Republic: the power of decision in these affairs was recognized as belonging to the President of the Community, that is to say the President of the French Republic, in whose election the States of the Community only participated in a very minor way. The Ministers to whom fell the duties of the common affairs were Ministers of the French Republic who were responsible for the corresponding affairs in France. Finally the common public services were mingled very largely with the French services.[3]

Yet, when the Agreements for Cooperation (*Les Accords de Coopération*) were signed, they covered most of the fields that had been reserved largely for the French State between 1958 and 1960. These fields were foreign policy, monetary affairs, defense, and various aspects of economic and financial arrangements; also policies for primary commodities and strategic materials, for justice, for higher education, and, finally, for the organization of international transport and telecommunications.[4] This was the beginning of the great change, as was evident at the time of independence, or soon thereafter, when most of the former colonies, except for Guinea,[5] signed cooperation agreements. These agreements of the "Entente States" (the Ivory Coast, Dahomey, Niger, and Upper Volta) and of Mauritania and the Cameroon were signed, at their request, after the proclamations of their independence, and also after the membership of each state in the United Nations had been secured. There was no reference to the Community in these cases. Thus these states were bound to France only by contractual governmental and predominantly bilateral agreements.[6] There were quadripartite agreements on defense among three of these Entente States (Ivory Coast, Dahomey, and Niger) and France. Upper Volta's only defense agreement concerned aerial overflight. All of the Entente States had agreements on raw materials and strategic products.[7] For these states and those previously in the Federation of French West Africa (Senegal, Mauritania, the Ivory Coast, Dahomey, and Upper Volta), but not for Mali, there were also agreements on economic aid and monetary matters, which were under the jurisdiction of the West African Monetary Union. Mali (the former French Soudan) did not join the monetary union and had differences also about political agreements. New plans were made with Mali after its short-lived federation with Senegal (the Mali federation) had split up.[8]

The states that had remained in the Community were Senegal, Central African Republic, Congo-Brazzaville, Chad, and Madagascar. They stayed somewhat closer to France and made agreements that concerned conciliation and the rights of nationals. For three of the states that had been in the Federation of French Equatorial Africa (the Central African Republic, Congo-Brazzaville, and Chad), there were agreements on defense, raw materials, strategic products, currency, economy, finance, and higher education. Gabon, the fourth state in the Federation, joined in these arrangements later.[9] In the cases of Togo and the Cameroon, the trusteeships over them, previously held by the United Nations, were removed as the states were granted independence. The agreements made in these two cases were similar to those of the Entente States.[10]

There was a general uniformity in the agreements of all the states, but there were allowances for individual differences. All were similar in form to those that had been in force in the Community. Certain additional juridical agreements differed in each case, but only in appearance, for, as Ligot wrote in 1964, the agreements of the Community and those of the Cooperation made later are similar[11] (though early in 1974 other agreements were made, some of these differing from the previous ones).[12]

When independence first came, it seemed that all of the new states needed both aid and protection from the mother country. The agreements were based on voluntary adhesion and could be altered. The states could become entirely independent without leaving the Community, in accordance with a revision of the Constitution in 1960.

This revision of the Constitution requires some explanation. As of August

1958, when the first draft of the Community left the Elysée, it was declared that an independent state would no longer belong to the Community and would not receive French aid. De Gaulle had believed that "if Confederation was allowed, the Federation would soon be a dead letter," for other countries, seeing the great advantages of confederation, would not remain in the federation. He had said: "I, de Gaulle, say 'Federation' and there we stop."[13] And he had added to the Consultative Constitutional Committee, "The referendum will tell us whether secession carries the day. But what is inconceivable is an independent state which France continues to help. If the choice is for independence, the government will draw, with regret, the conclusions that follow from the expression of that choice."[14]

But the General had reversed his stand by 1960. First came the modifications made on his trip around Africa. He had hinted at independence at Tananarive; then he talked with Barthélémy Boganda before speaking at Brazzaville and said there that the metropole would not oppose independence, but secession would be necessary to get it. Still, he said, after a certain time a referendum would settle that matter by agreement with the Community, and the metropole would not oppose independence, though it would retain the possibility of severing its bonds with a state. The menace of outside invasion must be avoided, but he did manage to give assurance of independence, though with no timing. Indeed, Gabriel d'Arboussier had told Sékou Touré before the referendum took place that independence had been conceded at Brazzaville.[15] Even in Guinea, de Gaulle spoke of whether the French and the Africans wanted "to engage each other in a Community for an uncertain length of time." So a loosening had begun in his thought. His change of attitude continued.

On November 10, 1958, de Gaulle said in a broadcast that all the states were in the Community because they had so chosen, and that all could leave when they chose to do so. "It is effective independence and guaranteed cooperation."[16] Soon, by early 1960, the Community had undergone a great change. In the case of the Mali Federation, the General conceded that it could become independent without forfeiting its membership in the Community.[17] Madagascar asked for a similar arrangement. In agreeing to these requests the General had moved toward confederalism. That could cause the entire Community to disintegrate as it had begun.[18] The situation was regularized quickly. An obedient Assembly changed the Constitution, voting that "a Member-State may, by way of agreements, become independent without thereby ceasing to belong to the Community" (Article 86, as amended by Constitutional Law of June 4, 1960).[19] A "Renewed Community" thus came into existence, "which was in fact a confederation, without common citizenship or common nationality."[20] It could only have "taken on a genuinely federal appearance" if, as the RDA had originally advocated, "there had been a federal parliament with a federal government responsible to it."[21]

There is no doubt that the reasons for the General's change were multiple. Jean Touchard, in a recent book, speaks of de Gaulle's pragmatism and empiricism and his acceptance of unavoidable revolutions without any nostalgia for the past.[22] There is no doubt that the General's belief in the force of circumstances affected him as it had always done. In addition, de Gaulle had already offered independence to Algeria. He was probably surprised that Guinea had managed to remain on its feet, but did he bother to retain more than irritation against Sékou Touré? One does not know—yet, certainly, there was extreme frigidity between the two men for some time, though Sékou Touré tried rather quickly to renew a cooperative arrangement with France. But Senghor, Tsiranana, and even Keita had supported de Gaulle in 1958, even though he knew they wanted immediate independence. We know, however, that General de Gaulle was anxious about Guinea's power to stay on its feet, and anxious, too, about how any further break with Guinea would affect the other states that had voted with France. Would they turn toward Russia if de Gaulle was too intransigent?[23] In short, he feared already for his Community. Now, an independent Guinea had tended to become glamorous and Sékou Touré became a hero in certain places. The very idea of young men in Nigeria wearing "Sékou Touré hats" must have been anathema to de Gaulle, though he tried to become "Olympianly aloof"![24] Still, he had come to perceive that if the Community were not federal, there was no point in having it. There was now no difference between the states in or out of the Community. Thus, the evolution in his thought took place.[25]

One writer not thought of as a Gaullist has referred to this change as "a remarkable personal evolution."[26] J.-B. Duroselle added later that the indispensable and generous work consisted in changing the relationships of domination into the relationships of cooperation.[27] And Teresa Hayter notes that the Cooperation agreements, the basis of aid to the fourteen states, represented an important concession by France on a point of principle. Whereas de Gaulle previously[28] was not willing to consider aiding an independent state, now he was prepared to continue to support the states financially, even though they had attained an independent status and some of them had left the Community formally.[29] It is easy to agree with Duroselle and Hayter that the change in the General's thinking was an unexpected and a very valuable evolution. Such an evolution of de Gaulle's thought must have cost him greatly, but it was certainly worth it. From that point on, the change to cooperation could proceed.

The agreements as they were put into effect were pragmatic and egalitarian in character. They were the basis of the new Cooperation that came out of the old colonial relationship. When they were signed, they ended the Community in its original form of 1958,[30] but Maurice Ligot, one of the most detailed writers on the subject, felt that this new form of "Cooperation" had to continue while need for it subsisted.[31]

Some former Community institutions remained: the presidency, though reduced in authority—it was now merely a moral magistracy—with no decision-making power. The General Secretariat remained to keep the president informed, a conference of chiefs of state met irregularly, the consultative

Senate and the Court of Arbitration existed in theory.[32] All of the new states were to have freedom of thought, science, religion, opinion, and assembly, and they were allowed to determine the rights of other states each on its own territory. Some meetings of the remaining states of the Community could and did occur on certain subjects.[33]

Some of the most important agreements concerned defense—sometimes both internal and external. They considered the way in which France could be involved in military installations, temporary or permanent, or in facilities for the use of French forces. In every state except Togo, a Council of Defense was set up. French forces, where they existed, were to have freedom of movement, but the French were responsible for infractions of order by their men. Under certain circumstances France would give military material or equipment, as well as personnel, to plan and train necessary forces. Technical and military aid were both involved.[34]

Where agreements dealt with raw materials and strategic products, there had to be consultation with France about them, and France was given priority in sales of such products and could limit their export to other countries when necessary; this restraint was particularly resented.[35]

Some attention was given to diplomatic affairs in the agreements, for France promised to represent the various states in other countries when asked to do so. It was stated that there should be consultation with her on foreign affairs.[36]

Financial, economic, and monetary matters were dealt with in agreements that attempted to coordinate them, when possible, in different states. France was given a privileged position in plans for productivity and in financial affairs. All of the states (except for Guinea, which had become free) were to be members of the franc zone, though Mali did not wish to be connected with the Monetary Union of West Africa.[37] France guaranteed the franc of the African states of the French Community (CFA, *Communauté Financière Africaine*) and its convertibility to the French franc, and France also granted financial aid for economic and social development. This was divided among the various forms of aid in capital, technical personnel, and educational and technical assistance. Treasury advances and foreign currency were sometimes used to help with budgets and with the setting up of national armies where necessary. Other agreements dealt with training of experts, credits, investments, etc.[38]

The most important agreements of all, however, were thought to be those planned to promote cultural cooperation. They dealt especially with the maintenance and expansion of the French language and culture, with the purpose, it was claimed, of developing the intellectual and political élite of Africa and Madagascar. The Cultural Agreements concerned especially stages for higher education, plans for training leaders and for setting up universities and higher technical schools for specialized purposes.[39]

In accordance with the recommendations of the Brazzaville Conference, France had tried in the late forties and fifties to extend primary education to all African children in the territories that were then under French control. They planned, too, to provide secondary, technical, and higher education for a much larger group. It was expected that the African élite would occupy many more posts than previously in administration, trade, and industry.[40] Part of the funds for this educational expansion would be obtained through FIDES (*Fonds d'Investissements et de Développement Economique et Sociale des Territoires d'Outre-Mer*), established in 1946. By 1957–58, Black African territories had 952,457 primary pupils, 32,643 in secondary and technical schools, and several hundred in higher education.[41] Higher educational institutions were established in Dakar in 1957 and in Brazzaville in 1959 for the students of the Federations of West and Equatorial Africa; and in 1961, a convention was established—the *Fondation de l'Enseignement Supérieur en Afrique Centrale* (FESAC). Included were a university center and an *Ecole Normale Supérieur,* and there was preparation for teachers in several centers in the four states, as well as in certain specialized institutions. France gave funds for buildings, equipment, and personnel, while UNESCO helped with the normal school.[42]

Political difficulties at Brazzaville, and the desire of many Africans to take their higher education in France, prevented these arrangements from taking root effectively. By 1971 interstate cooperation for higher education had broken down and FESAC was dissolved, giving way to a *Conseil Supérieur des Universités en Afrique Centrale.* Each state then attempted to add to its facilities with aid, sometimes from France, or even from the Soviet Union, Rumania, and the Common Market partners of France. But, as David Gardinier notes, "France has directly provided the bulk of aid to education" in these countries.[43]

Laurie J. Tracy remarked that education remained under the highly centralized metropolitan Ministry of National Education, though other aid programs were under the newly created Ministry of Cooperation. She cites three types of program in the administration of it in Africa, first the old French system with little but the classics given to the students, then a certain redefinition of the goals of African education, to which General de Gaulle did not object. Thus, finally, the absolute priority of the classic texts and diplomas was ended, and technical and vocational education began to be far more important. De Gaulle saw to it, she says, that larger amounts of funds were allocated to the development of two-year vocational programs at the French-supported universities of Abidjan, Dakar, Yaoundé, and Tananarive. In addition, there was a new program to disseminate French culture by libraries, bookmobiles, cultural centers, and theater companies, and aid was given to new periodicals. She does not, however, report any use of local languages. Instruction was still in French.[44]

Edward M. Corbett points out the need for reappraisal of the whole educational system in Africa, relaxing the humanistic values in favor of vocational and technical training, and relating it to rural needs. But he also speaks of French as the only language used in the schools, and the tight hold of the whole system under the French Ministry of Education. He concludes that French culture is becoming embedded more and more, and that it is not relevant to local societies, as one can well believe.[45] It is notable that in the issues of *Présence Africaine* that came out in 1966 and 1967 (Nos. 60 and 64) several articles show a real struggle to make education African.

Some educational agreements with the states were quadripartite, and it was made clear that France would aid in the development of teaching and would help to train Africans for that purpose. Each state would go first to the French government for recruitment of teaching personnel, inspectors, and examination juries.

There were some further agreements for judicial relationships, shipping, telecommunications, etc. France was expected to train technicians for these purposes and to plan progress for their use.[46]

Out of these agreements came the situation of the French presence in Black Africa since 1960, their political, financial, commercial, and cultural relationship. Where not entirely spelled out in the agreements, they resulted from them. As Corbett remarked, no area was overlooked.[47] They provide what appears at first sight to be a sort of straitjacket for the new states, but in view of some of the benefits they conferred and the relatively short time they have been in existence, it is impossible to judge them fairly as a whole at the present time.

The question of financial and economic aid to the new states was of great importance in the whole picture of the agreements. The aid to the young underdeveloped countries was given to help them to avoid isolation, to develop their organizations, to train their élites and advance their economic situations. But there is no doubt that it was also to keep them close to France, and, if possible, to give France a privileged position in Africa. The promises given, Ligot felt, must be respected.[48] However, it is fair at this point to say that Sylvain-Soriba Camara, in his valuable book on Guinea, says that Ligot gives, above all, the official position that French aid is a generous enterprise.[49] However, it is also fair to say that France has given to such aid a greater percentage of her gross national product than any other country, and this statement is confirmed by François Luchaire, who says that France has given more aid per capita to the underdeveloped countries than any other nation.[50]

Other writers point out different facets of the question of aid. Teresa Hayter says that some of the countries have become unduly dependent on France, and that this might be a danger. There were certainly historical sources for the French sense of responsibility for Africa—the documents of the French Empire, of the French Union, of Overseas France, and of the policy of assimilation. Behind all this lay the principles of the French Revolution as well as recent emotional links with France. It is only since independence that aid could be considered as an impulse toward self-sufficiency, and it was certainly a concession on the part of France to agree to aid countries already independent.[51]

Luchaire speaks of the fact that aid covered food, construction, services of technicians, cash or specie gifts, technical loans or training, commercial aid in procuring markets, customs advantages, support of prices, and military aid to set up national armies where necessary. Eighty percent of the aid went to states that had formerly been French colonies or trusteeships.[52] To sum it all up, from 1960 to 1964 France gave a yearly average of 283 million dollars to the Black African states, as compared to 22 million from other bilateral aid countries. From 1965 to 1968 the average of French gifts declined somewhat, but large-scale aid has continued in accordance with the needs of each country, and also in accordance with each country's relationship with France.[53] There was certainly some drop-off in aid, however, after 1964. Laurie Tracy refers to it as a "major policy shift" of General de Gaulle's government. There was certainly some criticism of aid by the general public in France, largely led by Raymond Cartier of *Paris Match*, then a very popular writer, who complained that the French were wasting their money outside France and that the government had not come clean about all the aid that was given. Possibly as a result of this criticism and because of the Jean-Marcel Jeanneney Report commissioned by the government and published in 1964 a few changes were made. Aid was widened to include certain disadvantaged countries not closely connected with France—among them India, Pakistan, and Latin America—and it was considered important that the European Economic Development Fund should shoulder some of the burden for Africa. Yet Hayter wrote in 1966 that the government had not put the Jeanneney proposals into effect "nor has it yet decided to do so."[54] Still, Tracy notes that General de Gaulle did succeed in persuading the EEC "to adopt the principle of multilateral responsibility for aid," and that "an overwhelming proportion" of the European Development Fund for Africa was allotted to the former French colonies of Africa.[55]

Aid comes from the French Treasury, which consents to advances from three funds: *Fonds d'Aide et de Coopération*, FAC (created in 1959, but it does not cover all French aid); *Fonds d'Investissements et de Dévelopment Economique et Social des Territoires d'Outre-Mer*, FIDES (phased out after FAC was created); and *Fonds d'Investissements des Départments d'Outre-Mer*, FIDOM. Other ministries involved have their own budgets which supply additional sums.[56] A *Caisse Centrale de Coopération Economique* controls disbursal of the funds that have been contributed for aid. The Ministries of Foreign Affairs, War, Economy and Finance, of State for the Overseas Territories, Transportation, and the Technical Ministries of Education and Public Works are involved. All this does not preclude the work of the Ministry of Cooperation. The prime minister of France and the minister of finance determine the broad divisions of the national budget.[57]

On the level of the presidency, the *Secrétariat Général pour la Communauté et les Affaires Africaines et Malgaches* was finally given a determining role. Credits were arranged with the Ministry of Cooperation, though voted previously by Parliament and disbursed by a *comité directeur*, with representatives from the Ministries of Finance and of Economic Affairs, and others from Parliament and the technical ministries. This directing committee alone can receive the requests of the states for aid, and these requests are then coordinated with all the ministries involved.[58] Plans for the use of funds must be furnished by those asking for them, and materials must come from the franc zone when available. The states must carry out the obligations they incurred when they asked for aid. All this is done with the proviso that the action must not injure France.[59]

Massive aid still seems to be necessary. President Houphouet-Boigny of the Ivory Coast said in 1969 it would be needed for twenty years more,[60] and President Hamani Diori of Niger made a similar statement to the author in an interview in November 1969. There was much complaint against the French at that time. There seems to be no doubt in the minds of some Africans that France keeps her predominant position in Africa because of the impressive amount of aid she contributes to all her former associates.[61] There is a good case for that attitude, but it does not take into account the social, cultural, and personal values that hold Africa and France together.

The question of management, not only of aid but of all the affairs of the African states in their relations with their former mother country, seems to be unduly complicated. Teresa Hayter wrote in 1966 that aid was administered by "a bewildering diversity of institutions and organizations" not yet integrated.[62] A few facts seem clear. The Ministry of Overseas France (of the rue Oudinot) died in 1958, and a General Secretariat for the States of the Community was set up, giving way with the demise of that first Community, in 1960, to the General Secretariat for the Community and for the African and Malgache States. At this time, FAC replaced FIDES. The Ministry of Cooperation was created in 1961, but in 1966, says Hayter, it was replaced by the Secretariat of State for Foreign Affairs in Charge of Cooperation, and was attached to the Ministry of Foreign Affairs in Paris. This was apparently an effort to give to the French Ministry of Foreign Affairs a more effective voice in African matters. However, the General Secretariat for the Community and for African and Malgaches Affairs of the Presidency continued to exist. It was headed by Jacques Foccart, who was the real political link between France and Africa until the end of President Pompidou's term of office. This secretariat kept the president of France informed about what went on in Africa, and it transmitted his directives to the African officials. So, from the political standpoint, French involvement in the African states continued to exist, though certain changes occurred in it after the election to the presidency of Valéry Giscard d'Estaing in 1974, when the new president made almost immediate changes in the structures of Cooperation.[63] However, the bonds between France and the states were always governed by the agreements that had been signed.

All the structures of the new states, including their constitutions, were set up on the French models. This was undoubtedly due to what Corbett calls the "French mind-set" in Africa,[64] a measure of French civilization that had become normal, at least among the French-trained leaders of Africa. Many French advisers remained in key positions in Africa, and the Africans apparently thought them necessary at the time when they received their political independence. Dependence on French techniques and technicians was general.[65] Corbett caps it all by saying, "Responsibility for major decisions on matters affecting Black Africa, and for maintaining close personal liaison with the top leaders, continues to be the formal prerogative of the President of the French Republic." Ligot thought this was no longer the case; but Corbett believed that desire for limitations of French control were growing, and that there was some resistance on the cultural front as well as some open complaints on many subjects related to French control.[66]

Though political, diplomatic, and defense measures were supposed to be dealt with by the Secretariat of State for Foreign Affairs in charge of Cooperation at the Quai d'Orsay, nearly all other subjects were under the Secretariat of the Presidency. The line between the two did not always seem clear. The prime minister of France at first had certain duties connected with Africa, at least until the Ministry of Cooperation was organized in 1960. A Council for African and Malgache Affairs, containing high French officials, was set up in 1961 to coordinate the role of the presidency with the other groups, and to make decisions not taken by the French ministries.[67]

It should be noted that the Jean-Marcel Jeanneney Report to the French Government of 1963 was intended to reorganize the management of Franco-African relations, but it was never really implemented. The report practically admitted that the French controlled Africa through the technical program, and it indicated (sadly) that France was profiting less and less by its trade with the former colonies, but that humanitarian reasons and the spread of French culture justified the continuance of Cooperation. Camara, in his book on Guinea, felt that this report never got beyond expressing the official position, though it did criticize Cooperation to a certain extent.[68]

In all of these extensive plans, the place and authority of France was felt, even though independence from her control had supposedly taken place in 1960 or before. The whole system was based on the *Loi-Cadre* of 1956 and the French Constitution of 1958 that had set up the Community, and high-level contacts later were kept up by frequent visits to France, when the African chiefs of state saw de Gaulle, Foccart, and other high French officials.[69] Corbett believed that all this was possible because all of the new states were committed to mass education with their models based on the French educational system, and that there was apparently no real indication of change. True, the aid and monetary policies were supposed to give a voice to the Africans, but the Ministry of Cooperation and FAC remained under French control. Still, the Africans did have representation on the board of the Central Banks of Africa and on certain commissions, though the French also had many members on them, and the number of Africans was limited. Some relaxation of French control took place due to the regulations of the Common Market, but, all in all, no monetary system in Africa was free of French control, with the exception of that of Guinea. French management of the banks was a key factor in importing. France was always undoubtedly powerful in financial matters.[70]

France was dominant, too, in African commerce and industry. There have been practically no Africans in industry and commerce except in humble capacities, and when independence came, there were no industries in African hands.[71] There had been some development of industry and a few new ventures

A reception for the leaders of the French African states, July 3, 1965. On General de Gaulle's right are Léon M'Ba of Gabon and Nicholas Grunetzky of Togo; on his left are Félix Houphouet-Boigny of the Ivory Coast, two African officials, and then Hamani Diori of the State of Niger next to Maurice Couve de Murville.

in the sixties, but French control remained overwhelming.[72] Still, emphasis on African participation in private industry is growing now in the late seventies.

The role of the French government in agriculture was even greater than in other aspects of the economy, and France has remained the major trade partner of its former territories.[73] In mining and oil concessions, France had a prior claim, and could block export to third countries if she needed their products for her own defense.[74]

One main means of control by France has existed in the technical assistance program. In the agreements that relate to such problems, France was a major source of influence. She has undertaken to provide expertise and training as the groundwork for economic development in the African states. It was part of the hard core of the Cooperation Agreements, for it provided teachers for the educational system and for scientific research; many Africans saw this as a powerful platform for the exercise of control by the French.[75]

At times the French have defended their actions in Cooperation rather well. In 1970, in a report to the *Académie des Sciences d'Outre-Mer*, Albert Charton, inspector general of public instruction, said that there had been "sensational progress" in education in Black Africa and Madagascar, now that the way was open for programs from the university level down to basic education, responding to "the pressing demand of the overseas populations." In Africa and Madagascar where aid had been received, there were 3 million primary pupils in the schools in 1970 (the date of the report), as against a little over 1.5 million in 1960. In secondary education, there were 215,000 pupils as against 67,200 in 1960. The same progress was taking place in higher education. The states of Africa were working to increase the rate of scholarship in their purlieus. In 1965, he said, the number of French *coopérants* working in Africa was 5,000, but of these only 1,600 were indigenous teachers. "The infantry of African teaching is still French," he said, "above all for the secondary level."[76] In 1972 Corbett spoke of 6,000 French nationals teaching in African secondary or higher level schools and of the fact that the large African universities are under French control. There were twice as many (teachers, technicians, administrators, etc.) south of the Sahara, he said, as before independence and in some countries even more than twice as many. In ten years, the French budget for education had tripled, up to $116 million a year, to cover primary and secondary schools and cultural activities of the type of the USIA.[77]

Before Corbett wrote in 1972, a French official, Georges Gorse, had prepared another long report, completed in June 1971, as a summation of the first ten years of Cooperation. Thus these facts were reported, practically in full, but never published by the government. That probably meant that there would be no great changes in the methods of Cooperation then in use, at least not at that time.[78] It was harsher on the management of Cooperation than the Jeanneney Report had been in 1963, stating that the aid given underdeveloped countries in general was insufficient and not well applied. He thought it should go to rural development, industrialization, education, and studies in demography.[79] Rurally, there was much to be done. There was need of a national market; an increase in food production and in variety of products; new priorities for cattle breeding, wheat, rice, and new crops; and coordination of educational activities that related to agriculture.[80] In industry, more non-agricultural products were needed, for only industry and tourism could produce more funds, and there was insufficient entrepreneurial activity for these purposes.[81]

In education, new teachers and better teacher training were needed, and responsibility for higher education should devolve upon the Africans.[82] Demographically speaking, there should be fewer births if the population was to be cared for. It was thought that fewer infant deaths might induce the people to want fewer children.[83]

Finally, as to the economy, there was a need to export more tools and to import fewer French products. France should stop increasing her gifts to the dominions and territories overseas and put more funds into Black Africa on a multiyear basis. A multilateral basis for aid was important.[84]

Gorse and his companions felt that there was a real crisis in Cooperation which they thought many in France did not fully understand. Up to 1970, the Agreements of Cooperation had sufficed, but after that, revision was called for. There seemed to be no doubt that France would continue in her projects for Cooperation, especially on the technical side.[85]

Since the report was not published by the government, it seems clear that the real necessity for these changes was not understood, at least during the presidency of Georges Pompidou, though he had spoken of need for flexibility. Apparently that was not enough. Indeed, the demands for change continued all through the early seventies. They came from Niger, the Congo, Mauritania, Madagascar, the Cameroon, and Dahomey. By 1974, negotiations for new agreements had been completed with several of these states (Mauritania, Madagascar, the Congo, and the Cameroon). A few changes or concessions were allowed by the French, especially on cultural matters with Madagascar, where the existence of the country's own language caused a strong reaction against the French cultural and educational policy. In Mauritania, Arabicization really meant cultural independence. It was agreed to take French land forces out of Madagascar, but agreements about defense and monetary arrangements were among the most difficult to obtain from France. In the end, Mauritania and Madagascar left the franc zone, but France retained control of the West African Central Bank. Some French teachers were posted elsewhere. The French reaction was calm and assured. There was no urgency. France had been committed to extension of her cultural and political influence in the Third World, and any decrease in aid expenditures would compromise this policy. She is certain to remain deeply involved in Africa.[86]

Obviously, there have been other vehement criticisms of the French position in Africa since the declarations of independence. Some of these are due to French interventions by force in the African states in the interests of political stabilization when governmental *coups* took place. Some critics relate these interventions to the economic potential of the states involved. France accepted the ousting of the political chiefs from Dahomey and the Middle Congo (Congo-Brazzaville) and the Central African Republic, where there was little economic value, but she did restore the president of Gabon, where there was lumber, oil, and uranium.[87] Nevertheless, a very high former official of the French government told the author recently that this was not true. The rule always applied was that intervention was used only when the state involved requested it.[88] What he did not say was that assistance was not always given when requested. Generally, Paris avoided power struggles in the interior of the states. For example, Fulbert Youlou's government was overthrown in the Congo, though he had asked for aid. In 1963, the French were asked to intervene in Togo, the Congo (Brazzaville), and Dahomey, but they refused to do so.[89]

At some point de Gaulle realized that intervention was making France unpopular, and just as he reduced the strength of the French military in Africa, so he was wary of using force to preserve regimes that seemed to him more favorable to France. As he perceived this and withdrew his forces, it became evident that he was not basing French influence in Africa on the military.[90] France and Africa today do not want to use military force to attain their ends,[91] and the French military presence in Africa steadily diminished under de Gaulle.[92] This was partly because of the use of more modern war materials, the need for economy stimulated by the preparation of France's "force de frappe," and also because there had been somewhat of a controversy over the French intervention in Gabon in February 1964. The motives there were the preservation, if possible, of stability, the uranium wealth of the state, and the effort to contain the opposition to President M'Ba because the insurgents had no popular backing.[93] In 1967 the Central African Republic asked for aid, though there was no real instability there. Troops were sent, but no action resulted. In de Gaulle's later years he tried to combat instability by withdrawal of aid or by other means, and he condemned interventions by other nations such as the United States in the Dominican Republic, thus making France appear to be the protector of African sovereignty. In other cases, he permitted internal takeovers of governments by new regimes, whether of his own shade of thought or not. It must be remembered that French intervention forces were a mere twenty-four hours away.[94]

Looking back over these interventions and other minor ones, it is hard to make a definite statement. Yes, the states asked for intervention, but whether they got it or not, was there evidence, as Corbett says, that the French did not tolerate coups against the current governments in states where there was military or economic potential?[95] On the other hand, Tracy says that "this change in French African policy from one of an active intruder in the African political scene, to one of interested observer" negates the belief of some people that French military interests dictated Gaullist policy in Africa. She adds:

> De Gaulle ordered the withdrawal of the vast majority of troops from Africa; he handed back the Mers-el-Kébir naval base and the Reggane atomic testing site to Algeria ten years in advance of the treaty deadline; and he dismantled all but four sub-Saharan African military bases. He was determined to maintain both his low military profile as a popularity device, and to develop the mobile intervention force as a "last ditch" to protect French citizens living in Africa from possible danger. This is not indicative of a policy of overt military prestige.[96]

Here again is a question that might better wait a while for decision, especially in view of the French interventions in Chad and Mauritania in the spring and early summer of 1978.

It should be noted, too, that there has been a change in the French use of force in Africa. After the Evian agreements about Algeria, 300,000 French troops were withdrawn from Africa, paring the force there to a minimum. In 1962 and 1963, 20,000 Africans were demobilized from the French army, and there were further reductions in 1964 and 1965.[97] There had been interventions in the Central African Republic (in 1960), in Chad (in 1963), in Mauritania (in 1961), and in both CAR and Gabon (in 1962). Nevertheless, France refused to intervene in Togo and the CAR in 1963, as well as in Dahomey.[98] Apparently the government feared that world opinion against intervention would have a bad effect on the French image. After this period, interventions became fewer, though France did support Bokassa in the CAR in 1967 and Tombalbaye in Chad in 1968. At this writing, in March 1978, it is unsettling to know that French soldiers are again in Chad, fighting against a "Libyan-backed" invasion, according to Western diplomatic sources.[99] There had been a request to France (from the chief of state of Chad, General Félix Maloumi) to withdraw all troops in the fall of 1975, and it was reported that all of them had left there by October

27 of that year.[100] However, the French government evidently sent in troops at a later time. Apparently, this was at the request of the chief of state of Chad, who remains in a perilous position.[101]

Obviously, these criticisms are ascribed to what is called "neocolonialism." Clearly, too, some of that must exist in France as elsewhere. Jeanneney, in his report of 1963, said that such accusations cannot be neglected.[102] And Albert Charton, the inspector of public instruction, speaking to the *Académie des Sciences d'Outre-Mer,* said that it was necessary to admit that "even with the most liberal representatives of colonization, with those who are most desirous of liberating men, there has been a kind of will-straining toward the conquest of souls." And then he asked: "What is the missionary spirit except the political action of charity?"[103] After all, what is "neocolonialism"? A good definition was given in a resolution passed by the All-African Peoples' Conference at Cairo, on March 23–31, 1961:

> The Conference considers "that Neo-Colonialism, which is the survival of the colonial system, in spite of formal recognition of political independence, in emerging countries which became the victims of an indirect and subtle form of domination by political, economic, social, military or technical [means], is the greatest thrust to African countries that have newly won their independence or those approaching this status."

Examples, it said, indicate that the colonial system and international imperialism, realizing their failure in facing the development of revolutionary movements in Africa, made use of many means to safeguard the essentials of their economic and military power, and when independence was inevitable, they tried to deprive it of its real essence by imposing unequal economic, military, and technical conventions, creating puppet governments, following false elections, or inventing constitutional formulas intended to hide the real discrimination favoring their own settlers.[104]

De Bosschère showed how the opponents of Cooperation attack its plans, finding in it a good chance for neocolonialism to extend its power through unlimited credits to irresponsible leaders of reforms, who use them for their own whims and contribute to their irresponsibility, thus alienating the countries in their charge. He said that 80 percent of the aid for underdeveloped countries was absorbed in the budget of the administration of the Cooperation. Its actions were presented as a natural effect of its generosity, but it could not hide the menace within its deeds.[105] It might be noted that de Bosschère did not go into the purposes of the budget, for it might well be used largely for the training of various sorts of technicians to aid the African countries in training their own men. We need only add that Kwame Nkrumah, writing about neocolonialism, said that it represented "imperialism in its final and perhaps most dangerous stage." He went on to say that the troops of the imperial power might garrison the new state and control the government of it, though more often the control was exercised through economic or monetary means, and foreign capital might also be used for exploitation rather than for development.

Finally, he thought that the danger to world peace sprang not from the action of those who would seek to end neocolonialism, but from the inaction of those who allowed it to continue.[106]

Over the years there was a great deal of criticism of this sort, but it is also true that some people have defended what colonization did for Africa. Governor-General André Soucadaux noted that colonization had become a myth, full of passion, and that many people would like to devour colonialists as at the beginning of the century they wanted to eat up the *curés*, the men of religion! He points out that the critics ignore the infrastructure that colonization brought to Africa, the roads, railroads, ports, aerodromes, schools, hospitals, and research centers established by the colonial power. Without being perfect, those institutions have responded to African needs and to continued development in that continent. He mentions, too, that in general famine and scarcity have disappeared, and some epidemics have been conquered. Further, if colonization has been the scapegoat, as Governor Robert Delavignette said, it has been partly, at least, because the changes it sponsored, especially those made by the funds of FAC and the *Fonds de Soutien* that did so much for the peasants, have gone unnoticed. The system, he said, deserves not to be misunderstood.[107] And Inspector Charton, on the same occasion as before, spoke of both the educational advance in Africa and of the cultural freedom gained—in its judicial character, in the sense of responsibility of the new states, and in the affirmation of the value of Third World civilizations. He admitted, however, that the aid methods should be revised.[108] One final word: Those against neocolonialism and those who have spoken in favor of some of colonization's benefits to Africa both proceeded from well-determined positions, and said what could be expected from them.

Here we come to the as yet unanswered question: How much of this tight control, this iron collar (*carcan*)—for that is the way a good many Africans feel about it—was due to General de Gaulle himself? The books about the Cooperation and the Agreements scarcely mention him, for management had passed, at least theoretically, into the hands of the General Secretariat, the French Foreign Affairs Ministry, and all the other agencies that had to do with the relations between Africa and France. We have, at least, a few sources to refer to.

First of all, we know something of the General's manner of working from his own writings. We know that, in general, when his ministers met twice a week (some of the time at least), they all sat around a table and each person present gave his opinion. And, "generally at the end of the session," he said, he gave his own opinion formulating the conclusions of the council meeting, and, if necessary, "settling the disputes." The decisions were then sent to the ministries, often in the form of ordinances or decrees. Texts formulated by René Cassin, the General's judicial expert, were then deliberated in council and finally published in the *Official Journal*.[109]

Clearly, this system allowed immense power to the General if he wanted to use it. It was undoubtedly one of the things that led to the common suspicion that he wanted to be a dictator, a suspicion that the General resented bitterly and denied on the grounds of his frequent appeals to the people by referendum.

There were other witnesses to his manner of working with Africa. Among them was Alain Plantey, a former ambassador and later secretary general for the Union of Western Europe. Plantey has written that the General, from the beginning of his power in 1958—or even before—followed, directed, and often led, sometimes day by day, the French policy toward Africa. African questions were among those most important to him, for he felt he had a strong bond with Africa. He studied the purposes, means, and stages through which the policies must proceed. In the course of time, the new system almost replaced the federalism the General had so desired, and cooperation became his great ambition. He felt that the states ought to be able to realize that decolonization was open, total, and without ulterior motives, and he tried to reduce the preponderance of France in men's minds. The sovereignty of the new states must be respected. They need not align their views with France.[110] Plantey went on to say that no convention was signed without the General's approval, and the men and institutions connected with the whole policy were part of the General's legacy to the foreign policy relating to the African states.[111]

Obviously, this account of the General's attitudes and actions comes entirely from the Gaullist side. Plantey made one or two comments that can be questioned. In his view, "no one in France or in foreign parts has taken exception because of its innovative and positive aspects" to the policy followed toward Africa. This policy, however one may view it, has certainly been criticized in all of its aspects. It is only natural that that should be so. Further, Plantey remarks that "France has seen former colonies transform themselves into sovereign recognized states, without this movement's involving so much as the breakage of their privileged bonds with her."[112] True, there is no doubt in the minds of many people that the giving of independence to the African states was one of the best and most successful of the General's actions, but it has certainly been criticized as neocolonialist in all of its aspects, and as to breakage of former relations, what about the case of Guinea?

According to Philippe Decraene, another well-known writer, it was commonly believed that African policy came directly from the General. Many of the chiefs of service at the Quai d'Orsay, where political affairs were settled soon after the beginning of the Cooperation, had been functionaries of France Overseas and knew Africa very well indeed. Nevertheless, he saw that "under the Gaullist regime, it was indeed the Elysée Palace that conceived, oriented, decided and led the African policy of France."[113] Decraene also referred to the misunderstandings about the Community and secession. Together with the General's "turning his back brutally" on Guinea, they opened a breach in the Community. However, Decraene admitted de Gaulle did respect the sovereignty of the states, and, except in Gabon in 1964 and in Chad in 1969, he never intervened to save a regime menaced by internal subversion. He always kept a choice place for African *Francophonie* in his policy, and he never reduced aid to Africa but maintained and diversified it, leaving it to the "astonishing continuity" of the next president of France, Georges Pompidou. Decraene did not explain the reduction in aid after 1964 except to note an increasing amount of aid to overseas departments.[114]

Recently, we have obtained further evidence as to how the General worked. Bernard Tricot, who was the secretary-general of the Presidency of the Republic during the last two years of de Gaulle's regime, wrote:

> For General de Gaulle, to decide, or, as he often said, to settle once and for all, was the supreme duty of a statesman.
>
> Whoever governs, must certainly consult, but "the essential point is that the decision should be taken and the deed accomplished: it is not possible to wait until everyone is in agreement." [Remark to Tricot by General de Gaulle.]
>
> "To hope and to expect unanimity would be to misunderstand the exigencies of the State, which is an institution of decision, of action, of ambition, expressing and serving only the national interest."[115]

This brief insight from one who was continuously with the General explains much of the speed of action and of planning that were such an intimate part of the General's personality.

Probably there is little doubt in the mind of anyone who has studied the General's life and character that he would have accepted the praise and blame due to this policy without flinching. Right or wrong, he believed in it and he wanted it to succeed. That was probably the key to his actions.

No doubt, de Gaulle felt he was right when he "refused to make any gesture that would make it easier for the president of Guinea to vote yes in the referendum of September 28, 1958. Whatever the reasons behind the conflict between France and her former colony of Guinea, it was a conflict that continued longer than any of the other conflicts of French decolonization."[116] Many have felt that the trouble was due to the confrontation of two strong personalities: General de Gaulle, who was bitter and stubborn at the time about the way he was treated at Conakry, and the president of Guinea, Ahmed Sékou Touré, who was at one and the same time president, prime minister, and secretary-general of the single and all-powerful *Parti Democratique de Guinée*, PDG.[117] However, S.-S. Camara, in the very valuable book on Guinea, felt that the difficulties were due to the institutions and politics of the countries involved.[118] Sékou Touré certainly felt they were due to imperialism in general and to French imperialism in particular. And Camara added that the opposition between the French and Guinean positions was irreducible.[119] On the other hand, General de Gaulle, equally certainly, felt that it was due to Sékou Touré's attitudes and actions. "There is a man we shall never get on with," said the General, after the confrontation in the old wooden Assembly Hall at Conakry.[120] Still, Camara had a point. France wished only to give internal autonomy in the bosom of a nonegalitarian system; she adopted a policy of *intransigeance* and showed a tenacious bitterness for some time toward Sékou Touré. On the other hand, Guinea had a nationalist, Pan-African, revolutionary policy, one that could not be adapted to the French position.[121] Camara said that General de Gaulle was unable to spare the sensibilities of those with whom he dealt, but he also admitted that Sékou Touré needed an outside enemy to make him able to deal with his internal troubles, and he admits, too, that the "personalization of power" in Guinea and the intolerant temperament of its president gave the confrontation of the two men an irrational and violent character. Camara referred to the conflict with France but also to the opposition within Guinea, and to those who had fled the country to escape the Touré regime. In replying to French propaganda that tried to isolate Guinea by presenting it as a bridgehead of communism in Africa, Touré exaggerated the reprisals and certain undeniable acts of sabotage used by the French before their departure from Guinea. Apparently Touré hoped to receive offers of cooperation from certain other great powers—in which he had some success.[122]

After the first break in relations at the end of September 1958, they were broken again in 1965 and 1971, these breaks being punctuated by accusations by Touré that assistance was given to plots against the government and even against Touré himself.[123] The whole story includes denunciations of France and arbitrary imprisonments, sometimes of Guinean nationals, and it is not clear whether Sékou Touré's outbursts were, as Camara thought, intentional political moves, or whether they were merely temperamental; and there has even been some uncertainty about the existence of the plots.[124] In any case, the party alone had come to control Guinea's destiny, and the party line was always thought to be correct and just. Guinea, in reality, was a "disguised dictatorship," said Claude Rivière in another recent book.[125]

Still, as of spring 1978, another attempt at reconciliation has been going on, with Guinea hoping to end its comparative isolation from France and from its two neighbors, Senegal and the Ivory Coast, with whom quarrels have been almost continuous over the years. Possibly this has been due to the greater stability and recent development in Guinea, and perhaps she may disprove Corbett's 1972 statement that there was little hope that Franco-Guinean relations could become normal.[126]

Thus General de Gaulle has been left with the largest part of the burden of praise or blame, for what his system of Cooperation has done for Africa. Those who arranged it and still continue to work for it have believed that it was a generous and beneficent process for Africa, and that it provided the new states with the means of continued progress toward becoming viable and successful African nations. Those who criticize it believe that it promoted and sustained the neocolonialism that is so much resented in Africa. As far back as the establishment of the original Community in 1958, one writer said that Sékou Touré "saw the Community for what it was, a method of sustaining colonialism."[127] The lines between approval and disapproval have been clearly drawn.

As to the General's ultimate responsibility as the real leader of Cooperation, there is no doubt that he thought that process necessary.[128] Edmond Jouve, who has studied de Gaulle for many years, has written that the General stressed this arrangement, feeling that no state could develop without such outside assistance. Interdependence is a fact that no one in the world today can escape, for, without it, every territory would be a prey to ignorance and would serve as a field of battle for all the imperialisms of the world. The objective was "coopération tous azimuts," in all quarters of the globe. The theme, said Jouve, "is omnipresent in the work and action of the General." And he quoted de Gaulle's proposal in a speech on March 25, 1959: "Why don't we erect all together a fraternal organization that would lend its aid to those others?" (i.e.,those who do not have what we have). Concretely, he went on, it would be suitable to use in common "a percentage of our raw materials, of our manufactured objects, of our food products, a number of our scientific, technical, and economic leaders, a section of our trucks, ships, airplanes, in order to conquer misery, to develop the value, and the resources, and to aid in the work of less developed peoples."[129]

These principles, these objectives, are indeed hard to fault. The Left, and even those who have criticized the neocolonialism of the present Cooperation, would probably agree with them, at least in principle. The difficulty, then, must be in the manner of working out the project. And that is probably where it was and is situated.

The testimonies to what the French have done for Africa since Independence are frequent and impressive. Ligot says:

> The short experience of independence seems to show that "the French contribution is more important and more disinterested than that of many others. The proof is that Mali has tried to avoid rupture with France so as to continue to profit by her technical, cultural and financial aid outside of any political bond."[130]

And again Duroselle and Meyriat, also in 1964, bore witness to its value:

> The contribution of General de Gaulle to the policy of decolonization was double. "On the one hand, he was the first who preceded the movement, and who would offer complete independence spontaneously from the time of the referendum of September 30, 1958. But, even more, having without doubt begun his intellectual reconversion before most of the French political leaders he knew how to change [public] opinion from the belief that decolonization was a series of humiliating defeats, into the belief that on the other hand it constituted an enterprise worthy of France and finally beneficent for her." The change in de Gaulle's thought followed by that of the immense majority of the French people is thus remarkable.[131]

And Hayter admits that the African states had been better administered under the French than they would otherwise have been. French aid was largely responsible for the economic growth that has taken place in Africa. She added that it was hard to see how there could be progress without France.[132]

Many other Africans have testified concerning the General's contributions to the freedom and well-being of Africa. President Houphouet-Boigny, in a speech at a luncheon for six African heads of state given by de Gaulle in July 1965, said:

> If we have been able to achieve some successful results, it is largely thanks to you, thanks to the living example which you represent in this hard and difficult world. It is thanks to you that we have been able to set our people on the path of liberty and happiness. You have been a sort of light-house for us. . . . We who are assembled

here and all the others—francophone and anglo-phone—who turn their eyes toward Paris, know as we do that you are our guarantee of peace and security. We should all like you to remain as long as possible at the head of France, and we should like to welcome you in each of our States where our good populations are impatient to see you and to give you a welcome—I do not want to exaggerate—which you have known nowhere, not even in France.[133]

Looking back over the important influences in the General's life, we find parental discipline, military training, time for reflection when he was withdrawn by imprisonment or lack of power from the central stage of France, and experience in dealing with governments in both his periods of management. Certainly these influences affected his decisions about the Community and the Agreements of Cooperation. He was intent on making decolonization succeed, and all of his past, it seems to this author, led him to require a measure of control, leading in turn to the accusations against him. The requirements he caused or allowed to be written into the Cooperation could not succeed without arousing continual criticism, especially after the first glow of political independence had worn off. In the first version of the Community, though by-passed by the agreements made after political independence had been granted, a large group of domains were beyond the competence of the Community to exercise, and many seemed to live on in the Cooperation. There was foreign policy, even though consultations of the states with France were supposed to be frequent and were important; defense, though requests by the states were necessary in order for France to utilize force in Africa; monetary matters, though the states could issue their own currency if they so desired; common economic and financial policy, though, for example, the development bank's fund for loans from the OECD was supposed to work through banks where the French played key roles; and there were also other financial restraints. Then there was an agricultural policy where French control was even greater than in other aspects of the economy; and raw materials, strategic products, higher education, and justice were all in the list that Yves Guéna gave as outside of the powers of the Community. In these latter matters Corbett thought that the need for restrictions was less obvious, and seemed aimed at "perpetuating a distinctive relationship that would ensure France a privileged position in each African state," though he admitted that all the states relied on France and her francs for expansion and for educational development.[134] Finally, as we have seen, there was an Executive Council, containing an uncertain number of Frenchmen, with its powers only "sketched in," a dangerous uncertainty.

These restrictions, and, no doubt, others that developed, would have brought trouble almost from the beginning. No nation out to procure real independence could be expected to like them, though it might feel that the time for protest had not yet come. The title of "neocolonialism" can cover them all, for they have given that impression. Even the Jeanneney Report of 1963 admitted that the accusation of neocolonialism could not be neglected, and after the Gaullist period and that of President Pompidou—so similar to it— had passed, the question comes to the fore even more forcibly.

Yet, again, we must consider the opposite attitude. Teresa Hayter said that French aid was better administered under the system set up than would otherwise have been the case, that the French were responsible for the economic growth in Africa, and that it was hard to see how progress would have taken place without France.[135] So, we are left with the most essential, the most inconclusive question of all—what would have happened in Africa if the Cooperation Agreements had not been signed? Most of the French would probably answer that question by saying that the situation would have been disastrous—that Guinea, taking off on her own but aided by various other nations, could not have provided a solution for the others. Many of the Africans, however, would probably say today that they would have been better without France. Summing it up, it seems that General de Gaulle would have been wiser to temper many of the agreements, to make them less strict, less absolute, less harsh-seeming in their control of the Africans. Yet even that would probably not have made the path to real independence—cultural, economic, and social— much more smooth, though it might have eased the way somewhat. Perhaps time had to pass before it could be seen just what Cooperation ought to be. President Pompidou thought of Cooperation as a basic element in French policy, not as a matter of expediency, noting, however, that the Africans wished to reject all colonial influence, and that their goal was constant.[136] There seems to have been no real change in Franco-African policy under the second president of the Fifth Republic. When President Giscard d'Estaing came into office in May 1974, his first moves were to close out the *Secrétariat d'Affaires Africaines et Malgache*, headed by Jacques Foccart, and to reinstate a Ministry of Cooperation, as it had been before 1966, when its functions had been taken over by the *Secrétariat d'Etat pour les Affaires Africaines et Malgaches* of the French Foreign Office.[137]

One of the first statements about Franco-African relations by President Giscard d'Estaing's administration was made by his then prime minister, Jacques Chirac, on February 7, 1975. He said that the use of the French language did not entail the disintegration of the many other languages in use in Africa. It was only a means to develop solidarity between African states, a way to accede speedily to the technique, thought, and creations of European and American countries, and a way in which those countries could understand the wishes and traditions of the Third World. France alone could not spread *francophonie;* it was a common responsibility for those who use French as a vehicle.[138] The insistence on the use of French had often been a grievance. Soon after, on February 28, 1975, came the Convention of Lomé, in Togo, when fifty-three countries signed the final document relating the African and other Third World countries to the EEC (European Economic Community). At Yaoundé in 1963 only nineteen countries had signed a similar pledge. At Lomé, equality between partners and international solidarity through dialogue were considered. In the early part of his *septennat* (seven-year term), President Giscard d'Estaing spoke at a conference at Bangui, capital of the Central African

Republic, and while he did not make any official statement about his African policy, he did show real friendship and a wish to communicate with the African masses.[139] A few months later, June 26 to July 2, 1975, *Le Monde* tells us that a Council on Cooperation had been held at the Elysée after consultation with almost a million people using "missions of dialogue." The Council's report prefigured that of Pierre Abelin, published in September of that year. It foresaw a reinforcement of Cooperation, and an active Third World policy that would devote 0.7 percent of the French gross national product to aid, this to be done in stages, for the percentages had slipped until, in 1974, less than 0.56 percent had been the figure for aid. This aid was to be given to the states that had signed agreements with France, though the Central Bureau planned to extend its work also to other countries. *Francophonie* was a positive matter that should lead to the training of more technicians and scientists. The states bound to France were not to be thought of as the private property of France (*chasse gardée*), however. The use of more multilateral aid would be considered. This report, a result of Pierre Abelin's dialogue teams, should make the French public more sensitive to matters of cooperation.[140] However, there was still insistence on *francophonie* as an objective.

Abelin's report added to what *Le Monde* had reported. It spoke of the desire to work together, for now there would be a zone open to the world, and an element of a new economic world order. At the conferences at Lomé and Bangui, it had been seen that the African states wished to continue with French support, but it would be essential to "remove the ambiguities of the post-colonial period" with a new Cooperation between sovereign partners and with Europe. The changes in international society would be important to consider, but France now saw her financial limits, and multilateral financing would be needed. There was realization that France was sometimes suspected of cultural imperialism and of abusing the economic interests of the countries she had controlled. However, the new Cooperation would be founded entirely on the common interest of the various partners. The solidarity of the francophone nations justified the use of French teaching. But the Cooperation must be fully explained to the peoples of Europe and the UN. It must be programmed with sufficient attention to training of the cooperants, better planning for them, and enough money to carry on its work. Nothing must be undertaken against the will of the governments involved. Happily, the young in France were already less likely to think of cooperation as neocolonialism. It was unjust to criticize France for giving her educational system to Africa, for she had given the best she had—so thought her leaders. There must be cooperation with UNESCO; and the whole organization of Cooperation must become a beneficent ensemble, so as to appear to be best adapted to the needs of the Africans and to engender no feeling that it was carried on for the benefit of the former colonizers, as Abelin and his associates believed it would otherwise be.[141] The report showed clearly the government's acceptance of the necessity of reorganization of the whole project and the need for a better public image.

The year 1976 began with the hope, expressed in *Le Monde Hebdomadaire*, that 1975 might come to be considered as Year I of real Decolonization. A new international order had been sketched in, partly by the opening of a dialogue between the industrialized countries and the Third World on the chief problems of the period. In 1975 the last great European empires, those of Portugal and Spain, had disintegrated. The year had also seen the end of the longest war of the century—that of Vietnam—and peace had finally come to that region, at least temporarily.[142] There was hope for the future, the writers in the paper thought.

Finally, at the beginning of May 1976, President Giscard d'Estaing spoke out further about Africa. He said that the coming conference with African chiefs of state, with its economic purposes, would nevertheless have a political atmosphere, to define how each one could contribute in establishing a more just economic world order, in agreeing to renounce certain advantages in favor of its partners. Decisions would be worldwide, but Franco-African cooperation would be the closest and most immediate reality. It would have two dimensions; one would be international, for France would not neglect the effort to install a new economic world order, and the other would be specific, in the relations that France would maintain with certain states. As to the Cultural and Technical Francophone Agency, he thought it was a good instrument. While *francophonie* and Cooperation sometimes coincided, there could not be an absolute correlation between them, and, in addition, it would be necessary to remove the notion of imperialism in all its forms from the concept of Cooperation, whether it be cultural imperialism or merely linguistic. The structures of Cooperation having been simplified by the suppression of the General Secretariat for African and Malgache Affairs, certain conflicts were still arising between the renewed Ministry of Cooperation and the Ministry of Foreign Affairs; and because of the number and the importance of the actions of Cooperation, a special organization was needed, so a Ministry of Cooperation must exist. Cooperation is only one aspect of our foreign policy, the president believed, for there is no permanent offer of cooperation with the whole world, but only with our friends, and that gives Cooperation its meaning. The president said he does not like the word "aid," but in a bilateral domain, France could do more for the African states, and for rural development. Bilateral cooperation was a factual solidarity, while multilateral cooperation was a worldwide expression beyond the power of anyone to accomplish. He ended with a wish to visit the states one by one.[143]

On May 10, 1976, at the opening of the Franco-African Summit meeting in Paris, the president added several points. He said that today, in a new spirit, we must construct an order acceptable to all, on bases that took into consideration the imperatives of world economic development. This, he said, is not only a humanitarian duty but a technical necessity, on which world equilibrium depends. France foresees that the developing countries should benefit by privileged conditions of liquid assets. The bond between aid to development and monetary creations would be a tangible manifestation of the will of the international community toward less favored nations. He affirmed his attachment and that of the French government to an active cooperation with the peoples of Africa. He reaffirmed, also, his wish to consecrate as soon as possible 0.7 percent of the French PNB to public aid for the Third World, this line to be followed by other industrialized nations. French Cooperation must be politically exemplary and economically efficient, adapting itself to the diversity of situations and to the degree of development of each nation. Africa, he said, must be left to the Africans, the only proper competition being the economic, social, and cultural development of the continent. As French Cooperation must permit each country to assume its own destiny, "France wishes," he said, and "I wish, that every State should reach that condition, and French aid is at your disposal if you wish it yourselves."[144]

A few months later, in August 1976, in Gabon, the president announced an exceptional promotional fund that would distribute a billion dollars in five years for common infrastructures for the least well equipped states of Africa. In addition, he made clear, France expects on a more modest scale to show her interest and sympathy for countries outside of her traditional field of action.[145]

The writer of the article on the president's speech, P.-J. Franceschini, added, "Suspected of political duplicity and commercial reservations, to dissipate this uneasiness, Paris ought to give its actions an image that is more coherent and more credible. Even the structure of French cooperation, which is largely bilateral, makes it suspect, and the priority of French market enterprises does not insure to our cooperation the reputation that its amplitude and its quality ought to give it."[146]

From these articles in *Le Monde Hebdomadaire*, it is clear that France has realized some of the mistakes made in the initial Agreements of Cooperation. In the spring of 1978, the French Press and Information Service has outlined the French position on military actions in Africa as:

1. to respect commitment to countries with which it has agreements;
2. to act only at the request of legitimate governments with internationally recognized borders;
3. to participate only in defense action, particularly when French nationals are in danger.

These statements show the realization by the French government of the criticisms of French interventions in the past.[147] We might ask whether Giscard d'Estaing can succeed in making his newer vision a reality. It is to be noted that the Africans do not want to leave the French orbit or to do without French aid, but they do want freedom in dealing with the former mother country, in spite of the great affection they have for General de Gaulle's memory and the belief in what he did for Africa when he gave political independence to all the states that had been French. Decolonization has now become an economic issue. Will it not become a linguistic one if the French try to insist on *francophonie?* De

Bosschère has said that the road to complete decolonization is a very long one indeed. Perhaps we may see the beginnings of other phases of the process, and those of us now present may not see the end of them. Still, the government of France has understood some of the criticisms of the present situation, and in the fund for the infrastructures of Africa it has made one positive proposal for the next years. Possibly that is all we can expect until time has brought to Africa more stability, fewer governmental coups, and greater calmness of spirit. If we think back to the innumerable phases the European countries went through for centuries before reaching their present rather uncertain tranquility, we may become more patient and more ready to wait for any final verdict on the work General de Gaulle and others tried to do in freeing Africa. The flaws and the virtues of their efforts will stand out more clearly with time. But the future can scarcely be even dreamed of today.

Notes

De Gaulle *Memoirs* refers to the English edition of General de Gaulle's *War Memoirs* (New York: Viking Press, 1955; Simon and Schuster, 1959 and 1960). *Mémoires* refers to the French edition (Paris: Plon, 1954, 1956, and 1959). The reason for using both editions is that the American edition does not contain the valuable documents.

In citations of French public documents, "Journal Officiel" is abbreviated as "J.O." *Journal de la France Combattante* is abbreviated as *J. O. Comb.*

Preface

1. De Bosschère, I, 9.
2. Coquery-Vidrovitch and Moniot, pp. 6, 7, 13.
3. Grimal, pp. 397, 398.

Introduction

1. Kohn, p. 5.
2. *Grand Larousse Encyclopédique* (1961 ed.), III (pages not numbered).
3. *Webster's New Collegiate Dictionary*, p. 221.
4. De Bosschère, I, 12.
5. *Grand Larousse Encyclopédique*, III.
6. Gardinier, in Dunner, *Handbook of World History*, p. 203.
7. *Webster's New Collegiate Dictionary*, p. 221.
8. Kohn, p. 2; Arnault, *Le Procès*, pp. 12, 25–27; de Bosschère, II, 15.
9. De Bosschère, I, 18, 21–22, 37, 45.
10. Ibid., p. 12.
11. White, Dissertation, chap. VII; Lansing, p. 97.
12. Moneta, pp. 18, 38, 146, 149, 301; Marshall, *The French Colonial Myth*, pp. 61, 244.
13. Marshall, *op. cit.*, pp. 63, 67.
14. Grimal, pp. 397–98.
15. De Bosschère, II, 15, 17, says the word "decolonization" was a neologism, born after the Second World War and consecrated at the Conference of Bandoung. It referred to deliverance from the past and to the future rejection of the colonizer's spirit and the habits inherited from him. Mohammed Gharsallah (*Revue Juridique et Politique d'Outre Mer*, no. 2, April-June 1963 p. 235) says Paul Mus was the first to use it.
16. De Bosschère, II, 22, mentions England's declaration about Egypt of 1922, and Lord Lloyd, p. 63, confirms Lord Allenby's recognition of Egypt as an independent sovereign state, but according to President Sadat, Egypt was anything but free in the thirties and forties when he grew up there (*Observer Review*, Sunday, March 12, 1978, pp. 29–30).
17. Grimal, pp. 397–98.
18. Guillebaud, p. 17, lists as still under French control: four Overseas Departments (Guadeloupe, Martinique, Réunion, Guyana); seven Overseas Territories (New Caledonia, French Polynesia, Wallis and Fortuna, Comoro Islands [partially independent since July 1975], Saint Pierre-Miquelon, Terres Australes and Antarctiques); one Condominium—Franco-British (the New Hebrides).

19. Other countries are still losing their colonies. As of March 27, 1978, the *International Herald Tribune* reports Belize (British Honduras) as on the way toward independence, having requested a multinational security force to replace the British garrison.

20. Césaire, *Discours sur le Colonialisme*, all; *Cahier d'un Retour au Pays Natal*, all; Memmi, all.

21. Gann and Duignan, *Burden of Empire*, pp. vi, vii.

22. Finbert, p. 60.

23. Kingsley, *Studies*, p. 20; Richard-Molard, *Le Monde Noir*, pp. 32, 34; Chailley, p. 20; Kingsley, *Travels*, pp. 101–3.

24. Coquery-Vidrovitch, *La Découverte*, pp. 192–204; Mannix, pp. 14–19; Chailley, pp. 18, 37; Gourou, pp. 7–8, 15, 24, 376–77; Suret-Canale, I, 25–46.

25. Suret-Canale, II, 503, quotes Dr. Mahé of the Medical School of Brest.

26. Deschamps, *L'Europe Découvre*, p. 23.

27. Arnault, *Le Procès*, pp. 25–27; C.-A. Julien, *Voyages*, pp. 10, 33–35.

28. Howard and Plumb, pp. 63–64.

29. Ibid., p. 65; "A" (of the Fathers of the Holy Ghost at Yaoundé), *Life of a Missionary*.

30. Among other countries so released before the sub-Saharan African states were Syria and Lebanon, 1945; India and Pakistan, 1944; the Philippines, 1946; Ceylon, 1947; Burma, 1948; Indonesia, 1949; Libya, 1951; Laos, Cambodia, and Vietnam, 1954; Sudan, Morocco, and Tunisia, 1956; Ghana and Malaysia, 1957; Singapore, 1958; Guinea, 1958.

1. The Life and Death of the First Colonial Empire of France

1. R. Cornevin, *Histoire*, II, 341; R. and M. Cornevin, pp. 184–85; R. Cornevin, "Navigations Dieppoises," *France-Eurafrique*, March 1965, pp. 35–39, and April 1965, pp. 2–4; Chailley, p. 85; Guénin, p. 20, cites Bethencourt; Coquery-Vidrovitch, *La Découverte*, pp. 33, 34, 39, 77, 90–92; David Henige, *Bulletin de l'Institut de l'Afrique Noire*, July-October 1963, p. 427 (title not given), cited by R. Cornevin in *France-Eurafrique*.

2. Shipley, pp. 13–14.

3. Ibid., pp. 7, 27.

4. Sédillot, II, 300; de Bosschère, I, 131–32; C.-A. Julien, *Voyages*, pp. 68, 69, 73; Merle, *L'Anticolonialisme*, p. 73, cites Voltaire; Coquery-Vidrovitch, p. 143; R. Cornevin, *Histoire*, II, 342.

5. Coquery-Vidrovitch, pp. 195–96, 206.

6. Ibid., p. 210; Shipley, pp. 14–15.

7. Mannix, p. 81.

8. C.-A. Julien, *Voyages*, pp. 69–73; R. Cornevin, *Histoire*, II, 318, 342; Chailley, pp. 85–86; de Gaulle, *Vers l'Armée*, p. 33.

9. De Gaulle, "La Doctrine a Priori ou Doctrine des Circonstances;" de Gaulle, *Mémoires*, I, 1–3; Sédillot, II, 299; Shipley, pp. 36, 40.

10. Hargreaves, *France and West Africa*, p. 54; Fage, pp. 70, 72; R. Cornevin, *Histoire*, II, 344; Deschamps, *Méthodes*, p. 34.

11. R. Cornevin, *Histoire*, II, 341, 343–45; Kingsley, *Studies*, p. 227; Chailley, pp. 97–99, 101–4; Hardy, *Histoire Sociale*, pp. 13–18, 24; Coquery-Vidrovitch, pp. 142–45; Deschamps, *Méthodes*, pp. 26–30, 34–35; Guénin, pp. 80, n. 1, 102–4.

12. Deschamps, *Madagascar*, p. 71.

13. R. Cornevin, *Histoire*, II, 341.

14. Deschamps, *Madagascar*, pp. 76, 77.

15. Coquery-Vidrovitch, pp. 144–45.

16. Deschamps, *Méthodes*, pp. 72–76.

17. Ibid., pp. 9, 11; Ardagh, p. 75.

18. Fage, pp. 14, 20–22, 43, 56, 71; Jahn, p. 99.

19. Chailley, pp. 26–32; Jahn, p. 26; Froelich, pp. 8–10; Griaule, p. 14.

20. Diop, pp. 16–17.

21. Chailley, pp. 32–35; N'Goma, "L'Islam Noir," pp. 333–34; Monteil, pp. 116–34; Guillaume, chap. II.

22. Chailley, pp. 38–43; Siril, "Civilisations Africaine," p. 73.

23. Chailley, pp. 44–49; Duchemin, "Comment il vit," pp. 50–54.

24. Hardy, "L'Ame Africaine," pp. 102–11; Welch, pp. 158–61; Davidson, *Mère Afrique*, pp. 93–94.

25. Stern, p. 268.

26. Lewis, *The Splendid Century*, pp. 48–51.

27. R. Cornevin, *Histoire*, II, 346.

28. Marx, bk. I, vol. III, p. 193.

29. Davidson, *History of West Africa*, pp. 209–10, 211–14, 295.

30. Davidson, *Slave Trade*, pp. 48–49.

31. Chailley, p. 136.

32. Ibid., pp. 137–39.

33. Ibid., pp. 108–10.

34. Ibid., pp. 92, 110–14, 116; Coquery-Vidrovitch, pp. 182–84; Deschamps, *Madagascar*, pp. 76–77, 80–83; Deschamps, *Les Pirates*, pp. 100–105; *Columbia Encyclopedia*, p. 1131.

35. R. Cornevin, *Histoire*, II, 350; Chaillot, p. 119.

36. Guénin, pp. 169–71; Deschamps, *Madagascar*, pp. 79–83.

37. Deschamps, *Méthodes*, p. 67.

38. De Saint-Pierre, letter XI, quoted by Merle, *L'Anticolonialisme*, pp. 98–101; Mercier, p. 82; Chailley, pp. 99, 105.

39. *Larousse Universel*, I, 666; Chailley, p. 87.

40. De Bosschère, I, 86.

41. Herskovits, *L'Héritage du Noir*, pp. 60–63; R. Cornevin, *Histoire*, II, 361–62; Mannix, pp. 1, 8, 9; Davidson, *Slave Trade*, p. 52.

42. R. Cornevin, *Histoire*, II, 366; R. and C. Oliver, pp. 60–66; Mannix, pp. 40, 92–95.

43. De Bosschère, I, 174; R. Cornevin, *Histoire*, II, 368–69. Mannix, pp. 60–68; Curtin, pp. xviii–xix, 167, 177, 200.

44. De Bosschère, I, 176; Mannix, pp. 101–3.

45. Mannix, pp. xiii–xiv.

46. Ibid., p. 287; de Bosschère, I, 73, 169–70, 179–80; Chailley, p. 87; Duverger, p. 32; Davidson, *Slave Trade*, pp. 62–63.

47. Davidson, *Slave Trade*, pp. 62–63, 72–75; Chailley, p. 99.

48. Ronsard, *Poésies*, "Complainte contre Fortune."

49. Rabelais, quoted by Pierre Lebon, *J.O. Consultative Assembée*, first special session, March 20, 1945.

50. Montaigne, "Des Cannibales," livre I, chap. XXXI.

51. Las Casas, cited by Merle, *L'Anticolonialisme*, pp. 9, 50–56.

52. Montesquieu, *Esprit des Lois*, XV, 5, XXI, 21; Deschamps, *Méthodes*, p. 76.

53. Raynal, *Histoire Philosophique*, 1770, cited by Merle, pp. 79–83; Deschamps, *Méthodes*, pp. 78–79; Mercier, p. 154; Confer, "French Colonial Ideas before 1789," p. 349.

54. Voltaire, *Essai sur les Moeurs*, chaps. CXLIX, 1756, CLI, 1761, CLII, 1701, quoted by Merle, pp. 72–76.

55. "Encyclopédistes," *Oxford Companion*, pp. 208, 245–47; *Dictionary of French Literature*, pp. 104–5.

56. De Saint-Pierre, *Paul et Virginie*, all; Merle on the Encyclopédistes, p. 118; Turgot, cited by Merle, p. 143.

57. Mercier, pp. 120–21, 188; R. Cornevin, *Histoire*, II, 440.

58. Deschamps, *Méthodes*, pp. 83–89; Merle, *L'Anticolonialisme*, pp. 190–93, cites Robespierre and article on Société des Amis des Noirs; Chailley, pp. 146–51.

59. Chailley, pp. 148–51; Hardy, *Histoire de la Colonisation*, p. 143; Talleyrand, "Essay on the advantages, etc."

60. Deschamps, *Méthodes*, pp. 90–97.

61. Ibid.

62. Ibid.; Chailley, p. 157.

2. The Gathering of the Second Colonial Empire of France: A Summary

1. Deschamps, *Méthodes*, pp. 96–97; Chailley, pp. 160–81.

2. Chailley, p. 228; Deschamps, *Méthodes*, pp. 94–98.

3. Chailley, pp. 161–62.

4. Ibid., p. 168.

5. Ibid., pp. 177–79; Durand, entire book; Deschamps, *L'Europe Découvre*, p. 114.

6. R. Cornevin, *Histoire*, II, 515.

7. Noguères, pp. 7–11.

8. Ibid., pp. 9–11, 13–14, 17–22, 25–28; Bury, p. 43; Bertier, pp. 434–36; Aron, p. 31; Cobban, II, 88–89.

9. Bertier, pp. 421, 436; Girardet, p. 6; Noguères, pp. 39–43, 70–71, 161, 208; Cobban, II, 89; P. Jullien, pp. 47, 49.

10. P. Jullien, pp. 55–59, 174; Noguères, pp. 182–86, 232–40, 246, 269–70, 272, 274.

11. Aron, pp. 35–42; C.-A. Julien, "Bugeaud," in *Les Techniciens.*

12. W. B. Cohen, p. 8.

13. Delavignette, "Faidherbe," in Julien (ed.), *Les Techniciens*, pp. 75–82, 88–91; Chailley, pp. 194–95, 199–200, 201–8, 212–17, 234–35; Kanya-Forstner, p. 29; Boni, pp. 97–98; Webster, Boahen and Idowu, pp. 22–25; Hardy, *L'Afrique Occidentale*, p. 43; Richard-Molard, *L'Afrique Occidentale Française*, p. 140; Suret-Canale, I, 199–201; R. Cornevin, *Histoire*, II, 512–13.

14. Girardet, pp. 24–25; Legendre, pp. 31–35; Ganiage, pp. 11, 26, 29, 31, 39–42; Murphy, pp. 226–27; R. Cornevin, *Histoire*, II, 446–52, 500, 509, 511, 530; Chailley, p. 167.

15. Girardet, pp. 25–28, 30–32, 39–44; Gabriel Charmes, *Journal des Débats,*August-October 1880; *R. des Deux Mondes*, November 1, 1883, pp. 49 ff., quotes Gaffarel, *Les Colonies Françaises,* pp. 35–36, 39, 43–44.

16. Chailley, p. 228; Girardet, pp. 32–35, R. Cornevin, *Histoire*, II, 52–53, 452, 500, 511; Kingsley, *Travels*, pp. 659–61.

17. R. Cornevin, *Histoire*, II, 514; Brunschwig, *Le Partage*, pp. 29–35; Robinson and Gallagher, pp. 166–78; Ganiage, p. 117; Chailley, pp. 22–23.

18. Musset, *A quoi Rêvent les Jeunes Filles?*, act 1, scene 4; Ferry, cited by Brunschwig, *Le Partage*, pp. 153–54; Girardet, pp. 44–46.

19. R. Cornevin, *Histoire*, II, 531, 534; Girardet, pp. 45, 67–78; Brunschwig, *Le Partage*, p. 35; Ganiage, p. 11; Langer, *European Alliances*, pp. 289–90; Kanya-Forstner, p. 206.

20. Ganiage, p. 117; Brunschwig, *L'Avènement*, pp. 134–36; R. Cornevin, *Histoire*, II, 500–503, 535.

21. R. Cornevin, *Histoire*, II, 498–99, 500–503, 535–36; Chavannes, "Savorgnan de Brazza," p. 242; Legendre, pp. 162–64; Brunschwig, *Le Partage*, pp. 46–47, 154–58.

22. Brunschwig, *Le Partage*, pp. 46–47, 154–58; R. Cornevin, *Histoire*, II, 503; Chavannes, pp. 243–45; de Vaulx, pp. 220–23.

23. Suret-Canale, I, 187, cites Augouard, *Twenty-Eight Years in the Congo*, II, 153–54; Mangin, *Souvenirs d'Afrique*, I, 28, cites Augouard.

24. Baratier, "Au Congo," in Guénin, pp. 314–15; Blanchard, "Administrateurs," p. 404; Froment-Guieysse, all; Legendre, pp. 165–68; Semidei, "De l'Empire," p. 64; Brunschwig, *L'Avènement*, p. 167; Chavannes, "Savorgnan de Brazza," p. 242.

25. Ganiage, pp. 21–24, 45–59; Girardet, pp. 46–50; Power, pp. 1, 50; *J.O. Chambre des Députés*, July 29, 1885; Brunschwig, *Mythes et Réalités*, p. 88; Hargreaves, *Prelude*, pp. 278–82; Chastenet, II, 154; Langer, *European Alliances*, pp. 286–87.

26. Brunschwig, *Le Partage*, pp. 51, 156–63; Crowe, pp. 23–24, 48, 78, 82, 102, 156; Hargreaves, *Prelude*, pp. 316–28; R. Cornevin, *Histoire*, II, 541–42; Langer, *European Alliances*, p. 306; Brunschwig, *Mythes et Réalités*, pp. 68–71, 112–28; Ganiage, pp. 118–19.

27. C.-A. Julien, in Delavignette and Julien (eds.), *Les Constructeurs*, pp. 382–88, 412–13; Kanya-Forstner, pp. 74–83; R. Cornevin, *Histoire*, II, 551–52; Rotberg, "African Nationalism," pp. 217–18; Gourou, pp. 94–96.

28. Kanya-Forstner, pp. 175–86, 195–208, 216–21, 236; Brunschwig, *Le Partage*, pp. 37–38; Crowder, *West Africa*, pp. 75, 84; Hargreaves, *France and West Africa*, p. 161; Brown, p. 47; Chailley, pp. 287, 298–300.

29. R. Cornevin, *Histoire*, II, 552–53; Brown, pp. 21, 34–35, 38, 40, 42–44, 49, 53–55, 59–60, 85, 89–92, 95–116, 126, 130–31, 133; Langer, *Imperialism*, pp. 129, 538, 540; Heggoy, pp. 34, 59, 122; J. Emily, in Guénin, pp. 343, 339–43; Robinson and Gallagher, p. 374; Ganiage, p. 220; Brunschwig, *Mythes and Réalités*, p. 108.

30. Heggoy, pp. 55, 122; Brown, pp. 38–40, 42–44, 50; Langer, *Imperialism*, p. 538.

31. Heggoy, pp. 55, 122; Brown, pp. 38–39, 42–44, 50; Langer, *Imperialism*, p. 538.

32. Heggoy, pp. 67, 112; Brown, pp. 51–53, 77–78, 85, 89, 92.

33. R. Cornevin, *Histoire*, II, 555.

34. Brunschwig, "French Exploitation," in Gann and Duignan, *Colonialism*, I, 139–40, 161; Langer, *Imperialism*, pp. 651–52; Crowder, *West Africa*, pp. 61–62, 128; Bury, pp. 209–10,

216–17; Newbury and Kanya-Forstner, "French Policy," p. 264; Hobson, *Imperialism*, chap. II; R. Cornevin, *Histoire*, II, 507–10.

35. Heggoy, pp. 34, 57, 59; Newbury and Kanya-Forstner, "French Policy," pp. 263–67, 275; Loutfi, pp. 19 (quotes Maupassant on racism), 65–66; Crowder, *West Africa*, pp. 10–16; Gann and Duignan, *Colonialism*, I, 113; Langer, *Imperialism*, pp. 559–63; Chailley, pp. 325–26; Brunschwig, "French Exploitation," p. 140.

36. Crowder, *Resistance*, pp. 1, 8–10, 119–20; Niane and Suret-Canale, p. 158; Baratier, pp. 5–7, 9–17.

37. Betts, pp. 12, 29 (cities Hanotaux, *L'Energie*, p. 365), 30; de Saussure, pp. 10, 18–20, 22–37, 45–50, 64, 73–75, 83–85, 109, 128–29, 294.

38. Louis, chaps. II-VIII.

39. Hobson, pp. xiv, 10–13, 27–40, 53–54, 130, 152, 196, 200, 228, 361, 368.

40. Zimmermann, "Le Colonisation Européene," pp. 629, 667, 669, 688, 689.

41. Harmand, pp. 4, 10–15, 18, 20–23, 152–58, 168–74.

42. Girardet, p. 304, note 7.

43. Grimal, pp. 31–38; Ligou, pp. 166, 221–22; Delaisi, Malraux and Galtier-Boissière, "Expeditions Coloniales," pp. 2–22; Girardet, pp. 89, 106–10; Goguel, p. 160; Langer, *Encyclopedia*, pp. 751, 920, 1094; White, Dissertation, pp. 353, 356, 358.

44. Emerson, pp. vii, 23, 24, 26, 27; Hardy, *Histoire Sociale*, pp. 213–20; Chailley, pp. 402–8; Crowder, *Resistance*, p. 264; Niane and Suret-Canale, p. 165; von Albertini, p. 266; Crowder, *West Africa*, pp. 263–66; Brunschwig, *Le Partage*, pp. 149–50; R. and M. Cornevin, pp. 331–33.

45. Merle, *L'Afrique Noire Contemporaine*, p. 91; Grimal, p. 19.

46. Delavignette, "The Territorial Administrator," pp. 83–96; Delavignette, *Service Africain*, pp. 17, 29–30; Betts, pp. 73–79; Delafosse, *Broussard*, p. 35; Deschamps, "The Colonial Vocation," *Bulletin du Comité de l'Afrique Française, Reseignements Coloniaux*, pp. 498–500; W. B. Cohen, pp. 14–15, 38, 44, 51; Crowder, *West Africa*, pp. 393–98; Burns, p. 104; Chailley, pp. 68–71; Delavignette, *L'Afrique Noire Française et son Destin*, pp. 43, 56.

47. "Rapport Joalland," in the Chamber of Deputies, November 30, 1900, pp. 570–71; Suret-Canale, I, 261–68 and 261 n. 2; Coquery-Vidrovitch, "French Colonization," pp. 171–72, 189–94; R. Cornevin, "Evolution des Chefferies," *Penant*, pp. 235–50; *Encyclopédie Mensuelle d'Outre-Mer*, October 1951, p. 278; Delavignette, *Service Africaine*, pp. 122–32; Villandre, pp. 28–29; Niane and Suret-Canale, p. 157; Crowder, *West Africa*, p. 188.

48. Mercier, p. 7; Crowder, *West Africa*, pp. 184–85; Chautemps, "Politique Indigène," in *Afrique Occidentale Française*, pp. 45–47, quoted by Crowder, *West Africa*, p. 187; W. B. Cohen, pp. 47, 60 (quotes Brazza to the minister of colonies, August 21, 1905), 62–64, 67–71, n. 43, n. 44.

49. De Gaulle, *Vers l'Armée*, pp. 21, 23, 36; *Le Fil de l'Epée*, pp. 21, 152; *La France et son Armée*, pp. 66, 158, 159; *Discours et Messages*, I, 374–75.

3. A Preparation for History

1. De Gaulle, *Le Fil de l'Epée*, p. 50.

2. Bouillon et al., pp. 5–14, 46–52, 92; Black and Helmreich, pp. 25, 30–33, 271–72.

3. Sarraut, speech at the Pagoda of Confucius, *L'Opinion* (Hanoi), May 7, 1919.

4. Clark, p. 5; Galante, p. 43; Bouillon et al., pp. 83–87.

5. Michelet, *La Querelle*, pp. 10–11.

6. Galante, p. 41.

7. Ibid., pp. 32–36; 40–44.

8. Ibid., p. 35.

9. Ibid., pp. 31, 34–36, 40–44.

10. Cattaui, p. 18; de Gaulle, *Discours et Messages*, I, 15–16.

11. Galante, pp. 19, 21, 43.

12. Ibid., pp. 31, 39–40.

13. De Gaulle, *Memoirs*, I, 3–4.

14. Galante, pp. 44–45, 64, 66.

15. Cattaui, p. 28.

16. Galante, p. 18.

17. Cattaui, p. 29.

18. Cattaui, pp. 28–33.

4. Ideas and the Man

1. Bemis, pp. 625–26, 641–44.

2. Bailey, p. 650.

3. Syrian letters and others about Syria in the Archives of the United States, Decimal File numbers 763.72119/3651, 763.72119/3661, 763.72119/7035 et al.; Sarraut, *Mise en Valeur*, entire book; Grimal, p. 69.

4. *The Oxford Dictionary; Nouveau Petit Larousse; Columbia Encyclopedia;* entries on colonies and colonialism.

5. Merle, *L'Anticolonialisme*, pp. 143, 149.

6. Colonel Brunau, interview with the author, February 1961.

7. Cattaui, p. 33; White, *Seeds*, pp. 26–27.

8. Bonheur, pp. 52–56; Cattaui, pp. 32, 41.

9. Cattaui, pp. 33, 41; Bonheur, pp. 52–58; de Gaulle, *La Discorde*, p. 2.

10. De Gaulle, *La Discorde*, pp. 242–43.

11. Dryden, "Annus Mirabilis"; de Gaulle (first article), "La Bataille de la Vistule," *R. de Paris*.

12. Pouget, "Le Commandant de Gaulle à Varsovie," pp. 10–12.

13. Cattaui, pp. 43–47.

14. Tournoux, *Pétain et de Gaulle*, p. 129; Hatch, pp. 56–57.

15. Bonheur, p. 69; Clark, p. 70; Grinnell-Milne, p. 56; Hatch, p. 53.

16. De Gaulle, "Le Rôle Historique des Places Françaises," *R. Milit. Franç.* See also de Gaulle, *Trois Etudes*, p. 9.

17. De Gaulle, *Trois Etudes*, p. 30.

18. De Gaulle, "Doctrine a Priori," *R. Milit. Franç.*, pp. 306–28.

19. Fisher, *Orbis*, p. 199; Holmes, *Newsweek*, February 15, 1971, p. 56.

20. De Gaulle, "Doctrine a Priori," p. 306.

21. De Gaulle, "L'Action de Guerre et le Chef," *R. Milit. Franç.*, pp. 299–316.

22. De Gaulle, "Le Flambeau," pp. 98–112; De Gaulle, "La Philosophie de Recrutement," pp. 507–18.

23. Clark, p. 70.

24. Bouillon et al., pp. 102–8, 177–78, 229–37.

5. The Descent to the Abyss

1. Galante, p. 68; Nachin, p. 56; Bonheur, p. 84.

2. De Gaulle and Yvon, p. viii; General Pierre Rondot, interview with the author, January 20, 1967.

3. Galante, p. 68.

4. De Gaulle, *Le Fil*, pp. ix, 142; "Le Flambeau," p. 112; Crawley, p. 22; Péguy, p. 275.

5. De Gaulle, "Combats du Temps de Paix," pp. 861–62.

6. De Gaulle, *Vers l'Armée de Métier*, pp. 90–91, 99–100.

7. Sarraut, *Grandeur*, pp. 14–19, 31, 69, 219, 281–85.

8. De Gaulle, *La France et son Armée*, p. 205.

9. Galante, p. 255; "Memorandum adressé par le Colonel Charles de Gaulle aux Généraux Gamelin, Weygand, et Georges et à MM. Daladier et Reynaud le 26 janvier, 1940," published in *Trois Etudes*, p. 163; d'Ormesson, "Le Général de Gaulle: Histoire et la légende," *Revue des Deux Mondes* p. 513.

10. Goodman, "The World through de Gaulle's Looking Glass," p. 99; Geneviève Anthonioz-de Gaulle, interview with the author, March 1967.

11. Sarraut, speech at the Pagoda of Confucius.

12. Snyder, *The Dynamics*, p. 110. This was evidently Count Honoré Gabriel Mirabeau, celebrated as a pro-Revolutionary orator and therefore opposed to Edmond Burke. Mirabeau's father, the Marquis de Mirabeau, had been an economist.

13. Bouillon et al., pp. 170–78, 226.

14. Michelet, *Le Gaullisme*, pp. 27–28.

6. The Broken Sword of France

1. Spears, pp. 303–4; Amouroux, "Le General m'avait raconté," pp. 114–15; White, *Seeds*, pp. 59–61; Galante, pp. 25–26.
2. De Gaulle, *Memoirs*, I, 78, 80–83; White, *Seeds*, pp. 58, 61, 62; *Noir et Blanc*, pp. 22–23.
3. References on June 18, 19, 22, 24, 26, July 2, 8, 23, 24 and later, in de Gaulle, *Discours et Messages*, I.
4. De Gaulle, *Memoirs*, I, 78, 83–84.
5. White, *Seeds*, pp. 159–60.
6. Dansette, p. 34; White, *Seeds*, pp. 161–62; Mordal, p. 72.
7. Sophie, pp. 39–41; White, *Seeds*, pp. 164–65.
8. Sophie, p. 22.
9. White, *Seeds*, p. 164.
10. Maurice, pp. 6–22; Weinstein, *Eboué*, pp. 33, 65, 85–89, 130, 139, 156, 165 ff., 173, 210.
11. Maurice, pp. 6–22.
12. Danton, Speech to Legislative Committee, *Le Moniteur*.
13. Maurice, p. 27.
14. Martin du Gard, p. 63.
15. White, *Seeds*, p. 171; de Larminat, p. 381, quoting from Laurentie; Martin du Gard, p. 59. (Even the Bureau of the Military Administrative Archives could not give this Marchand's first name.)
16. White, *Seeds*, pp. 166–67.
17. Mordal, p. 96.
18. Sophie, pp. 67, 68.
19. De Larminat, p. 381, quoting from Laurentie.
20. White, *Seeds*, p. 167; Mveng, pp. 401–2.
21. White, *Seeds*, pp. 167–68; de Gaulle, *Mémoires*, I, 289.
22. White, *Seeds*, p. 169.
23. De Gaulle, *Memoirs*, I, 112; Mveng, p. 402.
24. White, *Seeds*, p. 170.
25. Halleguen, p. 38; de Gaulle, *Memoirs*, I, 110.
26. De Larminat, pp. 131, 137–39, 143.
27. Ibid., pp. 125, 128–31; White, *Seeds*, p. 171.
28. White, *Seeds*, p. 171; de Larminat, pp. 143, 146–54.
29. De Larminat, pp. 147, 153–57.
30. Ibid., p. 156.
31. Ibid., pp. 149–59; White, *Seeds*, pp. 171–73, 406.
32. White, *Seeds*, pp. 171–73, 406.
33. De Larminat, p. 149.
34. Bury, p. 48; Soustelle, I, 124.
35. White, *Seeds*, pp. 174–75.
36. Ingold, p. 329.
37. De Larminat, pp. 182–93.
38. Ibid., pp. 195–203; White, *Seeds*, pp. 406–7.
39. De Larminat, p. 203.
40. Ibid., pp. 184–88, 193, 203.
41. Ibid., p. 119.
42. White, *Seeds*, p. 176.
43. De Larminat, p. 118.
44. Ibid., pp. 132–33.
45. Ibid., p. 390. De Larminat quotes Laurentie.
46. De Gaulle, *Discours et Messages*, I, 31–32.

7. Storm Clouds Gather and Retreat

1. Churchill, II, 489.
2. White, *Seeds*, XII, XIII.

3. Mordal, *La Bataille,* annex XI, pp. 308–9.
4. White, *Seeds,* pp. 194–201.
5. Ibid., pp. 191–93, quoting from Rouillon, *Les Compagnons,* pp. 69–72.
6. De Larminat, p. 172.
7. White, *Seeds,* p. 202; Funk, pp. 84, 133; de Gaulle, *Memoirs,* I, 129–30.
8. De Larminat, p. 171.
9. White, *Seeds,* p. 204.
10. De Gaulle, *Mémoires,* I, 303–5, 313–17.
11. *Time,* December 9, 1940, p. 27.
12. Weil-Curiel, pp. 224–25.
13. De Gaulle, *Discours et Messages,* I, 40–42.
14. Ibid., *Memoirs,* I, 106.
15. Ibid., *Discours et Messages,* I, 31, 32.
16. De Gaulle, quoted by d'Ormesson, *Revue des Deux Mondes,* p. 515.

8. The Road to Brazzaville

1. De Gaulle, *Discours et Messages,* I, 58, 80–81.
2. Grimal, p. 68.
3. De Gaulle, *Mémoires,* I, 389–92; *Memoirs,* I, 167–74.
4. De Gaulle, *Memoirs,* I, 85–86; White, *Seeds,* p. 238; Davet, pp. 16–17.
5. De Gaulle, *Memoirs,* I, 178, 182–84.
6. Ibid., *Mémoires,* I, 279–83; 412, 415, 431, 436.
7. White, *Seeds,* pp. 247–50.
8. Ibid., pp. 250–54.
9. Davet, pp. 213–14.
10. De Gaulle, *Memoirs,* I, 233–36.
11. Ibid., *Discours et Messages,* I, 216; *Mémoires,* I, 412, 415, 431, 436.
12. De Gaulle, *Discours et Messages,* I, 119–21.
13. De La Gorce, interview with the author, March 1966.
14. De Gaulle, *Discours et Messages,* I, 201–3, 216.
15. Ibid., pp. 211, 212.
16. Lorraine, pp. 90–91.
17. Mortimer, pp. 48–49.
18. De Gaulle, *Mémoires,* II, 62–63.
19. Mortimer, p. 29.
20. Ibid., p. 30; Grimal, p. 150.
21. Grimal, pp. 146–47.
22. Mortimer, p. 31.
23. Grimal, pp. 140, 147–56.
24. Maurice, p. 36.
25. Devèze, p. 178; Eboué, foreword.
26. Devèze, p. 175.
27. Eboué, p. 10.
28. Ibid., pp. 10–12.
29. Ibid., p. 58.
30. Devèze, p. 178.
31. M'Bokolo, "French Colonial Policy," p. 13.
32. Eboué, p. 59.
33. Maurice, pp. 46–48; *J. O. Comb.,* August 28, 1942, decrees 377, 378; June 15, 1943, decrees 1017; M'Bokolo, pp. 8, 18, 19, 21.
34. Thompson and Adloff, pp. 23–24.
35. Mordal, pp. 280–81.
36. Ageron, "De Gaulle et la Conférence de Brazzaville," p. 2, includes note of Gaston Palewski.
37. De Gaulle, *Memoirs,* II, 35–36; M'Bokolo, "French Colonial Policy," pp. 8, 13.
38. Arnault, *Du Colonialisme,* pp. 27–30.
39. General Georges Catroux, interview with the author, February 16, 1967; Claudius-Petit,

interview with the author, February 15, 1967; René Viard, *La Fin de l'Empire*, pp. 82–90; Hettier de Boislambert, interview with the author, February 17, 1967.

40. De Gaulle, *Memoirs*, II, 205–6.
41. Ibid., *Mémoires*, II, 608–9.
42. Ibid., *Memoirs*, II, 206–7.
43. Ibid.
44. Confer, pp. 38–39, 54–55, 98–99, 115–21; Grimal, p. 68.
45. De Gaulle, *Mémoires*, II, 183, 548–49.
46. Dehon, pp. 11–12; Aubame, p. 183; *J.O. de l'Assemblée Consultative Provisoire, Débats*, November 23, 1943, Session no. 10, pp. 14–15 and November 24, no. 11, p. 17.
47. *J. O. de l' Ass. Consult. Provis.*, Supplément, January 14, 1944, no. 23, p. 1.
48. Ibid., p. 4.
49. Ibid., pp. 5–7.
50. Ibid., pp. 1–8; W. B. Cohen, p. 75; *Larousse Méthodique* (1955) I, 369; *Larousse Universel* (1949) II, 376.
51. De Gaulle, *Memoirs*, II, 207.
52. *Supra*, chaps. II and VI; Funk, pp. 30, 33, 48, 62, 66, 104–8.
53. Ibid.
54. Black and Helmreich, p. 567; Bouillon et al., p. 271; Wilmot, p. 169.
55. Funk, pp. 160, 161.
56. De Gaulle, *Discours et Messages*, I, 217.

9. Nationalism in Africa—A Chain Reaction

1. Orwell, pp. 73–74, quoted in Snyder, *Dynamics of Nationalism*, pp. 23–25.
2. Rotberg, "African Nationalism," pp. 75–76; Foltz, p. 193; Andrew Cohen, p. 35.
3. Wallerstein, *The Road*, p. 42.
4. Coleman, "Nationalism in Tropical Africa," p. 410.
5. Ibid., p. 426.
6. Ibid., pp. 404–26; Coleman, *Nigeria*, p. 425.
7. Hardy, quoted by Zolberg, *One-Party Government*, p. 103.
8. Alduy, "La Naissance du Nationalisme Outre-Mer," pp. 123–37.
9. Grimal, pp. 72–73; Brace, pp. 59–61.
10. Langer, *Encyclopedia*, pp. 721–29, 732, 759–60, 943–44, 948.
11. Geneviève Anthonioz-de Gaulle, interview with the author, February 1967.
12. Grimal, p. 43.
13. Ligou, p. 223.
14. Grimal, pp. 43–47.
15. Brunschwig, *L'Avènement*, pp. 176–77, 179–80; Crowder, *West African Resistance*, pp. 1–3.
16. Legum, pp. 24–25.
17. Sarraut, speech at Pagoda of Confucius, May 1919.
18. Bidou, Gauvain and Seignobos, pp. 590–91, quoted in White, Dissertation, p. 304.
19. Wallerstein, *The Road*, p. 44; Crowder, *West African Resistance*, p. 379.
20. DuBois, 1969 ed., pp. 9–11.
21. Suret-Canale, I, 559; Padmore, p. 134.
22. Grimal, p. 18; Bemis, p. 645.
23. Suret-Canale, I, 559; Legum, p. 24.
24. Legum, pp. 25, 29–32; Makonnen, pp. 154, 163–66, 168.
25. Wallerstein, *Unity*, p. 13.
26. Crowder, *West Africa*, p. 407.
27. Padmore, p. 22.
28. Legum, pp. 25–27.
29. Padmore, p. 111.
30. Suret-Canale, I, 560–62.
31. Spengler, all; Stoddard, all.
32. Crowder, *West Africa*, pp. 18–19, 406–8; Hodgkin, p. 17.
33. Wallbank, pp. 51–52.

34. Crowder, "Independence as a Goal," quoted by W. H. Lewis, *French-Speaking Africa*, pp. 31–34; Crowder, *West Africa*, pp. 406–7.

35. Suret-Canale, I, 201.

36. Hanotaux, quoted by Grimal, p. 28; Lyautey, circular, "Le Coup de Barre," November 18, 1920, quoted by Grimal, p. 101.

37. Grimal, pp. 34–39.

38. Ibid., pp. 18–21; Mveng, p. 370.

39. Snyder, *Imperialism Reader*, pp. 420–21.

40. Grimal, pp. 24–25; Suret-Canale, II, 564–65; Mveng, p. 372.

41. Grimal, pp. 70–77.

42. Ibid., pp. 53–61, 78–91.

43. Deschamps, *Madagascar*, pp. 260–63.

44. Devèze, pp. 75–77; Suret-Canale, II, 418–22.

45. Devèze, pp. 75–77; Suret-Canale, II, 432–33; Crowder, *West Africa*, pp. 185–86.

46. Devèze, pp. 75–77; Crowder, *West Africa*, p. 438; Suret-Canale, II, 325.

47. Morgenthau, p. 4.

48. Suret-Canale, II, 548–49.

49. Ibid.

50. Crowder, *West Africa*, p. 416.

51. Johnson, pp. 155–65.

52. Suret-Canale, II, 548–51.

53. Guèye, pp. 54–56.

54. Ibid., p. 19.

55. Crowder, *West Africa*, pp. 441–43.

56. Wallerstein, "Voluntary Associations," in Coleman and Rosberg, p. 322.

57. Wallerstein, *The Road*, pp. 10, 107–23.

58. Crowder, *West Africa*, pp. 441–42.

59. Ibid., pp. 437–40.

60. Devèze, pp. 17, 20–21, 144; Mortimer, p. 45.

61. Devèze, p. 147.

62. Crowder, *West Africa*, p. 405.

63. Devèze, p. 147.

64. Legum, p. 30, quotes Padmore.

65. Hodgkin, pp. 17, 187; Balandier, "Etude des Nationalismes," pp. 382, 388; Sithole, p. 130.

66. Morgenthau, Introduction, p. xix.

67. Suret-Canale, II, 374, quotes Delavignette. *The Real Chiefs of the Empire* was suppressed by the Vichy government and later republished in France as *Service Africain* and in English as *Freedom and Authority in French West Africa*. Ibid., pp. 353, 379–80, 384.

68. Ibid., III, 39.

69. Ibid., II, 258–65; Sautter, "Notes sur la Construction," pp. 269, 273–84.

70. Ibid., pp. 263–66.

71. Morgenthau, p. 5.

72. Gide, pp. 67, 84–85, 143, 151, 158–59.

73. Ibid., p. 143.

74. Ibid., p. 151.

75. Ibid., pp. 158–59.

76. Londres, all; Moran, all.

77. Blet, III, 48, 54.

78. Deschamps, "France in Black Africa," in Gann and Duignan, *Colonialism in Africa*, II, pp. 238–42.

79. Ibid.

80. Morgenthau, Introduction, p. xix.

81. Deschamps, "France in Black Africa," pp. 242–44.

82. Ibid.

83. Ibid., pp. 244–46.

84. Chailley, pp. 418–22.

85. Delafosse, articles in *Renseignements Coloniaux* of the *Bulletin du Comité d'Afrique*, 1919, 1921, 1922.

86. Deschamps, "France in Black Africa," in Gann and Duignan, pp. 242–48; Chailley, pp. 422–31.

87. Sarraut, *Grandeur*, pp. 13, 15, 21, 31, 112, 215; *Annales de l'Assemblée de l'Union Française*, session of Wednesday, December 10, 1947.
88. Notes and Documents, no. 2508, p. 19.
89. Delavignette, *Les Paysans Noirs*, p. 258.
90. Suret-Canale, II, 562.
91. Damas, pp. 45–47.
92. Diop, in *A Book of African Verse*, pp. 27–28.
93. Césaire, *Cahier d'un Retour*, pp. 72–73.
94. Monnerville, "Ou va l'Union Française?" p. 10.

10 Brazzaville—An Uncertain Step into the Future

1. Tournoux, *Pétain and de Gaulle*, p. 310.
2. Interviews of the author with Jean Mialet, March 1967, General Catroux, February 16, 1967, et al.; M'Bokolo, "French Colonial Policy," p. 20.
3. Ageron, "De Gaulle et la Conférence de Brazzaville," p. 2.
4. De Gaulle, *Mémoires*, I, 219.
5. Ageron, "De Gaulle et la Conférence de Brazzaville," pp. 2–4.
6. Cissoko, "La Conférence de Brazzaville," pp. 13–15.
7. De Gaulle, *Mémoires d'Espoir*, I, 42, 87.
8. Marshall, "Free France in Africa," in Gifford and Lewis, pp. 733–36.
9. Tournoux, *La Tragédie*, p. 175; de Gaulle, *Mémoires d'Espoir*, pp. 42, 87.
10. De Gaulle, *Memoirs*, II, 207–8; Weinstein, p. 299.
11. Ageron, "De Gaulle et la Conférence de Brazzaville," p. 4.
12. Ibid., pp. 5–7.
13. Ibid., pp. 6–7.
14. De Gaulle, *Memoirs*, II, 207–8.
15. Weinstein, p. 298; de Gaulle, *Memoirs*, II, 210.
16. De Gaulle, *Memoirs*, II, 207; Weinstein, pp. 299–300.
17. Daruvar, p. 33.
18. Harmon, "Free France Booms."
19. Daruvar, p. 33.
20. Ibid.
21. Lorraine, p. 88.
22. Ibid.
23. Governor-General Laurentie, interview with the author, February 23, 1968. (While at Brazzaville, Laurentie was director of political affairs for Governor-General Eboué. Later he became governor-general.)
24. *Conférence de Brazzaville* (official report), pp. 88–111; Weinstein, p. 299.
25. *Conférence de Brazzaville*, pp. 88–111.
26. De Gaulle, *Mémoires*, II, 182–85.
27. De Gaulle, *Memoirs*, II, 172; *Mémoires*, II, 182; Weinstein, pp. 293, 298.
28. *Conférence de Brazzaville*, pp. 15–16.
29. Elgey, I, 310.
30. White, *Seeds*, p. 432; General Catroux, interview with the author, February 16, 1967.
31. Claudius-Petit, interview with the author, February 15, 1967.
32. *Conférence de Brazzaville*, pp. 17–26.
33. Ageron, "De Gaulle et la Conférence de Brazzaville," p. 4.
34. Ibid., p. 6.
35. Black and Helmreich, pp. 562–63; Bailey, pp. 838, 842.
36. De Gaulle, *Memoirs*, II, 92–94, 225–28, 268–71.
37. *Conférence de Brazzaville*, p. 22.
38. De Gaulle, *Memoirs*, II, 205–9.
39. Mortimer, p. 49.
40. Churchill, speech, November 10, 1942; Arnault, *Du Colonialisme*, p. 26.
41. *Conférence de Brazzaville*, pp. 23–26.
42. Barrès, pp. 29–30.

43. Renault-Roulier ["Rémy"], p. 69.
44. Weil-Curiel, pp. 224–27.
45. D'Astier, pp. 77–78.
46. Elgey, I, 40–46.
47. *Conférence de Brazzaville*, p. 48.
48. Ibid., pp. 22–31.
49. Lorraine, p. 88.
50. *Conférence de Brazzaville*, p. 32 (p. 35 in edition held by the University of Pennsylvania). The English word "self-governments" is in the French text—unusual in a French document. This edition, having belonged to D. S. White, is now in the European Seminar at Princeton University.
51. Viard, p. 14.
52. *Conférence de Brazzaville*, p. 32 (p. 35 in U. of P. ed.).
53. Ageron, "De Gaulle et la Conférence le Brazzaville," pp. 7, 8, and note, p. 8.
54. *Conférence de Brazzaville*, pp. 32–36 (U. of P., pp. 35–36).
55. Ibid.
56. Ibid., pp. 36–42 (U. of P., pp. 35–36).
57. Ibid., pp. 42–50 (U. of P., pp. 36–48).
58. Ibid., pp. 36–62 (U. of P., pp. 48–58).
59. Ibid., pp. 89–98 (U. of P., pp. 81–84).
60. Ibid., p. 110 (U. of P., pp. 95–105), quoting from Delafosse, *L'Ame Nègre*, p. 35.
61. Mortimer, p. 50.
62. *Conférence de Brazzaville*, report by Fily Dabo Sissoko, pp. 98–111 (U. of P., pp. 95–105).
63. Ibid., pp. 109–22 (U. of P., pp. 95–105); Hodgkin, p. 35.
64. *Conférence de Brazzaville*, pp. 63–70 (U. of P., pp. 61–66).
65. De Gaulle, *Memoirs*, II, 208–9.

11. Post Mortem on Brazzaville

1. Hayter, pp. 24–25.
2. Governor-General Laurentie, interview with the author, February 23, 1968.
3. De Gaulle, *Memoirs*, II, 208, or *Mémoires*, II, 185; M'Bokolo, "French Colonial Policy," p. 8.
4. Ageron, "De Gaulle et la Conférence de Brazzaville," p. 9.
5. Viard, pp. 14–15.
6. Mérat, pp. 43–44.
7. Ageron, "De Gaulle et la Conférence de Brazzaville," p. 7.
8. Ibid.
9. Thompson and Adloff, p. 24.
10. Guèye, pp. 162–65.
11. Viard, pp. 28–29.
12. *Conférence de Brazzaville*, pp. 112–31 (U. of P., pp. 109–22); Ageron, "De Gaulle et la Conférence de Brazzaville," p. 8.
13. *J.O. de l'Assemblée Consultative*, pp. 1–6.
14. Raymond Offroi, interview with the author, February 4, 1971.
15. Mérat, p. 43.
16. Arnault, *Du Colonialisme*, pp. 25–27.
17. Paul Devinat, interview with the author, February 13, 1967.
18. Maurice Schumann, minister of foreign affairs, interview with the author, March 8, 1968; Président Maurice Bayrou, vice-president of the Senate, interview with the author, January 29, 1968; Devèze, p. 182; General Pierre Rondot, interview with the author, January 20, 1967; Aubame, "La Conférence de Brazzaville," pp. 183–86.
19. Henri Laurentie, "L'Union Française devant le Monde," speech, March 14, 1946, to the *Ministère de la France d'Outre-Mer*.
20. Ageron, "De Gaulle et la Conférence de Brazzaville," p. 9, quotes Laurentie, *Renaissances*, March 1945.
21. Laurentie, speech at the Palais de Chaillot, January 28, 1945.
22. Laurentie, speech and discussion at the *Centre d'Etudes de Politique Etrangère*, February 9, 1945; Ageron, "De Gaulle et la Conférence de Brazzaville," p. 9, quotes Laurentie, *Renaissances*, March 1945.

23. Jean Mialet, judge of the *Cour des comptes*, interview with the author, March 1967; Lorraine, p. 88; Cissoko, "La Conférence de Brazzaville," pp. 13–15.

24. Ageron, "De Gaulle et la Conférence de Brazzaville," pp. 9–11.

25. Ibid., p. 11.

26. *J.O. de l'Assemblée Consultative Provisoire*, first extraordinary session, 1945, *Débats*, March 19, 1945, pp. 5, 556–60.

27. Ibid., pp. 559–64; M'Bokolo, "French Colonial Policy," pp. 23–24. List of new laws that were instituted after the end of the Conference of Brazzaville:

August 7 and 17, 1944. Laws introducing professional unions and inspection of work.

February 11, 1946. Abolition of forced labor.

February 20, 1946. Suppression of the *indigénat*.

April 30, 1946. Unification of justice.

May 7, 1946. Lamine Guèye Law extending French citizenship to the Overseas Territories without changing civil status of individuals.

October 7, 1946. Local assemblies created, representation in the French National Assembly granted and creation of the Council of the French Union. "Governors-general" become "ministers resident," and are responsible to the Assembly.

April 30, 1946. FIDES (*Fonds d'Investissement et de Développement*) set up with a ten-year plan from 1947 to 1956.

There were ambiguities, contradictions and delays in these laws. Some were extremely slow in being put into operation. M'Bokolo believes the laws went beyond the expectations of the blacks and of the French *colons*. They had not asked as much as the laws indicated. Reactions were slow. Still, the local and national assemblies developed the political life of the African colonies. The federal idea appeared to lose ground; the spirit remained the same. There were conflicts between an unwilling administration and those attempting to carry out the laws—and also between the hereditary chiefs and the newer *évolués* established by Eboué. After a time, in the fifties, there was more of a desire on all sides to get together (M'Bokolo, "French Colonial Policy," pp. 23–25, 29–31).

28. *J.O. de l'Assemblée Consultative Provisoire*, 2d extraordinary session, 1945, *Débats*, March 20, 1945, pp. 594–95.

29. M'Bokolo, "French Colonial Policy," p. 6.

30. Guèye, pp. 121, 136.

31. Kuoh-Moukouri, pp. 82–101.

12. Promises, Dreams, and First Fruits

1. De Gaulle, *Memoirs*, II, 270.

2. De Gaulle, *Mémoires*, II, 655–56; *Discours et Messages*, I, 415–22.

3. De Gaulle, *Mémoires*, II, 660; Tournoux, *La Tragédie*, pp. 49–50; von Albertini, pp. 22–25; Funk, pp. 84–87; Grimal, pp. 125–26.

4. De Gaulle, *Mémoires*, III, 340.

5. *J.O. de l'Assemblée Consultative Provisoire*, *Débats*, November 21, 22, 1944, pp. 311, 321, 322.

6. De Gaulle, *Mémoires*, III, 213.

7. Ibid., p. 340.

8. Delavignette, "French Colonial Policy," in Gann and Duignan, II, 253–56.

9. Ibid.

10. Devèze, pp. 185–86.

11. De Gaulle, *Memoirs*, III, 326.

12. Devèze, p. 207.

13. Ibid., pp. 210–11.

14. Ibid., pp. 185–86, 194; Mortimer, p. 54.

15. De Gaulle, *Mémoires*, III, 340.

16. Devèze, p. 207.

17. Mortimer, pp. 156–59.

18. Delavignette, "French Colonial Policy," in Gann and Duignan, II, 257–58.

19. Godechot, pp. 358–59.

20. Mortimer, p. 59 and n. 1.
21. Delavignette, "French Colonial Policy," p. 257; Suret-Canale, III, 29, says it was 64.
22. Suret-Canale, III, 29.
23. Milcent, p. 26, quoted by Suret-Canale, III, 30.
24. Suret-Canale, III, pp. 34, 35.
25. Guèye, p. 54.
26. Godechot, p. 360.
27. Chetrit and Timsit, pp. 3, 4; de Gaulle Memoirs, II, 362.

13. Two Constituent Assemblies Create a Union

1. Chauvel, II, 131.
2. De Gaulle, Memoirs, III, 315–23; Godechot, p. 360.
3. De Gaulle, Memoirs, III, 315–23; Chauvel, II, 135.
4. Suret-Canale, III, 36.
5. De Gaulle, Mémoires, III, 223–26, 554–55.
6. Vendroux, in L'Herne, Charles de Gaulle, pp. 129–31.
7. Suret-Canale, III, 36–38.
8. Devèze, pp. 222–23.
9. Godechot, pp. 361–62.
10. Devèze, pp. 264–65.
11. Suret-Canale, III, 39–44; Godechot, pp. 360–62; Guèye, p. 139.
12. Suret-Canale, III, 37–38.
13. Ibid., p. 49, n. 1.
14. De Gaulle, Extraits pour l'avenir, p. 75.
15. Devèze, pp. 272–73; Guèye, pp. 173–76.
16. Marshall, The French Colonial Myth, pp. 194–95, 206–7, 228, 270.
17. Suret-Canale III, 44–48.
18. Godechot, pp. 362–63; de Gaulle, Discours et Messages, II, 5–11; Chetrit and Timsit, pp. 1–5; de Gaulle, Mémoires, III, 647–52.
19. Suret-Canale, III, 52; Morgenthau, p. 86.
20. J.O. de l'Assemblée Nationale Constituante, II, 1946, pp. 3785–912.
21. Suret-Canale, III, 51–52.
22. Mortimer, p. 97, quotes from J.O. de l'Assemblée Nationale Constituante, II Débats, August 27, 1946.
23. J.O. de l'Assemblée Nationale Constituante, II, 1946, session of August 27, 1946, p. 3334; Séances de la Commission de la Constitution, II, 491, 506.
24. Ibid., pp. 478, 502.
25. Mortimer, p. 96.
26. Séances de la Commission de la Constitution, II, 510, 520, 524, 529.
27. Suret-Canale, III, 52, 53; Morgenthau, pp. 86–87; Foltz, p. 24.
28. De Gaulle, Discours et Messages, II, 18–23.
29. Ibid.
30. Ibid., pp. 26–33; Godechot, p. 363.
31. Chetrit and Timsit, p. 100; La France sera la France, p. 178; de Gaulle, Discours et Messages, II, 74–81.
32. Petit Larousse (ed. of 1959), p. 85.
33. Chetrit and Timsit, p. 13.
34. Elgey, article in Candide, November 16 and 23, 1961.
35. Godechot, pp. 364–66.
36. Williams, p. 424.
37. Chetrit and Timsit, p. 10.
38. La Roche and Gottmann, pp. 17–19, 32.
39. Hymans, pp. 149–52.
40. Petit Larousse (ed. of 1976), p. 422.
41. Larousse Universel, I, 716.
42. Petit Larousse, p. 240.

43. *Larousse Universel*, I, 415.
44. *Webster's New Collegiate Dictionary* (ed. of 1945), p. 236.
45. Chetrit and Timsit, pp. 96–102, 104.

14. In the Desert

1. De La Gorce, *De Gaulle entre Deux Mondes*, p. 464.
2. De Gaulle, *Discours et Messages*, II, 45–46.
3. De La Gorce, *De Gaulle entre Deux Mondes*, p. 478; Chetrit and Timsit, p. 16; Fauvet, p. 112.
4. Fauvet, p. 113.
5. Chetrit and Timsit, pp. 25–27, 32, 41, 89, 94, 98, 100.
6. Ibid., pp. 63, 100.
7. Ibid., pp. 32, 37, 60, 63, 90, 93, 94, 97–98.
8. De Gaulle, speech in Paris, August 18, 1947; Chetrit and Timsit, pp. 115–19.
9. De Gaulle, speech at Algiers, October 12, 1947.
10. Chetrit and Timsit, pp. 63–67
11. Ibid., pp. 100–101, 116, 122.
12. De Gaulle, press conference, March 16, 1950, *Discours et Messages*, II; Chetrit and Timsit, pp. 107, 109–11.
13. Chetrit and Timsit, pp. 101–2.
14. De Gaulle, *Memoirs*, II, 270.
15. Chetrit and Timsit, pp. 102–5.
16. Lacouture, *Malraux*, p. 342; Chetrit and Timsit, p. 104.
17. Brace, pp. 87–115; Chetrit and Timsit, pp. 105, 145–51, 160; Zolberg, *One-Party Government*, p. 210.
18. Germaine Tillion, interview with the author, March 16, 1974.
19. Singleton, "The Malagasy Republic"; Gaskill, "Madagascar."
20. "Madagascar, a Sketch," anonymous and dateless (loaned by the American Embassy at Tananarive).
21. Stibbe, all.
22. Ibid., preface, pp. 11–14.
23. Ibid., p. 10; Tronchon, pp. 13, 23, 159, 318.
24. Spacensky, p. 47.
25. Ibid., pp. 47–53.
26. Ibid., p. 268.
27. Deschamps, *Madagascar*, pp. 268–69.
28. Peter Walker, interview with the author, Tananarive, October 16, 1969.
29. Deschamps, *Madagascar*, p. 269.
30. Spacensky, pp. 62–67.
31. Deschamps, *Madagascar*, p. 270, n. 1.
32. Stibbe, pp. 17–20.
33. Spacensky, p. 70.
34. Munger, article in *Current Affairs Newsletter*.
35. Deschamps, *Madagascar*, p. 267.
36. Spacensky, pp. 69, 71.
37. Stibbe, pp. 22–72.
38. Spacensky, pp. 72, 74–75.
39. Stibbe, pp. 22–72.
40. Spacensky, pp. 69, 73.
41. Ibid., p. 77.
42. Stibbe, p. 8.
43. Munger, article.
44. Deschamps, *Madagascar*, p. 270; Munger, article.
45. Ki-Zerbo, pp. 589–92.
46. White, *Seeds*, p. 348.
47. Moreux, "Déviations des Nations Unies," December 29, 1945, p. 146; February 23, 1946, p. 171; Moreux quotes Laurentie in *Marchés Coloniaux*, no. 7 (1945), p. not given.

48. Marianne Cornevin, p. 119.
49. Foltz, pp. 15, 19; Rotberg, "African Nationalism," p. 78.
50. Zolberg, *Political Order*, pp. 12–13.
51. Foltz, pp. 49–55.
52. Ibid., p. 53.
53. RDA Report, p. 2.
54. Ibid., pp. 4, 5.
55. Ibid., p. 7.
56. Ibid., pp. 8–12.
57. Ibid., p. 22.
58. Ibid., first section.
59. Ibid., p. 15.
60. Ibid., pp. 49–95; Mortimer, p. 144.
61. RDA Report, first section and pp. 19–22.
62. Ibid., resolution of October 3, 1948, pp. 109–14.
63. De Gaulle, *Memoirs*, III, 312–33.
64. RDA Report, pp. 89–91, 112–13.
65. Morgenthau, pp. 88–98; von Albertini, p. 426.
66. Marianne Cornevin, pp. 188–89.
67. Wallerstein, *The Road*, p. 48.
68. Chetrit and Timsit, p. 36.
69. Foltz, pp. 63, 64.

15. The World from Colombey

1. Conte, pp. 7, 26, 36–37, 222, 226, 236.
2. Ibid., p. 315.
3. Ibid., pp. 284–96.
4. Spacensky, p. 201.
5. Elgey, II, 348.
6. Brace, pp. 69–72.
7. Ibid., pp. 80–92, 95–97.
8. Ibid., pp. 96–97.
9. *Larousse Universel*, p. 42.
10. Brace, pp. 107, 108.
11. Aron, p. 321.
12. Viansson-Ponté, I, 162.
13. De Gaulle, *Mémoires d'Espoir*, I, 16; *Memoirs*, II, 208.
14. Mortimer, pp. 201–5.
15. FIDES. *Fonds d'Investissements et de Développement Economique et Social des Territoires d'Outre-Mer*. This fund, financed from the metropolitan budget, was to make long-term loans for overseas development at a rate of 1 percent. In accepting it, the Assembly showed that it recognized a debt of gratitude to the Empire (or rather, as everyone was now careful to call it, the Union), which could not be paid in words; it at last admitted the necessity of a coherent overseas investment plan, the essential infrastructure for which could only be provided by a large initial public investment with no direct return (Mortimer, p. 76).
16. Ibid., pp. 241–42, 297–98, 341–42.
17. Ibid., pp. 212–18, 242–46.
18. Ibid., pp. 299–302, 336–40.
19. Ibid., pp. 336–40.
20. Morgenthau, p. 109.
21. Von Albertini, pp. 431–32.
22. Ibid., pp. 432–33.
23. Gaston Defferre, interview with the author, February 29, 1968.
24. Gaston Espinasse, interview with the author, March 7, 1968.
25. Interviews with the author: Martial de La Fournières, February, 1967; Bernard Tricot, February 27, 1971.
26. Interviews with the author: M. le Président Pierre Messmer, March 24, 1970; Gouverneur

Henri Laurentie, March 24, 1971; L'Ambassadeur Geoffroy de Courcel, April 1, 1968.
    27. Interviews with the author: Edouard Sablier, February 3, 1967; Gouverneur-Général Robert Delavignette, February 16, 1968.
    28. Foltz, p. 76; Morgenthau, p. 113.
    29. Zolberg, *One-Party Government,* p. 219.
    30. Morgenthau, p. 112.
    31. Mortimer, p. 181.
    32. Foltz, pp. 75–76 and n. 32; Morgenthau, p. 114.
    33. Morgenthau, p. 116.
    34. Ibid., pp. 111–15.
    35. Zolberg, *One-Party Government,* p. 210.
    36. Williams and Harrison, p. 61; Grimal, p. 350; interviews with the author: Le Président Boubakar Guèye, December, 1969; M. Onambélé, November 8, 1969; M. Le Ministre des Affaires Etrangères J. Rabemananjara, October 24, 1969; Le Président Houphouet-Boigny, March 28, 1972; Foltz, p. 75.
    37. Grosser, p. 262, quotes Bourguiba, *La Tunisie et la France,* pp. 190–99.
    38. Williams and Harrison, p. 32; Viansson-Ponté, p. 186; Givisiez, brief article in *Afrique Contemporaine,* December 1970, p. 21; de Gaulle, *Mémoires d'Espoir,* I, p. 17.
    39. Terrenoire, *De Gaulle et l'Algérie,* p. 48.
    40. Ibid., pp. 41, 42, 44.
    41. Ibid., p. 45, quotes Bourguiba, *L'Express,* June 21, 1957.
    42. Ibid., p. 11.
    43. Deputy Raymond Offroi, interview with the author, February 4, 1971.
    44. Terrenoire, *De Gaulle et l'Algérie,* p. 48.

16. The Climax of Decolonization

    1. De Gaulle, *Mémoires d'Espoir,* I, 23, 40.
    2. De Gaulle, *Discours et Messages,* III, 5.
    3. Ferniot, p. 376.
    4. Mortimer, pp. 304–5.
    5. Ferniot, p. 376.
    6. Werth, *The De Gaulle Revolution,* p. 250.
    7. Crowder, "Independence as a Goal," in Lewis, *French-Speaking Africa,* p. 33.
    8. Rous, pp. 15–22.
    9. Ibid., p. 21.
    10. Ibid., pp. 59–60.
    11. Reuters, *The New Africans,* p. 205.
    12. Mortimer, p. 145.
    13. Ibid., pp. 148–63, 178.
    14. Ibid., pp. 150–53.
    15. Ibid., pp. 145–48.
    16. *J. O. de l'Assemblée Nationale de la Côte d'Ivoire, Débats,* March 23, 1946, pp. 1028 ff., quoted by Morgenthau, pp. 4, 5.
    17. Paul Devinat, interview with the author, February 13, 1967.
    18. Guéna, pp. 59, 61.
    19. Ibid., p. 59.
    20. Morgenthau, pp. 115–17.
    21. Touré, p. 50.
    22. Crowder, in Lewis, *French-Speaking Africa,* p. 33.
    23. Mortimer, p. 317.
    24. Crowder, in Lewis, *French-Speaking Africa,* pp. 33–34.
    25. Touré, p. 71.
    26. De La Gorce, "La France et l'Afrique," p. 47.
    27. Mortimer, pp. 306–9; Guéna, p. 69.
    28. Ferniot, p. 119.
    29. Mortimer, p. 310.
    30. Ibid.

31. Camara, *Guinea Without France*, p. 326.

32. Guéna, pp. 68–69.

33. Chaffard, II, 189.

34. Mortimer, pp. 311–12.

35. Ibid., p. 312; Guéna, p. 74.

36. Mortimer, p. 313.

37. Chaffard, II, 190.

38. Werth, *The De Gaulle Revolution*, p. 252.

39. Guéna, p. 70.

40. Mortimer, p. 314.

41. Werth, *The De Gaulle Revolution*, p. 254.

42. Mortimer, pp. 314–15.

43. De Gaulle, speech at Brazzaville, August 24, 1958; Werth, *The De Gaulle Revolution*, pp. 254–55.

44. Mortimer, p. 316; Chaffard, II, 171.

45. Guéna, pp. 70–71.

46. Mortimer, II, 310, 315.

47. Chaffard, II, 193–95; de La Gorce, "La France et l'Afrique," p. 49.

48. Werth, *The De Gaulle Revolution*, p. 257; de La Gorce, "La France et l'Afrique," p. 49; Francis Guttmann, interview with the author, March 1970.

49. Zolberg, *Political Order*, pp. 43–46.

50. Touré, pp. 79–86.

51. Guéna, pp. 72–73.

52. Lacouture, *Cinq Hommes*, pp. 350–51.

53. Touré, pp. 87–90.

54. Lacouture, *Cinq Hommes*, p. 352.

55. De La Gorce, "La France et l'Afrique," p. 49.

56. Chaffard, II, 197.

57. Ibid., pp. 168, 176–77, 181–82.

58. Francis Guttmann, interview with the author, March 1970.

59. Chaffard, II, 168, 200.

60. Ibid., p. 181; I, 333.

61. Ibid., II, 192, 195.

62. Werth, *The De Gaulle Revolution*, p. 256.

63. Ibid., p. 257.

64. Chaffard, II, 165–67.

65. Mortimer, p. 317, cites Morgenthau, p. 162.

66. Chaffard, II, 165–67.

67. Werth, *The De Gaulle Revolution*, p. 257.

68. De Gaulle, speech at Dakar, August 26, 1958, *Discours et Messages*, III, 38, 39.

69. Chaffard, II, 168.

70. Werth, *The De Gaulle Revolution*, p. 252.

71. De Gaulle, *Discours et Messages*, III, 44–47.

72. De La Gorce, "La France et l'Afrique," pp. 47–48.

73. Terrenoire, *De Gaulle et l'Algérie*, p. 7.

74. Raymond Offroi, interview with the author, February 4, 1971.

75. De La Gorce, "La France et l'Afrique," p. 47.

76. Guéna, p. 62.

77. Chaffard, II, 191.

78. Mortimer, pp. 318–22.

79. Ibid., pp. 321–25.

80. Chaffard, II, 197–98, 206.

81. Mortimer, p. 329.

82. Chaffard, II, 210.

83. Interviews with the author: Francis Guttmann, March 1970; M. Lebel of the Foreign Office, January 26, 1967.

84. Mortimer, pp. 322, 324, 343.

85. Guéna, p. 86.

86. Chaffard, II, 212.

87. Ibid., p. 357.

88. Guéna, pp. 83–85; Chaffard, II, 235.

89. Mortimer, pp. 331–33.
90. Ibid., p. 331; Crowder, in Lewis, *French-Speaking Africa*, p. 35.
91. Chaffard, II, 217; Mortimer, p. 331.
92. De Gaulle, *Discours et Messages*, III, 58–59.
93. M. Lebel, interview with the author, January 26, 1967.
94. M. Tounkara, minister of information of Guinea, interview with the author, October 1966. A person very close to de Gaulle for a long time, whom the author has not permission to quote, said in the spring of 1978 that much of this talk of having denuded Guinea before leaving was not true.

17. The Life and Death of a Community

1. Plantey [Néra], pp. 21–24.
2. Yacono, p. 90.
3. Ibid., pp. 28–29. The "Entente States" were the Ivory Coast, Upper Volta, Niger and Dahomey. The short-lived Federation of Mali was composed of Senegal and Mali.
4. Guéna, pp. 78–79; Plantey [Néra], pp. 28–29.
5. Guéna, pp. 73–75.
6. Zolberg, *One-Party Government*, pp. 225–30.
7. Morgenthau, p. 118.
8. Ibid., p. 119.
9. Guéna, pp. 89–91.
10. Ibid., p. 91.
11. Ligot, p. 79.
12. Guéna, pp. 91–93.
13. Ibid., pp. 93–94.
14. Ibid., pp. 94–97.
15. Ibid., pp. 98–104.
16. Crowder, in Lewis, *French-Speaking Africa*, p. 38.
17. Guéna, pp. 106–11.
18. Zolberg, *One-Party Government*, pp. 232–37.
19. Ibid., pp. 111–16.
20. De La Gorce, "De Gaulle et la Décolonisation," pp. 50–51.
21. Guéna, pp. 116–20.
22. Ibid., pp. 120–28.
23. Ibid., pp. 128–39.
24. Ibid., pp. 139–44.
25. Ibid., pp. 144–49.
26. M. Cornevin, p. 222.
27. Guéna, pp. 158–66.
28. Ibid., pp. 166–88.
29. French Embassy, *Major Addresses of General de Gaulle*, press conference, November 10, 1959, pp. 57–66.
30. *Discours et Messages*, III, 139–42.
31. Ibid.
32. Speech of General de Gaulle, December 13, 1959, *Discours et Messages*, III, 151–54.
33. Ibid.
34. Speech at Limoux, February 26, 1960, French Press and Information Collection, New York.
35. Speech of January 29, 1960, *Discours et Messages*, III, 162–66.
36. Speech at Castres, February 26, 1960, French Press and Information Collection, New York.
37. Speech of June 14, 1960, *Major Addresses*, p. 82.
38. Press conference, September 5, 1960, *Major Addresses*, pp. 85–94; Terrenoire, *De Gaulle Vivant*, p. 87.
39. Press conference, September 5, 1960, *Major Addresses*, pp. 85–94; *Mémoires d'Espoir*, p. 16.
40. Press conference, April 11, 1961, *Major Addresses*, pp. 113–18.
41. Ibid.
42. Speech of September 5, 1961, *Major Addresses*, pp. 149–50.
43. Broadcast of March 26, 1962, *Major Addresses*, p. 168.

18. The Trial of the Spirit

1. De Gaulle, *Mémoires d'Espoir*, I, 41.
2. Pognon, p. 201.
3. De Gaulle, *Mémoires d'Espoir*, I, 41.
4. Ibid., p. 16 and chap. II.
5. Interview with the author, February 1967.
6. Arnault, *Du Colonialisme*, pp. 26–30.
7. Werth, *The De Gaulle Revolution*, p. 256, quotes Lacouture, source not given.
8. De Gaulle, *Le Fil*, p. 44.
9. M. Cornevin, pp. 215–16; de Gaulle, *Mémoires d'Espoir*, I, 41, 42, end of chapter.
10. De Gaulle, *Discours et Messages*, III, 108–10.
11. Crawley, p. 317.
12. Decraene, "La Politique Africaine du Général de Gaulle," p. 76.
13. Passeron, I, 482.
14. De La Gorce, p. 594; ibid., "De Gaulle et la Décolonisation," pp. 47–50; Viansson-Ponté, I, 95.
15. De La Gorce, "De Gaulle et la Décolonisation," pp. 47–48, 51; Delavignette, *Du Bon Usage*, p. 67; Jean Mialet, interview with the author, March 1967.
16. De Gaulle, *Mémoires d'Espoir*, I, 16.
17. Interview with the author, February 16, 1967.
18. M. Cornevin, p. 223.
19. Interviews of the author with President Senghor, December 5, 1969; Madame Lamine Guèye, December 11, 1969; General Catroux, February 16, 1967; Edouard Sablier, February 28, 1967.
20. Interview of January 1968, with a high government official.
21. Viard, pp. 148–56.
22. Von Albertini, p. 468.
23. Boubakar Guèye, vice-president of the Senegal Assembly, interview with the author, December 12, 1969.
24. Decraene, p. 75; de La Gorce, "De Gaulle et la Décolonisation," p. 53.
25. President Senghor, interview with the author, December 5, 1969; Senghor, I, pp. 394–95.
26. Werth, *De Gaulle*, p. 61.
27. Senghor, I, 394.
28. De Gaulle, *Vers l'Armée*, p. 182; Viansson-Ponté, I, 133.
29. Interview with the author, February 29, 1968.
30. Terrenoire, *De Gaulle et l'Algérie*, p. 194.
31. Ibid., pp. 224–25.
32. Von Albertini, p. 446; Claudius-Petit, interview with the author, February 15, 1967.
33. Edouard Sablier, interview with the author, February 23, 1967.
34. De La Gorce, "De Gaulle et la Décolonisation," p. 52.
35. De Gaulle, *Mémoires d'Espoir*, I, 42.
36. Semidei, "De l'Empire à la Décolonisation," p. 63; Herskovits, *Afrique et les Africains entre hier et demain*, chap. VI.
37. Guéna, pp. 187–89.
38. De La Gorce, "De Gaulle et la Décolonisation," p. 53.
39. Conte, p. 47.
40. Guéna, p. 182.
41. Tournoux, *Jamais Dit*, pp. 356–57.
42. RDA Report, p. 5.
43. Von Albertini, p. 443.
44. Montgomery, quoted by Davidson, *The African Past*, p. 39.
45. Ibid.
46. Toulat, p. 47.

19 After the Climax

1. The countries south of the Sahara that were granted political independence by France from 1958 through 1960 were: Guinea, which declared itself independent on September 28, 1958 by

refusing in the referendum set up by General de Gaulle to join the Community; Cameroon, independence received on January 1, 1960; Togo, April 27, 1960; Madagascar, June 26, 1960; Central African Republic—formerly Oubangui-Chari, July 12, 1960; Middle Congo—also called Congo-Brazzaville, July 12, 1960; Chad, August 15–17, 1960; Gabon, August 15–17, 1960; Dahomey, August 1, 1960; Niger, August 1, 1960; Upper Volta, August 5, 1960; the Ivory Coast, August 7, 1960; Senegal, September 11, 1960; Mali—formerly the French Soudan, September 23, 1960; Mauritania, November 28, 1960 (Grimal, pp. 397–98). French Somaliland (as the Republic of Djibouti) achieved independence on June 27, 1977.

2. Guy de Bosschère, II, 115, has written that decolonization is a neologism that appeared recently. It was born after the Second World Conflict from a movement that required a name. "To decolonize," he said, "is to combat the colonizer and get rid of him, but beyond that it is to reject him more radically still, with the spirit he represents and the habits inherited from him. It is to obtain independence by pacific or armed means, because real independence is a decisive victory over nominal independence."

David Gardinier, in his essay on "Decolonization" (in J. Dunner, *Handbook of World History*, p. 268) refers to the fact that Moritz Julius Bonn used the term in his article "Imperialism" in the *Encyclopedia of Social Sciences* in 1932, and that Henri Labouret popularized it in *Colonization, Colonialism, Decolonization* in 1952. In any case, it is a word that belongs largely to the second half of the twentieth century.

Governor-General Robert Delavignette's book of 1968, *Du Bon Usage de la Décolonisation*, also increased the use of the word—though it came out after the major decolonization took place.

3. Ligot, p. 17.

4. Hayter, p. 142.

5. Guinea signed some agreements with France in 1959 and again before the end of 1963, but most of them were not carried out due to the lack of normal relations between France and Guinea.

6. Ligot, pp. 21, 36, 39, 56, 57.

7. Ibid., pp. 36, 58, 59, and n. 3, n. 84.

8. Ibid., pp. 30, 53, 59, and n. 1, n. 104, n. 111.

9. Ibid., pp. 33, 34, 58, 59, and n. 2.

10. Ibid., pp. 38–42.

11. Ibid., p. 59; Hayter, p. 142.

12. Robarts, pp. 74, 80.

13. Mortimer, pp. 310–11.

14. Ibid.

15. Chaffard, II, 192–95.

16. Mortimer, p. 365.

17. De Bosschère, II, 194; Mortimer, pp. 363–66; Ligot, pp. 169–72. De Gaulle had at first refused to admit that the Federation of Mali existed, for it was not recognized by the Executive Council of the Community (at its third meeting on May 3, 1959) as having become a single state. However, at the fifth meeting of the Council in December 1959, it was recognized as a federation and admitted to independence without forfeiting its membership in the Community.

18. Mortimer, p. 366.

19. Ibid.; Ligot, p. 74.

20. Mortimer, p. 366.

21. Ibid., p. 362.

22. Touchard, p. 38.

23. Mortimer, p. 330.

24. Ibid., pp. 330–32.

25. Ibid., pp. 367–68.

26. Duroselle and Meyriat, p. 181.

27. Ibid., p. 184.

28. Mortimer, p. 311.

29. Hayter, p. 142.

30. Ligot, pp. 50, 56, 60–69, 70–75; Corbett, p. 3.

31. Ibid., pp. 64–65.

32. Ibid., pp. 73–75, 79. The author has found no indication that the Senate and the Court of Arbitration have been utilized.

33. Ibid. p. 79.

34. Ibid., pp. 84–91.

35. Ibid., p. 91; M'Bokolo, "French Colonial Policy," p. 40.

36. Ligot, pp. 92–93.

37. Ibid., p. 59.

38. Ibid., pp. 99–101, 103.

39. Ibid., pp. 104–10.

40. *Conférence de Brazzaville*, Section on Education.

41. Mortimer, p. 76.

42. Ministère de la France d'Outre-Mer, "Enseignement Outre-Mer," no. 10, December 1958; "Report of the Committee for the Modernization of Overseas Territories," in Scanlon, pp. 132–40.

43. Gardinier, "Schooling in the States of Equatorial Africa," pp. 525–27.

44. Tracy, pp. 21, 22.

45. Corbett, pp. 27, 28, 30, 33, 36, 40.

46. Ligot, pp. 111–18.

47. Corbett, p. 62.

48. Ligot, pp. 61–64, 144–46.

49. Camara, *Guinea Without France*, p. 292.

50. Ligot, p. 102; Luchaire, p. 97.

51. Hayter, pp. 17, 31, 142.

52. Luchaire, pp. 33–42, 94, 96.

53. Corbett, pp. 121, 135, and Table 3, based on OECD, which refers to 280 millions rather than 283 (with a note that certain totals have discrepancies because OECD has not updated all of them).

54. Tracy, pp. 42–43; Cartier, in *Paris-Match*, February-March 1964; Hayter, p. 95.

55. Tracy, p. 44.

56. Luchaire, pp. 90–93; Ligot, pp. 129, 130.

57. Hayter, pp. 85, 91; Ligot, pp. 131–32; Corbett, p. 62.

58. Ligot, pp. 125–31. Ligot, p. 128, says: "The Secretariat constituted the Cabinet of the President of the Republic. It is through it as an intermediary that the President's personal tie with the African and Malgache Chiefs of State is assured; . . . during the presidency of General de Gaulle, it can be considered as a presidential reserved section (*domaine réservé*) and it appears that the participation of the General Secretariat for the Community and African and Malgache Affairs in the conduct of the policy of cooperation is, in general, a determining factor."

59. Ibid., pp. 138–42.

60. Corbett, p. 143, words of Houphouet-Boigny quoted from *Le Moniteur Africain*, November 6, 1969, p. 5.

61. Corbett, pp. 119, 143.

62. Hayter, pp. 84, 85.

63. Ibid., pp. 146–47, 203; Corbett, pp. 51, 59, 62, 67–68.

64. Corbett, p. 1.

65. Ibid., pp. 62, 68, 89.

66. Ibid., pp. 8, 21, 59, 68, 69, 142–44. Corbett's book is dated 1972.

67. Ligot, pp. 128–29; Hayter, p. 143.

68. Corbett, pp. 3, 56; Hayter, pp. 94–95; Camara, p. 292.

69. Tracy, pp. 38–42; Corbett, pp. 4, 64.

70. Corbett, pp. 2, 85, 106, 114–15.

71. Ibid., pp. 85, 90, 115.

72. Ibid., pp. 92–112.

73. Ibid., pp. 99, 104.

74. Ibid., pp. 106–7.

75. Ibid., pp. 135–36.

76. Albert Charton, "Décolonisation et Coopération," pp. 175–76.

77. Corbett, pp. 1–3.

78. Robarts, p. 43.

79. Ibid., p. 44.

80. Ibid., pp. 45–47.

81. Ibid., pp. 49–50.

82. Ibid., pp. 51–53.

83. Ibid., p. 55.

84. Ibid., pp. 60–63.

85. Ibid., pp. 72–78.

86. Ibid., pp. 74–79.

87. Ibid., p. 6.

88. Interview of the author with a former high French official on April 24, 1978.

89. Corbett, pp. 63, 149; Tracy, p. 24, n. 48.

90. Tracy, pp. 25–26.

91. Corbett, p. 167.

92. Tracy, p. 22.

93. Ibid., pp. 22–24; Corbett, p. 13.

94. Tracy, pp. 24–25.

95. Corbett, p. 176.

96. Tracy, p. 26.

97. Ibid., p. 22.

98. Ibid., p. 26.

99. *International Herald Tribune*, March 25–26, 1978, p. 2.

100. *Afrique Contemporaine*, November-December, 1975, p. 26.

101. *Figaro*, April 27–28, 1978, p.1.

102. "Commission sur la Politique de Coopération avec les Pays en Voie de Développement," Documentation Française, *Rapport Jeanneney*, 1964, p. 33.

103. Charton, "Décolonisation et Coopération," p. 172.

104. Wallerstein, *Politics of Unity*, Appendix B.

105. De Bosschère, II, 259–60; Berque, Charnay, et al., "Le Neo-Colonialism: Essai de Définition," in *De l'Impérialisme à la Décolonisation*, p. 420.

106. Nkrumah, pp. ix, 259.

107. Soucadaux, "De la Colonisation à la Coopération," pp. 185–88.

108. Charton, "Décolonisation et Coopération," pp. 175–77, 179.

109. De Gaulle, *Mémoires*, II, 176.

110. Plantey, "L'Organisation de la Coopération avec les Pays d'Afrique Noire et Madagascar."

111. Ibid., *Espoir*, no. 13, pp. 45–46.

112. Ibid., *Espoir*, no. 12, p. 54.

113. Decraene, p. 75.

114. Ibid., pp. 77–79, 82, 89.

115. Tricot, "Processus de Prise de Décision," in *De Gaulle et le Service de l'Etat*, pp. 28–29.

116. Camara, p. 235; Tricot, pp. 28–29.

117. Rivière, p. 96.

118. Camara, pp. 15, 16, 102.

119. Ibid., pp. 17, 235.

120. Mortimer, p. 316.

121. Camara, pp. 117, 233, 237.

122. Ibid., pp. 128, 130, 131, 132, 236, 239; *supra*, chap. 16, n. 94.

123. Rivière, pp. 123, 171; *Monde Hebdomadaire*, July 10–16, 1973, p. 3.

124. Camara, pp. 156, 160; Rivière, p. 123.

125. Rivière, pp. 79, 92, 245.

126. *Figaro*, March 21, 1978, p. 10; *Demain l'Afrique*, no. 8, April 1978, pp. 27–34; Camara, p. 245; Corbett, p. 72.

127. Schwab, p. 4.

128. Corbett, p. 77.

129. Jouve, "De Gaulle, Giscard et la Coopération," pp. 21–23. Jouve quotes from the General's speeches from 1941 to 1963. He notes that the General became more insistent on cooperation after 1960. He had also mentioned a similar idea in *Le Fil de l'Epée* of 1932.

130. Ligot, p. 64.

131. Duroselle and Meyriat, pp. 182–83.

132. Hayter, p. 104.

133. Ibid., p. 32.

134. Guéna, pp. 73–75, gives the list of domains in which the Community was not competent to act; Hayter, p. 143; Corbett, pp. 62, 99, 119. Corbett did not go into the final questions on Guéna's list—those of exterior transportation and telecommunications.

135. Hayter, pp. 203–4.

136. Corbett, pp. 121, 162.

137. *Afrique Contemporaine: Documents d'Afrique Noire et de Madagascar* 14, no. 78 (March-April 1975), statements of February 7, 1975, p. 14.

138. Ibid., pp. 13–14.

139. *Le Monde*, June 26 to July 2, 1975, p. 4, article by Philippe Decraene.

140. Ibid.; Abelin, "Rapport sur la Politique Française de Coopération," p. 78. (The report is long

and has been synthesized rather than quoted page by page. Its chief interest for the purposes of this volume lies in the perception of the criticisms that were now directed toward the whole subject of cooperation. In addition to that it asked for a more adequate administration and better planning.)

141. *Le Monde Hebdomadaire*, January 1–7, 1976, p. 1.

142. Ibid., April 29-May 5, 1976, pp. 1–3. Speeches of President Giscard d'Estaing reported by Philippe Decraene.

143. Ibid., May 6–12, 1976.

144. Ibid., August 6–11, 1976, p. 1.

145. Ibid., p. 6. Statement by P.-J. Franceschini, in article about President Giscard d'Estaing.

146. Ibid.

147. French Embassy, Press and Information Division, July 1978, pp. 78/7.

Bibliography

Books and Articles in Books Cited in the Text*

"A," of the Fathers of the Holy Ghost at Yaoundé. *Life of a Missionary.*

Albertini, Rudolph von. *Decolonization: The Administration and Future of the Colonies.* Translated by Francesca Garvie. New York: Doubleday, 1971.

Ardagh, John. *The New French Revolution.* New York: Harper & Row, 1968.

Arnault, Jacques. *Du Colonialisme au Socialisme.* Paris: Editions Sociales, 1966.

——. *Le Procès du Colonialisme.* Paris: Editions Sociales, 1958.

Aron, Robert. *Les Origines de la Guerre d'Algérie: Textes et Documents.* Paris: Fayard, 1962.

d'Astier, Emmanuel. *Sept Fois Sept Jours.* Paris: Editions de Minuit, 1947.

Augouard, Msgr. *Twenty-eight Years in the Congo.* Vol. 2, n.d. In Suret-Canale, vol. 1 (q.v.).

Bailey, Thomas A. *A Diplomatic History of the American People.* 3d ed. New York: Crofts, 1947.

Baratier, Général. *Au Congo: Souvenir de la Mission Marchand.* Paris: Fayard, n.d.

Barrès, Philippe. *Charles de Gaulle.* New York: Brentano, 1941.

Bemis, Samuel Flagg. *A Diplomatic History of the United States.* Rev. ed. New York: Holt, 1946.

Berque, Jacques; Charnay, Jean-Paul; et al. *De l'Impérialisme à la Décolonisation.* Paris: Les Editions de Minuit, 1965.

Bertier de Sauvigny, Guillaume. *The Bourbon Restoration.* Translated by Lynn M. Case. Philadelphia: University of Pennsylvania Press, 1966.

Béthencourt, Jean de (Sieur de). "Histoire de la Conquête des Canaries, 1402–05." In G. Guénin, *L'Epopée Coloniale de la France: Racontée par les Contemporains* (q.v.).

Betts, Raymond F. *Assimilation and Association in French Colonial Theory 1890–1914.* New York: Columbia University Press, 1961.

Bidou, H.; Gauvain, A.; and Seignobos, C. Edited by E. Lavisse. *Histoire de France Contemporaine.* 10 vols. *La Grande Guerre,* vol. 9. Paris: Hachette, 1922.

Black, C. E., and Helmreich, E. C. *Twentieth Century Europe.* New York: Knopf, 1963.

Blet, Henri. *France d'Outre-Mer: L'Oeuvre Colonial de la Troisième République.* Paris: Arthaud, 1950.

Bonheur, Gaston. *Charles de Gaulle: Biographie.* Paris: Gallimard, 1958.

Boni, Nazi. *Histoire Synthétique de l'Afrique Resistante.* Paris: Présence Africaine, 1971.

Bonn, Moritz Julius. "Imperialism." In *Encyclopedia of the Social Sciences.* New York: Macmillan, 1932.

Bosschère, Guy de. *Les Versants de l'Histoire.* 2 vols. *Autopsie de la Colonisation,* vol. 1. *De la Décolonisation,* vol. 2. Paris: Albin Michel, 1967, 1969.

Bouillon, J.; Sorlin, P.; and Rudel, J. *Le Monde Contemporain.* Paris: Bordas, 1968.

---

*"Presses Universitaires Françaises" is abbreviated as P.U.F.

Bourguiba, H. *La Tunisie et la France.* Paris: Julliard, 1954.

Brace, Richard M. *Morocco-Algeria-Tunisia.* Englewood Cliffs, N.J.: Prentice-Hall, 1964.

Brown, Roger Glenn. *Fashoda Reconsidered: The Impact of Domestic Politics on French Policy in Africa 1893–1898.* Baltimore: Johns Hopkins Press, 1969.

Brunschwig, Henri. *L'Avènement de l'Afrique Noire.* Paris: Colin, 1963.

——. "French Exploitation and Conquest in Tropical Africa." In Gann and Duignan, *Colonialism in Africa 1870–1960,* vol. 1 (q.v.).

——. *Mythés et Réalités de l'Imperialisme Français 1871–1914.* Paris: Colin, 1960.

——. *Le Partage de l'Afrique Noire.* Paris: Flammarion, 1971.

Burns, Alan. *Le Préjugé de race et de couleur.* Paris: Payot, 1949.

Bury, J. P. T. *France: 1840–1914.* Philadelphia: University of Pennsylvania Press, 1949.

Camara, Sylvain-Soriba. *La Guinée sans la France.* Paris: Fondation Nationale des Sciences Politiques, 1976.

Cattaui, Georges. *Charles de Gaulle: d'Homme et son Destin.* Paris: Fayard, 1960.

Césaire, Aimé. *Cahier d'un Retour au Pays Natal.* 2d ed. Paris: Présence Africaine, 1956.

——. *Discours sur le Colonialisme.* Paris: Présence Africaine, 1963.

Chaffard, Georges. *Les Carnets Secrets de la Décolonisation.* 2 vols. Paris: Calmann-Lévy, 1965, 1967.

Chailley, Marcel. *Histoire de l'Afrique Occidentale Française.* Paris: Berger-Levrault, 1968.

Chastenet, Jacques. *Histoire de la Troisième République.* 7 vols. *La République des Républicains,* vol. 2. Paris: Hachette, 1954.

Chautemps, Félix. "Politique Indigène." In *L'Afrique Occidentale Française.* Paris, 1913. Quoted by Michael Crowder, in *West Africa Under Colonial Rule.*

Chauvel, Jean. *Commentaire II. D'Alger à Berne.* Paris: Fayard, 1972.

Chetrit, Elie, and Timsit, Jean-Pierre. "La Retraite au Désert ou la Pensée du Général de Gaulle de 1946 à 1958." Dissertation presented at l'Institut d'Etudes Politiques de l'Université de Paris, April 1, 1962.

Churchill, Winston S. *The Second World War.* 6 vols. Boston: Houghton Mifflin, 1952–54.

Clark, Stanley. *The Man Who Is France.* New York: Dodd, Mead, 1963.

Cobban, Alfred. *A History of Modern France 1799–1945.* Vol. 2. Baltimore: Penguin Books, 1961.

Cohen, Andrew. *British Policy in Changing Africa.* Evanston, Ill.: Northwestern University Press, 1959.

Cohen, William B. *Rulers of Empire: The French Colonial Service in Africa.* Stanford, Calif.: Hoover Institution Press, 1971.

Coleman, James S. *Nigeria: Background to Nationalism.* Berkeley: University of California Press, 1958.

——, and Rosberg, Carl G., Jr., eds. *Political Parties and National Integration in Tropical Africa.* Berkeley: University of California Press, 1966.

Columbia Encyclopedia. 3d ed. New York: Columbia University Press, 1963.

Confer, Vincent. *France and Algeria: The Problem of Civil and Political Reform 1870–1920.* Syracuse, N.Y.: Syracuse University Press, 1966.

Conte, Arthur. *Bandoung: Tournant de l'Histoire.* Paris: Robert Laffont, 1965.

Coquery-Vidrovitch, Catherine. *La Découverte de l'Afrique: l'Afrique Noire Atlantique des Origines au XVIIIe Siècle.* Paris: Julliard, 1965.

——. "French Colonization in Africa to 1920: Administration and Economic Development." In Gann and Duignan, *Colonialism in Africa 1870–1960,* vol. 1 (q.v.).

——, and Moniot, H. *L'Afrique Noire de 1800 à Nos Jours.* Paris: P.U.F., 1974.

Corbett, Edward M. *The French Presence in Black Africa.* Washington, D.C.: Black Orpheus Press, 1972.

Cornevin, Marianne. *Histoire de l'Afrique Contemporaine: De la 2ᵉ Guerre Mondiale à Nos Jours.* Paris: Payot, 1972.

Cornevin, Robert. *Histoire de l'Afrique.* 3 vols. *Des Origines au 16ᵉ Siècle,* vol. 1. *Du Tournant de Seizième au Tournant du XXᵉ,* vol. 2. *Colonisation, Décolonisation, Indépendance,* vol. 3. Paris: Payot, 1961, 1962, 1975.

—— et Marianne. *Histoire de l'Afrique des Origines à nos jours.* Paris: Payot, 1964.

Crawley, Aidan, *De Gaulle: A Biography.* Indianapolis; Ind.: Bobbs-Merrill, 1969.

Crowder, Michael. "Independence as a Goal in French West African Politics." In W. H. Lewis, *French-Speaking Africa.*

——. *West Africa Under Colonial Rule.* Evanston, Ill.: Northwestern University Press, 1968.

——. *West African Resistance: The Military Response to Colonial Occupation.* New York: Africana Publishing Co., 1971.

Crowe, Sybil F. *The Berlin West African Conference, 1884–1885.* London: Longman's, Green, 1942.

Curtin, Philip D. *The Atlantic Slave Trade: A Census.* Madison: University of Wisconsin Press, 1969.

Dansette, Adrien. *Leclerc.* Paris: Flammarion, 1952.

Damas, Léon-Gontran. *Pigments.* Paris: Présence Africaine. 1937.

Daruvar, Yves de. *De Londres à Tunisie: Carnet de route de la France Libre.* Paris: Charles Lavanzelle, 1945.

Davet, Michel-Christian. *La Double Affaire de Syrie.* Paris: Fayard, 1967.

Davidson, Basil. *The African Slave Trade.* Boston: Little, Brown, 1961.

——. *Mère Afrique.* Paris: P.U.F., 1965.

——, with F. K. Buah and advice of Ade Ajayi. *A History of West Africa to the Nineteenth Century.* Garden City, N.Y.: Doubleday, 1966. This is a revised version of *The Growth of African Civilization: West Africa, 1000 to 1800.* London: Longman's, 1965.

Dehon, Émile. *La Nouvelle Politique Coloniale de la France.* Paris: Flammarion, 1945.

Delafosse, Maurice. *L'Ame Nègre.* Paris: Payot, 1922.

——. *Broussard ou les Etats d'Ame d'un Colonial.* Paris: Larose, 1923.

Delavignette, Robert. *L'Afrique Noire Française et son Destin.* Paris: Gallimard, 1962.

——. *Du Bon Usage de la Décolonisation.* Paris: Casterman, 1968.

——. *Freedom and Authority in French West Africa.* London: Oxford University Press, 1950.

——. "French Colonial Policy, 1945–60." In Gann and Duignan, *Colonialism in Africa, 1870–1960,* vol. 2 (q.v.).

——. *Les Paysans Noirs.* New ed. Paris: Stock, 1947.

——. *Service Africain.* Paris: Gallimard, 1946. Published first as *Les Vrais Chefs de l'Empire* and in English as *Freedom and Authority in French West Africa.*

——, and Julien, Charles-André, eds. *Les Constructeurs de la France Outre-Mer.* Paris: Corréa, 1946.

Deschamps, Hubert-Jules. *L'Europe Découvre l'Afrique.* Paris: Berger-Levrault, 1967.

——. "France in Black Africa." In Gann and Duignan, *Colonialism in Africa 1870–1960,* vol. 1 (q.v.).

——. *Histoire de Madagascar.* Paris: Berger-Levrault, 1965.

——. *Les Méthodes et Doctrines Coloniales de la France.* Paris: Colin, 1953.

——. *Les Pirates à Madagascar au 17ᵉ et 18ᵉ Siècles.* Paris: Berger-Levrault, 1949.

Devèze, Michel. *La France d'Outre-Mer: De l'Empire Coloniale à l'Union Française.* Paris: Hachette, 1948.

Dictionary of French Literature. Sidney D. Braun, ed. New York: Philosophical Library, 1958.

Diop, Birago. Poem, "Breath." In *A Book of African Verse,* John Reed and Clive Wake, eds. (q.v.).

——. "Souffles." *Leurres et Lueurs*. Paris: Présence Africaine.

Dryden, John. *Annus Mirabilis*, clv. In *Oxford Dictionary of Quotations*. 2d ed. Oxford, England: Oxford University Press, 1941.

DuBois, W. E. B. *The World and Africa*. New York: Viking Press, 1947.

Dunner, Joseph. *Handbook of World History: Concepts and Issues*. New York: Philosophical Library, 1967.

Durand, Oswald. *René Caillié à Tombouctou*. Paris: Mame, 1944.

Duroselle, J.-B., and Meyriat, Jean. *Les Politiques Nationales envers les Jeunes Etats*. Paris: Colin, 1964.

Duverger, Maurice. *Introduction à la Politique*. Paris: Gallimard, 1964.

Eboué, Félix. *La Nouvelle Politique Indigène de l'Afrique Equatoriale Française*. Brazzaville: Pfister Printing Press, 1941.

Elgey, Georgette. *La République des Illusions 1945–1951: La Vie Secrète de la IVe République*, vol. 1. *La République des Contradictions 1951–1954*, vol. 2. Paris: Fayard, 1965, 1968.

Emerson, Rupert. *From Empire to Nation: The Rise to Self-Assertion of Asian and African Peoples*. Cambridge, Mass.: Harvard University Press, 1967.

Emily, J. *Travel Journal of the Marchand Mission*. Paris: Hachette, 1913.

Encyclopedia Brittanica, vol. IX, 1964.

Fage, J. D. *A History of West Africa: An Introductory Survey*. 4th ed. Cambridge: Cambridge University Press, 1969.

Fauvet, Jacques. *La Quatrième République*. Paris: Fayard, 1959.

Ferniot, Jean. *De Gaulle et le 13 mai*. Paris: Plon, 1965.

Finbert, Elian-J. *The Book of Negro Wisdom*. Paris: Laffont, 1950.

Fisher, H. A. L., ed. *History of Europe*. New York: Charles Scribner's Sons, 1926.

Foltz, William J. *From French West Africa to the Mali Federation*. New Haven, Conn.: Yale University Press, 1965.

French Embassy. Press and Information Service, New York. *Major Addresses, Statements and Press Conferences of General Charles de Gaulle*. New York, 1964.

Froelich, J. C. *Animismes—les Religions Paiënnes de l'Afrique de l'Ouest*. Paris: Edition de l'Orante, 1964.

Froment-Guieysse, G. *Brazza et ses Compagnons*. Paris: Editions de l'Empire, 1945.

Funk, Arthur L. *Charles de Gaulle: The Crucial Years*. Norman: University of Oklahoma Press, 1959.

Gaffarel, Paul. *Les Colonies Françaises*. Paris: F. Alcan, 1899.

Galante, Pierre, *Le Général: les Siens, les Autres et Lui-Même*. Paris: Presses de la Cité, 1968.

Ganiage, Jean. *L'Expansion Coloniale de la France sous la Troisième République*. Paris: Payot, 1968.

Gann, L. H., and Duignan, Peter. *Burden of Empire: An Appraisal of Western Colonialism in Africa South of the Sahara*. New York: Praeger, 1967.

——. *Colonialism in Africa, 1870–1960*. 3 vols. *The History and Politics of Colonialism, 1870–1914*, vol. 1. *The History and Politics of Colonialism, 1914–1960*, vol. 2. *Profiles of Change: African Society and Colonial Rule*, edited by Victor Turner, vol. 3. Cambridge, England: Cambridge University Press, 1969, 1970, 1971.

Gardinier, David E. "Decolonization." In Dunner, *Handbook of World History*.

Gaulle, Charles de. *La Discorde chez l'Ennemi*. 2d ed. Paris: Berger-Levrault, 1944.

——. *Discours et Messages*. 5 vols. *Pendant la Guerre 1940–45*, vol. 1. *Dans l'Attente, 1945–58*, vol. 2. *Avec le Renouveau, 1958–62*, vol. 3. *Pour l'Effort, 1962–65*, vol. 4. *Vers le Terms, 1966–69*, vol. 5. Paris: Plon, 1970.

——. Discours au Madagascar et en Afrique Noire, August 1958, October 1958. In *Discours et Messages*, vol. 3.

——. *Le Fil de l'Epée*. Paris: Berger-Levrault, 1932.

——. *La France et son Armée.* Paris: Plon, 1938.
——. *Mémoires d'Espoir.* 2 vols. *Le Renouveau: 1958–62,* vol. 1. *L'Effort: 1962. . . . ,* vol. 2. Paris: Plon, 1970, 1971.
——. *Mémoires de Guerre.* 3 vols. *L'Appel: 1940–42,* vol. 1. *L'Unité: 1942–44,* vol. 2. *L'Salut: 1944–46,* vol. 3. Paris: Plon, 1954, 1956, 1959.
——. Memorandum addressed by Colonel Charles de Gaulle to Generals Gamelin, Weygand and Georges and to Messieurs Daladier and Reynaud, January 26, 1940. In *Trois Etudes* (q.v.).
——. *Trois Etudes.* Paris: Berger-Levrault, 1945.
——. *Vers l'Armée de Métier.* Orig. pub. 1934. 2d ed. Paris: Berger-Levrault, 1944.
——. *The War Memoirs of Charles de Gaulle.* 3 vols. *The Call to Honor: 1940–42,* translated by Jonathan Griffin, vol. 1. New York: Viking Press, 1955. *Unity: 1942–44,* translated by Richard Howard, vol. 2. New York: Simon and Schuster, 1959. *Salvation: 1944–46,* translated by Richard Howard, vol. 3. New York: Simon and Schuster, 1960.
——, Chef de Bataillon Breveté, and Yvon, Chef de Bataillon Breveté, de l'Etat Major des Troupes Françaises du Levant. *Histoire des Troupes Françaises du Levant.* Paris: Imprimerie Nationale, 1931.
Gide, André. *Travels in the Congo.* Contains *To the Congo* and *Back from Chad.* Berkeley and Los Angeles: University of California Press, 1962.
Gifford, Prosser, and Lewis, William Roger, eds. *France and Britain in Africa: Imperial Rivalry and Colonial Rule.* New Haven and London: Yale University Press, 1971.
Girardet, Raoul. *L'Idée Coloniale en France de 1871 à 1962.* Paris: La Table Ronde, 1972.
Godechot, Jacques. *Les Constitutions de la France depuis 1789.* Paris: Garnier-Flammarion, 1970.
Goguel, François. *France Under the Fourth Republic.* Ithaca, N.Y.: Cornell University Press, 1952.
Gourou, Pierre. *L'Afrique.* Paris: Hachette, 1970.
Grande Encyclopédie: Inventaire raisonné des sciences, des lettres et des arts, vol. XVII. Paris, 1895.
Grand Larousse Encyclopédique, vol. III. Paris: Librairie Larousse, 1961.
Griaule, Marcel. *Dieu d'Eau: Entretiens avec Ogotemmêli.* Paris: Fayard, 1966.
Grimal, Henri. *La Décolonisation 1919–1963.* Paris: Colin, 1965.
Grinnell-Milne, Duncan. *The Triumph of Integrity.* New York: Macmillan, 1962.
Grosser, Alfred. *La Quatrième République et sa Politique Extérieure.* Paris: Colin, 1961.
Guéna, Yves. *Historique de la Communauté.* Paris: Fayard, 1962.
Guénin, G. *L'Epopée Coloniale de la France: Racontée par les Contemporains.* Paris: Larose, 1932.
Guèye, Lamine. *Itinéraire Africain.* Paris: Présence Africaine, 1966.
Guillaume, Alfred. *L'Islam.* Baltimore: Penguin Books, 1954.
Guillebaud, Jean-Claude, *Les Confettis de l'Empire.* Paris: Seuil, 1976.
Halleguen, Joseph. *Aux Quatre Vents du Gaullisme.* Paris: Dervy, 1953.
Hanotaux, Gabriel. *L'Energie Française.* Paris: Flammarion, 1902.
——. *Pour l'Empire Colonial Français.* Paris, 1933.
Hardy, Georges. *L'Afrique Occidentale Française: Etude et Textes.* Paris: Laurens, 1937.
——. *Histoire de la Colonisation Française.* 1st ed. 1928. Paris: Larose, 1943.
——. *Histoire Sociale de la Colonisation Française.* Paris: Larose, 1958.
Hargreaves, John D., ed. *France and West Africa: An Anthology of Historical Documents.* New York: Macmillan, 1969.
——. *Prelude to the Partition of West Africa.* London: Macmillan, 1963.
Harmand, Jules. *Domination et Colonisation.* Paris: Flammarion, 1910.
Hatch, Alden, *The De Gaulle Nobody Knows.* New York: Hawthorn Books, 1960.

Hayter, Teresa. *French Aid.* London: Overseas Development Institute, 1966.

Heggoy, Alf Andrew. *The African Policies of Gabriel Hanotaux 1894–98.* Athens: University of Georgia Press, 1972.

Herskovits, Melville J. *L'Afrique et les Africains entre hier et demain.* Paris: Payot, 1965.

——. *L'Héritage du Noir.* Translated by Arnold Grévy. First published as *The Myth of the Negro Past.* Paris: Présence Africaine, 1966.

Hobson, J. A. *Imperialism: A Study.* London: Allen and Unwin, 1902.

Hodgkin, T. *Nationalism in Colonial Africa.* New York: New York University Press, 1957.

Howard C., and Plumb, J. *West African Discoverers.* London: Oxford University Press, 1951.

Hymans, Jacques. *Léopold Sédar Senghor: An Intellectual Biography.* Edinburgh: Edinburgh University Press, 1971.

Ingold, François-Joseph-Jean. *Le Chemin: Tempêtes, Escales, Victoires.* Paris, 1958.

Institut Charles de Gaulle. *Charles de Gaulle: Extraits pour l'Avenir.* Paris: Berger-Levrault et Plon, 1973.

Jahn, Janheinz. *Muntu: An Outline of New African Culture.* New York: Grove Press, 1961.

Johnson, G. Wesley. *The Emergence of Black Politics in Senegal: The Struggle for Power in the Four Communes.* Stamford, Calif.: Stamford University Press, 1971.

Julien, Charles-André. *Les Voyages de Découverte et les Premiers Etablissements du XVe et XVIe Siècles.* Paris: P.U.F., 1948.

——, ed. *Les Techniciens de la Colonisation au XIXe et XXe Siècles.* Articles on Faidherbe, Bugeaud, Gallieni, Lyautey, et al. Paris: P.U.F., 1947.

Jullien, Pierre. *Journal de la Prise d'Alger 1830 du Capitaine Matterer.* Paris: Editions de Paris, 1960.

Kanya-Forstner, A. S. *The Conquest of the Western Sudan: A Study in French Military Imperialism.* Cambridge, England: Cambridge University Press, 1969.

Kingsley, Mary. *Travels in West Africa.* 3d ed. London: F. Cass & Co., 1965.

——. *West African Studies.* 3d ed. London: F. Cass & Co., 1964.

Ki-Zerbo, Joseph. *Histoire de l'Afrique Noire.* Paris: Hatier, 1972.

Kohn, Hans. "Reflections on Colonialism." In Strausz-Hupé and Hazard, *The Idea of Colonialism* (q.v.).

Kuoh-Moukouri, Jacques. *Doigts Noirs.* Montréal: Editions à la Page, 1963.

Labouret, Henri. *Colonisation, Colonialisme, Décolonisation.* Paris: Larose, 1952.

Lacouture, Jean. *Cinq Hommes et la France.* Paris: Seuil, 1961.

——. *Malraux.* Paris: Seuil, 1973.

La Gorce, Paul-Marie de. *De Gaulle entre deux Mondes: Une Vie et Une Epoque.* Paris: Fayard, 1964.

Langer, William L. *The Diplomacy of Imperialism.* New York: Knopf, 1951.

——. *An Encyclopedia of World History.* 2d ed. Boston: Houghton Mifflin, 1948.

——. *European Alliances and Alignments.* New York: Knopf, 1950.

Lansing, Robert. *The Peace Negotiations: A Personal Narrative.* Boston: Houghton Mifflin, 1921.

Larminat, René-Marie-Edgard de. *Chroniques Irrévérencieuses.* Paris: Plon, 1962.

La Roche, Jean de, and Gottmann, Jean. *La Fédération Française: Contacts et Civilisations d'Outre-Mer.* Montréal: Editions de l'Arbre, 1945.

Larousse Méthodique. Vol. 1. Paris: Librairie Larousse, 1955.

Larousse Universel. 2 vols. Paris: Librairie Larousse, 1948.

Las Casas, Bartholomé de. *Mémoire adressée au Roi. Lettre Dédicacé au Prince des Asturies,* 1542. In Merle, *L'Anticolonialisme de Las Casas à Marx* (q.v.).

Laurentie, Gouverneur-Général Henri. "Le Refus de Tchad." In de Larminat, *Chroniques Irrévérencieuses* (q.v.).

Legendre, P. *La Conquête de la France Africaine.* Paris: Paclot et Cie., n.d.

Legum, Colin. *Panafricanism: A Short Political Guide.* New York: Praeger, 1965.

Lewis, William H. *French-Speaking Africa: The Search for Identity.* New York: Walker, 1965.

——. *The Splendid Century.* New York: William Sloane, 1954.

Ligot, Maurice. *Les Accords de Coopération entre la France et les Etats Africains et Malgache.* Paris: La Documentation Française, 1964.

Ligou, Daniel. *Histoire du Socialisme en France, 1871–1961.* Paris: P.U.F., 1962.

Lloyd, Lord. *Egypt Since Cromer.* London: Macmillan, 1934.

Londres, Albert. *Terre d'Ebène: La Traite des Noirs.* Paris: Albin Michel, 1929.

Louis, Paul. *Le Colonialisme.* Paris: Societé Nouvelle de Librairie et d'Edition, 1905.

Loutfi, Martine Astier. *Littérature et Colonialisme: Expansion Coloniale vue dans la Littérature Romanesque Française 1871–1914.* Paris: Mouton, 1971.

Luchaire, François. *L'Aide aux Pays sous-développés.* Paris: P.U.F., Que Sais-je Edition no. 1227, 1966.

Makonnen, Ras. *Pan-Africanism from Within.* Nairobi: Oxford University Press, 1973.

Mangin, Général Charles. *Souvenirs d'Afrique: Lettres et Carnets de Route.* Paris: Denöel et Steele, 1936.

Mannix, Daniel P., with Conley, Malcolm. *Black Cargoes: A History of the Atlantic Slave Trade 1518–1865.* New York: Viking Press, 1962.

Marshall, D. Bruce. "Free France in Africa." In Gifford and Lewis, *France and Britain in Africa* (q.v.).

——. *The French Colonial Myth and Constitution-making in the Fourth Republic.* New Haven and London: Yale University Press, 1973.

Martin du Gard, Maurice. *La Carte Impériale: Histoire de la France Outre-Mer, 1940–45.* Paris: Editions André Bonne, 1949.

Marx, Karl. *Le Capital.* Oeuvres de Karl Marx. Paris: La Pleiade, n.d.

Maurice, Albert. *Félix Eboué, sa Vie, son Oeuvre.* Brussels: Institut Royal Colonial Belge, 1954.

Memmi, Albert. *Portrait du Colonisé: Précédé du Portrait du Colonisateur.* Paris: J. J. Pauvert, 1966.

Mérat, Louis. *Fictions et Réalités Coloniales.* Paris: Librairie du Recueil Sirey, 1947.

Mercier, Roger. *L'Afrique Noire dans la Littérature Française: Les Premières Images XVIIᵉ - XVIIIᵉ siècles.* Dakar: Universitaire de Dakar, 1962.

Merle, Marcel. *L'Anticolonialisme de Las Casas à Marx.* Paris: Colin, 1969.

——, director. *L'Afrique Noire Contemporaine.* Paris: Colin, 1968.

Michelet, Edmond. *Le Gaullisme: Passionante Aventure.* Paris: Fayard, 1962.

——. *La Querelle de la Fidelité.* Paris: Fayard, 1971.

Milcent, Ernest. *L'A.O.F. entre en Scène.* Paris: Témoignage Chrétien, 1958.

Ministère des Colonies. *La Conférence Africaine Française de Brazzaville, 30 janvier, 1944–8 février, 1944.* Paris: Ministère des Colonies, 1945.

Moneta, Jacob. *Le Parti Communiste Français et la Question Coloniale.* Paris: Maspéro, 1971.

Montaigne, Michel de. *Les Essais.* Paris: Guernier, n.d.

Monteil, Vincent. *L'Islam Noir.* Paris: Editions du Seuil, 1971.

Montesquieu, Baron de (Charles de Secondat). *De l'Esprit des Lois.* 1748.

Moran, Denise. *Tchad.* Paris: Gallimard, 1934.

Mordal, Jacques. *La Bataille de Dakar.* Paris: Ozanne, 1956.

Morgenthau, Ruth Schachter. *Political Parties in French-Speaking West Africa.* Oxford: Clarendon Press, 1964.

Mortimer, Edward. *France and the Africans: A Political History 1944–60.* London: Faber & Faber, 1969.

Murphy, Agnes. *The Ideology of French Imperialism.* Washington, D.C.: Press of Catholic University of America, 1948.

Musset, Alfred de. *A Quoi rêvent les Jeunes Filles?* c. 1840.

Mveng, Engelbert. *Histoire du Cameroun.* Paris: Présence Africaine, 1963.

Nachin, Lucien. *Charles de Gaulle: Général de France.* Paris: Editions Colbert, 1944.

Néra, Gilles. See Plantey.

Niane, Djibril Tamsir, and Suret-Canale, Jean. *Histoire de l'Afrique Occidentale.* Paris: Présence Africaine, 1965.

Nkrumah, Kwame. *Neo-Colonialism: The Last Stage of Imperialism.* London: Nelson, 1965.

Noguères, Henri. *L'Expédition d'Alger, 1830.* Paris: Julliard, 1962.

Nouveau Petit Larousse. Paris: Librairie Larousse, 1959.

Oliver, Roland, and Oliver, Caroline. *Africa in the Days of Exploration.* Englewood Cliffs, N.J.: Prentice-Hall, Spectrum Books, 1965.

Orwell, George. *Such, Such Were the Joys.* New York, 1953.

Oxford Companion to French Literature. Oxford: Harvey and Haseltine, 1959.

Oxford Universal Dictionary. Rev. ed. Oxford: Clarendon Press, 1955.

Padmore, George. *Panafricanisme ou Communisme?* Paris: Présence Africaine, 1960.

Passeron, André. 2 vols. *De Gaulle Parle: des Institutions, de l'Algérie, de l'Armée, des Affaires Etrangères, de la Communauté, de l'Economie, et des Questions Sociales,* vol. 1. Paris: Plon, 1962. *De Gaulle Parle: 1962–1966,* vol. 2. Paris: Fayard, 1966.

Péguy, Charles. *Basic Vérités.* Translated by Ann and Julien Green. New York: Random Books, 1943.

Petit Larousse. Paris: Librairie Larousse, 1959, 1976.

Plantey, Alain [Gilles Néra]. *La Communauté.* Paris: P.U.F., 1960.

Pognon, Edmond. *De Gaulle et l'Histoire de France.* Paris: Michel, 1970.

Power, Thomas J. *Jules Ferry and the Renaissance of French Imperialism.* New York: King's Crown Press, 1944.

Rassemblement du Peuple Français. *La France sera la France: Ce que veut Charles de Gaulle.* Paris: R.P.F., 1951.

Raynal, Abbé Guillaume Thomas. *Histoire Philosophique et Politique des Establissements et du Commerce Européen dans les Deux Indes.* Published 1770. Edition de Gabriel Esquer, under the title *L'Anticolonialisme au XVIIIᵉ siècle.* Paris: P.U.F., 1951.

Reed, John, and Wake, Clive, eds. *A Book of African Verse.* London: Heinemann Educational Books, 1964. Poem, "Breath," by Birago Diop.

"Rémy." See Renault-Roulier.

Renault-Roulier, Gilbert ["Rémy]. *De Gaulle: Cet Inconnu.* Monte Carlo: Raoul Solar, 1947.

Reuters News Agency. *The New Africans: A Guide to the Contemporary History of Emergent Africa and Its Leaders.* New York: Putnam, 1967.

Richard-Molard, Jacques. *L'Afrique Occidentale Française.* Paris: Berger-Levrault, 1949, 1952.

Rivière, Claude. *Guinea: The Mobilization of a People.* Translated by Virginia Thompson and Richard Adloff. Ithaca, N.Y.: Cornell University Press, 1977.

Robarts, R. C. (1974). "French Development Assistance: A Study in Policy and Administration." Sage Professional Papers in Administrative and Policy Studies, I, 03001. Beverly Hills and London: Sage Publications.

Robinson, Ronald, and Gallagher, John. *Africa and the Victorians: The Official Mind of Imperialism.* London, 1961.

Ronsard, Pierre. *Poèsies.* "Complainte contre Fortune." Mid-16th century.

Rouillon, Léon. *Les Compagnons du Premier Jour.* Paris: Les Editions du XXᵉ Siècle, 1952.

Rous, Jean. *Léopold Sédar Senghor: Un Président de L'Afrique Nouvelle.* Paris: John Didier, 1967.

Saint-Pierre, Bernardin de. "Etudes de la Nature 1784." Cited by Merle, *L'Anticolonialisme de Las Casas à Marx.*
——. *Paul et Virginie.* 1st ed. 1787. New York: C. R. Lockwood, 1852.
Sarraut, Albert, *Grandeur et Servitude Coloniale.* Paris: Editions du Sagittaire, 1931.
——. *La Mise en Valeur des Colonies Françaises.* Paris: Payot, 1922.
Saussure, Léopold de. *La Psychologie de la Colonisation Française dans ses Rapports avec les Sociétiés Indigènes.* Paris: Alcan, 1899.
Scanlon, David. *Traditions of African Education.* New York: Teacher's College Press, 1964.
Schwab, Morton. *The Political Relationship between France and her former Colonies in the sub-Saharan Region since 1958.* Atlanta, Ga.: Emory University, Political Science, 1968.
Sédillot, René. *Histoire des Colonisations.* Paris: Fayard, 1958.
Senghor, Léopold Sédar. 2 vols. *Liberté I: Négritude et Humanisme. Liberté II: Nation et Voie Africaine du Socialisme.* Paris: Seuil, 1964, 1971.
Shipley, A. Dorothy. "The Renaissance at Dieppe." Master's thesis, Columbia University, 1920.
Sithole, Ndabaningi. *African Nationalism.* London: Oxford University Press, 1969.
Snyder, Louis L. *The Dynamics of Nationalism.* Princeton, N.J.: Van Nostrand, 1964.
Snyder, Louis L., et al. *The Imperialism Reader: Documents and Readings on Modern Expansionism.* Princeton, N.J.: Van Nostrand, 1962.
Sophie, Ulrich. *Le Gouverneur-Général Félix Eboué.* 2d ed. Paris: Larose, 1950.
Soustelle, Jacques. *Envers et Contre Tout.* 2 vols. *De Londres à Alger,* vol. 1. *D'Alger à Paris,* vol. 2. Sources et Paris: Larose, 1947, 1950.
Spacensky, Alain. *Madagascar: Cinquante Ans de Vie Politique.* Paris: Nouvelles Editions Latines, 1970.
Spears, Sir Edward. *Assignment to Catastrophe.* New York: Hill and Wang, 1955.
Spengler, Oswald. *The Decline of the West.* Published in German, 1918. New York: Knopf, 1928.
Stern, Jacques. *The French Colonies: Past and Future.* Translated by Norbert Guterman. New York: Didier, 1944.
Stibbe, Pierre. *Justice pour les Malgaches.* Paris: Seuil, 1954.
Stoddard, Lothrop. *The Rising Tide of Color against White World Supremacy.* New York: Charles Scribner's Sons, 1920. Also published as *Le Flot Montant des Races de Couleur contre la Suprématie du Monde Blanc.* London, 1921.
Strausz-Hupé, Robert, and Hazard, Harry W. *The Idea of Colonialism.* New York: Praeger, 1958.
Suret-Canale, Jean. *Afrique Noire.* 3 vols. *Géographie, Civilisations, Histoire,* vol. 1. *L'Ere Coloniale,* vol. 2. *De la Colonisation aux Indépendances,* vol. 3. Paris: Editions Sociales, 1961, 1964, 1972.
Terrenoire, Louis. *De Gaulle et l'Algérie: Témoignage pour l'Histoire.* Paris: Fayard, 1964.
——. *De Gaulle Vivant.* Paris: Plon, 1971.
Thompson, Virginia, and Adloff, Richard. *The Emerging States of French Equatorial Africa.* Stanford, Calif.: Stanford University Press, 1960.
Touchard, Jean. *Le Gaullisme, 1940–1969.* Paris: Seuil, 1978.
Toulat, Jean. *Français d'aujourd'hui en Afrique Noire.* Paris: Perrin, 1966.
Tournoux, J.-R. *Jamais Dit.* Paris: Plon, 1971.
——. *Pétain et De Gaulle.* Paris: Plon, 1964.
——. *La Tragédie du Général.* Paris: Plon, 1967.
Touré, Sékou. *Expérience Guinéenne et Unité Africaine.* Paris: Présence Africaine, 1962.
Tracy, Laurie J. "France, de Gaulle and the Former African Colonies." Honors thesis,

Southern Connecticut State College, Department of Political Science, 1974.

Tricot, Bernard, ed. *De Gaulle et le Service de l'Etat*. Paris: Plon, Collection *Espoir*, 1977.

Tronchon, Jacques. *L'Insurrection Malgache de 1947*. Paris: Maspéro, 1974.

Turgot, Anne-Robert-Jacques. *Oeuvres*. Paris: Guillaumin, 1844.

Vaulx, Bernard de. *En Afrique 5000 ans d'exploitation*. Paris: Fayard, 1960.

Vendroux, Jacques. "Le Sens de l'Avenir," in L'Herne, *Charles de Gaulle*. Paris: Editions de l'Herne, 1973.

Viansson-Ponté, Pierre. *Histoire de la République Gaullienne*. 2 vols. *La Fin d'une Epoque, Mai, 1958-Juillet, 1962*, vol. 1. *Le Temps des Orphelins, Eté, 1962-Avril, 1969*, vol. 2. Paris: Fayard, 1970, 1971.

Viard, René. *La Fin de l'Empire Colonial Français*. Paris: Maisonneuve et Larose, 1963.

Villandre, Jean-Jacques. "Chefferies Traditionnelles en Afrique de l'Ouest Française." Doctoral dissertation, University of Paris, Faculty of Law, 1950.

Voltaire. *Essai sur les Moeurs*. 1756. Cited by Merle, *L'Anticolonialisme de Las Casas à Marx* (q.v.).

Wallbank, T. Walter. *Contemporary Africa*. Princeton, N.J.: Van Nostrand, 1956.

Wallerstein, Immanuel. *Africa, The Politics of Unity: An Analysis of a Contemporary Social Movement*. New York: Random House, 1967.

——. *The Road to Independence: Ghana and the Ivory Coast*. Paris: Mouton, 1964.

——. "Voluntary Associations." In Coleman and Rosberg, *Political Parties and National Integration in Tropical Africa* (q.v.).

Webster, J. B.; Boahen, A. A.; and Idowu, H. O. *History of West Africa: The Revolutionary Years*. New York: Praeger, 1967.

Webster's New Collegiate Dictionary. Springfield, Mass.: G. C. Merriam Co., 1975.

Weil-Curiel, André. *Le Jour se lève à Londres*. Paris: Editions du Myrte, 1945.

Weinstein, Brian. *Eboué*. New York: Oxford University Press, 1972.

Welch, Galbraith. *Africa Before They Came*. New York: William Morrow, 1965.

Werth, Alexander. *De Gaulle: A Political Biography*. New York: Simon and Schuster, 1965, 1966.

——. *The De Gaulle Revolution*. London: Robert Hale, 1960.

White, Dorothy Shipley. "Franco-American Relations in 1917–18: War Aims and Peace Prospects." Ph.D. dissertation, University of Pennsylvania, 1954.

——. *Seeds of Discord: De Gaulle, Free France and the Allies*. Syracuse, N.Y.: Syracuse University Press, 1964. Published as *Les Origines de la Discorde: de Gaulle, la France Libre et les Alliés*. Paris: Editions Trèvise, 1967.

Williams, Philip. *Politics in Post-War France: Parties and the Fourth Republic*. London: Longman's, Green, 1954.

Williams, Philip, and Harrison, Martin. *De Gaulle's Republic*. London: Longman's, 1960.

Wilmot, Chester. *The Struggle for Europe*. New York: Harper & Row, 1952.

Yacono, X. *Histoire de la Colonisation Française*. Paris, P.U.F. Série Que Sais-je, 1969.

Zolberg, Aristide R. *Creating Political Order: The Party-States of West Africa*. Chicago: Rand McNally, 1966.

——. *One-Party Government in the Ivory Coast*. Princeton, N.J.: Princeton University Press, 1969.

Selected Bibliography Consulted but Not Cited

Adloff, Richard. *West Africa Yesterday and Today*. New York: Holt, Rinehart and Winston, 1964.

Ahidjo Ahmadou. *As Told by Ahmadou Ahidjo.* Monte Carlo, 1968.

Alduy, Paul. *L'Union Française: Mission de la France.* Paris: Fasquelle, 1948.

Ameillot, B. *La Guinée: Bilan d'une Indépendance.* Paris: Maspéro, 1964.

d'Arboussier, Gabriel. *L'Afrique vers l'Unité.* Paris: Editions St. Paul, 1961.

Aron, Robert. *An Explanation of de Gaulle.* Translated by Marianne Sinclair. New York: Harper and Row, 1966.

d'Astier, Emmanuel. *Les Grands.* Paris: Gallimard, 1961.

Baratier, Colonel. *A Travers l'Afrique.* Paris: Fayard, n.d.

Baumann, H., and Westermann, D. *Les Peuples et les Civilisations: Les Langues et l'Education.* Paris: Payot, 1962.

Bernstein, Serge. *La Décolonisation et ses Problèmes.* Paris: Colin, 1969.

Berthelot, Yves, and Fossi, Giulio. *Pour une Nouvelle Coopération.* Paris: P.U.F., 1975.

Blanchet, André. *L'Itinéraire des Partis Africains depuis Bamako.* Paris: Plon, 1958.

Boiteau, Pierre. *Contribution à l'Histoire de la Nation Malgache.* Paris: Editions Sociales, 1958.

Bovill, E. W. *The Golden Trade of the Moors.* London: Oxford University Press, 1958.

Brunschwig, Henri. *Brazza: Explorateur.* L'Ogooué, 1875–79. Paris: Mouton, 1966.

Cédétim. *L'Imperialisme Français.* Paris: Maspéro, 1978.

Cheverny, Lucien. *Eloge du Colonialisme.* Paris: Julliard, 1961.

Cissoko, Sékéné-Mody. *Histoire de l'Afrique Occidentale: Moyen âge et temps modernes. VIIe siècle-1850.* Paris: Présence Africaine, 1966.

Coquery-Vidrovitch, Catherine. *L'Afrique Noire de 1800 à Nos Jours.* Paris: P.U.F., 1974.

Crozier, Brian. *Neo-Colonialism.* London: Bodley Head, 1964.

Davidson, Basil. *The African Past.* Published also as *Mère Afrique.* New York: Grosset & Dunlap, 1964.

Delavignette, Robert. "Christianisme et Colonialisme." In *Je sais, je crois, Encyclopédie du Catholique an XXème Siècle,* 9ème partie, *Les Problèmes du Monde et de l'Eglise.*

Deschamps, Hubert-Jules. *La Communauté Française.* Amicale des Elèves de l'Institut d'Etudes Politique de Paris, 1958–59.

——. *L'Eveil Politique Africain.* Paris: Presses Universitaire Françaises. Série Que Sais-je?, 1952.

——. *La Fin des Empires Coloniaux.* Paris: P.U.F. Série Que Sais-je?, 1959.

——. *The French Union.* Paris: Berger-Levrault, 1956. Originally published as *L'Union Française: Histoire, Institutions, Réalités.* Paris: Berger-Levrault, 1952.

Dumon, Frédéric. *La Communauté Franco-Africaine, Malgache: Origines, Institutions, Evolution.* Bruxelles: Université Libre, Institut de Sociologie Solvay, octobre 1958–juin 1960.

Dunner, Joseph. *Dictionary of Political Science.* New York: Philosophical Library, 1964.

Folliet, Joseph. *La Travail Forcé aux Colonies.* Paris: Les Editions du Cerf, 1934.

Fouchet, Christian. *Au Service du Général de Gaulle.* Paris: Plon, 1971.

Fougeyrollas, Pierre. *De la Décolonisation à la Coopération.* Afrique-Documents no. 73, 2ème cahier, 1964. Place of publication not given.

Gaffarel, Paul. *La Politique Coloniale en France de 1789 à 1830.* Paris: Alcan, 1908.

Garas, Félix. *Charles de Gaulle: Seul contre les Pouvoirs.* Paris: Julliard, 1957.

Gardinier, David E. *Cameroon: United Nations Challenge to French Policy.* London: Oxford University Press, 1963.

Gaulle, Charles de. Discours à Tahiti, Papeete, et al., août-septembre, 1956. Trip to the Pacific islands. In *Chronologie de la Vie du Général de Gaulle.* Paris: Plon, 1973.

Guèye, Lamine. "Confession de Foi: Elections Législative du novembre, 1946." Unpublished article loaned to the author by Madame Lamine Guèye.

———. *Etapes et Perspectives de l'Union Française.* Paris: Editions de l'Union Française, 1955.

Hailey [W. M.], Lord. *An African Survey: A Study of Problems Arising in Africa South of the Sahara.* Rev. ed. London: Oxford University Press, 1957.

Hama, Boubou. *Kotia-Nima: Rencontre avec l'Europe.* Vienne-Ligugé: Publication de la République du Niger, 1969.

Hardy, Georges. *La Politique Coloniale et le Partage de la Terre aux XIXe et XXe Siècles.* Paris: Albin Michel, 1937.

Hargreaves, John D. *West Africa: The Former French States.* Englewood Cliffs, N.J.: Prentice-Hall, 1967.

Henige, David. *Colonial Governors in History in Africa: A Journal of Method.* Waltham, Mass.: African Studies Association.

Hettier de Boislambert, Claude. *Les Fers de l'Espoir.* Paris: Plon, 1978.

Hoffman, Stanley; Kindleberger, C. P.; Wylie, L.; Pitts, J. J.; Duroselle, J.-B.; and Goguel, F. *In Search of France.* Cambridge, Mass.: Harvard University Press, 1963.

Kolodziej, Edward A. *French International Policy under de Gaulle and Pompidou: The Politics of Grandeur.* Ithaca, 1974.

Kulski, W. W. *De Gaulle and the World: The Foreign Policy of the Fifth Republic.* Syracuse, N.Y.: Syracuse University Press, 1966.

Labat, René. *Le Gabon devant le Gaullisme.* Bordeaux: Edition Delmas, 1941.

Lacouture, Jean. *De Gaulle.* Paris: Seuil, 1965.

Lapie, Pierre-Olivier. *De Léon Blum à de Gaulle.* Paris: Fayard, 1971.

La Roche, Jean de. *Le Gouverneur Félix Eboué.* Paris: Hachette, 1957.

Laurentie, Henri. "Développement de la Politique Coloniale Française en matière internationale de 1940 à 1945." Discussion at the Centre d'Etudes de Politique Etrangère, February 9, 1945. Taped.

Leroy-Beaulieu, Paul. *De la Colonisation chez les Peuples Modernes.* 4th ed. Paris: Guillomin, 1898.

Le Vine, Victor T. *The Cameroons from Mandate to Independence.* Berkeley and Los Angeles: University of California Press, 1964.

Mabileau, A., and Meyriat, J. *Décolonisation et Régimes Politiques en Afrique Noire.* Paris: Armand Colin, 1967.

Mahé de la Bourdonnais, B. F. *Mémoires Historiques.* 2d ed. Paris: Savine, 1892.

Malraux, André. *Antimémoires.* Paris: Gallimard, 1967.

Mannoni, Dominique O. *La Psychologie de la Colonisation.* Paris: Editions du Seuil, 1950.

Mannoni, Eugène. *Moi, Général de Gaulle.* Paris: Seuil, 1964.

Mauriac, Claude. *Un Autre de Gaulle: Journal, 1944-54.* Paris: Hachette, 1970.

Mauril, M. H. *Dans la Brousse Africaine.* Dammarie-des Lys (S. M.), 1951.

Merlo, Jean. "Sources Populaire de l'Idéologie de l'Indépendance en Afrique Noire." Thèse de doctorat. Paris, Centre de Recherches Africaines.

Morse, Edward L. *Foreign Policy and Interdependence in Gaullist France.* Princeton, N.J.: Princeton University Press, 1973.

d'Octon, Vigné. *Les Crimes Coloniaux de la Troisième République.* Paris: Editions de la Guerre Sociale, 1911.

Paden, John N., and Soja, Edward W. *The African Experience.* "The Impact of Colonialism" by Michael Crowder. Evanston, Ill.: Northwestern University Press, 1970.

Plantey, Alain. *Indépendance et Coopération.* Paris: Librairie Générale de Droit et de Jurisprudence, 1965.

Renan, Ernest. *Qu'est-ce qu'une Nation?* Paris: Calmann-Lévy, 1882.

Rey, Pierre Philippe. *Colonialisme, Néo-Colonialisme: Transition au Capitalisme.* Paris: Maspéro, 1971.

Roberts, Stephen H. *History of French Colonial Policy, 1870–1925*. London: P. S. King and Son, 1929.
Robinson, Kenneth. "Political Development in French West Africa." In Calvin W. Stillman, ed. *Africa in the Modern World*. Chicago: University of Chicago Press, 1955.
Rous, Jean. *Chronique de la Décolonisation*. Paris: Présence Africaine, 1965.
Scherk, Nikolaus. "La Coopération avec la France et la Souveraineté des Etats Francophones Africains et Malgaches." Dissertation presented at l'Institut Politique de l'Université de Paris, March, 1968.
Schoelcher, Victor. *Esclavage et Colonisation*. Paris: P.U.F., 1948.
Schoenbrun, David. *The Three Lives of Charles de Gaulle*. New York: Athenaeum, 1966.
Shepherd, George W., Jr. *The Politics of African Nationalism*. New York: Praeger, 1962.
Sicé, Médicin Général Adolphe. *L'A.E.F. et la Cameroun au Service de la France*. Paris: P.U.F., 1946.
Spears, Sir Edward. *Two Men Who Saved France: Pétain, 1917, De Gaulle, 1940*. London: Eyre and Spottiswood, 1966.
Tevoedjre, Albert. *L'Afrique Révoltée*. Paris: Présence Africaine, 1958.
Thompson, Virginia, and Adloff, Richard. *French West Africa*. London: Geo. Allen and Unwin, 1958.
Thornton, A. P. *Doctrines of Imperialism*. New York: John Wiley and Sons, 1965.
Tramond, Renée. *La Merveilleuse Epopée d'A. M. Javouhey*. Namur: Editions du Soleil Levant, 1964.
Vaucel, Médicin-Général. *La France d'Outre-Mer dans la Guerre: Documents*. Paris: Office Français d'Edition, 1945.
Viansson-Ponté, Pierre. *Les Gaullistes: Rituel et Annuaire*. Paris: Seuil, 1963.
Viorst, Milton. *Hostile Allies: Roosevelt and de Gaulle*. New York: Macmillan, 1965.
Wallerstein, Immanuel. *The Politics of Independence*. New York: Random House, 1961.
Wiedner, Donald L. *A History of Africa South of the Sahara*. New York: Knopf, 1962.
Young, Crawford. "Decolonization in Africa." Typescript at Hoover Institution, Stanford, Calif.

Periodicals, Miscellaneous Articles, and Sources not Otherwise Classified

Abelin, Pierre. "Rapport sur la Politique Française de Coopération." *La Documentation Française*, September, 1975.
Ageron, Charles-Robert. "De Gaulle et la Conférence de Brazzaville." Typed article for the Institut Charles de Gaulle, June 1978.
Afrique Contemporaine. "L'Afrique Australe," 14, no. 82 (November–December 1975), special number. "La Convention C.E.E.-A.C.P. 28 février, 1975," 14, no. 78 (March–April 1975). "L'Informatique en Afrique," 16, no. 95 (January–February 1978), part 2, special number.
Alduy, Paul. "La Naissance du Nationalisme Outre-Mer." Colston Papers. *Principles and Methods of Colonial Administration*. London: Butterworth's Scientific Publications, 1950.
Aubame, J. "La Conférence de Brazzaville." *Encyclopédie Coloniale et Maritime*, no. 5 (1950).
Balandier, Georges. "Contribution à l'Etude des Nationalismes en Afrique Noire." *Zaïre* 8, no. 1 (April 1954).

———. "Messianismes et Nationalismes en Afrique Noire." *Cahiers Internationales de Sociologie* 8, no. 14.

Blanchard, Marcel. "Administrateurs d'Afrique Noire." *Revue d'Histoire des Colonies,* no. 11 (1953).

Brévié, Gouverneur-Général Jules. Circulaire sur la Politique et Administration Indigènes en Afrique Occidentale Française. 1935.

Brunschwig, Henri. "Colonisation et Décolonisation: Vocabulaire de Politique Coloniale." *Cahiers d'Etudes Africaines* 1 (1960).

———. "Les Technocrates de l'Impérialisme." *Revue Française d'Histoire d'Outre-Mer* 53 (1966).

Bulletin du Comité d'Afrique Française et du Maroc. Supplément: Renseignements Coloniaux, 1919, 1921, 1922.

Camara, Sylvain-Soriba. "Les Origines du Conflit Franco-Guinéen." *Revue Françaises d'Etudes Politiques Africaines,* June 1975.

Cartier, Raymond. *Paris-Match,* nos. 777, 778, 779 (February 28, March 7, March 14, 1964).

Charmes, Gabriel. *Journal des Débats,* August–October 1880.

———. "La Politique Coloniale." *Revue des Deux Mondes,* November 1, 1883.

Charton, Albert (inspector general of public education). "Décolonisation et Coopération dans le Domaine culturel." *Comptes-rendus mensuels de l'Académie des Sciences d'Outre-Mer,* vol. XXX, session of May 8, 1970.

Chauleur, P. "La Guinée de M. Sékou Touré." *Etudes* 347 (November 1977).

Chavannes, Charles de. "Savorgnan de Brazza." *Bulletin du Comité d'Afrique et le Comité du Maroc. Rensiegnements Coloniaux et Documents,* no. 5 (May 1931).

Cissoko, Sékéné Mody. "La Conférence de Brazzaville: Prélude à l'Independance de l'Afrique." *Bingo,* no. 184 (May 1968).

Coleman, James S. "Nationalism in Tropical Africa." *American Political Science Review* 48, no. 2 (June 1954). Republished in his *Political Change in Underdeveloped Countries.* New York and London: John Wiley & Sons, 1962.

Comptes-Rendus du 2ème Congrés des Ecrivains et Artistes Noirs tenu à Rome, 1959. *Présence Africaine,* nos. 24–25 (February–May 1959).

Confer, Vincent. "French Colonial Ideas before 1789." *French Historical Studies* 3, no. 3 (Spring 1964).

Cornevin, Robert. "Evolution des Chefferies Traditionnelles en Afrique Noire." *Penant,* nos. 686, 687, 688 (1961).

———. "Le Problème des Navigations Dieppoises au XIVème Siècle." *France-Eurafrique,* nos. 160, 161 (March and April 1965).

Curton, E. de. "Vers une Union Fédérale Française." *Renaissance,* no. 12 (July 1945).

Danton, Georges-Jacques. Speech to Legislative Committee of General Defense, September 2, 1792. *Le Moniteur,* September 4, 1792.

Debré, Michel. "L'Europe et l'Union Française." *Marchés Coloniaux* 9e année, no. 377 (January 31, 1953).

Decraene, Philippe. Articles on Giscard d'Estaing and Africa and on Niger. *Monde Hebdomadaire,* June 26 to July 2, 1975.

———. "La Politique Africaine du Général de Gaulle." *Revue Française d'Etudes Politiques Africaine,* no. 47, November 1969.

Delafosse, Maurice. "Le Congrés Panafricain." *Bulletin de l'Afrique Française. Renseignements Coloniaux,* nos. 3, 4 (1919).

———. "Les Points Sombres de l'Horizon." *Bulletin de l'Afrique Française. Renseignements Coloniaux,* 1922.

———. Article sur la politique indigène. *Bulletin du Comité de l'Afrique Française et du Maroc. Renseignements Coloniaux,* 1921.

Delaisi, Malraux, and Galtier-Boissière. "*Expéditions Coloniales: leurs dessous, leurs atrocités.*" *Crapouillot,* special number (January 1936).

Delavignette, Robert. "L'Administrateur Territorial en Afrique Noire Française." *Revue des Travaux de l'Académie des Sciences Morales et Politiques* 118ème année, 4ème série, 1er semestre (1965).

——. L'Oeuvre de nos Administrateurs." *Tropiques*, no. 419 (July 1959).

——. "La Politique de Marius Moutet au Ministère des Colonies." *Cahiers de la Fondation Nationale des Sciences Politiques*, no. 155 (1967).

Demain l'Afrique, April 8, 1978. Paul Bernetel, "Editorial: Opportunités." Edouard J. Maunick, "Les bons Baisers de Monrovia."

Deschamps, Hubert-Jules. "La Vocation Coloniale et le Métier d'Administrateur." *Bulletin du Comité d'Afrique Française et du Maroc. Renseignements Coloniaux*, no. 9 (1931).

Destanne de Bernis, Gérard. "Décolonisation de la France." *Esprit*, no. 10 (October 1961).

Didier, H. "Aperçu sur le Syndicalisme en Afrique Noire." *Encyclopédie Mensuelle d'Outre-Mer*, December 1955.

La Documentation Française. *Notes, Documentations et Etudes*. "Le Contenu de la Coopération," no. 3330 (October 1966). "Service de Coopération Culturel," no. 3787 (May 4, 1971).

Domenach, Jean-Marie. "Dernières Chances de l'Union Française." *Esprit* 17, special number 157 (July 1949).

DuBois, W. E. Burghardt. "France's Black Citizens in West Africa." *Current History* 21, no. 4 (July 1925).

Duchemin, J. G. "Comment il vit." *Présence Africaine: Le Monde Noir*, special number 8–9 (1950).

Elgey, Georgette. Articles in *Candide*, November 16 and 23, 1961.

"Les Empires Coloniaux et leur Avenir." *Renaissance* 1, special number 3, 4 (March 1944).

"Les Etudiants nous Parlent." *Revue Juridique et Politique de l'Union Française* 7 (1953).

Le Figaro, April 27–28, 1978. Also article by Jean-Marc Kalflèche, "Guinée: plus d'Obstacle au Rapprochement avec la France," March 21, 1978.

Fisher, H. A. L. *Orbis* 11, no. 1 (Spring 1967).

Fougeyrollas, Pierre. "De la Colonisation à la Coopération." *Afrique Documents Bimestriels*, no. 73, 2e Cahier (1964).

Francheschini, P.-J. Article on Giscard d'Estaing in Gabon, *Monde Hebdomadaire*, August 6–11, 1976.

Gandolfi, A. "Les Accords de Coopération en Politique Etrangère." *Revue Juridique et Politique d'Outre-Mer*, no. 2, April–June 1963.

Gardinier, David E. "Schooling in the States of Equatorial Africa." *Revue Canadienne des Etudes Africaines* 7, no. 3, 1974.

Gaskill, Gordon. "Madagascar: Island of Riddles." Undated, written for the *Readers Digest*. Loaned by the American Embassy, Tananarive, Madagascar.

Gaulle, Charles de. "L'Action de Guerre et le Chef." *Revue Militaire Française* 27 (March 1, 1928).

——. "La Bataille de la Vistule: Carnet de Campagne d'un Officier Français." *Revue de Paris* 27, no. 21 (November 14, 1920).

——. "Combats du Temps de Paix." *Revue d'Infanterie*, May 1932.

——. "La Doctrine a Priori." *Revue Militaire Française* 15 (March 1, 1925).

——. "Le Flambeau." *Revue Militaire Française*, new series 24, no. 23 (March 1 and April 1, 1927).

——. "La Philosophie du Recrutement." *Revue d'Infanterie*, April 1, 1929.

——. "Le Rôle Historique des Places Françaises." *Revue Militaire Française* 18, no. 54 (January 21, 1925).

——. Speeches.

Algiers, October 12, 1947. Bibliothèque Nationale. Reserve.
Assemblée Nationale de Mauritanie, December 10, 1959.
Castres, February 26, 1960. French Press and Information Collection.
Dakar, August 26, 1958.
Limoux, February 26, 1960. French Press and Information Collection.
Nouakchott, Mauritanie, October 12, 1959.
Paris, August 18, 1947. Bibliothèque Nationale. Reserve.
——. Press conferences. March 10, 16, 1950.
"De Gaulle et l'Afrique." *Bingo. Le Mensuel du Monde Noir*, no. 156 (January 1966).
"De Gaulle et l'Union Française." *Marchés Coloniaux* 5, no. 210 (November 19, 1949).
Gharsallah, Mohammed. "Réflexions sur la Décolonisation." *Revue Juridique et Politique d'Outre-Mer*, no. 2, April–June 1963.
Giviziez, André. *Afrique Contemporaine*, no. 52 (December 1970).
Goodman, Eliot R. "The World through de Gaulle's Looking-Glass." *Orbis* 11, no. 1 (Spring 1967).
Grosser, Alfred. "Sept années de Gaullisme." *Témoignage Chrétien*, November 1965.
Hardy, Georges. "L'Ame Africaine." *La Revue des Vivants* 4, no. 1 (January 1930).
——. "La Psychologie des Populations Coloniales." *Revue de Psychologie des Peuples* 2, no. 3 (July 1947).
Harmon, Dudley. "Free France Booms in Africa." *Christian Science Monitor*, January 7, 9, 10, 1942.
Hayter, Teresa. "French Aid to Africa: Its Scope and Achievements." *International Affairs 4* (April 1965).
Henige, David. (Title not given.) *Bulletin de l'Institut d'Afrique Noire*, nos. 3, 4 (July, October 1963). Cited by R. Cornevin in *France-Eurafrique*.
"Histoire d'un Referendum." *Bingo*, no. 70 (November 1958).
Hodgkin, T., and Schacter, R. M. "French-Speaking West Africa in Transition." *International Conciliation*, no. 528 (May 1960).
Hoffmann, Stanley, and Hoffmann, Inge. "The Will to Grandeur: De Gaulle as Political Artist." *Daedalus: Journal of the American Academy of Arts and Sciences* (Summer 1968).
Holmes, Oliver Wendell. Quoted by *Newsweek*, February 15, 1971.
International Herald Tribune, March 25–26, 1978.
Jeanneney, Jean-Marcel. "Rapport de la Commission sur la Politique de Coopération avec les pays en voie de Développement." *La Documentation Française*, 1964.
Johnson, G. Wesley. "The Ascendency of Blaise Diagne and the Beginning of African Politics in Senegal." *Africa, Journal of the International African Institute* 36, no. 3 (July 1966).
Joseph, Richard. "The German Question in French Cameroun." *Comparative Studies of Society and History* 17, issue 1 (January 1975).
Journal Officiel des Communautés Européennes. "Les Conventions adoptées à Yaoundé." French language edition no. 93 (June 11, 1964).
Jouve, Edmond. "De Gaulle, Giscard et la Coopération." *L'Appel*, no. 22 (January–February 1976).
——. "Charles de Gaulle et la Coopération." *Espoir*, no. 21, 1977.
Kohn, Hans. "Napoleon and the Age of Nationalism." *Journal of Modern History* 22 (1950).
Kolodziej, Edward A. "France Ensnared. French Strategic Policy and Bloc Politics after 1968." *Orbis* 15 (Winter 1972).
——. "Revolt and Revisionism in the Gaullist Global Vision. Analysis of French Strategic Policy." *Journal of Politics* 33 (May 1971).
Labouret, Henri. "Les Problèmes de l'Education Indigène." *Bulletin de l'Afrique Française: Renseignements Coloniaux et Documents* 49, nos. 8–9 (1939).

La Gorce, Paul-Marie de. "La France et l'Afrique." *Revue Française d'Etudes Politiques Africaines*, no. 60 (December 1970).

———. "De Gaulle et la Décolonisation de l'Afrique Noire." *Revue Française d'Etudes Politiques Africains*, no. 60 (December 1970).

Lapie, Pierre Olivier (Gouverneur). "Fin de l'Ere Coloniale?" *Chemins du Monde*, no. 5 (1948).

Laurentie, Henri. "Eboué: Le Grand Français." *Renaissance*, no. 6 (August 1944).

———. "Notes sur une Philosophie de la Politique Coloniale Française." *Renaissance*, nos. 3–4 (March 1944).

———. "Pour ou contre le Colonialisme." *Renaissance*, no. 15 (October 1945).

Ligot, Maurice. "La Coopération Militaire dans les Accords." *Revue Juridique et Politique d'Outre-Mer*, no. 4, 1963.

———. "Vue générale sur les Accords de Coopération." *Revue Juridique et Politique d'Outre-Mer*, new series, 16 (1962).

Lorraine, Jacques. "La Conférence de Brazzaville." *Renaissance*, no. 3–4 (March 1944).

Lyautey, Louis-Hubert, Maréchal de France. "Le Coup de Barre." November 18, 1920.

"Madagascar: A Sketch." Anonymous and dateless. Loaned by the American Embassy, Tananarive, Madagascar.

Marchés Tropicaux 14, no. 669 (September, 1958). Article on African independence.

M'Bokolo, Elikia. "French Colonial Policy in Equatorial Africa in the 1940's and 1950's." Provisional sketch for the Conference, "Transfer of Power in Africa," Bellagio, September 30–October 4, 1977.

Merle, Marcel. "La Communauté Française Africaine." *Revue de l'Action Populaire*, June 1960.

Ministère de la France d'Outre-Mer. "Enseignement Outre-Mer," no. 10 (December 1958).

Le Monde. "Efforts to get on with Sékou Touré," March 10, 1978. Also article by Pierre Lefranc, "Les Critères du Gaullisme," February 8, 1978.

Le Monde Hebdomadaire. Articles on Giscard d'Estaing and Africa and on Niger by Philippe Decraene, June 26–July 2, 1975. France and Guinea and chronology of their relations, July 10–16, 1975. The Comoros independence of July 6, 1976, in issue of January 1–7, 1976. Giscard and Cooperation, April 29–May 5, 1976. Giscard's Declaration on Africa, May 6–12, 1976. P.-J. Francheschini on Giscard in Gabon, August 6–11, 1976.

Monnerville, Gaston. "Où va l'Union Française? Du Colonialisme à l'Association." *La Nef* 12, no. 9 (June 1955). Paris: Julliard-Nouvelle Série.

Moreux, René. "Déviations des Nations Unies." *Marchés Coloniaux*, December 29, 1945, February 23, 1946, December 10, 1949. Cites Gouverneur Laurentie in no. 7 (1945).

Munger, Edwin S. Article on Madagascar in the *Current Affairs Newsletter*, no. ESM 35 of the American Field Service Staff. No date on the paper. Apparently written in 1952, as it refers to the rebellion as of five years before.

Newbury, C. W., and Kanya-Forstner, A. "French Policy and the Origins of the Scramble for Africa." *Journal of African History* 10, no. 2 (1969).

N'Goma, Albert. "L'Islam Noir." *Présence Africaine: Le Monde Noir*, special number 8–9 (1950).

Noir et Blanc. "Le Guide." Special number published in November 1970, after General de Gaulle's death.

d'Ormesson, Wladimir. "Le Général de Gaulle: Histoire et la Légende." *Revue des Deux Mondes*, no. 12 (1970).

Perham Margery. "The Psychology of African Nationalism." *Optima*, March 1960.

Plantey, Alain. "L'Organisation de la Coopération avec les Pays d'Afrique Noire et de Madagascar." *Espoir* 12, 13 (October, December 1975).

Pleven, René. "Préface, 16 mars. 1944." *Renaissance* 1, no. 364 (March 1944).

Pouget, J. "Le Commandant de Gaulle à Varsovie." *Figaro Littéraire*, no. 1103 (June 5–11, 1967).

Presse et Information des Communautés Européennes. "La Communauté aujourd'hui et demain." Paris: rue des Bellesfeuilles, 1978.

"Le Problème des Chefferies en Afrique Noire." *Notes Documentaires et Etudes*, no. 2508 (February 19, 1959).

Publication Officielle des Communautés Européennes. "La Communauté aujourd'hui et demain." n.d.

Quermonne, Jean-Louis. "Nouvelles Institutions Politiques." *Revue de l'Action Populaire*, no. 139 (June 1960).

Rassemblement Démocratique Africain. "Le Rassemblement Democratique Africain dans la Lutte Impérialiste." Report of the Comité de Coordination du R.D.A., 1948. Mimeographed.

"Restez avec nous. Il se fait tard." *Marchés Tropicaux* 15, année, no. 736 (December 19, 1959).

Richard-Molard, Jacques. "Terres de Démesure." *Présence Africaine: Le Monde Noir*, special number 8–9 (1950).

Rotberg, Robert I. "The Rise of African Nationalism: The Case of East and Central Africa." *World Politics* 15, no. 1 (1962).

Rous, Jean. "Que veulent-ils?" *Esprit* 17, special number 157 (July 1949).

Sarraut, Albert. Speech at the Pagoda of Confucius. *L'Opinion* (Hanoï), May 7, 1919.

Sautter, Gilles. "Notes sur la Construction du Chemin de Fer Congo-Océan 1921–34." *Cahiers d'Etudes Africaines* 7, no. 26 (1967), 2ᵉ cahier.

Schumann, Maurice. If God lets me live.—De Gaulle. *Réalités*, March 1960.

Semidei, Manuela. "De l'Empire à la Décolonisation à travers les manuels scolaires français." *Revue Française de Science Politique* 16 (February 1, 1966).

Senghor, Léopold Sédar. "Ce que l'Afrique attend de l'Europe." *Marchés Coloniaux du Monde* 11, no. 496 (May 14, 1955).

———. "Comment nous sommes devenus ce que nous sommes." *Afrique Action*, no. 16 (January 30, 1967).

Singleton, Carey B. "The Malagasy Republic: A Land with Agricultural Production despite Massive Erosion." Loaned by the American Embassy, Tananarive, Madagascar.

Siril, Abou. "Les Civilisations Africaines." *Présence Africaine: Le Monde Noir*, special number 8–9 (1950).

Soucadaux, André. "De la Colonisation à la Coopération: Evolution des Faits, Persistance (et Influence) des Mythes and des Complexes." *Comptes-rendus mensuels de l'Académie des Sciences d'Outre-Mer* 30, session of May 8, 1970.

Talleyrand, citoyen (Talleyrand-Perigord, Charles Maurice de, Prince de Benevent). "Essai sur les advantages à retirer de colonies nouvelles dans les circonstances présentes." *Mémoires de l'Institut National de Sciences et Arts* 2, read at the public meeting of 15 messidor, an 5 (1798–1804).

United States of America. National Archives, Washington, D.C. *U.S. Department of State: Correspondence, Decimal File, 1918.* Syrian letters. Nos. 763.72119/3651, 763.72119/7035, et al.

Viard, Paul-Emile. "Essai d'une Organisation Constitutionnelle de la Communauté Française." *Renaissance*, nos. 3–4 (March 1944).

Zimmermann, Maurice. "La Colonisation Européenne dans le Monde." *Revue de Géographie Annuelle*, no. 2 (1908). Paris: Delagrave.

French Public Documents

Journal Officiel de la France Libre. Débats. Décrets.

Journal Officiel de la France Combattante. Débats. Décrets.

Journal Officiel de l'Assemblée Consultative Provisoire. Débats. Documents. Supplément.

Journal Officiel de l'Assemblée Nationale Constituante, I, 1945–1946. Débats. Documents. Séances de la Commission de la Constitution. Décrets.

Journal Officiel de l'Assemblée Nationale Constituante, II. Débats. Séances de la Commission de la Constitution. Annexes. Décrets. Composition de l'Assemblée Nationale de la IVe République.

Journal Officiel de l'Assemblée Nationale, Troisième République. Chambre des Députés. Débats. Speech of Georges Clemenceau, March 29, 1885.

Journal Officiel de l'Assemblée Nationale, Troisième République. Chambre des Députés. Débats, June 20, 1885.

Journal Officiel de l'Assemblée Nationale, Troisième République. Chambre des Députés. Rapport Joalland, November 30, 1900.

Journal Officiel de l'Assemblée de l'Union Française. Annales: Session of Wednesday, December 10, 1947. Speech by Albert Sarraut, président d'âge.

Journal Officiel de la République Française, no. 1100 (1957). Réformes Outre-Mer. Law no. 56–619, June 23, 1956, and Applied decrees.

Journal Officiel de l'Assembleé Nationale de la Côte d'Ivoire. Débats, March 23, 1946.

Conseil d'Etat. Annuaires. Procès Verbaux. Etudes et Documents.

Service d'Information de la France Libre, 1941. *Documents d'Information.* Also *Les Documents 1942–43* et *Les Dépêches Parisiennes.*

French Embassy. Press and Information Division, New York. 1978.

Index